AF786630

European Monetary Integration

Springer
Berlin
Heidelberg
New York
Barcelona
Budapest
Hong Kong
London
Milan
Paris
Santa Clara
Singapore
Tokyo

Paul J. J. Welfens (Ed.)

European Monetary Integration

EMS Developments and International Post-Maastricht Perspectives

Third, Revised and Enlarged Edition

With 14 Figures
and 26 Tables

Springer

Professor Dr. Paul J. J. Welfens
University of Potsdam
Wirtschafts- und Sozialwissenschaftliche Fakultät
Lehrstuhl Wirtschaftspolitik/Internationale Wirtschaftsbeziehungen
August-Bebel-Straße 89
D-14482 Potsdam, Germany

Cataloging-in-Publication Data applied for

Die Deutsche Bibliothek - CIP-Einheitsaufnahme

European monetary integration : EMS developments and international post-Maastricht perspectives ; with 26 tables / Paul J. J. Welfens (ed.). - 3., rev. and enl. ed. - Berlin ; Heidelberg ; New York ; Barcelona ; Budapest ; Hong Kong ; London ; Milan ; Paris ; Santa Clara ; Singapore ; Tokyo : Springer, 1996
ISBN-13:978-3-642-79971-6
NE: Welfens, Paul J. J. [Hrsg.]

ISBN-13:978-3-642-79971-6 e-ISBN-13:978-3-642-79969-3
DOI: 10.1007/978-3-642-79969-3

This work is subject to copyright. All rights are reserved, whether the whole or part of the material is concerned, specifically the rights of translation, reprinting, reuse of illustrations, recitation, broadcasting, reproduction on microfilms or in other ways, and storage in data banks. Duplication of this publication or parts thereof is only permitted under the provisions of the German Copyright Law of September 9, 1965, in its version of June 24, 1985, and a copyright fee must always be paid. Violations fall under the prosecution act of the German Copyright Law.

© Springer-Verlag Berlin · Heidelberg 1991, 1994, 1996
Softcover reprint of the hardcover 3rd edition 1996

The use of registered names, trademarks, etc. in this publication does not imply, even in the absence of a specific statement, that such names are exempt from the relevant protective laws and regulations and therefore free for general use.

43/2202 - 5 4 3 2 1 0 - Printed on acid-free paper

Towards European Monetary Union (Preface to the Third Edition)

The editor is pleased that the second edition quickly is followed by a third one which covers one more additional aspect at the end of the book - that of the "demand for money and currency substitution in Europe" which deals with the question to which extent factors due to currency substitution have affected German demand for money. The Bundesbank's reading of recent empirical analysis is that for its own policy stance currency substitution in the private sector is of minor importance. However, the DM - as noted by the Bundesbank itself - plays an increasing role in Eastern Europe. Currency substitution is confirmed by money demand functions which show a significant negative sign for the expected depreciation rate and the foreign interest rate. If domestic and foreign money are substitutes a rise of the opportunity cost of holding domestic money balances should reduce the demand for money. Since the expected depreciation rate cannot be observed expectations have to be modelled. It is, however, uncertain whether or not the exchange rate regime - e.g. defined by the width of the parity band - is affecting expectation formation. A broader parity reinforces the "random walk case" of exchange rate developments such that short-sighted governments will not have to fear the sanction of currency depreciations. It is, however, doubtful that capital markets and currency markets are efficient in a strict sense.

Renewed national monetary policy autonomy in countries with greater exchange rate flexibility and less pressure to follow the credible anti-inflation course of the Bundesbank and - after its independence - of the Banque de France is not without costs since higher nominal and real interest rates are faced by inflation-prone countries as well as countries which have a track record of frequent (and strong) currency depreciations. The interest rate premium vis-à-vis German interest rates is considerable in some EU countries, and with increasing financial liberalization in the course of the single EU market the premium could rise further. The single EU market in effect is reinforced by deregulation and major privatizations in EU countries which raise the pressure to achieve competitive rates of return by exploiting investment opportunities abroad. High nominal interest rates have negative welfare effects because they reduce the real demand for money, and higher real interest rates reduce investment and output growth. For some countries high nominal interest rates can hardly be avoided - the choice is between short term rates and long term rates. Fearing a currency depreciation interest rates are raised by the monetary authorities in order to attract higher short-term capital inflows, or a currency depreciation is accepted, but this raises fear of rising inflation and thus drives up long term interest rates. With the unfolding of the single EU market dynamics more and more goods and services are tradables such that exchange rate movements will affect an even broader range of goods and services.

With Austria, Finland and Sweden as new member states, the EFTA enlargement of 1995 adds three small open economies which have an impressive record of price stability and full employment - except for recent events in Sweden and Finland. The latter strongly suffered from the implosion of the former USSR and the disintegration of the CMEA; while Finland would have met the Maastricht criteria in 1990 its performance with respect to deficit-GNP ratios and even debt-GDP ratios of 1994 violated the threshold values for membership in an EU monetary union. This shows how fast external shocks can change the macroeconomic performance for worse. By contrast, Ireland's policy record of the early 1990s shows a dramatic improvement in the debt-GDP figure. Major problems remain in Italy which, however, after a steep fall of the Lira in 1993/94, showed an impressive export boom which suggests that a real depreciation is effective in improving the trade balance in the medium term. However, currency depreciation means major financial losses for foreigners who had invested in Italian bonds; financial investors will require higher real interest rates to compensate for the exchange rate risk. For Spain similar problems are relevant, except that Spain attracts much higher foreign direct investment inflows than Italy. Since a considerable share of Spain's inward foreign direct investment stock is from non-devaluing EU partner countries - Germany, the Netherlands and France - a currency depreciation stimulates further FDI inflows from these countries as German, Dutch and French firms will try to maintain export markets by expanding the production base in Spain. Attacting FDI inflows as a consequence of a depreciation is a rather **favorable** endogenous market response since the output potential is increased; countries which have only a small stock of inward FDI would have to rely more on short term capital inflows and a reduction of domestic absorption.

Since it is more difficult to increase internal price flexibility than to devalue a currency (and accept the rise of interest rates and the consequences for investment and government debt) depreciation is an important instrument for countries with unsolved social conflicts - both high and sustained deficit-GNP ratios and high inflation rates are indicative of such problems. With the newly established political independence of central banks in the EU there are reduced options of cutting the debt burden via an inflationary policy. Thus the need to reduce public expenditures, to generate extra revenues via privatizations and to raise taxes is increasing in some EU countries. The ultimate test for EMU membership remains, however, the ability to restore full employment in the Community. This challenge is not too difficult a problem if regionally differentiated incentive compatible contribution rates to the unemployment insurance scheme would be applied - i.e. higher rates for regions with high unemployment rates and above average unemployment duration. With stable North-South unemployment differentials - e.g. as in the context of Italy, Germany or the UK - uniform contribution rates are simply a hidden regional transfer mechanism.

Wage policies in small open economies are less difficult to gear towards a path consistent with low inflation rates than big economies for which the home market is dominating. Firms from small open economies typically are price takers in world markets so that firms will strongly reject wage claims exceeding productivity gains. In big countries (big) firms will be inclined to accept higher nominal wage claims less reluctantly because each firm anticipates that other firms in the industry will face similar wage pressures which will translate into increasing market prices at home - thus effectively reducing the pinch of generous nominal wage hikes. This mechanism is important for the enlarged EU because enlargement further lifts the share of intraregional trade in the EU so that the EU becomes more like a big economy which is rather closed towards the rest of the world. Therefore low inflation rates in a monetary (European) union will become more difficult to achieve than a low average EU inflation rate in the mid-1990s; or, to put it differently, the same low EU inflation rate in a monetary union can only be achieved if the monetary constitution is very firmly designed in a way that emphasizes the priority goal of price stability. To fully implement such emphasis will, however, be impossible if looming political conflicts - such as inflation versus unemployment - are faced in many EU member states. For this reason it is very important to solve the unemployment problems in western Europe, where governments and peoples have become used to non-clearing labor markets.

Germany which suffered from a transitory increase in public deficits in the context of German unification faces more favorable prospects since high (even double digit) economic growth in eastern Germany contributes to overall German growth and raises present and future tax revenues. Moreover, the inflation rate in Germany declined to below 3 % in early 1995 such that the Bundesbank's policy credibility is strengthened. The inflation rate in neighboring France is still lower and indeed the lowest in France in more than three decades, but France is facing the problem of double digit unemployment rates which impairs prospects for economic growth and thereby causes convergence problems between Germany and France. Fragile financial market institutions (e.g. CL in France; Baring case in the UK) could undermine confidence of investors in various currencies. Finally, political stability is important as is clearly shown by the fall of the Italian Lira in early 1995 when the Dini government was coping with the legacy of the Berlusconi government that had emerged out of a shattered system of political parties in Italy. Spanish developments point to the importance of stable government, too, but the Spanish peseta fell victim to the "network effect" of devaluation. With the Italian lira falling for political reasons and the prospects for Italian exports rising speculative pressure on the Spanish peseta built up - not least because Spanish export segments strongly overlap with major Italian exports of goods and services. What holds for Spain with respect to Italy is true mutatis mutandis for Portugal with respect to Spain, so that the Peseta devaluation (by 7%) of March 1995 was accompanied by a 3.5% devaluation of the escudo. Nevertheless, Spain entered the wide 6% ERM band in June 1989 and managed to stay in the ERM, while Sterling entered (with the same band) in October 1990, but left in September 1992 - together with the Lira. The Escudo which entered the ERM in April 1992 with the wide 6% ERM band also stayed in the ERM. The Peseta looks weak with respect to the series of devaluations: September 1992 by 5%, Nov. 1992 (together with the escudo) by 6%, in May 1993 by 8% and in March 1995 by 7% (escudo by 6.5% in May 1993 and 3.5% in March 1995). Both relatively high inflation rates as well as devaluations in major competing countries - Italy in the case of Spain - force devaluations upon a country. The Irish pound in turn is bound to suffer if the British pound's rate is falling (the Irish pound was devalued by 10% in February 1993). As the UK is Ireland's major trading partner a falling pound drives up prices of imported consumers goods from Britain which creates wage pressure and raises prices of imported intermediate inputs as well as investment goods from the UK; this implies a deterioration of Irish export price competitiveness, and a similar mechanism applies to Ireland's exports side. The rising intra-EU trade network which is fostered by the single market dynamics implies major problems for currency union if major EU countries are not participating. France, Germany, the Benelux countries plus Austria might be a viable core of a currency union, but for France it would be difficult to see Italy and Spain staying out.

On top of the trade network problems in the EU there is the DM-dollar problem, namely that an international excess supply of dollars (e.g. triggered by the Mexican tequila shock of 1994/95 when Mexico and other Latin American central banks sold dollars to stabilize their respective currency) translates into an uneven excess demand for EU currencies. Given the disparity of countries, monetary stability records and internationalization of industries, the DM is the preferred currency in Europe. This well-known fact could be reinforced by German unification which tends to bring about a revaluation of the DM in the long term.

Widening the ERM bands to 15% in August 1993 has not brought greater stability to the EMS. However, widening the parity band certainly is useful in a period of tremendously increased capital mobility. A transitory stage towards monetary union could be that all EU countries join the exchange rate mechanism, but choose different band classes: class a which is zero, class b which is 6% and c which is 15%; it is doubtful that east European countries could join the club in the 1990s. The formation of a core monetary union is likely to be accompanied by a devaluation of the currencies of countries staying out. This will generate pressure for political reforms.

Conflicts over policy priorities and diverging economic performance will make the 1996 intergovernmental conference ("Maastricht II") a difficult issue. This conference will not only face Franco-German differences in economic policy stances but more fundamental ones between the western European continent and the UK. From an economic point of view the main reason not to advance quickly with the monetary union project is the stubbornly high unemployment rates in EU countries which implies that the inception of EMU would be burdened with a conflict of full employment versus price stability. Before establishing monetary union - preferably within a small group of EU countries at first - labor market equilibrium should be restored. The German government is reluctant to surrender the DM for a future ECU of unproven stability (the ECU lost 20% vis-à-vis the DM in the two decades after 1979). 1997 is unlikely to be the date for EMU since only indulgent reading of the convergence criteria could bring about such an early switch to monetary union in the EU. For a well prepared EMU 1999 could be the magic date for countries in which low inflation, reduced unemployment and broad political consensus provide a basis to move towards stage III of the EU's monetary integration process.

The Maastricht Treaty is strict in the convergence criteria for the inflation rate (not more than 1.5 percentage points above the inflation rate of the three best countries) and the nominal interest rate (not more than two percentage points above the three countries with the lowest inflation rate); however, there is discretion with respect to the fiscal convergence criteria (debt-GNP rate not higher than 60%) and the deficit-GNP rate (not higher than 3%). Countries which violate the fiscal convergence criteria but have shown strong progress in bringing down the respective indicators could be eligible for monetary union. In a strict sense Germany and Luxembourg were the only countries fulfilling the convergence criteria in 1994, but the EU convergence report concluded that Ireland's progress in bringing down the debt-GNP ratio could be interpreted as being compatible with the debt-GNP convergence criterion. The fifth criterion for entering monetary union is that no devaluation - referring to ERM currencies within the standard margin - should have occurred at the initiative of the respective country. With the 15% margins having silently become the new standard margins, the convergence criteria indirectly became softer than initially. It would be useful to restore a more narrow margin for at least a minority of countries soon. It is unlikely that 1997 could be the date ("X") for starting monetary union because the required majority of countries will probably not fulfill the five criteria. 1999 could bring monetary union of a minority of EU countries whose currencies would then constitute the new ECU (it will have the same value as the old ECU). Switching to the ECU - so far a basket of EU currencies with an interest rate on ECU bonds much above DM denominated bonds - has to be prepared for both the banking system and the private sector where it seems clear that a big bang would be appropriate. While banks and firms should be able to switch to the new currency on date X, old and new notes and coins could circulate for about a year in parallel. One major challenge remains unsolved: interest rates on the new ECU should be lower or close to DM interest rates at date X - this implies that only a small group of EU countries would start with EMU. Otherwise banks, firms and private households holding assets in DM could suffer a loss of monetary wealth, following an interest rate increase, which would make the ECU unpopular in Germany, the Netherlands and Austria in particular (lower profit taxes as a consequence of depreciations on assets held would be a secondary problem). Those taking out mortgages for building homes should be alerted to the problems of switching to the ECU so that monetary union will not lead to redistributions of income and wealth in the EU. Compensating tax rules might be considered, but indeed there is the challenge to choose the date and the policy approach for the European System of Central Banks in a way that brings down interest rates to the DM level. The German Ministry of Finance should start issuing "basket bonds" which will contain several varieties of low EU inflation currencies so that market participants have an option to buy long term bonds whose value will not fall at date X. EMU has to be prepared technically, politically and economically. *Potsdam, March 1995* *Paul J.J. Welfens*

Preface to the Second Edition

The European Monetary System emerged as an attempt to save some of the positive features of the Bretton Woods System which in turn started out as a kind of gold standard in which the US dollar replaced gold. Fixed exchange rates were considered to be beneficial for the growth of trade and international investment, but also to allow a smooth financing of cyclical or structural balance of payments disequilibriums. From its start in 1979 to 1989 the EMS worked rather well although the system initially learned only from crises (e.g. in 1983 the franc devaluation). With German unification in 1990 the EMS faced a new challenge because the Bundesbank faced difficulties in controlling the money supply and maintaining low inflation rates. Until unification the Bundesbank's DM (no. 2 in world currency markets) provided the anchor of the system - in the sense that German interest rates were the bottom of EC interest rates and that Germany's inflation rate was always among the lowest in the EC - and most EC central banks deliberately followed the Bundesbank's policy. In 1990 the UK joined the European Exchange Rate System at a unilaterally set exchange rate which was to last only until the autumn of 1992 when the EMS faced a tough crisis because of increased misalignment caused by divergent inflation rates in the EC and by speculation about the failure of the Maastricht Treaty. The first Danish referendum on the EC turned out negative by a 51:49 margin of no-votes so that the whole ratification process seemed to be endangered - with a pending case before Germany's Constitutional Court the Maastricht Treaty still faces an uncertain fate at the time of this writing. The Maastricht Treaty was signed on February 7, 1992 and swift ratification (within one year) was expected for a treaty which radically changed the Rome Treaties of 1957. The Maastricht Treaty states in Article B:
The Union shall set itself the following objectives: - to promote economic and social progress which is balanced and sustainable, in particular through the creating of an area without internal frontiers, through the strengthening of economic and social cohesion and through the establishment of economic and monetary union, ultimately a single currency in accordance with the provisions of this Treaty...The objectives of the Union shall be achieved as provided in this Treaty and in accordance with the conditions and the timetable set out therein while respecting the principle of subsidiarity as defined in Article 3b ("In areas which do not fall within its exclusive competence, the Community shall take action, in accordance with the principle of subsidiarity, only if and in so far as the objectives of the proposed action cannot be sufficiently achieved by the Member States and can therefore, by reason of the scale or effects of the proposed action, be better achieved by the Community").
Article 4a states: *A European System of Central Banks (hereinafter referred to as "ESCB") and a European Central Bank (hereinafter referred to as "ECB") shall be established in accordance with the procedures laid down in this Treaty: they shall act within the limits of the powers conferred upon them by this Treaty and by the Statute of the ESCB and of the ECB ...annexed thereto.*

The Maastricht Treaty envisaged nothing less than the creation of a common central bank and an EC currency by the late 1990s, and this itself would be a radical change for people and governments in Europe who were used to having their own national currency (plus central bank) and pursuing national monetary policies for the sake of national policy goals - including inflationary war financing.

The Maastricht negotiations already showed that the EC12 club could not achieve consensus. The British government obtained the concession that the Protocol on Social Policy should not apply to the UK and Northern Ireland. Policy preferences were obviously too divergent in the field of social policies, where the British position was in favor of maintaining full national autonomy and rather weak social policies which should translate into lower total wage costs - an important advantage for the UK as an investment location. Danish voters at the other extreme were afraid that Maastricht would undermine the mainly tax financed extensive social benefits. For opposite reasons the British and the Danish government were weak supporters of the treaty whose ratification seemed to be cleared after the positive second Danish referendum in 1993.

It is an open question whether a European Monetary Union with a common central bank could really work in a system of weak political integration. Does a technically functional EC central banking system need support in the sense that efficient intra-EC political clearing mechanisms have to be established so that the ECB would not face the risk to come under political fire from all sides in both recessions and inflationary periods? What were the reasons of the EMS crisis of 1992/93; what have European governments learned from this and is monetary integration really complementary to EC real integration (integration of goods markets and factor markets); which main international aspects of EMU are to be considered? Paul Welfens looks into these issues in the first chapter. Randall Henning expands on some of the issues raised.

Michael Klein's focus is on the long term developments in the EMS which went through several stages of turbulence and tranquility. The paper analyzes the relationship between economic liberalization and macroeconomic coordination. Vittorio Grilli's comments on this paper take into account the asymmetries of EC currencies as imperfect substitutes to the dollar. Karl Otto Pöhl as the president of the Deutsche Bundesbank when he presented a dinner speech at the AICGS and published the article *Basic Features of a European Monetary Order* provided a clear-cut description of the required pillars of a viable EC integration (it is no secret that Mr. Pöhl has favored starting EC monetary union as a smaller club of EC member countries). The successor of his successor, Mr. Tietmeyer is now heading the Deutsche Bundesbank through a period of German and EC political turbulence. Daniel Gros and Niels Thygesen write about the strategy of EC monetary integration and the pros (and cons) of EC monetary integration. They emphasize that irrevocably fixed exchange rates mean something different than a single currency, and they develop a pragmatic view of the process towards European currency unification. The basic message is that establishing a balance of costs and benefits of monetary union is difficult but that increasing EC integration should reinforce the benefits. Alan G. Isaac sounds in his comments a rather cautious note - Isaac rightly doubted that "current parity commitments are irrevocable".

Manfred Willms' paper takes up the critical issue of German monetary unification and European monetary union, which were seen by many observers as parallel events. Drawing on the optimum currency area literature Willms argues that political reasons and high labor mobility made the case of a quick

German monetary union while EC monetary integration should proceed much more slowly. John Williamson's comments and Manfred Willms' contribution are likely to have been a favorable piece at the Deutsche Bundesbank because it is implicitly suggested that an optimum currency area is the largest area that the Bundesbank can control as a the central bank. Franco Reither's contribution focuses on liberalization and regulation in the process of financial market integration; EC financial markets have rapidly developed as have international financial markets where trading volumes are exploding. Regulating financial markets has always been a crucial problem in capitalist systems and Reither and Sydney Key, the discussant emphasize the EC's two-pronged approach. Peter Bofinger's contribution is on the crucial problems of coordinating monetary policy in the transition stage to full monetary union. Basic principles of monetary policy in an integrated EC are discussed. With hindsight this transition stage could be much longer than anticipated earlier and a "permanent transition stage" can indeed not be ruled out. Horst Ungerer's comments also focus on the crucial rules for the transition period. The contribution *"Creating a European Central Bank after 1992: Issues of EC Monetary Integration and Problems of Institutional Innovation"* focuses on some basic questions of creating a European central bank after 1992. Paul Welfens raises the issue of German dominance, the problems of integrating the UK into the EMS and some topics of EC central bank formation as they were perceived in May 1990 when the American Institute for Contemporary German Studies hosted a conference on *"European Monetary Integration: From German Dominance to an EC Central Bank?"*. George M. von Furstenberg's comments argue - among other things - that for a future ECU the Swiss Franc should remain a yardstick for currency competition. Given the fact that the Swiss referendum on joining the European Economic Area turned out negative in late 1992 the Swiss franc indeed is likely to play such a role. Jürgen von Hagen and Michele Fratianni introduce some public choice aspects into the debate on public debt policies and monetary policies in the EC. This increasingly important issue will remain high on the agenda in the 1990s because reduced tax rates on capital income in the EC and the rising deficits in major EC countries - most notably Germany, Italy and the UK - raise fears that politicians could exploit monetary integration as a means to more easily finance higher public deficits. Von Hagen and Fratianni take a closer look at the US experience with deficit policies at the state levels and arrive at the conclusion that although monetary union effectively replaces currency competition with the collusion of central bankers EMU could improve the quality of monetary policy under certain circumstances. Robert Solomon gives his critical comments. New questions of fiscal policy have emerged in the context of EC monetary integration after Maastricht where the EC set up a new cohesion fund for those regions with incomes under 90 % of the EC average - provided measures are embedded in attempts for increased convergence. Fiscal federalism is a major topic in both North America and the EC: What role fiscal policies have for income smoothing and reducing regional disparities is crucial for the EC whose internal market dynamics could cause both increased problems of cyclical synchronization of national business cycles as well as rising regional disparities. Paul Masson and Tamim Bayoumi focus on these issues and give a rich set of data as well as a summary of empirical evidence, and Susan Collins gives a brief discussion of selected issues. Stephen Overturf's contribution *"The European Community as an Optimum Currency Area"* takes a fresh look at the issue of optimum currency areas, where his focus is on the McKinnon criterion. Using a model involving adjustment in general, and the costs of price instability in particular, Overturf empirically demonstrates that openness is a useful guide for deciding on greater exchange rate fixity. For the EC the question of currency areas will indeed be crucial since significant benefits would support the viability of the new envisaged central banking system; unfortunately there is little reason to believe that the various criteria of optimum currency areas will be simultaneously met in the EC integration process, and it is also unclear whether a non-optimum EC currency area would require (at what welfare costs?) higher real dollar exchange rate flexibility. Karen Johnson's discussion of the paper provides interesting perspectives on this issue. The first chapter and the two chapters at the end are revised papers from a panel presented at the third biennial international conference of the European Economic Studies Association which took place on May 27-29, 1993, in Washington DC.

This second edition of a book whose focus is on European monetary integration reflects only part of the broader discussion of a complex politico-economic problem in a rapidly changing Europe. The transition to full European monetary union could undermine the working and benefits of the EC internal market if misalignment, recurrent exchange rate instability and very restrictive fiscal policies were adopted in Europe. However, if the transition is organized smoothly and if no major external shocks occur the way to EMU could indeed strengthen single market dynamics. The Brussels EC meeting which introduced wide 15 % margins for ERM countries points to major problems of combining the single market, full capital mobility and exchange rate stability.

I am particularly grateful to Gerry Livingston, AICGS/The Johns Hopkins University, for continuing support for my projects concerning European integration where a strong focus is on the special role of the new Germany in that process. Tim Yarling's excellent editorial support is also gratefully acknowledged. Münster, August 2, 1993 *Paul J.J. Welfens*

Preface to the First Edition

The European integration process has entered a critical stage in 1990. The EC 1992 program means not only the creation of a single EC market for goods and services, but also the liberalization of financial markets in a period characterized by high interdependency, innovativeness and transitory volatility in global financial markets. The removal of capital controls in the EC should contribute to increased efficiency of intra-EC resource allocation, but at the same time national economic policies are increasingly exposed to shifts and shocks from financial markets. This creates a greater need for monetary cooperation in the EC, where the Delors Report has suggested a specific sequencing of tighter monetary cooperation and integration. Achieving EC monetary integration - both in the sense of monetary coordination in a fixed exchange rate regime and institutional integration - requires exploring unchartered waters. Theoretical and practical issues arise, for which the problems of institutional innovation in a highly sensitive field of economic policy are considerable. The intergovernmental conference to be held in Rome in 1990/91 will deal with a host of complicated issues that concern the further development of economic and monetary union in the EC.

To fully exploit the benefits of a greater European market requires to some extent price and exchange rate stability that would enhance the functioning of the price mechanism in a liberalizing single EC market which is still characterized by different currencies as well as diverging policy preferences with respect to price stability, unemployment rates and economic growth. Moreover, the regulations of financial markets differ significantly across EC countries, and the removal of capital controls is likely to enhance the competition of regulatory regimes which are expected to strike a balance between efficiency and stability. The European deregulation experience might well offer conclusions for other major players in the global financial markets. Financial and monetary stability in Europe very much depend upon the type of monetary regime chosen and the degree of integration accomplished.

In 1990 the German-German monetary unification provided an unanticipated case study for some problems centered around monetary integration and currency unification. One aspect played a particular role for the intra-German process: East Germany's decision to give up its own currency and thereby to forego the policy instrument of exchange rate changes as a means of maintaining price competitiveness was valued against the advantages of obtaining West Germany's fully convertible currency with its strong record of price stability. Access to world markets, a functional market system, improved expectations for growth (and hence reduced pressure for migration) are expected from the availability of a convertible currency known for its qualities as a means of national/international exchange and as a reliable store of value that encourages working and saving activities.

The Deutsche Bundesbank, characterized by some unique institutional traits among European central banks - foremost its political independence - swiftly organized the transition to a greater Deutsche mark area that was so obviously desired by the two German governments. The Bundesbank might thereby further increase its weight in EC monetary policy which still consists of national policy-makers but has strongly been influenced by the Bundesbank; some observers have argued that the Bundesbank dominated monetary policy in the EC in the 1980s, and the desire to establish a generally accepted monetary balance of power among major EC countries is certainly one element in the search for new institutional arrangements for monetary policy in Europe. The adoption of stage I of the Delors Report on July 1, 1990, and the envisaged realization of stage II in 1994 are signs of visible progress in the European Monetary System. A comprehensive assessment of the costs and benefits of EC monetary integration will be published by the Commission in the coming weeks.

The implicit adjustment pressures felt in other EC countries as a consequence of German monetary policy often has created political conflicts, but it has over time also contributed to a wider acceptance of the merits of a policy of monetary stability. Whether the envisaged monetary integration process in the EC could emulate the Bundesbank model is an open question. The policy strategies chosen and the institutions created EC-wide will determine whether Western Europe can be an area of price stability which is so vital for long term economic growth and the functioning of the price mechanism. In Eastern Europe, where market-oriented countries now face the quest for growth, full employment and price stability, the EC monetary integration process and the role of the Bundesbank in particular will be carefully watched.

These major topics of EC monetary integration were treated in the conference *EUROPEAN MONETARY INTEGRATION From German Dominance to an EC Central Bank*. This conference - taking place on May 8 - was organized under the auspices of the American Institute for Contemporary German Studies (AICGS) at The Johns Hopkins University. The revised papers presented at this conference and the comments by the discussants as well as the speech of Karl Otto Pöhl, President of the Deutsche Bundesbank (and President of the European Committee of Central Bank Governors), are presented in this proceedings volume.

I am particularly grateful to the Institute's Director, Robert Gerald Livingston, who generously encouraged and supported the idea of a conference on European monetary integration. It is part of a series of Germany-related seminars, conferences and research activities in economics, political science and the humanities upon which the AICGS has a continuous focus. Tim Yarling provided valuable research support and assistance in the editing process of this volume. I am also grateful to Lynn van Norstrand who ensured continuous staff support. Last but not least I wish to express my gratitude to American Airlines, Dresdner Bank and Lufthansa which in cooperation with a generous grant from the German Marshall Fund provided the financial basis for our conference. I am also indebted to the Olin Foundation.

All participants of the conference received a 5 ECU coin, minted in Belgium where it is legal tender. To hand out a symbolic honorarium in the form of a multinational coin is an optimistic view that Western Europe is heading towards a common currency. My personal experience with the coin - it failed the convertibility test in Washington where I could not convince a taxi driver to take me to the IMF building - might represent a minor aspect of the problems of creating a new accepted currency, but a prudent institutional arrangement for monetary policy and a stability-oriented policy can clearly be expected to be able to establish a European currency of high qualities in the 1990s. The institutional features of the Bundesbank model might point to the kind of success-promising blueprint which a stability-oriented monetary policy for the whole of Europe would need. If the Old World can set an example of successful institutional innovation in monetary policy it might also provide a precedent for combining economic integration with greater macroeconomic stability.

Washington D.C., October 1990 *Paul J.J. Welfens*

TABLE OF CONTENTS

Paul J.J. Welfens

EUROPEAN MONETARY UNION: POST-MAASTRICHT PERSPECTIVES ON MONETARY AND REAL INTEGRATION IN EUROPE

1. European Monetary Integration after Maastricht

With the Maastricht Treaty signed on February 7, 1992, the EC member countries seemed to be heading not only for the single market as of January 1, 1993, but also towards monetary union by the end of the 1990s. However, within months the EC was facing (i) a confidence crisis on the side of market participants, (ii) an economic policy crisis in the sense of diverging views on the desired policy course in major EC countries and (iii) a growing concern that too rigid fiscal policy convergence criteria of the Maastricht Treaty would restrict the room to maneuver at the start of single market. The start of the single market was surprisingly characterized by slow growth and strong pressures for structural adjustment in all EC countries.

The Bundesbank faced problems with respect to monetary policy leadership in Europe because Germany's inflation rate reached 4 % in 1992 and most of 1993. This is high by German standards and hence creates fear that the Bundesbank will pursue restrictive monetary policies which reduce German inflation a bit but other EC countries' growth prospects strongly. Moreover, in 1992 only Italy, Spain, Portugal, Ireland and Greece had a consumer inflation rate higher than that in (Western) Germany. Germany's monetary leadership faced external criticism on its policies, while central banks in other EC countries, notably in France and Belgium, prepared for political independence which no longer makes the Bundesbank's institutional position look unique in Europe.

The confidence crisis in the EMS developed when the narrowly failed Danish referendum on Maastricht in June 1992 raised questions about the viability of the whole Maastricht Treaty in which not only European Monetary Union was a major element, but EC Political Union - meaning common defence policies and common foreign policies. Danish voters' resistance obviously was focussing more on Political Union and the quest for national autonomy in this field than on monetary policy. When French President Mitterand called for a referendum on the Maastricht Treaty and opinion polls suggested a narrow outcome, speculative attacks against various currencies mounted; these attacks were partly the reverse side of a move into the DM in an EC political environment in which a future ECU had become doubtful. DM denominated assets had in their own right become increasingly attractive in 1992 when Germany's Bundesbank, eager to demonstrate stability-oriented monetary leadership - in contrast to alleged excessive fiscal deficits of the Bonn government for the sake of German unification - raised the discount rate to a post-1949 record level; all this occurred while US short term interest rates were hitting record lows so that massive US capital outflows were strongly and disproportionately attracted by DM denominated assets. Speculative capital flows increased in a maximum damage EC environment, namely in a setting characterized by newly established full capital mobility in all EC countries (except for Spain, Portugal and Greece) on the one hand, and, on the other hand, the anticipated unfolding of the single EC market which implied free trade not only in commodities, but also in financial and nonfinancial services and the free movement of labor and capital.

Various aspects of EMU have been analyzed in recent literature where emphasis has been placed on both institutional problems of monetary policy in the EC (e.g. *Hasse and Schäfer 1990; Weber 1991; Kenen 1992; Fratianni, von Hagen and Waller 1992; Canzoneri, Grilli and Masson 1992; Kösters 1993; Goldstein et al. 1993*) and problems of optimal currency area in the EC (*Eichengreen 1990; Menkhoff and Sell 1992; De Grauwe 1992; Fratinanni and von Hagen 1992; Smeets 1993*). While some critics argue that the EC is not an optimum currency union and hence monetary unification is an economic mistake, other critical observers suggest that the transition towards full EMU is full of risks and should be prolonged because of the structural adjustment needs stemming from the single market project and the new EC problems faced in the context of systemic transformation and economic opening up in Eastern Europe (*Welfens 1992b; 1993a*). In the subsequent analysis we will focus on the autumn crisis of 1992 (section 1) in order to draw some lessons for sustainable transition policies in the EC; in section 2 the Maastricht approach to EMU is analyzed and the link between the single market and monetary integration is analyzed. Finally, some issues of the transition to EMU are addressed and the question is raised whether or not Germany and the Bundesbank are likely to shape a viable EMU.

1.1 The Ratification Crisis

Facing an uncertain and delayed ratification of the Maastricht Treaty raised serious stability problems in the EMS in 1992/93. In autumn 1992 a major crisis in the EMS erupted when the Italian Lira and the British Pound left the Exchange Rate Mechanism, their exchange rates were allowed to float and the Spanish Peseta and the Portuguese Escudo were devalued. Competitive devaluations in Iceland - with some advocates of devaluation pointing to competition of Iceland's fishing fleet against Spain's fleet - and Ireland occurred at the turn of 1992/93; Ireland's strong trade links with the U.K. almost forced it to shadow the Pound's 20 percent devaluation within three months. Ireland tried to defend the Punt parity with triple digit interest rates as had been the case in Sweden a few months earlier. Finland's, Sweden's and Norway's unilateral pegging of their respective exchange rates to the ECU was not viable in the heavy weather of speculative attacks and high nominal and real interest rates in late 1992. Finland's double digit unemployment rate, partly caused by the collapse of the USSR and its strong trade links with it, induced Finland to switch back to floating again, while Sweden tried to defend parity for a few weeks with record interest rates. These record rates were necessary to compensate those holding Swedish Kronas instead of DM in an exchange rate crisis/an anticipated devaluation (note that a 4 percent devaluation taking place over a two-day weekend will result in an annualized yield of some 750 percent for those borrowing Kronas on Friday - prior to devaluation - and repaying the Krona loan with depreciated currency after they had converted DM assets into Kronas on Monday; hence a "weekend devaluation probability" of 0.15 or 0.5 requires two-day annualized Krona rates of about 100 % or 300 %, respectively). Watching Finland's exports and stock market index benefitting from devaluation, while Swedish industry suffered from record nominal and real short term interest rates, the government of Sweden finally decided to also return to floating. Norway did the same. Speculative attacks against the French Franc were countered in France by high interest rate policies and government's arm-twisting of state banks, by Bundesbank intervention (including public statements) in favor of the Franc and, finally, by a first reduction of Germany's discount rate in January 1993 which was followed by several other small interest rate reductions; on July 1, 1993 the discount rate was reduced by half a percentage point to 6.75 %. French interest rates could be strongly reduced after the new conservative government took over, but in real terms long term interest rates remain at high levels in France. Short term rates fell below German levels in mid-1993, but nominal interest rates remained slightly higher than in Germany. The 10-year yield spread over German bonds has fallen back dramatically in early 1993. French inflation was 200 basis points below German inflation in 1993.

From the Bundesbank's point of view the virtue of small reductions in the discount and lombard rate is consistent to the extent that this policy fuels anticipation of further future interest rate reductions and does not undermine the prospects for a decrease in the long term inflation rate. Both effects can reduce real long term interest rates strongly, and long term interest rates are more important in German financial markets - and for investment - than short term interest rates. Lower real interest rates also support the Bundesbank's goal to induce the government to reduce government borrowing which sharply increased in the context of German unification and is considered as a potential threat for anti-inflationary monetary policy.

By contrast, British financial markets are characterized by a dominance of short term borrowing, and long term interest rates are often adjustable so that short term interest rates are truly dominating. The U.K. as well as Italy (and some other EC countries) face a much higher vulnerability to short term interest rate shocks than Germany, the Netherlands, Belgium or France. Theory suggests that low inflation rates will increase the average maturity of bonds and generally will encourage more long term financing. The diverging historical inflation records of EC countries thus influence the term structure of financial markets and this in turn creates vulnerability to short term interest rate shocks for some countries whereas others are more robust in this respect. Countries in which dominant short term interest rates coincide with a high debt GNP ratio (as in Italy and Greece) are most exposed to interest rate shocks arising from Germany's monetary policy reactions. Moreover, such countries then obviously cannot afford to defend overvalued currencies by a high interest rate policy over the long term.

High capital mobility and considerable intra-EC interest differentials played a significant role in the ERM crisis of 1992. In the UK, interest rates were 6 percentage points higher than German rates between 1987 and 1990, and the differential came down quickly after the pound's entry into the ERM in late 1990. In Italy, the interest differential peaked at 8 points in mid-1987 and declined to some 2 percentage points by mid-1991, while in Spain the differential against German rates came down from 7 percentage points in the period 1987-90 to about 300 basis points in late 1991:

A distinguishing feature of the ...crisis in Europe, compared with earlier realignments and speculative attacks, is the magnitude of capital flows precipitated by fears of realignment...Also, in the "convergence play" strategy, institutional investors had sought to exploit the existing interest differentials within Europe, given the perception that the macroeconomic performance of ERM member countries would gradually converge. They pursued this strategy, for example, by borrowing funds in the countries with relatively low interest rates such as Germany, and by investing in high-yield countries such as Italy and Spain. An investor who believed that interest rates would gradually converge toward the levels observed in the low-interest rate countries without exchange rate realignment on the way, would invest in long-term, high-yielding securities in anticipation of earning significant capital gains as interest rates fell (Goldstein et al. 1993, p.49).

After the negative Danish referendum on Maastricht in June and in anticipation of a narrow result at the French referendum in September 1992, the Maastricht plan for a future EC currency became less credible and by the same token the idea of a dominating DM more likely. In a period of high DM interest rates the movement out of ECU assets, out of dollar assets and out of weak EMS currencies, but moving into DM assets became appealing. Italy's currency was the first country to fall victim to its accumulated currency overvaluation and the rising DM attractiveness which had been reinforced by Germany's high interest rate policy adopted in 1992 as a means to reduce inflationary pressures (with inflation running at 4 %) and to signal to the Bonn government that fiscal restraint was necessary. The role of the DM as an international reserve asset had strongly increased since 1973 and its share in world currency reserves - reaching over 15 % by the late 1980s (*Issing 1992*) - could be expected to increase at the expense of the ECU or even the dollar if Maastricht failed.

Italy's foreign exchange reserves had already been melting away in the first half of 1992 and therefore the lira devaluation was inevitable. On September 14 the lira was devalued by 7 %, and three days later the Peseta followed with a 5 % devaluation (later followed by a second and third devaluation), while the Pound Sterling and the Lira left the exchange rate mechanism. *The Bank of International Settlements (1993, p.188)* noted:

The Bank of England later published an estimate of the volume of official intervention which had taken place over the four months to end-September: the figure was over $ 160 billion, most of which had been accounted for by sales of Deutsche Mark. For the period June-December the Bank of Italy estimated that total intervention in defence of exchange rates had been about $ 200 billion, of which half had taken place in September alone...Nevertheless, exchange rate pressures persisted into October and, particularly, November. Many currencies were involved, including sterling, as UK interest rates were lowered. In mid-November Swedish Government failed to obtain the necessary all-party support for its new fiscal austerity package. The market's response was instantaneous...The authorities decided to let the krona float. It was later announced that over six days the currency outflow had been the equivalent of $ 26 billion, or 11 % of Sweden's GNP. The comparable intervention figure during the three weeks of the September crisis had been .. over half this amount.

The Bundesbank's "interview policy" - indicating in mid-September that a broader EMS realignment was adequate - might indeed have weakened the British pound. However, as the following Tab. 1 shows the Pound indeed was overvalued and rumors hardly would have affected its position if this had not been the case. Compare 1987.IV (the last realignment prior to 1992 was in early 1987) and the index for 1992.II showing a strong overvaluation of the Lira and the Pound Sterling. For the Lira the overvaluation was about 13 %, for the Pound about 9 %, much in contrast to the Irish Punt, the Danish Crown, the Belgian Franc and the French Franc whose real exchange rates had changed only slightly in the period 1987 to mid-1992. Postponed adjustment requirements and fundamental changes, including considerations of relative political instability, led to sharp devaluations of the Lira and the Pound, once it was decided to let the two currencies float. Vis-à-vis the DM the Lira and the Pound Sterling lost about 25 % within three months. Joint German-French measures to defend the Franc in the run-up to the French parliamentary elections in early 1993 were justified by underlying fundamentals to a large extent. However, while French nominal and real interest rates came down after the French election real long term interest rates remained about one percentage point above the German real interest rate; compared to 1989 the Franco German real interest rate differential was nearly halved. This could undermine the DM's anchor role in the EMS: German interest rates were the lowest in the EC, and the DM is an international reserve currency.

If one takes the simple monetarist exchange rate model which relies on purchasing power parity $p= e +p^*$ (P,P* denote the domestic and foreign price level, respectively, E the nominal exchange rate; small letters denote logarithms of the variable), money market equilibrium $\ln M - p = \Omega y - \sigma i$ (M=money stock; Ω=income elasticity of the money demand; σ=interest semi elasticity of the money demand (which is, according to *Kremers/Lane (1990)*, about 2 in the EC , i=nominal interest rate in %) and interest rate parity $i = i^* + a$ (i^*= foreign interest rate and a is the expected devaluation rate) the nominal equilibrium exchange rate will be: (1) $e = \ln M - \Omega y + \sigma i^* + \sigma a - p^*$

If we assume a symmetric money demand function abroad (starred variables) and money market equilibrium abroad $\ln M^* - p^* = \Omega y^* - \sigma i^*$ the fundamental monetarist equilibrium equation is $e = \ln M - \ln M^* - \Omega(y - y^*) + \sigma(i - i^*)$. From a German perspective the Bundesbank's high interest rate policy which forced other EC countries to increase their nominal interest rates overproportionately as well as high German economic growth in 1990/91 - or unification induced higher growth in the 1990s - would indicate a need for a DM revaluation.

Tab. 1: Real DM-Exchange Rate Index [P/eP*: (1972) = 100; on the basis of consumer prices] Vis-à-Vis EMS Countries#

	Pound Sterl.	Ital. Lira	Ir. Punt	Dan. Crown	Belg. Franc	Fr. Franc	Guil-der	Port. Escu.	Pese-ta	US $
1973.IV	121.3	123.4	118.2	103.3	109.2	107.9	102.6	104.1	104.8	125
1979.IV	102.8	126.9	107.2	93.3	94.2	102.7	93.9	111.0	84.0	142
1981.IV	80.9	114.1	86.7	91.1	95.1	95.8	91.7	90.8	81.8	102
1982.IV	81.8	110.2	84.8	94.7	105.9	103.0	91.4	100.7	84.6	92
1985.IV	83.3	103.2	80.0	89.8	100.1	96.3	93.0	97.1	86.3	85
1987.IV	96.1	101.3	87.3	07.9	100.9	101.0	93.6	103.5	82.8	122
1988.IV	86.2	99.2	86.2	85.6	101.3	100.9	94.5	97.0	78.0	114
1990.IV	84.2	94.0	85.1	84.3	98.2	98.5	96.3	86.0	69.9	128
1992.II	83.8	92.1	86.0	87.2	100.4	100.3	96.5	74.8	67.9	121
% change										
'92/'87*	-12.8	-9.1	-1.5	-0.8	-0.5	-0.7	3.1	-27.7	-18.0	-0.2
'92/1972	-16.2	-7.9	-14.0	-13.8	+0.4	+0.3	-3.5	-25.2	-32.1	21.3

#: Except for Greece *: *percent change of IInd quarter 1992 vis-à-vis IVth quarter 1987; own computation, based on Bundesbank statistics.*

Chances to save the pound parity by orchestrated intervention were minimal because once a currency has reached its lower margin in the parity grid even massive interventions are insufficient in view of the huge market volume. Only if the British economy had been able to easily get along with very high real interest rates as a means to defend the Pound had there been a slight chance for defending the overvalued British currency. In the UK capital mobility had increased in the 1980s. In the U.K. pensions funds' shares of investments abroad increased from 6 to 20 % in the period 1980-92 (*Blitz 1992*; see also on the rising internationalization Tab. A1). With a rising number of EC countries in the ERM the uncovered interest rate parity $i=i^* + R + a$ (a=expected devaluation rate) was increasingly bound to lead to contradictions with purchasing power parity. The interest rate i was determined by adding a risk premium R (depending on the respective country, the width of the parity band) to the DM interest rate i^{DM} - which set the floor for long term interest rates in the EC - such that real interest rates r_j in each of Germany's EC partner countries would exceed German rates strongly if inflation was below that in Germany; but a high r reduces growth - this represents costs of monetary integration - and this could weaken the currency. Facing already a 10 % unemployment rate in 1992 the UK, Italy and France became subject to speculative attacks. The UK and Italy left the ERM in late 1992, while the attacks against the FF/other currencies brought the EMS "reform" of August 1, 1993. In a dramatic EC meeting in Brussels a widening of the parity band was adopted, namely ±15 % for the period until the end-'93; only for the Guilder-DM parity the band of ±2.25 % was maintained. The Brussels meeting was organized at the request of Germany. The Bundesbank - for fear of German inflation and excess liquidity - had refused on Thurday, July 29, to reduce the discount rate; this decision reinforced speculation against the FF and other currencies such that on the following day massive interventions of the Bundesbank became necessary as EC currencies under attack had to be supported once the ERM floor rate had been reached. This foreign exchange market intervention created excess liquidity such that the Bundesbank faced a true dilemma. The rationale of the Brussels decision was: (i) to decouple EC interest rates from high interest rates in Germany so that France and other ERM countries could reduce interest rates; (ii) to allow the Bundesbank to regain control of the money supply; (iii) to raise the risk for speculators (but now there is the risk of overshooting); (iv) to allow markets to determine exchange rates.

Currency Substitution

Indirect currency substitution played a major role in the September 1992 crisis in the EMS. With nominal interest rates in the U.S. at very low levels and German rates at post-1945 record levels the interest differential generated transatlantic passat-like winds: short term capital was massively moved out of the US dollar to be poured into DM denominated assets (DM interest rates exceeded US interest rates in 1971, too). As a consequence of massive capital inflows German interest rates started to slightly fall in late 1992. Since the Bundesbank refused to lower the discount rate and because inflationary expectations were running at unchanged high levels of around 4 % in 1992/93 nominal interest rates in Germany were unlikely to come down quickly, and indications for rising US interest rates remained weak even after the Clinton administration took office in the US. Transatlantic interest rate differentials disproportionately affect the $-DM exchange rate in Europe because the DM is a closer substitute to the dollar than any other European currency. This in itself is bound to create tensions within the EMS, a link analyzed earlier by *Giavazzi and Giovannini (1986)*.

It is unclear which mechanisms account for the uneven tensions within the EMS. Two hypotheses may be advanced: (i) Since in integrated European capital markets Germany's EC partner countries (more strictly the ERM partner countries) have to raise nominal interest rates parallel to the German interest rate, the economic situation in each country is critical: countries with high budget deficits or high unemployment rates can hardly be expected to be able to live with higher real interest rates. Italy with its double problem of high budget deficits and high unemployment therefore could only devalue, and finally leave the ERM. (ii) Countries which are major producers and exporters of innovative capital equipment - such as Germany, the Netherlands, Austria and Switzerland - are less likely to be forced to devalue in a period of rising European real interest rates because the European-wide need to match higher real interest rates with a rising marginal product of capital can be achieved not only by reducing output, but also by accelerating capital modernization. While for nonproducers of capital equipment in Europe high real interest rates imply only the pain of lower investment-output ratio and increased budget problems for government, countries which are major producers of capital equipment and known for a high supply side flexibility will face smaller economic problems in periods of higher real interest rates. (iii) European countries differ in their international net creditor status. Countries with a net creditor position are likely to partly benefit from rising interest income from abroad in periods of high real interest rates. As regards the credibility of policy measures defending an overvalued parity speculators will take these aspects into account. The less favorable (i)-(iii) are for a given country and the higher the initial overvaluation, the less risky it is to mount speculative attacks against a certain currency.

1.2 Competitive Devaluations

The devaluation of one currency (country A) can trigger a cascade of devaluations in other countries B-Z. If A has strong trade links with B and a strong overlap in exports on third country markets B is likely to respond to A's devaluation with a devaluation, too; and similar arguments could apply to B with respect to C...Z. A clear example is the link between Spain and Portugal in May 1993 when the Peseta was devalued by 8 %, while the Escudo was devalued by 6.5 % (in the 6 % devaluation of the Peseta in November the Escudo also had followed suit). Another example is the pair U.K. and Ireland. The Pound devaluation and the fall of the Sterling exchange rate after the switch to floating implied that the Irish Punt bound to be devaluated, and it probably was only the political indeterminacy of pending elections in late 1992 that postponed the 10 % devaluation of the Punt to as late as January 30, 1993. The lira devaluation weakened the Iberian currencies because part of Italian exports show a strong overlap with Spanish and Portuguese exports; indeed the Peseta was devalued twice, and the Escudo - having entered the ERM in 1992 - was devalued, too. Finally, the Swedish strategy of unilaterally pegging its currency to the ECU became unfeasible not only because the weak Swedish economy could not survive short term interest rates of up to 500 %, but also because the Finnish decision to switch from pegging to floating in autumn 1992 was bound to erode Swedish export positions in all markets with direct competition against Finnish exporters. "Hyper interest rates" can occur during an exchange rate crisis and during policy switching.

What happened in 1992 was not very different from the crisis of the French Franc in 1983 when France devalued on Monday, March 21 - after the FF had reached annualized interest rates of 350 % during the week before. The 1983 devaluation of 3.75 % vis-à-vis the DM took place over a two-day weekend and implied an annualized yield of 675% for those happy speculators who borrowed Francs on Friday in order to convert them into DM over the weekend, and repaying the FF loan with depreciated currency. Market signals had strongly suggested an impending devaluation. Dealers in foreign exchange who assumed over a given weekend a 0.5 probability of a 3.75% devaluation would be willing to hold a short term FF position - rather than a DM position - only if markets offered two-day interest rates of some 300 % at an annual rate. Anticipated policy switching is an important theoretical issue and is covered in the analysis of *Garber and Flood (1993)*.

The EMS had narrowly escaped a full disintegration in a period where it was supposed to develop toward European Monetary Union with irrevocably fixed exchange rates. In the U.K. interest rates had strongly been reduced immediately after the switch to floating and for some time it seemed that countries following the British course of floating would benefit in a similar way; indeed, it seemed that a situation similar to 1931 had occurred when the U.K. gave up the gold standard and the pre-World War I parity (reestablished, based on a deflationary process, in 1925) and devalued the Pound by some 30 %, with more than 20 countries from the Pound block following suit, thereby leaving the gold block France, Switzerland, the Netherlands, Belgium and Poland plus Germany and Italy - the latter two introducing capital controls - in a situation of overvalued currencies, rising real interest rates and rapidly falling industrial output. Sharp devaluations impose a shock-like adjustment pressure on the EC; this holds even if devaluation is consistent with PPP, but it clearly makes a difference whether there is a continuous adjustment (or no adjustment need) or a sudden exchange rate adjustment which corrects accumulated inflation differentials over an extended period.

The basic problem in the EMS in 1992 was not devaluation itself, but the order of magnitude which basically reflected cumulated inflation differentials of the U.K. and Italy vis-à-vis Germany. Several observers had pointed out early on that the pound had entered the ERM at too high an exchange rate and that sustaining inflation differentials were, of course, not consistent with fixed nominal exchange rates (*e.g. Dornbusch 1991; Welfens 1991*, this volume).

What seemed surprising, however, was the political self-blocade implicit in one of the convergence criteria of the Maastricht Treaty which stipulated, among other criteria, that no devaluation should have occurred for two consecutive years if an EC country was to enter stage III of Economic and Monetary Union. Instead of interpreting this clause as freedom to devalue if necessary in the first half of the 1990s, most governments obviously were determined to fix parities already well before the immediate run-up to stage III envisaged for 1997 or 1999 in the Maastricht Treaty. Had the U.K. devalued by a small percentage in 1991 and Italy accepted a real devaluation when it entered the narrow band in the EMS in 1990, speculators would have found their victims in much better shape. Record German interest rates as a consequence of German unification and - this should be emphasized - persistent Italian deficits that remained at the equivalent of 2 % of EC GNP posed difficult problems for all EC countries, but countries with overvalued currencies were unable to weather this interest rate shock in a period of confidence crisis and rising capital mobility. Competitive devaluations undermined European free trade and thus caused market disintegration in the 1930s in Europe when misalignment (overvaluation of the Franc, undervaluation of the Pound and the sterling bloc) distorted trade and allocation, while encouraging compensating tariff policies and regional block building.

Monetary institutions in Europe have a long record of slowly learning about feasible and necessary policy strategies consistent with sustained growth and price stability. Maintaining an overvalued currency over many years is not only a trait of the 1980s but can be found in the 1920s, too. E.g. British policy inconsistency in exchange rate policies indeed has a long record if one recalls the return to the pre-World War I gold parity of the Pound in 1925 which had to be sharply devalued by 1931, and one may also recall the aborted move to convertibility in 1947. Misalignment and inadequate policies are certainly not a British specialty, but adequate policies of reserve currency countries are of significant internal and external importance in all exchange rate regimes. With respect to the EMS the German Bundesbank still has to prove that it can exert monetary leadership that takes into account both national and EC aspects. The Bundesbank can, however, claim that in spring 1990 it suggested considering a realignment but EC partners - especially France and the U.K. - were unwilling to really envisage a timely revaluation of the DM. Creating closer similarities in the institutional setup of central banks might reinforce the willingness to cooperate in a consistent manner. From this perspective the French move towards an independent central bank could indeed facilitate German-French monetary cooperation, and if the U.K. and Italy cannot follow in institutional central bank reform quickly the interests of both countries might become less taken into account in the future by German-French monetary policy strategies; moreover, both the Pound and the Lira are likely to face an eroding position in international currency markets if central bank independence cannot be established relatively fast.

Misalignment risks are prevalent in the EC in the 1990s. If major EC countries should face unemployment problems at the same time competitive devaluations as well as overshooting phenomena (a typical problem of transitory or permanent floating) could destroy not only the European Monetary System but also the single market. Governments that face devaluations in competing countries but want to avoid devaluation themselves could quickly face pressure to reimpose nontariff and tariff barriers in the EC. Finally, increased use of EC funds (EC cohesion fund) for structural and regional policies could become a means of compensating adverse exchange rate effects.

1.3 Some Problems with the Maastricht Design of EMU

The Maastricht Treaty emphasizes price stability as the priority goal of a future EC central banking system. Germany's political preferences as well as the institutional model of the Deutsche Bundesbank have strongly influenced the envisaged main goal and EC central banking design. If the Bundesbank would be replaced by the European System of Central Banks (ESCB) in accord with the Maastricht Treaty the Federal Republic of Germany would lose its monetary autonomy and the DM, while there would be an uncertain gain from currency union in the EC; however, part of the Maastricht dividend for the FRG obviously was the support of France - and other EC member countries - for German unification in 1990.

The Maastricht Treaty envisages, following the Delors Report, a three stage approach to EMU. A first stage - already started on July 1, 1990 and lasting until end-1993 - will bring full capital mobility as well as increasing policy coordination. The latter could require some EC countries to submit convergence programs that shows ways for achieving the convergence criteria of the Maastricht Treaty: a deficit GNP ratio of below 3 percent, a debt-GNP ratio not exceeding 60 %, an inflation rate that must not exceed the average of those three countries with the lowest inflation rate by more than 1.5 percentage points and a nominal long term interest rate (bond rate) which should not exceed the rate in the three countries with the lowest inflation rate by more than 2 percentage points. Since the nominal interest rate is the result of the "market real interest rate" plus the expected inflation rate, one may argue that the interest rate criterion emphasizes that convergence in actual inflation rates should be accompanied by convergence in expected inflation rates. This in turn is consistent with real interest parity. The fact that the ERM crisis in autumn 1992 brought a transitory reinforcement of capital controls in some EC countries (Spain, Portugal, Ireland) shows that even stage I is difficult to realize. As regards the desired membership of all EC countries in the ERM - within the narrow band - Italy's and the UK's leaving (as well as the wider ±15 % margin adopted August 1, 1993) of the EMS clearly is the opposite of the development to be achieved.

In Stage II of EMU a new institution will be created: the European Monetary Institute (EMI) as the successor organization of the EC committee of central bank governors and the European Fund for Foreign Exchange Cooperation. EMI will be responsible for coordinating monetary policies. The responsibility for monetary policy will remain at the national level which could mean that German monetary policy will continue its strong impact upon EC monetary policy. The EMI will undertake preparatory steps for stage III which could start as early as 1997; 1999 is the alternative date. For Italy, Greece, Spain and Portugal stage III would bring an important change with respect to central bank financing of government budget deficits. Direct monetary financing of government budget deficits will be no longer possible; technically this will even affect the German government which formerly could draw short-term credits from the central bank (within certain limits) in order to bridge the period between major tax receipt dates. National central banks will obtain political independence; at the latest this measure must be at the beginning of stage III. In 1992/93 the Benelux countries, France and Spain have prepared steps towards central bank independence. Governments face the risk of losing some seigniorage gains if one assumes that independent central banks will adopt a less inflationary monetary policy than otherwise; however, governments could gain from lower nominal and real interest rates to the extent that market participants associate an independent central bank with less unstable monetary policies, declining uncertainty and therefore finally reduced interest rates. Risk premiums could decline and possibly lower real interest rates could stimulate growth.

At the end of stage II the Council of Economics and Finance Ministers (ECOFIN) will evaluate whether progress in achieving the convergence criteria has been achieved. Based on the ECOFIN report about the fulfillment of convergence criteria the EC Council will decide with qualified majority until end-1996 whether a majority of countries has achieved convergence and whether it is useful for the EC to enter stage III of EMU; if so, a date for entry in stage III will be fixed. An additional criterion for would-be members in stage III of monetary union is that two years prior to the ECOFIN report no devaluation of the respective currency has occurred. This clause has stimulated the tabooing of devaluations in stage I beyond the normal political reluctance to devalue a currency whose parity is often held to have a political value of its own. The Maastricht Treaty did not emphasize the necessity to regularly adjust parities - e.g. within small margins, in annual intervals - during the transition period 1990-95. The dynamics of the single EC market and the structural adjustments resulting from the unfolding of the EC '93 project indeed suggest that real exchange rate adjustment will be necessary in the 1990s within the EMS. If the 1997 date cannot be realized the Maastricht Treaty proposes another convergence report in 1998. In accordance with this report EMU III will enter into force for at least two countries on January 1, 1999, and a European Central Bank (ECB) will be established as of July 1, 1998; a possible option to fulfill the Treaty, while avoiding sharp conflicts about a revision of the Treaty, could be that the currency union between Belgium and Luxembourg would be the two countries to introduce the ECU in 1999. The revision clause of the Maastricht Treaty leaves open whether the EC government conference of 1996 will introduce some refinements with respect to the switch to stage III. In stage III the ESCB will be established (most anticipate its seat will be in Germany). Since in stage II the currencies will be defined that will compose the "new ECU", the enlargement of the EC by some EFTA members should be settled by then. The ECU will become a real currency in stage III.

Fig. 1: Stages of European Monetary Union According to the Maastricht Treaty

STAGE I (July 1, 1990 - end-1993)

1a) Full liberalization of the capital account in all EC countries; transition periods for Greece, Spain and Portugal (the latter until 1995, due to provisions in the treaties of the Iberian enlargement of the EC).

1b) Increasing macroeconomic policy coordination of EC member countries, which are expected to develop convergence programs.

1c) All EC currencies should be integrated in the ERM: standard parity margin of ± 2.25%.

STAGE II (1994 to end-1996 or end-1998)

2a) Creation of the European Monetary Institute (EMI) as the successor organization of the EC committee of central bank governors and the European Fund for Foreign Exchange Cooperation. EMI will be responsible for coordinating monetary policies, but responsibility for monetary policy will remain at the national level. EMI will prepare stage III.

2b) Direct monetary financing of government budget deficits no longer possible;

2c) Central banks will obtain political independence; at the latest at the beginning of III.

2d) The weights of the currencies in the ECU are irrevocably fixed which makes the mid-1990s critical with respect to EC enlargement.

2e) The Council of Economics and Finance Ministers (ECOFIN) will evaluate whether progress in achieving the convergence criteria has been achieved; moreover, ECOFIN will report whether a majority of countries havs achieved convergence, and based on this report the EC Council will decide with qualified majority until end-1996 whether it is useful for the EC to enter stage III of EMU; if so, a date for entry in stage III will be fixed. After another convergence report EMU III will enter into force for at least two countries on January 1, 1999, and a European Central Bank (ECB) will be established as of July 1, 1998.

Stage III/Final Stage (at the earliest as of 1/1/1997) - Creation of the ESCB

(3a) The ESCB will be established. Paid-up equity capital according to equal weights for national shares of GNP and the population in the respective EC total.

(3b) Freezing of parities with a zero margin. ECU will become a real currency.

(3c) Governments will agree on guidelines for fiscal policies and economic policies.

STATUTE OF EUROPEAN CENTRAL BANKING SYSTEM (EUROPEAN CENTRAL BANK + NATIONAL CENTRAL BANKS): *MAIN GOAL IS PRICE LEVEL STABILITY;* Position of the ESCB: a) functionally independent. b) no-bailout clause for other EC member countries' debt. The ECB Council consists of the six members of the ECB Directorate - who have to be appointed unanimously - plus the national central bank presidents. c) operationally independent ESCB which means that monetary policy (indicators and instruments) will be chosen by the ESCB; d) personally independent which is achieved by eight year terms for the board members - no reelection possible; national central bank presidents must have at least a five year term.

The convergence criteria chosen are clear, but first one can object that they are not really hard targets because the EC summit could always argue in a somewhat arbitrary way that sufficient progress has been achieved by member countries which have failed to meet convergence targets; second some criteria are doubtful and partly lack convincing economic justification.

An inflation rate convergence criterion certainly is a useful requirement if the goal of price stability is to be achievable in the first critical stage of the ESCB which will face the natural credibility problem of a newly created institution. Even if it is modelled on the German Bundesbank (which until 1957 was a "Bank deutscher Länder" - Bank of German States - which in turn was modelled on the US Federal Reserve System) it is obvious that market participants would strongly doubt the goal of price stability if the initial stage III club would consist of countries with strongly diverging inflation rates. The inflation criterion and the interest rate criterion are convincing ideas for countries that want to establish a low-inflation community at the final stage of EMU - and want to maintain price stability; it is, however, doubtful whether high real interest rates that characterized almost all EC members in 1992 would be an ideal starting position for a stability oriented EMU. Low real interest rates and high growth rates which would reduce unemployment are desirable if a discussion about an inflation unemployment trade off in the initial stage of EC monetary union is not to undermine the credibility of EC monetary policy.

The debt-GNP ratio of 60 % is quite doubtful as a convergence criterion because it is reflecting past policies rather than future sound policy strategies. The 60 % ratio was chosen (*Matthes 1992*) because this was the average EC ratio prevailing during the period of the government conference leading to the Maastricht Treaty; and the 3 % deficit-GNP ratio is a corollary of the 60 % debt-GNP ratio because only with that upper limit on national deficit-GNP ratios can those countries which currently strongly exceed the 60 % debt limit expect to achieve that ratio in the long term. Given the fact that Italy, Belgium and Greece strongly exceed the 100 % margin with respect to the debt-GDP ratio (Tab. 2) - reflecting in part past political mismanagement - it is clear that massive surpluses would have to be reached in the 1990s if these countries were to at least strongly move towards the 60 % debt figure.

Tab. 2: Fulfillment or Nonfulfillment of EMU Convergence Criteria
(reference values are for 1992, hypothetical scenario; brackets indicate fulfillment)

	%-change of consumer prices	public debt in % of GDP	budget deficit; % of GDP	interest rate on bonds(%)	[real interest rate]#
Reference	3.3	60	-3	10.0	6.7
FR	[2.6]	[50.1]	[-2.8]	[9.0]	6.4
FRG*	4.0	[43.3]	-3.2	[8.0]	3.2
B	[2.4]	132.2	-6.7	[8.7]	5.3
NL	[3.1]	79.8	-3.5	[8.2]	5.1
DK	[2.1]	74.0	[-2.3]	[8.9]	6.8
LX	3.4	[6.8]	[-0.4]	[7.9]	4.5
IR	[2.9]	99.0	[-2.5]	[9.1]	6.2
UK	5.1	[45.9]	-6.1	[9.1]	4.0
SP	6.0	[47.4]	-4.6	12.2	6.2
P	9.1	66.2	-5.6	11.7	2.6
IT	5.3	106.8	-10.5	12.4	7.1
GR**	16.0	106.7	-13.4	19.0	3.0

* 1992 inflation rate for Western Germany; ** discount rate (no long term interest rate available since maturities are short).
# interest rate minus inflation rate

Source: Deutsche Bundesbank, Monatsberichte, 1993; EC Commission

The Netherlands, Denmark and Ireland face less dramatic problems in this respect although they also exceeded the critical limit in 1992. A more generous debt-GNP limit in combination with a relatively strict deficit-GNP medium term limit would have been more adequate if at the same time the crucial indicator, unemployment rate, had been additionally taken into account. In order to establish policy credibility and reputation it would be of paramount importance that an EC central bank is not facing serious conflict-prone trade-offs between inflation and unemployment. If major EC countries have high unemployment rates in the beginning of the ESCB the looming policy conflict will undermine anti-inflation policy credibility so that actual anti-inflation measures will have to be more drastic than otherwise; moreover, if price stability can only be achieved at the price of mass unemployment in the EC after 2000 - similar to the British case of the 1920s when pre-World War I parity could only be achieved via deflationary policy and mass unemployment - the political acceptance of the ESCB is bound to suffer; indeed the whole EC integration could unravel in such a situation.

Are debt limits necessary at all? The answer for countries embedded in an institution as big as the EC is yes unless one would think that the no-bailout clause contained in the Maastricht Treaty (and in other countries in constitutional rules) is credible ex post and ex ante; if, however, a country would face bankruptcy and politico-economic disruptions the other EC member countries could certainly not simply watch the unfolding of serious negative spillovers of debt default. In the 1970s thc city of New York went bankrupt despite provisions that the city of New York must have a balanced budget over thc medium run, and the federal government bailed out the city. A similar inconsistency between ex ante bail out and ex post bail out is likely with respect to the relations between the EC layer and EC countries (*Lane 1993*).

Since markets discriminate only very weakly among sovereign borrowers a limit on deficit GNP ratios seems to be adequate because with the switch to monetary union the disciplinary force of potential devaluation can no longer check excessive borrowing by individual EC countries; the alternative to check government borrowing via the political process lets one expect poor results in an EC monetary union because borrowing in some EC countries (Italy, Belgium, Greece, and possibly others, too) has been excessive during certain periods.

Judging by the low debt-GNP ratio of Switzerland only small countries with strong requirements on state and central government to get explicit voters' support on tax and debt issues are able to avoid excessive public debt. The latter may be defined by a situation in which the social rate of return of expenditures financed through government borrowing is lower than the real interest rate. Given the many problems to ensure efficient government programs the social return on investment of many government programs is probably close to zero and rarely can one expect a competitive return on investment. This is not to say that government borrowing for fighting recessions could not be justified on economic grounds, but the poor track record of governments actually repaying debt during boom situations raises doubts about the ability of political systems to adopt prudent intertemporal financing and expenditure schemes.

2. The Single Market Program and EC Monetary Integration

Many arguments for the complementarity of the single market and of EC monetary integration were presented by EC representatives (*EC Commission 1990*; *Matthes and Italianer 1991*). E.g., price transparency will increase in the case of monetary union and this could reinforce the benefits of the single market and intensified competition, respectively; and the existence of a single market will reinforce the global position of a fully convertible ECU in world currency markets such that the demand for ECU-denominated assets outside the EC will increase. Subsequently, we will take a closer look at possible links between the single market and EMU.

2.1 The Single Market and Monetary Union

Significance of the Single Market from a Monetary Perspective

As of January 1, 1993 a single market has been established in the EC (disregarding some still valid exceptions). The free movement of goods, services, labor and capital is shaping a new competitive environment in the EC. For a system of fixed exchange rates full capital account mobility is, of course, critical. Since political risk plays no role in EC countries one may assume that financial assets denominated in different EC countries are very close substitutes, and this implies in the context of full capital mobility that nominal interest rate differentials across EC countries adhering to the ERM will have to reduce further. The nominal interest rate differential for countries in the narrow parity band cannot exceed 4.5 percentage points if nominal interest parity holds; this margin can be exceeded if there is speculation on parity changes and if capital mobility or asset substitutability is effectively impaired by government regulations concerning requirements for insurance companies or pensions funds to hold a minimum share of domestic assets; or if state banks - as in the case of France - are not characterized by the pursuit of profits only, but have to consider the wishes of the Ministry of Finance. The single market implies that public procurement will no longer discriminate against firms from other EC countries, and in general intensified competition after the removal of non-tariff barriers implies that the share of tradable goods and tradable services in GNP should increase and arbitrage intensify.

Stronger Interest Rate Convergence in the EC

A stricter nominal interest parity - assuming reduced devaluation risk on the way to stage III of EMU - and the stricter validity of the law of one price imply that real interest rates at home (r) and abroad (r*; abroad means here in a different EC country) will show a stronger convergence than before. Since real capital also has become more mobile in the 1980s and the early 1990s - that is, there is a rising role of foreign direct investments (FDI) in the EC - one may conclude that real interest rate convergence should indeed be reinforced in the single market. Rising FDI flows will reinforce the long term tendency of the marginal product of capital at home Y_K and abroad Y_{K*} to become equal. Intra-FDI flows are not the only important factor for the equalization of marginal products within the EC. Extra-FDI inflows - mainly from the US and Japan - could also play a role for the equalization of the marginal product of capital across EC countries, where one would expect in the case of an ECU revaluation vis-à-vis the dollar (following the move to EMU III) that extra-FDI inflows into the EC will reduce; this will hold if one follows, *mutatis mutandis*, the imperfect capital market view of *Froot and Stein (1991)* who argued that a devaluation of the dollar stimulates in a world of imperfect capital markets US FDI inflows.

Increasing capital mobility in EC financial markets and the intensified inflation rate convergence imply a stricter convergence of real interest rates on financial assets (r, r*), while at the same time profit maximization of investors implies $r=Y_K$ and $r^*=Y_K^*$. The implication is that long term real interest rates should converge in EC countries, so that divergent long term interest rates can only reflect different inflationary expectations and diverging degrees of policy credibility. Germany with its independent and credible central bank should therefore enjoy the advantage of lower long term nominal inflation rates - compared to EC countries with a politically dependent central bank. Germany also enjoys the advantage that the DM is a major international reserve asset, so that interest rates can be lower than in other EC countries. The DM's share in world reserves rose from 1 % in 1974 to almost 20 % in 1993. German unification offers new opportunities to reinforce the share of DM invoicing in Germany's imports and exports. Moreover, some multinational companies favor the DM as a means of account and transaction in Europe: DOW Chemicals declared in late 1992 that they would switch to DM-based invoicing throughout the EC.

A faster nominal interest rate convergence in the EC implies that one major determinant of the demand for money in EC countries is converging. This should facilitate monetary policy, although different income elasticities in the demand for money are likely to persist across EC countries. In Europe money demand functions differ with respect to income elasticity, where e.g. Belgium and Germany had an income elasticity close to 1 and 1.2, respectively, while the U.K. recorded an elasticity of 1.89 (*Butter and Fase 1981*). A parallel recession in the U.K. and Germany would therefore reduce the demand for money in the U.K. much more than in Germany which would imply pressure on the pound sterling - even if inflation rates in the U.K. and Germany were the same. Moreover, the British economy's share in trade with the US is much higher than in any other EC country so that the US business cycle drives a wedge between the UK and the continental EC countries. Such shifts in monetary demand require offsetting interest rate policies in the EMS. In a monetary union with a single currency and fully integrated money markets such intra-EC shifts in money demand would no longer be a problem (except for EC external exchange rates). The potential gains from EMU and monetary union are therefore clearly related to the problems of the EMS with increasing capital mobility and rising financial market competition (due to the single market project). Nominal interest rate convergence could be undermined by broader parity margins. If rising capital mobility requires to a widening of the parity band for some ERM countries - say $\pm$ 6 % - such that intra-EC trade with these countries would face higher transaction costs the opportunity costs of limited goods market integration could become so high that the switch to monetary union becomes attractive. Hence the EC's leading trading countries would be prime candidates for a small EC monetary union. Finally, if rising real interest rates in the EC and the pressure from the convergence criteria would force governments to sharply reduce welfare state benefits political support for EC integration could reduce unless a broad reform of social policies is envisaged.

Trade, Investment and Exchange Rate Volatility

Exchange rate stability will not in itself strongly support the creation of intra-EC trade and intra-EC investment if one is to follow standard empirical analysis (*e.g. Bailey and Tavlas 1988; 1991; Gotur 1985*). However, exchange rate instability in the EC cannot be seen as an isolated political issue; high exchange rate instability could lead to a collapse of the EMS and this could be the start of full EC disintegration.

Trade and FDI go together in the EC, but trade links were typically established before major FDI links (*Molle and Morsink 1991*). In the single market intensified FDI flows could in turn stimulate the expansion of intra-EC trade. One must not overlook that portfolio capital flows have significantly contributed to EC equity capital in the 1980s (see Tab. 3). In the second half of the 1980s portfolio capital flows sharply increased as a source of equity capital, compared to EC inflows of foreign direct investment; in some years portfolio capital inflows reached about 50 % of FDI inflows. Therefore - and taking into account that full capital mobility will characterize the EC in the 1990s - reduced exchange rate volatility in the ERM could indeed stimulate an optimum capital allocation in the EC market; there is no doubt that portfolio capital flows are strongly influenced by exchange rate changes and exchange rate expectations. Misalignment and overshooting effects in foreign exchange markets could distort capital allocation in the single EC market which then would translate into lower positive growth effects than would have been recorded otherwise.

Tab. 3: Foreign Direct Investment (FDI) and Portfolio Capital Flows in Industrial Countries, 1975-91
($ bill.,annual averages; outflows/inflows divergence due to divergent statistical coverage)

	1975-79	1980-84	1985-89	1990	1991
FDI outflows total	34.7	41.0	128.4	209.5	165.3
EC	14.1	20.9	59.4	97.5	80.5
FDI inflows tot. (a_1)	19.9	36.2	98.1	148.7	115.2
EC (a_2)	11.4	14.2	38.4	85.9	67.7
a_2/a_1 in %	*57.3%*	*39.2%*	*39.1%*	*57.8%*	*58.8%*
portfolio capital outflows total	12.4	41.8	176.8	151.6	277.6
EC	3.8	18.9	62.6	79.8	144.0
portfolio capital inflows total	**25.0**	**57.8**	**186.0**	**159.1**	**388.7**
EC	8.5	17.7	70.4	94.4	173.7
equity capital inflows, total (b_1)	3.7	10.8	31.4	-16.0	90.1
b_1 in % of a_1:	*18.6%*	*29.8%*	*26.7%*	-	*57.1%*
EC (b_2)	2.2	2.1	22.7	11.5	32.1
b_2 in % of a_2:	*19.3%*	*14.8%*	*59.1%*	*13.4%*	*47.4%*

Note: Total EC FDI stock (inward) in 1988: $ 399 bill., of which 160 bill. as intra-EC FDI; average annual flows in 1985-89: $ 20 bill.; stock of EC FDI (outward) in 1988: $ 492 bill. of which $ 160 bill. as intra-EC stock. About 50 % of EC FDI inward flows were from extra-EC sources in the second half of the 1980s, down from a much higher share in the late 1970s and the first half of the 1980s.

Source: BIS (1992) Annual Report, Basel; EUROSTAT (1990), Provisional Report, Luxembourg, August 1990; YANNOPOULOS (1992); own calculation

Reforming the EMS?

It is doubtful that a tightening of margins could improve the functioning of the EMS and the ERM because increased capital mobility makes narrower margins more difficult to defend; theoretical arguments also suggest that tighter margins will not be beneficial for the EMS (*Canzoneri and Diba 1992*). Moreover, the ERM has effectively reinforced policy coordination and made policy responses more similar within the EC (*Bayoumi 1992*). Widening margins might reduce the necessity to intervene, but it could also reduce the pressure for stronger monetary cooperation in the EC. More frequent small realignments and a feasible strategy for stage III could be the superior alternative to EMS reforms through changing margins.

Credibility Debate

More stable economic policies and better coordinated policies could be an indirect result of EC monetary integration, and this in turn could translate into higher economic growth as policy-induced fluctuations are reduced. *Giavazzi and Pagano* (1988) have emphasized the credibility argument of fixed exchange rates, namely that countries which otherwise have a pro-inflationary policy bias could enjoy an enhanced policy credibility - hence a smaller rise of unemployment during disinflation - if the currency is pegged to a country with a stable monetary policy and a good inflation record; entering the ERM also reduced nominal and real interest rates in the UK in 1990. This argument applies some basic ideas of *Kydland/Prescott (1977)* and of *Barro and Gordon (1983)* to the question of exchange rate arrangements in Western Europe. Indeed the costs of disinflation seem to be lower when certain EC countries peg their currency to the DM. However, once low inflation rates have been achieved there is no extra gain for economic policy makers. Too strong a reduction of inflation rates - below what nationally would be an optimal inflation rate under fiscal revenue aspects (given tax structures, marginal tax collection costs and options for seigniorage gains) - could create accentuated social conflicts concerning the income distribution between labor and capital as well as acceptable tax burdens, and such conflicts in turn could weaken growth.

Inflation and Growth

There is empirical evidence for a negative correlation between inflation and economic growth (*Grimes 1991*); basic economic theory supports this view as long as the reduction of real interest rates in periods of modest inflation rates and the induced higher investments are not dominating the distortionary effects of inflationary misallocation. The traditional welfare analysis of inflation puts the focus on the impact of changing nominal interest rates on the real demand of money M/P (*Tatom 1976*); the welfare costs H of inflation in the traditional analysis are $H = \sigma(m_0/i_0)\pi(\pi/2 + r)$, where π is the inflation rate, σ the interest elasticity of money demand, m=M/P and i (r) the nominal interest rate (real interest rate). A refined approach would have to include the question whether the inflation induced change in real output Y is positive or negative. The welfare loss relative to GNP, h, then is given - with V defined as Y/m - by $h= V_0^{-1}\sigma(1/i_0)\pi(\pi/2 + r) - [(\delta m/\delta Y)(\delta Y/\delta\pi)][(Y_0/m_0)(m_0/Y_0]$, where the term in squared brackets simply is used to introduce the income elasticity of the demand for money $E_{m,Y}$ so that we get with Y_π denoting $\delta Y/\delta\pi$:

$$h= V_0^{-1}\sigma(1/i_0)\pi(\pi/2 + r) - (m_0 Y_\pi E_{m,Y})$$

An increase (a fall) of Y shifts in i,M/P space the money demand schedule to the right (left) so that a negative sign of Y_π would imply an additional welfare loss of inflation - see appendix 2. The impact of lower inflation rates on real output growth in the EC is unclear because in some EC countries higher inflation rates were a social mollifier in the struggle for income between capital and labor. The removal of barriers for free capital flows and the higher capital mobility resulting from privatization and increased competitive pressure in the EC single market already have aggravated conflicts between capital and labor - within labor between insiders with relatively protected workplaces in the firm and outsiders with their uncertain job positions.

Gains from EMU

The Report of the EC COMMISSION (1990, p.81., p.89, p. 186) has argued that static and dynamic gains from economic and monetary union could reach between 3.6% and 16.3% of EC GDP; the direct monetary union gains from the elimination of transaction costs and hedging costs are estimated to be about 0.4 % of EC-GDP; an upper limit for the welfare benefit of reduced inflation is 0.3 % of Community GDP; the seigniorage revenues from potential shifts in international cash holdings in favor of the ECU amount to about 0.05 % of EC GDP so that monetary union would bring a benefit of about 1 % of GDP. This could be more than the benefits from the single market which the *Cecchini (1988)* Report estimated to yield one-off benefits of 2.5-6.5 % of Community GDP. There might be also dynamic gains from increased competition, improved policy coordination in the EC and higher economic growth in a regime of lower inflation rates (see appendix 3). However, higher price transparency could also imply higher wage transparency which in turn could create in a North-South context of the EC problems akin to those encountered in a West-East context after German unification. Greater wage transparency could create intensified upward wage pressure in low income EC countries where wage claims might outpace productivity growth. The dynamic gains from monetary union are assumed to accrue via reduced EC real interest rates, the elimination of intra-EC exchange rate uncertainty and gains from a greater (reduced) role of the ECU (dollar) in international financial markets and in central banks' international reserve management worldwide. The Cecchini Report had argued that static efficiency gains from the single market program would amount to 2.5-6.5% of EC GDP so that the EC Commission's analysis of monetary union effects implies that monetary union would have greater positive effects than the removal of non-tariff barriers in the EC.

One caveat with respect to gains from a changing global reserve composition concerns the fact that a reduced number of EC currencies will induce non-EC countries to cut the amount of overall EC currency holdings (*Kenen 1992*). In addition to this one may raise the question how external exchange rate volatility and the level of the real ECU exchange rate will be affected by EC monetary union. The new type of global currency competition in an oligopolistic setting will affect volatility - with uncertain a priori effects. The real income effect of monetary union and the change in the average EC interest elasticity in the demand for money will affect the level of the real ECU exchange rate vis-à-vis the dollar and the yen. A real depreciation of the ECU is likely to attract higher FDI inflows from the USA and Japan so that Western Europe would benefit from heavy FDI inflows in a similar way as the US in the second half of the 1980s. Implicitly the Froot Stein argument of imperfect capital markets is used here. If the ECU would face a real appreciation which is the view consistent with the report of the EC Commission the real depreciation of the dollar would stimulate EC FDI outflows to the US and reduce US outflows to the EC where economic growth would then be lower than otherwise. As regards EMU benefits there are three final caveats from a global perspective: EC currency unification could mean a lower intensity in global currency competition and could therefore bring higher inflation worldwide; the degree of competition will depend, among other things, on G-7 collaboration. Second, on the way to EC monetary union rising intra-EC policy conflicts and higher EC unemployment could reduce effective demand in the EC which in turn would reduce the export potential of the US and other countries so that global output could be negatively affected; under such circumstances the benefits from improved G-7 coordination might also be worse than before monetary union. Finally, and this seems to be the biggest risk of EMU, prudential supervision in the EC could become weaker under the impact of competitive deregulation and the principle of home country supervision. Internal or external shocks could then destabilize the financial and real sphere of EC countries (and the whole OECD area) more than when EC financial markets, separated by national currencies, would have allowed mitigating shocks by different national shock absorbers and economic policies.

2.2 Problems with the Kenen Criterion

A critically important question refers to the impact of the EC single market and the ongoing real integration for adequate monetary integration in the Community. If the unfolding of the single EC market reinforces the case for monetary union the EC 1992 program would indeed suggest that this program and monetary union are complementary elements (as suggested by the EC COMMISSION). However, from the perspective of the optimum currency literature there is one basic reservation, namely the question whether or not the Kenen criterion (*Kenen 1969*) will be violated by the dynamics of the single market. The Kenen criterion argues that a highly diversified production and export structure reduces the significance of the exchange rate as a policy instrument because a high degree of diversification makes it likely that random external shocks will tend to cancel out at the aggregate export or import level. The developments in industrial diversification in both "old" EC members and in Spain, Portugal and Greece as EC latecomers do suggest that integration might go along as much with increasing national specialization in some cases as with increasing diversification in other cases (Tab. 4). To the extent that the single market program means creating huge EC markets with a greater emphasis on economies of scale one would indeed expect that intra-EC specialization should play a considerable role in the 1990s. Tab. 4 shows in column 1 that the degree of economic openness supports the case of monetary integration in the EC.

Tab. 4: Industrial Specialization Degree h and Intensity of Structural Change (ß: moving 5-year average in degrees) in Selected Countries

Degree of Specialization is defined as $h = 100\left(1 + \frac{\Sigma s_i \ln s_i}{h_{max}}\right)$

where s_i is the share of value-added of industry i and h_{max} is the number of industries existing (h=0, if all industry shares are equal; h=100 if there is only one industry).

Degree of Structural Change: $\cos \beta = \frac{\Sigma s_i(t) s_i(t-1)}{[(\Sigma s_i(t)^2)(\Sigma s_i(t-1)^2]^{0.5}}$

COUNTRY X/Yratio [man.indu./Y,%]	1980 degree of specialization of industry (structrual change)	1985	1989	89/80 change	1989 merch. exports/GNP [intra EC#]	1981 export concentration index(0≥k≤1)	1989	change 89/81
GE 38.5	12.1	14.5	15.4	+	26	.062	.085	+
[31.1]	(2.7)	(3.5)	(1.9)		[55/52]			
F 22.7	10.4	11.1	11.4	+	19	.054	.059	+
[21.3]	(3.7)	(2.8)	(2.6)		[63/60]			
I 18.5	10.1	10.9	10.8	+	17	.063	.056	-
[23.2]	(2.8)	(6.1)	(2.1)		[59/58]			
NL 56.1	15.4	16.0	15.2	-	47	.124	.066	-
[20.2]	(2.8)	(3.4)	(2.3)		[77/64]			
B 71.5	12.5	14.0	13.8	+	61##	##.096	.104	+
[23.3]	(2.6)	(2.8)	(2.2)		[75/73]##			
L 72.2	37.0	34.0	24.3	-	n.a.	n.a.	n.a.	
[28.4]	(3.1)	(3.0)	(5.8)		n.a.			
UK 23.6	11.1	11.9	12.1	+	21	.083	.060	-
[20.4]	(3.8)	(2.6)	(2.0)		[53/52]			
DK 37.9	14.4	14.9	14.6	+	26	.075	.074	-
[15.8]	(3.0)	(3.0)	(2.2)		[52/52]			
IR 69.6	14.9	18.8	21.0	+	57	.121	.132	+
[25.6]	(4.5)	(4.5)	(4.1)		[75/67]			
SP 17.4	*8.4*	*8.5*	*9.8*	+	*15*	*.079*	*.104*	+
[25.8]	*(5.5)*	*(3.4)*	*(4.9)*		*[70/60]*			
P 36.6	*11.2*	*10.4*	*10.5*	-	*35*	*.094*	*.103*	+
[26.7]	*(5.3)*	*(7.0)*	*(5.2)*		*[61/70]*			
GR 21.9	*10.5*	*11.8*	*12.1*	+	*22*	*.167*	*.144*	-
[15.3]	*(3.6)*	*(4.4)*	*(4.1)*		*[64/64]*			
USA	**11.9**	**13.5**	**12.4**	**+**	**8**	**.064**	**.088**	**+**
[19.4]	**(2.9)**	**(3.4)**	**(3.1)**					

share of intra-EC merchandise exports/intra-EC imports in 1990; k = normalized Hirschmann index scaled to fall in the interval 0, 1(maximum concentration) on the basis of 3 digit SITC/2(i=1-239 groups); ##=B+Lux.

$$k_j = \frac{[\sqrt{\Sigma (x_i/X)^2}] - \sqrt{1/239}}{1-\sqrt{1/239}} \quad \text{where } X = \sum_{i=1}^{239} x_i;\ x = \text{exports};\ j = \text{countries}$$

* 1989, ** including Luxembourg; Note: X/Y ratio= exports of goods and services/GNP (B,L,P,GR,IR: 1990, otherwise 1991) x=merchandise exports x* = merchandise imports; *[share of manufacturing industry in GNP Y in %]; Source: UNIDO (1992), GATT (1992) and OECD, Directions of Trade, own calculations.*

However, export-GNP shares are still surprisingly low in France, Italy and Spain, where state-ownership of firms (in Italy also protection through kick-backs) restricted import competition and discouraged firms' drive for exporting. One may note that the share of intra-EC trade is lowest in the U.K. and Denmark, where the resistance against EC deepening is particularly strong - although as regards social policies the U.K. and Denmark are opposed to Maastricht for opposite reasons: Denmark wants to keep high standards in social policies; the U.K. would like to maintain its low level of social policies and the apparent advantage of low unit labor costs. The degree of specialization in industry has not increased in all EC countries in the 1980s, and the same is true with respect to export concentration. The single EC market could indeed reinforce the degree of specialization in some countries since improved opportunities for exploiting economies of scale by concentrating production in a few countries will be exploited by multinational companies facing fierce competition in the EC. At the same time increasing intra-industry trade could mitigate tendencies towards increasing specialization.

3. Transition Problems towards EMU

In the single market intensified price arbitrage and reduced scope for intra-EC price discrimination (along traditional political border lines) will reinforce the tendency for ERM countries to exhibit a common tradables inflation rate. With a given relative price of tradables to nontradables this implies a common inflation rate or at least a faster convergence towards common inflation rates. The price of nontradables will rise relative to tradables in the course of economic catching-up in southern EC countries (Spain and Portugal). *Balassa (1961)* and *Kravis and Lipsey* (1988) provide arguments and empirical evidence that the ratio of the price of nontradables to tradables is a positive function of per capita income. Relative price shifts significantly affect regional price levels in the case of the US, too (*Tootell 1992*). One may add the hypothesis that relative wealth positions in the EC influence relative prices in the same direction as relative income positions. In EC regions with a quasi-current account surplus the prices of immobile assets will increase as their owners - with a preference to live in a prospering region - build up a net creditor position vis-à-vis people in regions with a current account deficit. One should therefore not be surprised that some inflation differential will persist among EC countries even in the long term.

Tradables vs. Nontradables: Divergent Sectoral Inflation Rates

The consumer price inflation rate for tradables in the EC reached 3.2% in 1992, while that for nontradable goods and services was more than twice as high (6.6%; see Tab. 5). This difference might transitorily even widen if the single market program brings about closer integrated markets for tradables such that major firms in these markets would all have lower market shares than in the more segmented pre-1992 markets in the EC. The EC central bank governors' report for 1992 has drawn attention to the divergence between the development of prices of tradables and nontradables and has argued that strengthening competition policies and providing less protection for traditionally sheltered industries could reduce not only the differential between the dynamics of tradables and nontradables, but might indeed contribute to reducing the overall inflation rates in some EC countries and thus indirectly support a downward convergence process (Tab. 5). Defining $P=(P^N)^{ß}(P^T)^{(1-ß)}$ and assuming that the law of one price holds for tradables ($E=P^T/P^{T*}$) we obtain $E=P^T/P^{T*}=[P(P^T/P^N)^{ß}]/[P^*(P^{T*}/P^{N*})^{ß*}]$ which shows that the nominal exchange rate E depends both on relative price level developments and on relative shifts in the price of tradables to nontradables - shifts which can be influenced by economic catching-up processes which induce relatively high increases of the nontradables price P^N (e.g. in Southern EC countries); slow productivity growth caused by price cartels in the service sector (even relevant in the Netherlands as it turned out in 1993) could be an alternative explanation. Assuming that the marginal product rule $W/P^T=z^T$ and $W/P^N=z^N$ holds (similarly for nominal wages W* abroad, where we assume $ß=ß^*$) then the relative change of the equilibrium exchange rate is:

(2) $dE/E = \pi-\pi^* + (1-ß)[(z^{T*}-z^T)+(z^N-z^{N*})]$

In the single market there is a need for changes of EP*/P as long as intra-EC differentials in labor productivity in the tradables sector ($z^{T*}-z^T$) and the nontradables sector (z^N-z^{N*}) persist, and a change of E is necessary even if the inflation rate at home (π) is the same as abroad (π^*). If tradables are heterogeneous one gets $E=\phi P^T/P^{T*}$, where ϕ could depend on relative product innovativeness (Q/Q*). As a country's industry is moving up on the technology ladder - relative to its competitors - its terms of trade will improve because the share of goods fetching high prices with high Schumpeterian rents will increase.

Tab. 5: Consumer Price Inflation (%) for Tradables and Nontradables in the EC
(p.a. changes; countries ordered in accordance to the sectoral price differential in '92)

	(A, 1992) Nontradables and Services	(B, 1992) Traded Goods	(A)-(B) Difference	Average Differential: Period 1982-86	1987-91
Italy	7.5	2.8	4.7	4.5	4.2
Greece	19.2	14.7	4.5	0.3	5.5
Spain	8.8	4.5	4.3	0.3	5.3
Portugal	11.2	7.4	3.8	1.1	3.3
U.K.	7.3	3.8	3.5	1.4	2.0
Denmark	3.5	0.2	3.3	0.9	1.3
France	4.5	1.6	2.9	1.0	3.3
Germany (W.)	5.5	2.7	2.8	1.6	1.2
Belgium	4.2	2.4	1.8	-0.7	0.1
Netherl.	4.1	2.6	1.5	1.4	1.5
Ireland	3.9	2.5	1.4	2.8	1.5
EC Average	*6.6*	*3.2*	*3.4*	*1.8*	*2.8*
EC Stand. Dev.	*2.4*	*1.9*	*0.5*	*1.4*	*1.5*

Source: Committee of EC Central Bank Gov. (1993), Annual Report 1992, Basel.

Industrial economics suggests that mark-up rates in markets with standardized products are a positive function of market shares so that falling market shares would imply reduced mark up rates - as soon as intra-EC mergers and acquisitions raise market shares the prices of tradables could transitorily increase faster or at least almost as fast as those of nontradable goods and services. Privatization of industry in EC countries with high shares of state-owned industry in industrial output could indeed be one key to more competition in the supply of industrial services from national markets. Moreover, the privatization of state-owned firms in the services industry (telecom, insurance companies, utilities) as well as the increased competition from the single market program and the greater mobility of the users of services could reduce nontradables inflation rates. In this respect developments in Italy, France, Spain and Portugal which all have envisaged broader privatization plans in 1992/93 will be interesting to watch in the 1990s. This reinforces uncovered interest rate parity $i=i^*+a$, namely to the extent that banks/insurance companies are privatized.

3.1 Conflicts of Interest and Asymmetric Adjustment Capability

In a period of high dynamics in international financial markets and great political uncertainties throughout Europe it would be wise to create a reliable and functional ESCB, not an additional source of uncertainty and political conflict which - in a stage of rising European nationalism - could lead to destabilization of the whole EC integration process. Europe has faced several stages of monetary integration after 1945 (see appendix 2), and EMU could be a final stage or just one step too much.

On the way to monetary union there remain potential conflicts of interests within the EC12 group. In 1991 - prior to the recession 1992/93 - unemployment rates strongly differed among EC countries, where the figures for the five big economies were in the range of 4.5 % (Germany) to 17.5 % in Spain; France, Italy and the U.K. all recorded figures around 10 % and thus were close to the EC average. A 10 % average unemployment rate in the EC points to serious labor market clearing problems, while the divergent national figures of the big economies suggest that national perceptions of the desirability to exploit short term inflation unemployment trade-offs might differ among EC members strongly. Since stage III of EMU would imply giving up the exchange rate instrument - within the EC - insufficient labor market clearing could become an even more serious problem for the EC in the future. An even more important field of interest could be the sensitivity of public budgets to interest rate changes. The ratio of interest expenditures to government outlays exceeded 10 % in Portugal, Ireland, Italy, Belgium and Greece, while in the U.K., Germany and France it was in the range of 4-5 %. Interest rate shocks as well as high interest rate policies are not too difficult to absorb in the latter countries. Indeed real interest rates in the 1990s could remain high not only because of an increased global savings shortage (as compared to the 1970s and the early 1980s), but also because high marginal products of capital in the single market as well as in North America and some Asian NICs create upward pressure on real bond interest rates. High real interest rates would make compliance with deficit and debt convergence indicators impossible to achieve for Ireland, Italy, Belgium and Greece - and possibly also Portugal which, however, can still improve its position through a massive privatization program. The role of interest rates in credit allocation generally increased in the 1980s *(OECD,1993).*

A small monetary union that would be comprised of only five or six countries at first - Germany, France, the Benelux countries, and possibly Italy (to start with the old group that formed the EC in 1957) - could be a feasible and sustained EMU club. *Neumann and Von Hagen* (1992) found that Germany and the Benelux countries - with a caveat also France - showed a similar degree of real exchange rate flexibility (which could come from nominal exchange rate changes as well as from national price level changes) as the West German Länder showed "real exchange rate flexibility" within Germany's common currency area. The real exchange rate is the price index of a country relative to the price index of the rest of the world, and within a country it is the regional price index relative to the national price index. High real exchange rate flexibility is necessary to absorb shocks and shifts, and if the ERM members France, Benelux and Germany (plus Austria) show as high a real exchange flexibility via changing prices as Germany's regions show one may assume that giving up the exchange rate instrument does not significantly worsen real exchange rate flexibility.

However, for a small union comprised of 5-7 member countries it is quite difficult to see how the club members could fulfill the convergence criteria. Discretionary decision-making by the EC council could finally solve this contradiction, but EC countries left behind could feel excluded on arbitrary grounds. Hence as regards the crucial debt and deficit criteria a market-oriented escape clause could be useful which would stipulate that all countries whose government debt has been rated AA (or better) for at least two consecutive years - prior to the ECOFIN reporting - can be considered as having passed the debt convergence test. A paradox improvement of national debt ratings could occur immediately after full EMU membership becomes apparent because markets might anticipate an effective future EC bailout behavior - in contrast to all declared ex ante no-bail out clauses. If a small EC monetary union were to exert a dominant impact on monetary policy in the single market the union must not be too small in the sense that only if at least half of monetary growth in the EC is directly controlled (Tab. 6) would one expect that other EC countries which have pegged their parities to the UNION will be dominated by the union's stability-oriented monetary policy. Non-union members would have to bear the burden of adjustment if there were tensions in the rest-EMS.

Tab. 6: Selected Divergence Indicators for EC Countries, 1991/1992
(figures are in %, except for the population which is in Mill.; real unit labor cost index 1980=100; 1990 per capita income based on World Bank, at purchasing power rates)

	##Unemployment Rate '91 (Real Unit Labor Costs)	Public Interest Ratio*	M3**-Growth 1992	M3/M^{EC} Shares (ECU-Weights)	Inflation 1992	Population (Per c. Income)
FRG**	4.5 (92.0)	4.7	8.8	22.9 (30.1)	4.0	79.1 (100)
F	10.3 (90.0)	5.1	4.7	16.7 (19.0)	2.6	58.2 (93)
B	7.7 (88.2)	20.2	6.2	3.0*# (7.6)	2.4	10.3*# (79)
NL	6.3 (86.9)	9.7	4.9	5.5 (9.4)	3.1	14.8 (90)
DK	11.1 (89.0)	6.5	3.3	1.8 (2.45)	2.1	5.1 (94)
I	9.9 (97.0)	17.8	7.8	16.7 (10.15)	5.3	57.5 (89)
UK	10.5 (99.7)	3.7	5.5	22.4 (13.0)	5.1	57.2 (92)
IR	16.8 (83.5)	13.5	3.7	0.4 (1.1)	2.9	3.5 (52)
SP	17.5 (83.4)	6.0	5.9	7.6 (5.3)	6.0	38.9 (66)
P	3.8 (85.7)	10.0#*	25.3	1.0 (0.8)	9.1	10.5 (49)
GR	4.6 (96.0)	25.1	-	0.9 (0.8)	16.1	10.0 (45)
EC	9.4	-	6.7#	100.0		343.1

M3/M^{EC} indicates for 1991 the shares of national monetary aggregates in EC total M3; weights in ECU basket according to revision of July 19, 1989.
* interest expenditures in % of general government expenditures; growth rates for broad monetary aggregate; *# including Luxembourg (share of 1 % in M3/M^{EC});
#* own estimate; ** West Germany, except for population figure; # without Greece;
OECD standardized unemployment rates for 1992.II (Italy, Portugal and Greece: I. quarter); real unit labor costs from unit labor costs/GNP deflator; index 1980=100.

Sources: OECD (1992), Main Economic Indicators; OECD; Economist (1992, Sept. 19 and 26), IMF, International Financial Statistics und Eurostat, Luxembourg; EC Commission (1992), European Economy, Supplement A, No.5/6 1992; WELCKER, J. and NERGE, C. (1992), Spanien müßte mehr abführen, als es vom Kohäsionsfond erhielte, Handelsblatt, 8/6/91, Nr. 150, 11; WORLD BANK (1992), World Development Report, New York, Tab. 30, Deutsche Bundesbank, Monatsberichte, March 1993, EC Commission.

Overambitious goals for creating an EC monetary union with all member states at the outset bear in it the seed of future disintegration. It is not the intra-EC divergence of national per capita income which makes monetary union of all EC members a problem (one may recall that German monetary union of 1871 was compatible with considerable intra-German divergences, ranging from a per capita income of about 65 in East Prussia and West Prussia to 186 in Hamburg in 1913; *Borchardt 1968*). The problem is the divergence of policy preferences and desired policy strategies. Moreover, some countries - such as Italy, Greece and Belgium - are more exposed to adverse interest rate shocks than EC members with low debt-GNP ratios (see the public interest ratios in Tab. 6).

The lack of an EC public that would serve as a clearing mechanism for opposing national policy preferences can be considered as a crucial problem for achieving a viable monetary union in the EC. In critical situations in which the West German government clearly would have desired a more loose monetary policy than that actually realized the German public was the supporter of last resort for the stability-oriented Bundesbank which may be assumed to have a more long term policy orientation than the federal government with its typical focus on the next election campaign. As long as a genuine EC public is not existing, EMU might not be able to weather political storms or EC external economic shocks. Higher margins (±4 %) might be useful in such a situation and allow avoiding excessively high interest rates cum EC economic stagnation.

Some observers (e.g. *Seidel 1992*) argue that as long as political union has not made considerable progress - say with EC based political parties - an EC central bank faces the risk of coming under political fire from all sides; from those governments which would like to see a more accommodative monetary policy, but also from those which consider the EC central bank's commitment to anti-inflationary policy as insufficient. A functional system of cross-national interest clearing in the EC is indeed necessary for a viable monetary union. One might argue that the formation of Euronationals (*Klein and Welfens 1992*) in the context of the unfolding of the single EC market and the increasing mobility of labor in the EC could support such a process. However, labor mobility in the EC is only about 1/3 of that in Japan and the US (*OECD 1987,* p.136). Moreover, rising intra-EC labor mobility is a problem in a period of rising nationalism.

G-7 Coordination

If the ESCB were not firmly rooted in the EC institutional fabric and enjoyed the support of all major EC countries' governments G-7 coordination in monetary and fiscal policy could become less effective than it used to be - much in contrast to what US or Japanese central bankers might expect. To the extent that US and Japanese policy makers expect to gain from a stability-oriented EC monetary policy external support for the ESCB could support the position of an EC central bank in the first crucial stage III of EMU. However, at least from a US point of view a strong and stable ECU is not ideal because the ECU would then endanger the still dominant position of the US dollar as a reserve asset and vehicle currency in international financial markets (on G-7 monetary policy divergence see *Henning 1993*). This conflict would not be strong if world trade and world investment would grow quickly so that a convertible ECU's position would build on the increase in international demand for reserves rather than on mainly substituting dollar denominated assets in the stock of international reserves. If an initially stable ECU could be established the dollar would depreciate which could let the US benefit both because of rising exports and - following the FROOT-STEIN argument - because of higher FDI inflows from the EC. For the EC this could mean suffering from increasing unemployment, especially if Japanese and Chinese export surpluses vis-à-vis the EC would further increase from already high levels at the start of the single EC market. This scenario as well as the economic opening up of Eastern Europe which confronts the EC for the first time with proximate low wage competition point to the enormous need for structural adjustment in the EC - a need not really recognized by policymakers.

3.2 Institutional Aspects

A major problem concerning decision-making in the ESCB is related to the fact that the six members of the directorate will be unanimously elected by the EC Council for an 8 year term, while the other members of the central bank council are the presidents of the participating central banks. The directorate is likely to enjoy greater political independence than the presidents of the national central banks and therefore the likelihood that the ESCB will adopt inflationary policies under political pressure in EC member countries is the greater the more EC countries join the ESCB in an early stage and the more these countries are interested in inflationary monetary policies. If not more than six countries enter stage III, the members of the directorate could always bloc a pro-inflationary policy course since the central bank council will decide with simple majority; a majority of EC member countries would be 7 (the number will change after EC enlargement).

Neglected Problems in the Maastricht Treaty?

As more and more central banks in the EC gain political independence one may wonder whether or not two major problems of capitalism should be addressed more explicitly in a revised Maastricht Treaty - in the context of the revision talks scheduled for 1996 in accordance with the Maastricht Treaty: (i) The risk of deflationary policies might seem to represent a rather opaque danger for the real economy in the EC, but as the US central bank has shown in the Great Depression a deflationary policy course (whether really intended or not) cannot be ruled out a priori. (ii) The risk of insufficient regulation of highly developed and volatile financial markets cannot be overlooked in the EC. The S&L crisis in the US in the 1980s has shown that poor and uncoordinated financial regulation can create high wealth losses, create widespread uncertainty and transitorily impair economic growth. Two EC reports on the ERM and a study commissioned by the G-10 group (presented in May 1993) argued that there was no need for a reform of the ERM. The report, however, argues that the high volume of foreign exchange markets - reaching almost $ 900 bill. in daily turnover in the early 1990s - requires attempts by all ERM partners to pursue monetary policies that are consistent with fundamental economic variables and are conducive to price stability. Intensified monetary cooperation is required.

Creating a monetary union creates specific problems, some of which are highlighted by the Belgium-Luxembourg currency union which dates back to 1921. Even after more than 75 years there are practical convertibility problems that are caused by the fact that banknotes in the two countries look different (while the parity is 1:1 and the unit of account the same); if one takes Luxembourg banknotes - Luxembourg francs - to Belgium in order to buy goods or acquire assets Belgium people often refuse to accept these banknotes. Hence there is a practical convertibility problem which results in transaction costs.

3.3 Some German Points of View

In Germany the Maastricht Treaty has created a vivid discussion among academics, the banking community and the general public about EC monetary union. Economists from academia were not really involved in the pre-Maastricht decision-making of the German government and hence it is not surprising that after Maastricht the government faces a majority of critical economists. The banking community has always supported EMU, possibly because they expect profitable opportunities to expand in a common currency area whose functioning would follow the well-known lines of Bundesbank policies. An initially very supportive business community has become more skeptical in Germany in 1992/93 because a stability-oriented ESCB seems to be more difficult to establish than anticipated in 1990 and because German exporters' and importers' advantage of invoicing in the home currency (DM) is no longer a source of comparative advantage if all EC countries are members of an ECU/ESCB club.

There are three forces which could destroy the EMS: The Bundesbank - which never liked the EMS system - with a high interest rate policy (indirectly motivated by German unification) which induces devaluation pressures on other EC currencies; the mighty speculators whose power is increased by the EC's switch to full capital mobility, the single market and privatization projects in major EC countries; and inadequate macroeconomic policies in EC countries.

The Brussels *ad hoc* reform of the EMS showed that not only EC monetary union is a delicate issue. The transition stage in a period of higher capital mobility and increased internal and external adjustment pressure is a strategic topic for EMU. With parity margins of 15 % the EMS is almost floating, and the advantages of fixed exchange rates, downward inflationary convergence and increased policy credibility were given up in a critical situation. More exchange rate flexibility is indeed useful in a situation of asymmetric shocks (German unification, CMEA disintegration and EC single market dynamics) and high unemployment rates in all major EC countries. However, after a transition period of much greater flexibility reduced parity bands should be introduced (maybe with margins of ± 4 %). The Brussels meeting of Sunday, August 1, 1993 proved that the EC partners have the political will to save the EMS; however, crisis management was no swift reaction. According to the Financial Times of August 3, 1993 the monetary committee's meeting (on Saturday) brought only an agreement to preserve the ERM and its central parity grid. When the ECOFIN met on Sunday, Germany's proposal for solving the crisis was to widen the margins in the EMS. France absolutely refused to devalue the FF, and Germany insisted that the Bundesbank could not be expected to provide unlimited intervention. A Franco-German proposal that the DM should leave the ERM (for a certain period) turned out to be not feasible. The Netherlands which has traditionally maintained a currency parity with the DM, signalled that it intended to follow the Germans out of the ERM. Reacting to this Dutch move Belgium+Luxembourg and Denmark indicated that they, too, wanted to leave the ERM. France was facing the strange option to be left behind with Portugal and Spain - the latter two enjoying the $\pm$ 6 % parity band. This solution would have resulted in a kind of two-tier snake arrangement, and France certainly was not eager to create the impression that the "franc fort" policy (maintaining the DM-FF parity) had failed. At the same time the French government faced a public opinion which favored lower interest rates and employment growth over the goal of exchange rate stability. The final solution was to adopt a fluctuation band of 15 % for all ERM currencies. The effective revaluation of the DM could reduce import prices and reduce inflationary pressures in Germany so that the Bundesbank in turn could adopt a policy of more quickly reducing interest rates. However, given the fact that about 50 % of all prices are state-administered prices or prices strongly influenced by government procurement a fast reduction of German inflation is unlikely; this holds especially because excessive monetary growth of 1991/92 will translate with a lag into inflation in 1993/94. EC monetary problems can only be overcome if labor market clearing is reinforced and economic growth is increased. Growth rates could be depressed by exchange rate uncertainty and shocks (*e.g.* German unification).

The collapse of the CMEA, the USSR and the Warsaw Treaty Organization mean that Germany and the other EC countries have lost an external catalyst for political cooperation in Western Europe, and indeed in all EC countries the political focus is strongly back on the national interest ("where is my net gain?") and sometimes nationalistic perspectives influence politics again. Weakening EC cohesion could indeed result not only from increasing internal political conflicts in the EC12 group, but EC widening could furthermore weaken the political cohesion as decision-making becomes more complicated, ineffective and inefficient in an enlarged Community. If political unification or at least stable and efficient political schemes for achieving intra-community consensus, competition and coordination were a prerequisite for a viable currency union or unification, EC widening - whether towards Scandinavia or central and eastern Europe - would be the wrong step. Hence facing a trade-off situation of EC deepening (monetary union) vs. EC widening Germany might find that its politico-economic gains from EC enlargement are considerable, but those from EC deepening quite uncertain. By itself Germany is unlikely to give up the idea of EC monetary union and strongly emphasizes potential opportunities in central and eastern Europe, although the ex-CMEA area offers new opportunities not only for exporting goods and acquiring firms, but also for exporting the Bundesbank model to the increasing number of countries plagued by hyperinflation and the desire to establish a stable currency. On balance a united Germany - facing enormous adjustment problems in the context of unification (*Welfens 1992a*) - cannot gain much from central and eastern Europe because in economic terms the region is poor and has limited prospects for a successful economic opening-up. However, transforming economies in the ex-CMEA could reduce EC cohesion and change German policy perspectives indirectly (*Welfens 1992b, 1993a*). If Germany's main EC partner, France, would face serious agricultural and industrial adjustment problems as a consequence of the economic opening up and transformation of former CMEA countries this would raise pressure on Germany to step up its net contributions to the EC budget - while the contribution of France would reduce; this could sharply intensify the German discussion about the gains from EC membership. From an economic point of view Germany's gains from higher trade through EC membership clearly override the fiscal contributions, but in the political debate the gains from trade are underestimated because they are spread over millions of products and millions of consumers/investors, while the contributions are clearly visible. Germany's prospects to impose its monetary policy course on other EC countries has improved after German unification. Germany's firms traditionally faced lower wage pressure than EC rivals in the 1980s and if Germany can restore its lead in price stability in the even more competitive single market in the 1990s the political pressure in other EC countries to match low German inflation rates will be reinforced (see Tab. A2). German firms already account for shares of 20-30 % in EC partners' imports in 1990; exceptions with lower shares are the U.K., Ireland, Spain and Portugal. Moreover, a united Germany as an export market is crucially important for all EC countries.

References

BAILEY, M.J. and TAVLAS, G.S. (1988), Trade and Investment under Floating Exchange Rates: The U.S. Experience, CATO Journal, Vol. 8, 421-442.
BAILEY, M.J. and TAVLAS, G.S. (1991), Exchange Rate Variability and Direct Investment, Annals of the American Academy of Political and Social Science, 516, July, 106-116.
BALASSA, B. (1961), The Theory of Economic Integration, London: Irwin.
BARRO, R. and GORDON, D. (1983), Rules, Discretion and Reputation in a Model of Monetary Policy, Journal of Monetary Economics, July, 101-121.
BAYOUMI, T. (1992), The Effect of the ERM on Participating Economies, IMF Staff Papers, Vol. 39, 330-356.
BIS (BANK OF INTERNATIONAL SETTLEMENTS, 1992), 62. Jahresbericht, Basle.
BIS (1993), 63rd Annual Report 1993, Basle.
BLITZ, J. (1992), How Central Banks Ran into the Hedge, Financial Times (30 Sept.), London.
BORCHARDT, K. (1968), Regionale Wachstumsdifferenzierung in Deutschland im 19. Jahrhundert unter besonderer Berücksichtigung des West-Ost-Gefälles, in: LÜTGE, F., ed., Wirtschaftliche und soziale Probleme der gewerblichen Entwicklung im 15-16. und 19. Jahrhundert, Stuttgart: 115-123.
BUTTER, F.A.G. den and FASE, M.M.G. (1981), The Demand for Money in EEC Countries, in: Journal of Monetary Economics, Vol. 8, 201-230.
CANZONERI, M.B. and DIBA, B.T. (1992), The Inflation Discipline of Currency Substitution, European Economic Review, Vol. 36, 827-846.
CANZONERI, M.B.; GRILLI, V. and MASSON, P.R., eds. (1992), Establishing a Central Bank: Issues in Europe and Lessons from the US, Cambridge: Cambrige University Press.
CECCHINI, P. (1988), Europa '92. Der Vorteil des Binnenmarktes, Baden-Baden: Nomos.
DE GRAUWE, P. (1992), The Economics of Monetary Integration, London: Oxford UP.
DE GRAUWE, P. (1989), International Trade and Economic Growth in the European Monetary System, European Economic Review, Vol. 31, 389-398.
DEUTSCHE BUNDESBANK (1992), Geschäftsbericht der Deutschen Bundesbank für das Jahr 1991, Frankfurt/M.
DORNBUSCH, R. (1991), Problems of European Monetary Integration, in: Giovannini, A. and Mayer, C., eds., European Financial Integration, 305-327.
EC COMMISSION (1990), One Market, one Money, No. 44, Luxembourg.
EC COMMISSION (1992), European Economy, Supplement A, No.5/6 1992.
EICHENGREEN, B. (1990), One Money for Europe? Lessons from the US Currency Union, Economic Policy, No. 10, 177-188.
EUROSTAT (1990), Provisional Report by Christine Spanneut on Direct Investment in the European Community, Luxembourg, August 1990.
FRATIANNI, M. and VON HAGEN, J. (1992), The EMS and European Monetary Union, Boulder, Co.: Westview.
FRATIANNI, M., VON HAGEN, J. and WALLER, C. (1992), The Maastricht Way to EMU, Essays in International Finance, No. 187, International Finance Section, Princeton University, June.

FROOT, K.A. and STEIN, J.C. (1991), Exchange Rates and Foreign Direct Investment: An Imperfect Capital Markets Approach, Quarterly Journal of Economics, November, 1191-1217.

GARBER, P. and FLOOD, R. (1993), Policy Switching, Cambridge: MIT Press.

GIAVAZZI, F. and GIOVANNINI, A. (1986), The EMS and the Dollar, Economic Policy, 1986/2, 455-473.

GIAVAZZI, F. and PAGANO, M. (1988), The Advantage of Tying One's Hands: EMS Discipline and Central Bank Credibility, European Economic Review, Vol. 32, 1055-1082.

GOLDSTEIN, M. et al. (1993), International Capital Markets, Part I., Washington: IMF.

GOTUR, P. (1985), Effects of Exchange Rate Volatility on Trade, IMF Staff Papers, Vol. 32, 475-511.

GRIMES, A. (1991), The Effects of Inflation on Growth: Some International Evidence, Weltwirtschaftliches Archiv, Vol. 127, 631-700.

HASSE, R.H. and SCHÄFER, W. (1990), Europäische Zentralbank, Göttingen:

HENNING, R. (1993), International Monetary Policymaking in the United States, Germany and Japan, Washington DC: Institute for International Economics.

ISSING, O. (1992), Institutionen und Evolution im internationalen Währungssystem - Zur Entwicklung der Reservewährungen, in: GÖRGENS, E. und TUCHTFELDT, E., Ed., Die Zukunft der wirtschaftlichen Entwicklung - Perspektiven und Probleme, Bern: Haupt, 343-361.

KENEN, P. (1992), EMU after Maastricht, Washington DC: Group of Thirty.

KENEN, P. (1969), The Theory of Optimum Currency Areas: An Eclectic View, in: MUNDELL, R. and SWOBODA, A., Ed., Monetary Problems in the International Economy, Chicago: University of Chicago Press.

KLEIN, M. and WELFENS, P.J.J., Eds. (1992), Multinationals in the New Europe and Global Trade, Heidelberg: Springer.

KÖSTERS, W. (1993), On the Stability Conception of the Maastricht Treaty: Interpretation and Critical Assessment, Ruhr-Universität Bochum, mimeo.

KRAVIS, I. and LIPSEY, R. (1988), National Price Levels and the Price of Tradables and Nontradables, American Economic Review, P&P, Vol. 78, 474-478.

KREMERS, J. and LANE, T. (1990), Economic and Monetary Integration and the Aggregate Demand for Money in the EMS, IMF Working Paper 90/23, Washington DC.

KYDLAND, F. and PRESCOTT, E. (1977), Rules Rather than Discretion: The Inconsistency of Optimal Plans, Journal of Political Economy.

LANE, T. (1993), Market Discipline, IMF Working Paper, WP/92/42, Washington DC, forthcoming in IMF Staff Papers.

MATTHES, H. (1992), Adäquate Regeln für die Fiskalpolitik der EG-Länder, Wirtschaftsdienst, 1992/VII, 409-414.

MATTHES, H. and ITALIANER, A. (1991), Ist die Gemeinschaft ein optimaler Währungsraum, in: WEBER, M., Ed. (1991), Europa auf dem Weg zur Währungsunion, Darmstadt: Wissensch. Buchgesellschaft, 70-103.

MENKHOFF, L. and SELL, F.L. (1992), Überlegungen zu einem optimalen DM-Währungsraum, Zeitschrift für Wirtschafts- und Sozialwissenschaften, Vol. 112, 379-400.

MOLLE, W. and MORSINK, R. (1991), Intra-European Direct Investment, in: BURGENMEIER, B. and MUCCHIELLI, J.L., eds. (1991), Multinationals and Europe 1992, London: Routledge, 81-101.

OECD (1987), Structural Adjustment and Economic Performance, Paris.
OECD (1992), Main Economic Indicators, Paris.
OECD (1993), OECD Economic Outlook, June, Paris.
SEIDEL, M. (1992), Verfassungsrechtliche Probleme der Wirtschafts- und Währungsunion, List Forum, Bd. 18, 219-231.
SMEETS, H.-D. (1993), Monetäre Integration in Europa - Vom EWS zur Währungsunion, forthcoming: in GRÖNER, H. and SCHÜLLER, A., eds., Europäische Integration als ordnungspolitische Aufgabe, Stuttgart: Fischer.
TATOM, J.A. (1976), The Welfare Cost of Inflation, Federal Reserve Bank of St. Louis Economic Review, Vol. 56, Nov., 9-22.
TOOTELL, M.B. (1992), Purchasing Power Parity within the United States, New England Economic Review, July/August, 15-24.
VON HAGEN, J. and NEUMANN, M.J.J. (1992), Real Exchange Rates Within and Between Currency Areas: How Far Away is EMU?, CEPR Discussion Paper No. 660, London.
WEBER, M., Ed. (1991), Europa auf dem Weg zur Währungsunion, Darmstadt: Wiss. Buchgesellschaft.
WELCKER, J. (1992), Das Europäische System der Zentralbanken, Wissenschaftliche Hefte No. 1, Landeszentralbank im Saarland, Saarbrücken.
WELCKER, J. and NERGE, C. (1992), Spanien müßte mehr abführen, als es vom Kohäsionsfond erhielte, Handelsblatt, 8/6/91, Nr. 150, 11, Düsseldorf.
WELFENS, P.J.J., Ed. (1992a), Economic Aspects of German Unification, New York: Springer.
WELFENS, P.J.J. (1992b), Market-oriented Systemic Transformations in Eastern Europe, Heidelberg: Springer.
WELFENS, P.J.J. (1993a), The Single Market and the Eastern Enlargement of the EC, New York and Heidelberg: Springer.
WELFENS, P.J.J. (1993b), A Short History of European Monetary Integration, paper presented at Institut Universitaire International Luxembourg, forthcoming in: WILLMS, M., ed., European Monetary Union.
WORLD BANK (1992), World Development Report, New York.
YANNOPOULOS, G. N. (1992), Multinational Corporations and the Single European Market, University of Reading Discussion Paper No. 45, Reading.

Appendix 1:

Tab. A1: Increasing Financial Internationalization: Cross-border Transactions in Bonds and Stocks

(Gross purchases and sales of securities between residents and non-residents in % of GNP)

	1970	1975	1980	1985	1990
US	2.8	4.2	9.3	36.4	92.5
Japan	n.a.	1.5	7.0	60.5	118.6
FRG	3.3	5.1	7.5	33.9	57.5
F	n.a.	n.a.	8.4*	21.4	53.3
IT	n.a.	0.9	1.1	4.0	26.7
UK	n.a.	n.a.	n.a.	367.5	690.1
Canada	5.7	3.3	9.6	26.7	63.8

* 1982
Source: BIS (1992), 62nd Annual Report, Basle.

Tab. A2: Germany's Leverage Through Trade: EC Countries and US, 1973-1990

	FRG's Import Pressure (% in Country's Imp.)				FRG's Importance as Export Market (Share of Exports to FRG)					
	1973	1979	1990	79-90 swing	1973	1979	1990	79-90 swing	Germany's** Trade Exp.	Share Imp.
B+L	24.9	22.0	24.1	+2.1	23.6	22.5	21.3	-1.2	7.4	7.2
NL	27.1	24.2	25.8	+1.6	32.8	30.5	27.8	-2.7	8.4	10.1
DK	20.4	19.7	22.8	+2.9	13.2	17.5	19.9	+2.4	1.9	2.0
F	22.7	18.0	19.0	+1.0	19.3	17.2	17.4	+0.2	13.0	11.8
IT	20.3	17.2	21.3	+4.1	21.7	18.9	19.1	+0.2	9.3	9.4
GR	19.5	15.9	20.8	+4.9	21.5	19.3	22.2	+2.9	1.0	0.6
P	14.5	12.4	14.4	+2.0	7.5	12.7	16.7	+4.0	0.9	0.9
SP	13.6	9.6	16.5	+6.9	11.7	10.3	13.5	+3.2	3.5	2.4
IR	8.2	7.5	8.4	+0.9	6.2	8.8	11.7	+2.9	0.4	0.9
UK	8.5	12.0	15.9	+3.9	6.3	9.9	12.7	+2.8	8.5	6.7
US	7.7	5.4	5.7	+0.3	5.3	4.7	4.8	+0.1	7.3	6.7

** Share in German total merchandise exports and imports, 1991

OECD (1992), Foreign Trade Statistics, Series, A, Paris; Deutsche Bundesbank (1992), Statistische Beihefte zu den Monatsberichten der Deutschen Bundesbank, Reihe 3, Juli, own calculation.

Appendix 2; Fig. A1: Historical Steps of European Monetary Integration

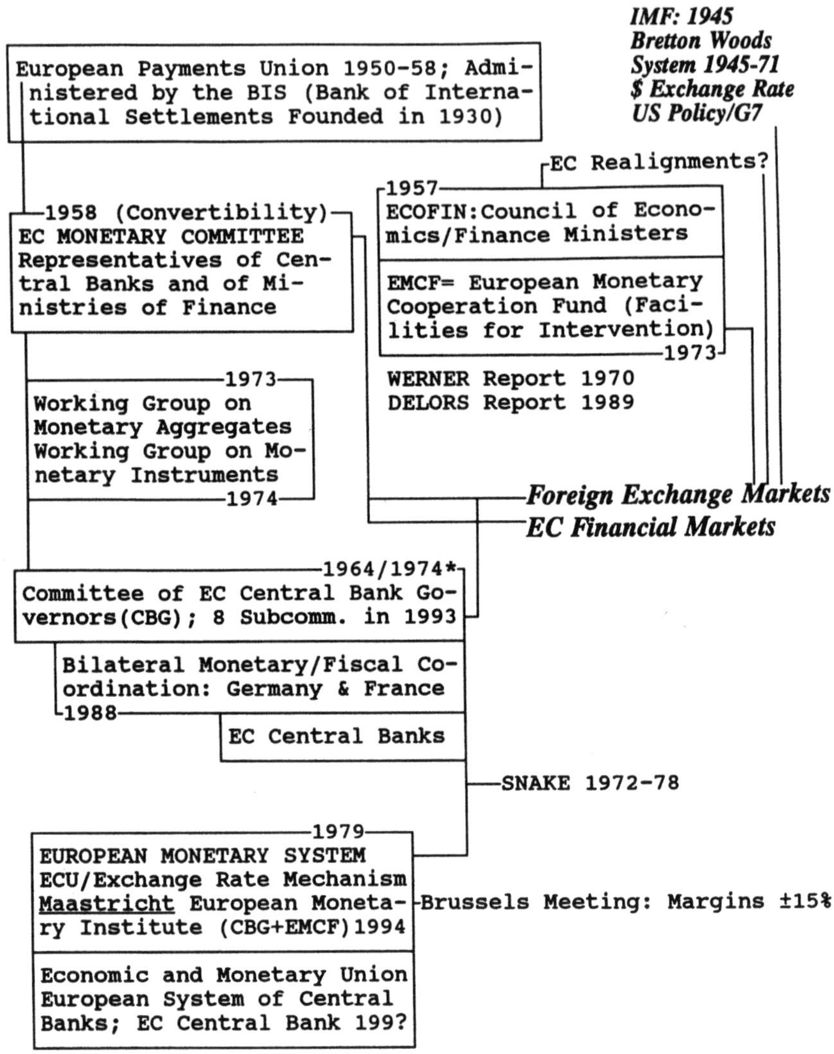

** founded in 1964, but major activities only have developed since 1974 when the EC Council declared convergence of economic policies to be a priority of EC economic policies*

Source: adapted from WELFENS (1993b)

Appendix 3: A Graphical Analysis of Benefits from Monetary Integration

Benefits from holding money can be analyzed with emphasis on the role of money as a production factor which allows increasing aggregate output or a consumption good *sui generis*. In an n country world the switch to a single currency would obviously minimize information costs in international transactions and contribute to increased competition in financial markets so that the interest rates i at home and i* abroad will equalize. However, at the same time there would be no longer any competing monies which lets economists expect that the quality of money issued would deteriorate because of reduced international political competition. There would be a higher world inflation rate than otherwise and hence a higher nominal interest rate i which is composed of the real interest rate r and the expected inflation rate π'. With a standard nominal money demand function $M^d = Pm(i)Y$ the real demand for money $m^d (= M^d/P)$ would reduce if nominal interest rates rise; increased opportunity costs of holding money will induce individuals to try to reduce real money balances through increased spending on goods or acquisition of other assets. With a lower nominal interest rate - whether caused by a lower r or a lower inflation rate π - the real money demand will increase.

The "consumer rent", reflecting the value of liquidity services, accruing to individuals holding money would increase (from the triangle CAB to CA'B'); a stability-oriented monetary integration should bring about an equalization of interest rates at home and abroad at lower levels ($i_1 = i^*_1$ instead of i_0, i_0^* initially). Conversely, under weak monetary integration or in an inflationary union economic growth could reduce. In a money supply regime which brings about lower inflation rates the nominal interest rate will reduce and output should increase from Y_0 to Y_1 (rightward shift of the m^d schedule which could also become more flat if increased competition in markets provides new highly liquid interest-bearing assets) because relative price signals are less confused with inflationary price changes so that the investment becomes more effective. Higher inflation rates typically go along with a greater volatility of inflation and a shortening of investment horizons which can be seen from the decline of bond maturities in high inflation periods. Low inflation directly raises the demand for money via lower nominal interest rates but also via a more effective allocation process and higher trade growth. The demand for money shifts outward and benefits from monetary integration/lower inflation are not only the area AA'BB' in country I; one has to add the area B'CDE . A similar reasoning holds for country II. In a two country model monetary integration would be an economic success if the combined real demand for money in country I and II would be higher than before monetary integration: say, m_3, m^*_3 instead of m_0, m^*_0 (with downward wage rigidity the transition towards m_3, m^*_3 could create one-off costs in the form of unemployment resulting from the transitional pressure on P: M will increase faster than P). Note that the consumer surplus has also increased in both countries. If monetary union would lead to higher π interest rates would converge at a higher level; hence m, m* would reduce.

Fig. A2: Monetary Integration-Real Money Demand in Country I and Country II

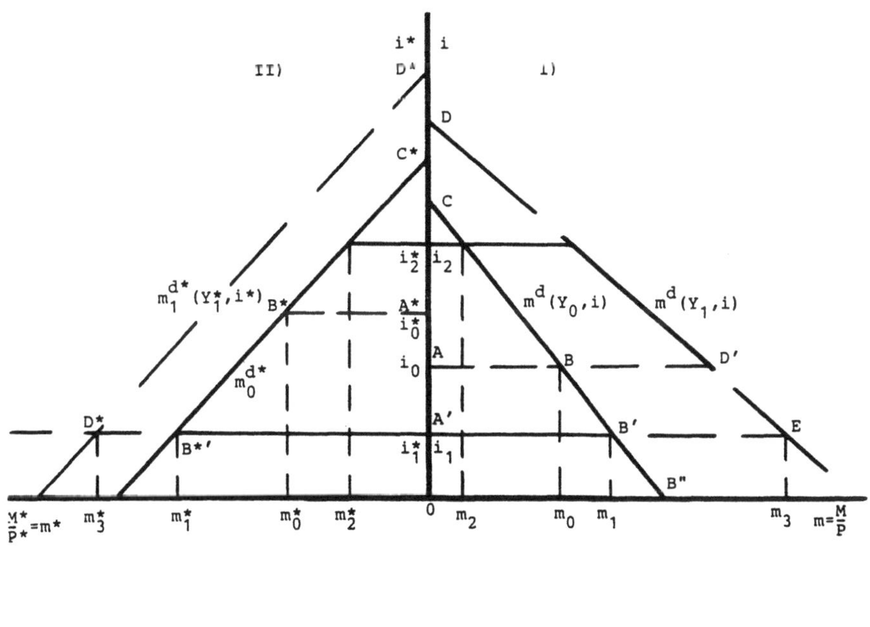

C. Randall Henning

Comments on:
European Monetary Union: Post-Maastricht Perspectives on Monetary and Real Integration in Europe

I am pleased to comment on the paper by Professor Welfens on European economic and monetary union (EMU). The paper, which covers a lot of ground and contains many intriguing ideas, is primarily critical of EMU on economic policy grounds and pessimistic about its future. With the exception of a few pages which acknowledge some of the benefits of monetary. unification, the Welfens paper lists the reasons as to why EMU is costly and politically difficult.

I agree that there are formidable obstacles to realizing a one-speed vision of EMU. As a political scientist, I will not challenge the economic arguments presented here. But, I want to offer constructive feedback to the author and make a general appeal about evaluating EMU by registering a disagreement with *the way the problem is posed*.

I will begin with the general appeal to those who conduct economic evaluations of EMU. Many analysts arrive at a negative assessment of monetary union on the basis of the assumption that monetary union will be single-speed. Naturally, when we group the high-inflation, southern European countries with the low-inflation northern countries, the obstacles to monetary union appear formidable indeed.

The heterogeneity of the twelve members of the Community increases the likelihood that the effects of external shocks will be asymmetrical among them. Although Europe is moving toward the single market, inflexibility in labor markets will continue to impede adjustment. The absence of a robust European system of automatic fiscal transfers between countries, analogous to those within countries, ensures that countries will bear by far the largest shares of the costs of adjustment themselves. These problems are well known.

When the assumption that EMU must be single-speed is relaxed, however, and we acknowledge that monetary union is in fact a *multi-speed* project, many of the costs appear much smaller and more manageable. It was for this reason that the multi-speed arrangement was built into the Maastricht Treaty during the intergovernmental conference in 1991. Criticizing the economic merits of a one-speed monetary union is an easy task. Proponents of a multi-speed monetary union, in which the low-inflation, northern European countries first form a union around the Franco-German core, have a stronger case.

Economic and monetary union must be a multi-speed affair for two relatively simple reasons which stem from the pivotal role of Germany. First, to be meaningful, EMU must include Germany. Second, Germany will not enter into a monetary union that includes members which have not demonstrated (not simply promised) a stability-orientation in macroeconomic policy and dedication to low inflation. The fact that Germany does not meet the convergence criteria in the Maastricht Treaty on inflation and deficits will probably not change this attitude. Because many countries within the Community cannot satisfy Germany on these grounds during this decade, a multi-speed system is the only way monetary union can happen.

The European Council has repeatedly professed that EMU is a one-speed affair. But, by all the evidence - which is further developed in the Welfens paper - this is simply not now credible. I reason, therefore, that when analysts design their studies they should dismiss the one-speed vision as economically unrealistic and focus on (1) the viability of monetary union among the hard, central core countries (including Austria) and (2) the relationship of the core to the "second-speed" countries and the process by which the latter could be eventually incorporated into the union.

The southern countries within the Community will resist the multi-speed approach to monetary unification. The one-speed union is clearly their first preference. But, the operative question is, what are their second and third preferences? I argue that, in the preference ordering of the southern countries, letting the northern, hard core proceed with monetary union and then joining them later is superior to no monetary union at all for the foreseeable future. The southern countries have a strong incentive to disguise their preferences so as to extract the maximum side payment for their accession to the multi-speed approach. But, once the Maastricht Treaty is fully ratified - assuming it is fully ratified - the European discussion on this issue will become much more realistic.

Let me refer to the couple of specific examples from the Welfens paper, cases where making the distinction between a one-speed and a multi-speed monetary union is important to our assessment of its desirability.

First, the paper portrays the Autumn 1992 currency crisis as a case of competitive devaluation of currencies. However, the paper also acknowledges, indeed stresses, that the British pound, Italian lira, Spanish peseta, Portuguese escudo each appreciated substantially in real terms within the ERM since the last realignment prior to the crisis. This was the result of substantially higher inflation in these countries compared to Germany. The devaluations of the peseta and the escudo within the ERM and the depreciation of the pound and lira outside the ERM were appropriate responses to prior overvaluation. Though they created competitiveness problems for countries such as France, these devaluations cannot be described as unfair.

Second, though the Autumn 1992 currency crisis was a setback for European monetary integration, the episode has redeeming features when we accept that a multi-speed approach is desirable. The crisis achieved a necessary realignment, which was best accomplished sooner rather than later. The crisis stripped away those currencies which could not be part of a stability-oriented monetary union at an early point, separating the fast-track from the slower-track. If the pound and the lira re-enter the ERM at more appropriate central parities, the crisis will have laid the basis for a more stable system and for more convergent macroeconomic policies in the future.

Third, the paper examines problems in the Maastricht design for EMU, citing in particular the debt/GNP ratio among the convergence criteria. Again, acknowledging the multi-speed nature of the process changes the assessment. Those governments which abuse their borrowing status will not be admitted into the monetary union and are far less likely to be bailed out. Fiscal rectitude, above all, is the *sine qua non* for admission into the union in Germany's eyes, notwithstanding Germany's own fiscal transgressions.

Fourth, the paper draws attention to the difference in the rates of inflation in the tradables and nontradables sectors in the EC member countries. Welfens argues that the countries in which the relative price of nontradables to tradables rises fastest - Italy, Greece, Spain, Portugal and the UK - need stronger competition policies. But, it is precisely these countries which are candidates for exclusion from the fast-track toward monetary union.

Finally, the paper addresses the institutional aspects of monetary policymaking after monetary union is achieved. It raises the specter of political influence over monetary policy through government control of national central banks which will vote in the governing bodies of the European System of Central Banks (ESCB). However, again, countries without independent central banks will not be admitted into the monetary union. This is a serious institutional problem within member countries, but it will not be a problem at the European level under the Maastricht institutional architecture. The ESCB, in fact, might well be considerably more independent within the European monetary union than the Bundesbank is within Germany!

Michael W. Klein

THE EUROPEAN MONETARY SYSTEM AND EUROPEAN INTEGRATION: AN EVALUATION

1. Introduction

National borders are becoming increasingly faint on the economic map of Europe. The 1989 Delors Commission report calls for both liberalization of goods and factor markets as well as increased coordination of macroeconomic policies among members of the European Community. The process of economic integration of goods and factor markets is to culminate with the removal of obstacles to trade, labor movements and capital movements within Europe by 1992. The logical extension of the process of macroeconomic coordination, begun by the institution of the European Monetary System (EMS) in 1979, is the proposed European Central Bank. These movements, while continuing the trans-national European policies that began with the Treaty of Rome in 1957, represent significant new steps down the path towards European integration.

The processes of extending macroeconomic coordination and furthering economic liberalization are distinct, though each impinges on the other. A stable macroeconomic environment is necessary for economic liberalization to proceed. The suspension of economic liberalization, especially as regards the liberalization of financial capital movements, may be necessary in the early stages of macroeconomic coordination although later economic liberalization may advance the process of macroeconomic coordination. In this paper we focus on the relationship between economic liberalization and macroeconomic coordination.

We first consider the experience of macroeconomic coordination in Europe and examine the extent of convergence of important macroeconomic variables before and after the institution of the EMS. We then survey some theoretical and empirical research on the manner in which macroeconomic convergence has been fostered by the EMS and the possible links between macroeconomic coordination and economic integration.

2. European Macroeconomic Convergence

International monetary arrangements that stabilize European cross exchange rates promote the liberalization of intra-European trade and foster the viability of certain institutional elements of the European Community. The importance of exchange rate stability reflects the extent to which the economies of the members of the European Community are interdependent. For example, trade among members of the European Economic Community accounted for over half of all trade by EC countries in 1970, and for almost 60% of all EC trade in 1986 (from European Economy, no. 34, November 1987, cited in *Giavazzi/Giovannini 1989*). A particularly important institutional element of the European Community that requires exchange rate stability is the insulation of agricultural commodity prices from currency movements through subsidies. The costs of these subsidies, which represent one-third of the cost of the common agricultural policy, increase with realignments due to certain asymmetries between their imposition and their removal.

The specter of the dissolution of European integration arises when the international monetary system fails to provide a stable economic environment. The most dramatic example of this occurred during the interwar period when currency instability led to a destabilization of the balance of payments of European countries and a subsequent suspension of European economic integration. The wide exchange rate fluctuations, competitive depreciations, massive unemployment and collapsing financial markets of the interwar period served as an object lesson to the architects of the post-war Bretton Woods system. The manifestation of their concerns was the construction of a system of fixed exchange rates which was an attempt to avoid the destabilization associated with the currency movements of the interwar period.

The stability of intra-European exchange rates during the Bretton Woods period fostered the development of the European customs union and the common agricultural market. As currencies became less stable in the late 1960s and the early 1970s, these developments toward economic integration were threatened. The manner in which exchange rate stability began to unravel at the end of the 1960s is demonstrated in Figure 1 in which we present the annual percentage changes of the bilateral German real exchange rates with France, Italy, the

Netherlands and the United States. During the period 1962 to 1969, the annual percentage change in the bilateral real exchange rate of the Deutsche Mark against the Franc, the Lira and the Guilder did not exceed 2.5%, 3.3%, and 3.6%, respectively. In contrast, the annual percentage change in these bilateral real exchange rates in 1970 were 10.9%, 5.5% and 6.5%, respectively.

The threat posed to European economic integration by divergent responses within Europe to the collapse of the Bretton Woods system prompted early calls for European monetary integration (*Johnson 1973*). The actual response to the suspension of the dollar standard was less ambitious than full European monetary integration. This half-step, however, did not provide a full measure of stability. The "snake-in-the-tunnel," instituted in April 1972 as an alternative to the 1971 Smithsonian agreements, established exchange rate bands centered around each currency's bilateral dollar exchange rate. The width of these bands was 4.5% around the central parity. This proved too wide for the smooth functioning of the common market and in March 1973, as the dollar began to depreciate against European currencies, the center could not hold and the snake began to float.

The "floating snake" lasted until 1979, but its membership was limited to Germany, the Netherlands, Denmark, Norway, Sweden, Belgium and Luxembourg. France left the snake in January 1974 and an attempt to rejoin in the summer of 1975 lasted for only eight months. Italy quit the snake before it began to float, and the United Kingdom was a member for only two months in 1972. The relatively poor performance of the "snake" can be attributed to its asymmetric exchange rate mechanism, whereby all intervention was undertaken by the central bank of the weak currency, and the lack of adequate financing to survive exchange rate crises. These institutional factors promoted a lack of credibility in the system which, in turn, contributed to the inability of the system to survive exchange rate crises. (*Thygesen 1979*, cited in *Giavazzi/Giovannini 1989*).

Figure 1
Deutschemark Real Exchange Rates

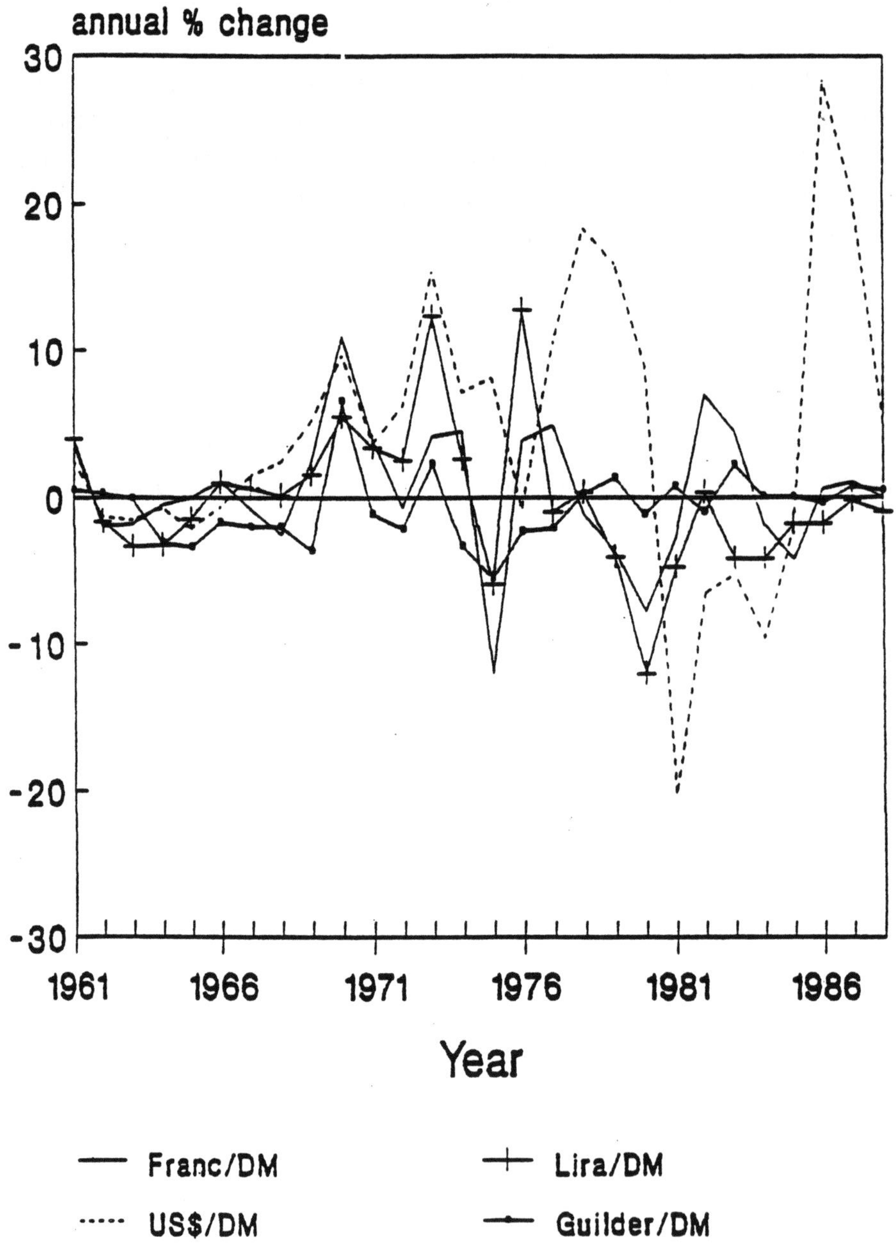

While membership in the floating snake was circumscribed, real exchange rate variability among its members did seem to be lower than real exchange rate variability between members and non-members. Inspection of Figure 1 suggests that there was greater stability of the real exchange rate of the Deutsche Mark against the Guilder than the Deutsche Mark against the Franc, the Dollar or the Lira during the period of the floating snake, a difference across currencies that was not apparent in the 1960s. Even so, the general increase in real exchange rate instability in the 1970s extended to members of the floating snake. For example, the smallest annual percentage change in the Guilder real exchange rate against the Deutsche Mark between 1972 and 1978 was still greater than the annual percentage change for six of the years of the 1960s.

Against the backdrop of the instability of the 1970s, the EMS began in March 1979 with all of the EC countries but for Great Britain participating in the exchange rate mechanism. The EMS, by providing a nominal anchor that stabilized expectations about exchange rates, reduced uncertainty concerning nominal exchange rate movements. This is demonstrated in Figures 2 which plots the squared monthly forecast error of the Guilder, the Franc and the Lira against the Deutsche Mark. After the beginning of 1979, the forecast errors of the Lira and the Franc against the Deutsche Mark decreased. The forecast error of the Guilder against the Deutsche Mark was lower than that of the Franc or the Lira. The Guilder forecast error was not markedly affected by the institution of the EMS, perhaps because membership in the floating snake provided the same type of credible nominal anchor subsequently provided by the EMS. The decrease in the forecast error of the Lira and Franc exchange rates at the end of 1979 was not matched by a decrease in the forecast error of these two currencies against the Dollar, as demonstrated in Figure 3. Indeed, the forecast errors of each currency against the Dollar increased beginning in late 1979.

Convergence in inflation rates in the EMS is an important prerequisite for the liberalization of the capital account. Unless inflation rates converge, a fixed exchange rate system will require continual realignments to preserve real exchange rate stability. The prospect of realignments, however, leads to speculative outflows from high-inflation countries and speculative inflows

Figure 2
Deutschemark Forecast Errors

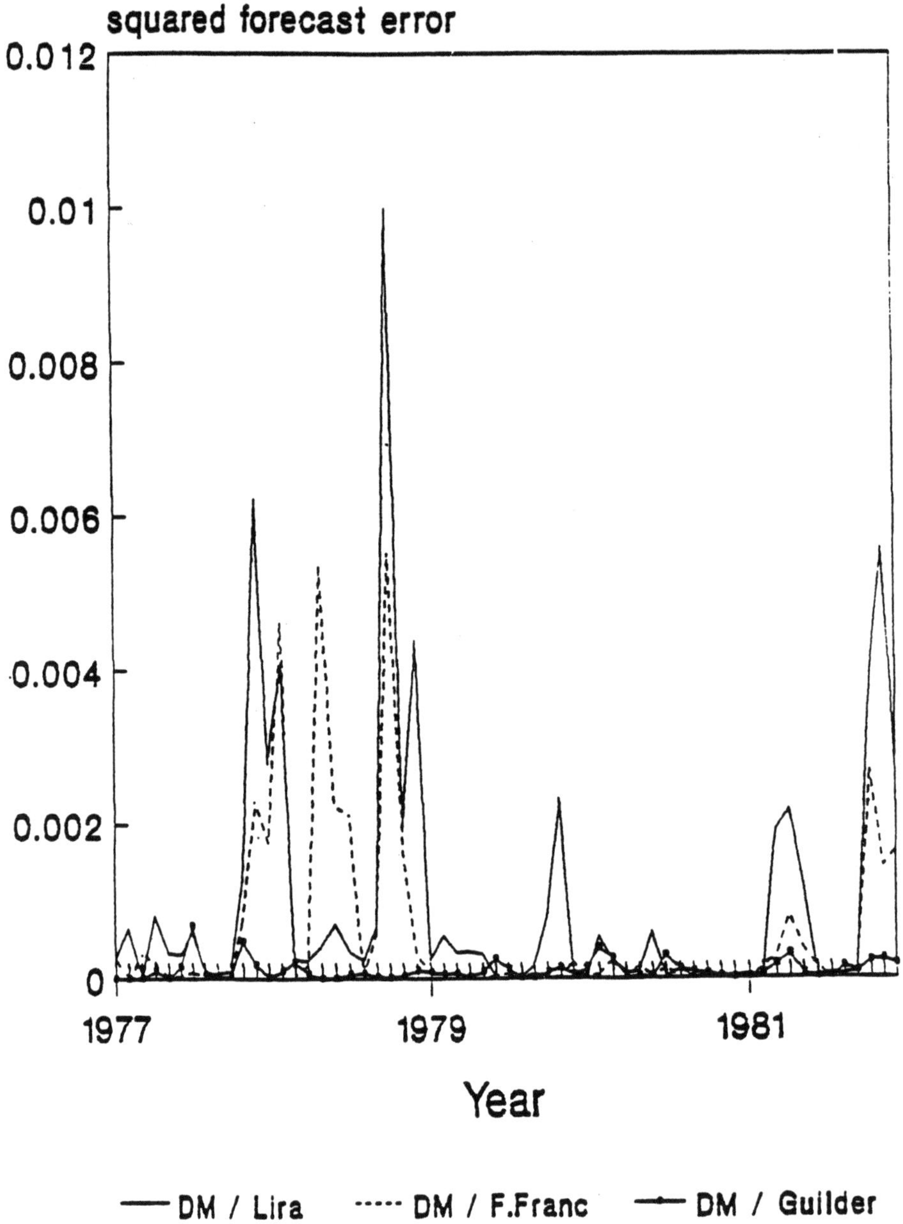

Figure 3
Dollar Forecast Errors

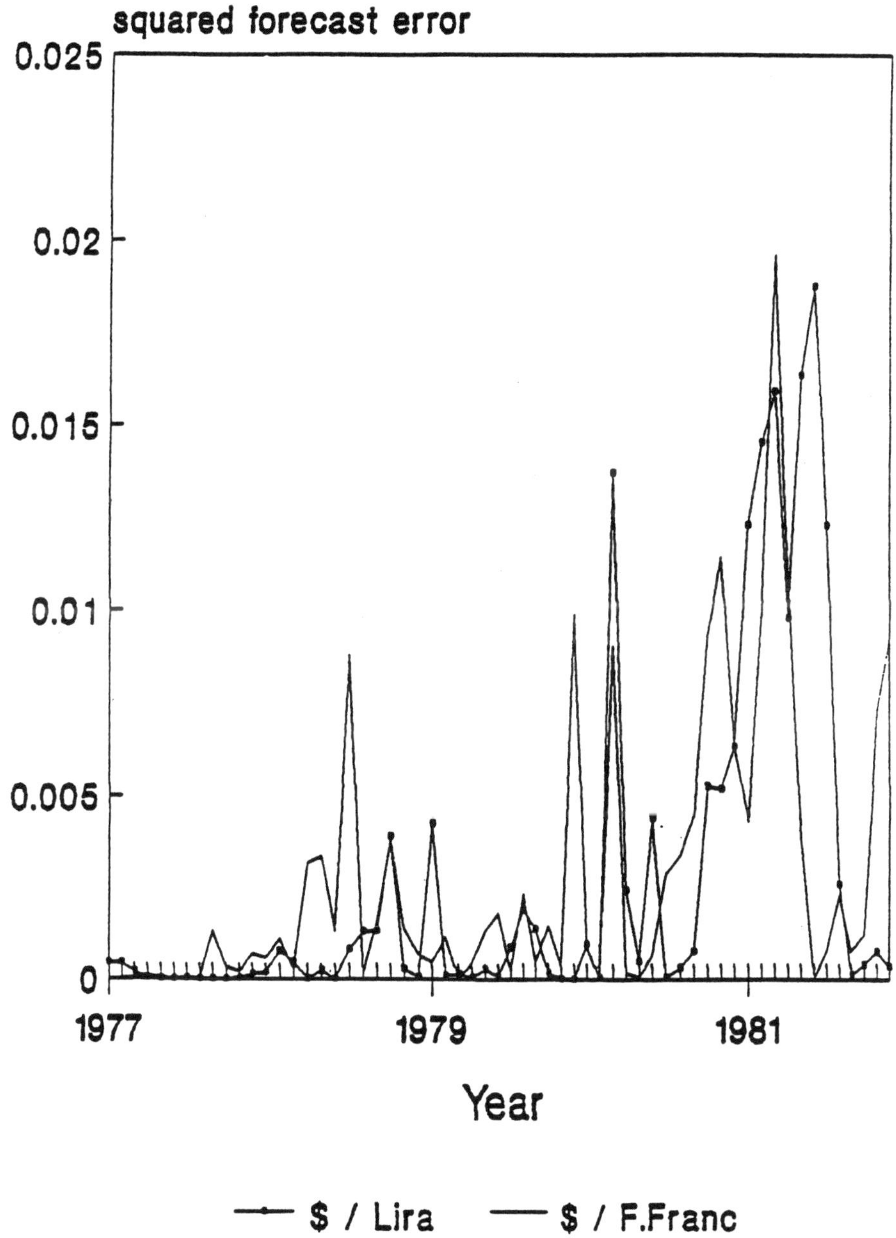

into low-inflation countries. These potentially destabilizing capital flows could only be quelled through the use of capital controls. Thus, divergent inflation rates in a fixed exchange rate system will force either the imposition of controls on trade in goods and services to counteract the effects of divergent real exchange rates, or the imposition of controls in financial markets, which otherwise would be characterized by instability reflecting anticipation of frequent realignments.

The time series of CPI Inflation rates for a variety of countries are presented in Figure 4. The data in this figure demonstrate a trend towards disinflation within the EMS during the 1980s. In 1978, inflation averaged 7.2% among those countries which would form the EMS while a decade later inflation in the EMS averaged 2.5%. The figure also demonstrates the convergence of inflation rates within the EMS. In 1978, the lowest inflation rate among the countries that would form the EMS was Germany's 2.7% rate while the 12% Italian inflation rate was the highest. By 1988, the range had narrowed, with the lowest inflation rate 0.7% in the Netherlands and the highest inflation rate 5% in Italy.

The extent to which the institution of the EMS has contributed to the disinflation in Europe is the subject of both theoretical and empirical research. Theory suggests the advantages to a country of aligning its monetary policy with that of a country with a reputation for a strong disinflationary policy (*Giavazzi/Pagano 1988*). Empirical research has investigated whether the EMS contributed to disinflation in Europe. *Ungerer et al. (1986)* study a time series cross-section of inflation rates and find that membership in the EMS facilitated disinflation in the 1980s. Reference to Figure 4, however, demonstrates that the 1980s disinflation also occurred in the United States and the United Kingdom. *Collins (1988)* demonstrates that the post-1979 shift in inflation was not limited to countries that are members of the EMS and that membership in the EMS provides no additional explanatory power to the determination of post-1979 inflation rates.

Inspection of Figure 4 suggests that inflation rates in the EMS have converged toward the German inflation rate during the 1980s. This may reflect an asymmetry in policy determination in the EMS in which monetary

Figure 4
Inflation Rates

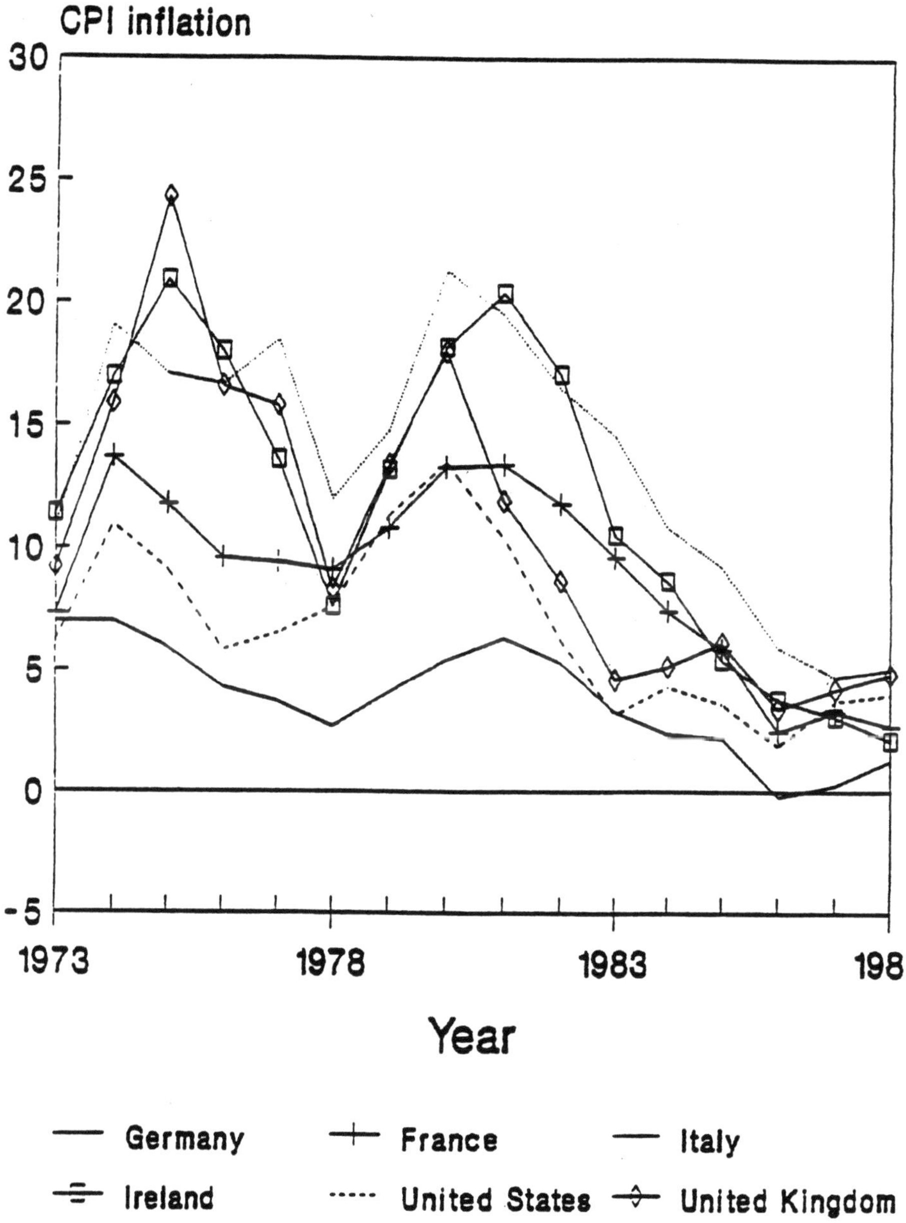

policy for all members is determined by the Bundesbank. Evidence supporting the hypothesis of German monetary hegemony is provided by data on intervention in exchange markets. The EMS requires intervention when currencies reach the edge of their permissible bands. Germany undertook 9% of the total amount of this so-called marginal intervention between March 1979 and March 1985 while France accounted for 31% of marginal intervention during this period. The difference in the burden of intervention across countries is even more marked for the period April 1985 to April 1986 when intervention by Germany and by France constituted 3% and 86%, respectively, of all intervention occurring at the margin. Germany undertook no intramarginal intervention during either of these periods (*Giavazzi/Giovannini 1989*).

Other approaches that attempt to determine the degree of symmetry in the EMS include studies focusing on realignment data and studies estimating central bank reaction functions. *Honohan/McNelis (1989)* find no evidence that EMS realignments significantly affect the level or the ability to forecast the Dollar / Deutsche Mark exchange rate although the level and the ability to forecast Dollar exchange rates of other currencies are significantly affected by realignments. They conclude from this that the Deutsche Mark serves as the dominant EMS currency. *Giovannini (1986)* estimates central bank reaction functions but, because of the difficulty of setting up these tests, the evidence from them is not conclusive.

The convergence of inflation rates in the EMS has been correlated with a convergence of seigniorage revenues. Figure 5 presents data on seigniorage relative to GDP since the collapse of the Bretton Woods system for four EMS countries (seigniorage relative to GDP is defined as the change in reserve money divided by nominal GDP, as in *Fischer 1982*). Seigniorage in Italy and Ireland has decreased during the 1980s to rates comparable (and, for Ireland, below) those in France and Germany. In 1978, at the eve of the EMS, seigniorage in Italy was 4.5% of GDP, representing 13.2% of all government revenue. In 1988, seigniorage in Italy had fallen to 1.3% of GDP, which represented 3.2% of total government revenue.

Figure 5
Seignorage in EMS Countries

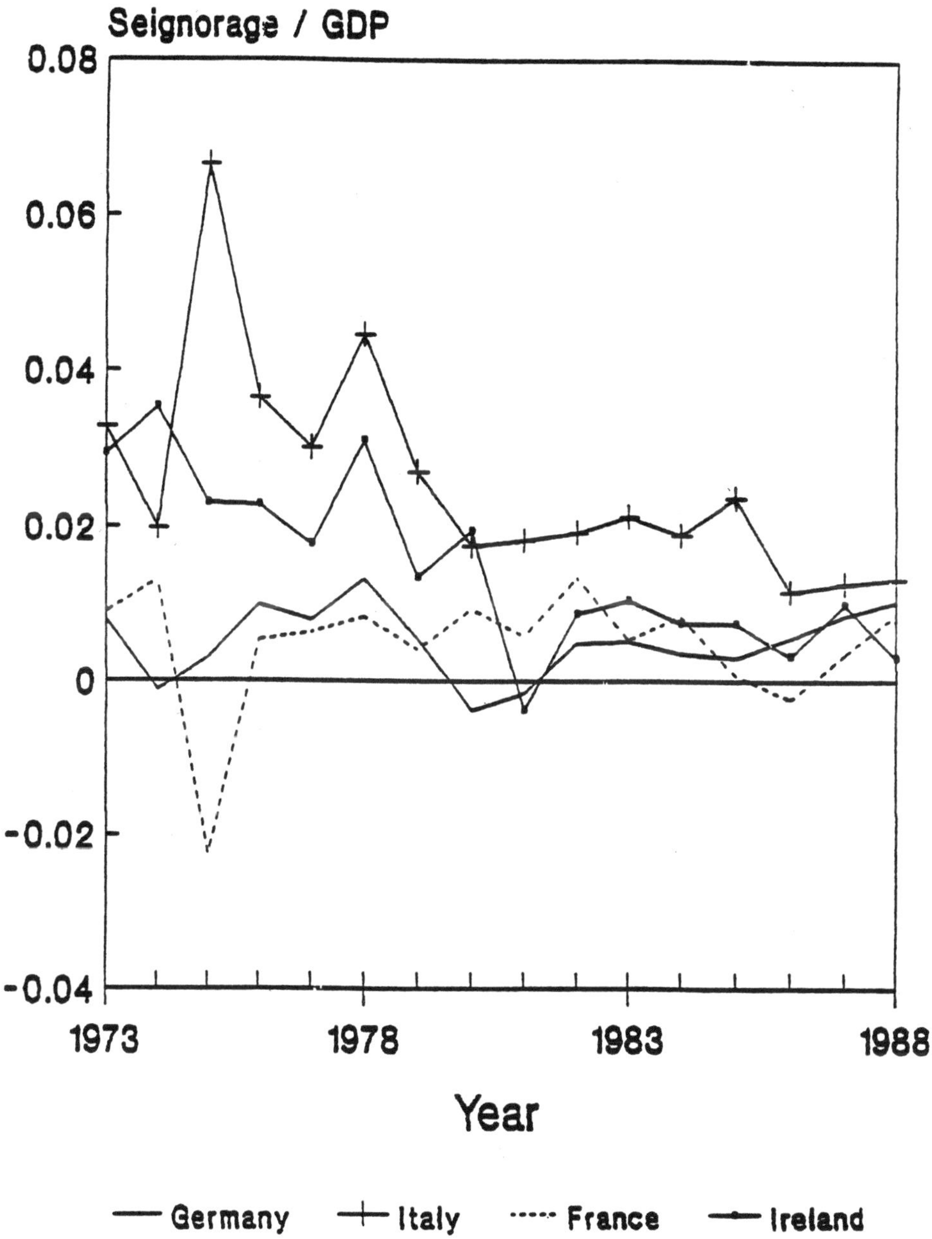

Differences in seigniorage revenues across countries may reflect differences in the ability of various governments to collect taxes. Seigniorage may be a relatively efficient method of raising revenues in an economy with a substantial underground component in which an income tax or a value-added tax cannot be easily assessed (*Canzoneri/Rogers 1990*). Evidence is presented in *Grilli (1989)* that fails to reject the hypothesis that the governments of the countries presented in Figure 5 used seigniorage in a manner consistent with the optimal seigniorage theory of *Phelps (1973)*, although the evidence does not support this result for other EMS countries. The continued presence of divergent rates of seigniorage has led to calls for a European exchange rate system based upon a crawling peg rather than fixed exchange rates to enable countries to have different rates of seigniorage (*Dornbusch 1988*).

The constraint imposed by the EMS on divergent rates of seigniorage may be particularly important when considering the membership of new countries. Figure 6 shows seigniorage relative to GDP for four countries; Italy, Spain, Greece and Portugal. Seigniorage in Italy, which is the highest among the original members of the EMS, has generally been less than seigniorage in Greece, Spain or Portugal since 1979. The Spanish peseta became part of the EMS exchange rate mechanism in July 1989, three-and-a-half years after Spain joined the EEC. Seigniorage in Spain increased between 1985 and 1987, but, perhaps in anticipation of becoming part of the ERM, the seigniorage rate was cut in half between 1987 and 1988. Greece became a member of the EEC at the beginning of 1981, and Portugal joined at the beginning of 1986, although neither country has yet joined the exchange rate mechanism. Seigniorage in these countries has been greater than seigniorage in Italy (and thus in other EMS countries) since 1986.

The constraint imposed by a monetary union on seigniorage differentials among its members is directly related to the requirements it places on fiscal convergence. While all governments face a budget constraint, membership in a fixed exchange rate system introduces another binding obligation, one that prevents budget deficits within a monetary union from being monetized at different rates. Capital controls can somewhat relieve this constraint by allowing for differential inflation rates (and preventing speculative capital movements) among members. But, in the absence of capital controls, long

Figure 6
Seignorage: Italy and Non-EMS Countries

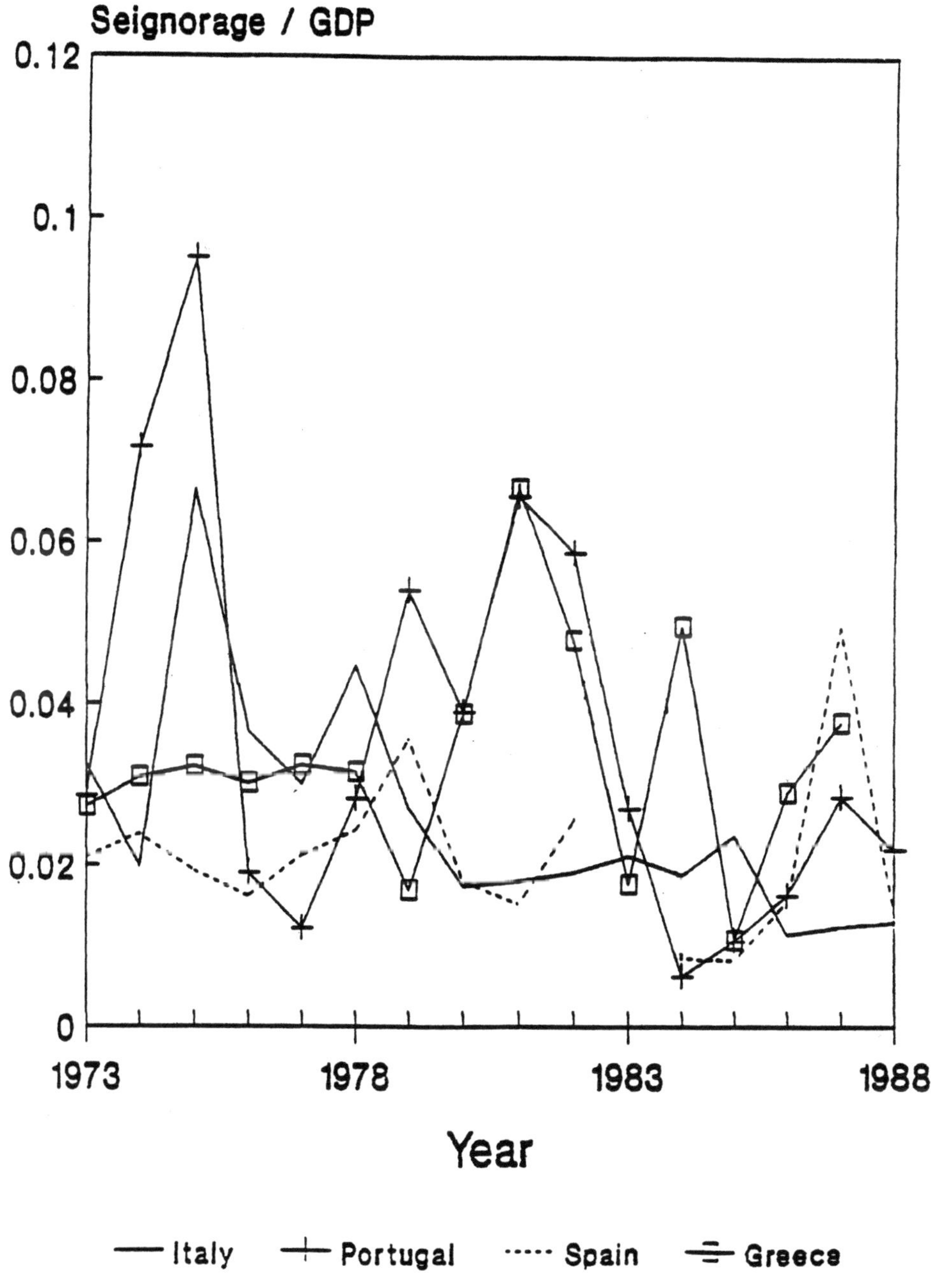

run expected deficits must be equalized across countries. These deficits (relative to GDP) also cannot reflect different combinations of expenditures and taxes (relative to GDP) across countries if physical capital and labor are internationally mobile since these factors of production will, to a certain extent, seek the area of highest after-tax returns (*Eichengreen 1990*).

While constraints on seigniorage revenues limit deficits of members of a monetary union, externalities associated with debt financing may encourage borrowing by its member governments. Consider the case of a perfectly credible fixed exchange rate system in which the bonds of the member governments are perfect substitutes. The interest rate on these government bonds will be the same since there is no exchange rate risk. An increase in borrowing by any one member increases the interest rate on all bonds. Thus, the cost of borrowing by any one member is shared by all members. This free-rider problem tends to increase the amount of borrowing among the members of a fixed exchange rate system (*Casella/Feinstein 1989*).

The evidence presented in this section supports the proposition that there has been a convergence in inflation and a corresponding stabilization of real exchange rates among the members of the EMS since its founding. An institutional fact that further bolsters this argument is the reduction in the frequency of realignments in the EMS in recent years. As discussed in the next section, the experience with realignments draws attention to the linkages between macroeconomic coordination and the integration of markets.

3. Macroeconomic Convergence and Economic Integration

The twin goals of macroeconomic coordination and economic integration were not compatible when the EMS began in 1979 since its initial survival required a lack of integration of national financial markets. At its founding, five of the seven members of the EMS had tight capital controls in place. The *devise titre* in France limited residents to purchasing foreign exchange only from other residents. Italian residents paid a high tax on the purchase of foreign securities. Belgium and Luxembourg had a two-tiered exchange rate system. Germany instituted administrative controls on capital inflows. There has been a progressive easing of capital controls since 1985, and all controls are scheduled to be lifted by July 1990 when the EC Directive on capital market liberalization will take effect throughout the community.

The suspension of financial market integration at the beginning of the EMS was necessary to prevent speculative capital flows in response to the anticipation of realignments. These anticipations were well-founded since there were frequent realignments during the early years of the EMS. The seven realignments between 1979 and 1983 were necessary responses to persistent inflation differentials among EMS members. The progressive convergence of inflation rates among members of the EMS since 1979 has reduced the need for realignments. After the two central parity realignments in 1986, there were no further realignments for over three years. The January 1990 realignment, moreover, was undertaken to facilitate a more narrow 2.25% exchange rate band for the lira from its former width of 6%.

The easing of capital controls, initially facilitated by a reduction in the frequency of realignments, may have subsequently served to reduce the need for realignments. *Giavazzi/Spaventa (1990)* argue that financial liberalization has led to greater exchange rate fixity since the cost of realignments when capital controls are not in place is greater than when capital controls shield the foreign assets of member countries' central banks. Markets realize this and assign a smaller probability to realignments occurring which, in turn, reduces the frequency of realignments. Evidence supporting this hypothesis is provided by the convergence of the variability of onshore and offshore interest rates. Giavazzi and Spaventa point out that the variability of the Eurofranc and Eurolira rates fell 250% between the 1983 to 1987 and the 1988 to 1989 periods. This fall cannot be fully explained by general movements in interest rate variability since the variability of the Deutsche Mark Eurorate fell by 50% between these periods. Inspection of bid-ask spreads also rejects the hypothesis that the change in volatility reflects a change in the "thinness" of the Eurobond market.

While Giavazzi and Spaventa focus on the evolution of expectations during the development of the EMS, research initiated by *Krugman (1990)* focuses on the manner in which an exchange rate target zone affects exchange rate dynamics through its effect on expectations. The exchange rate is a forward-looking variable and its value depends upon the value of fundamentals as well as its own expected rate of change. A target zone limits the admissible range of values of the fundamental, thus linking the expected change of the fundamental, as well as the exchange rate, to its current realization. The result is that a target zone stabilizes the exchange rate by mitigating its expected change which attenuates the relationship between fundamentals and the exchange rate, even absent any actual intervention. In a full macroeconomic model, the stabilizing effect of the target zone on the nominal exchange rate also extends to the real exchange rate and output (*Klein 1990*).

Support for these theoretical conclusions is provided by empirical research that focuses on the effects of exchange rate regimes on macroeconomic variables. *Artis/Taylor (1988, p. 202)* find "..unequivocal evidence that the ERM has brought about a reduction in both the conditional and the unconditional variance of exchange rate changes - and, far from having purchased this reduction at the cost of increased interest rate volatility, there is also some evidence of a reduction in the volatility of interest rates for ERM members." They attribute this result to the effects of exchange rate policies on credibility.

Svensson (1989) considers the theoretical effects of an exchange rate target zone on the variability of the interest rate differential. He demonstrates that the instantaneous variability of the interest rate differential decreases as the exchange rate band gets wider. The asymptotic variance of the interest rate differential depends upon the width of the band (as well as parameters such as the semi-elasticity of money demand). In the case of a band width comparable to that in the EMS, the asymptotic variance of the interest differential increases with wider bands and decreases with narrower bands.

Baxter/Stockman (1989) find that real exchange rates were more volatile in the post-1973 period than in the pre-1973 period, even among countries that would later become members of the EMS. They do not, however, consider the performance of the EMS separately from the general post-Bretton Woods experience. Reference to Figure 1 suggests that the volatility of the Deutsche Mark bilateral real exchange rate against the franc, lira and guilder was higher during the period between 1973 and 1979 than during the period of the EMS.

While empirical evidence suggests that the EMS has served to reduce the volatility of bilateral real exchange rates among its members, the impact of exchange rate volatility on other variables is far from clear. Theory suggests that an increase in exchange rate volatility may diminish the amount of international trade undertaken by risk-averse firms and thus be negatively correlated with the volume of trade (*Hooper/Kohlhagen 1978*). Evidence of the significance of this effect, at least for nominal exchange rate volatility, is not forthcoming. There is some stronger evidence that real exchange rate volatility is negatively correlated with the volume of trade (*Cushman 1981*) and that trade is diverted towards partners with lower bilateral real exchange rate volatility (*Cushman 1986*). Other research, however, fails to find evidence that exchange rate volatility is negatively correlated with the volume of international trade (see *IMF 1985*; *Bailey/Tavlas/Ulan 1987*).

A possible reason for the lack of consistent evidence on the effect of exchange rate volatility on trade is that export supply by risk-neutral firms may increase in the face of an increase in volatility. An increase in exchange rate volatility raises the expected return to an exporter in much the same way that an increase in the variance of the payoff of a bet raises the expected return of that bet. There is evidence that exchange rate volatility does lead to lower export prices (*Giovannini 1988*) for certain categories of exports from Japan to the U.S. and higher export volumes for disaggregated categories of U.S. bilateral exports to other industrial countries (*Klein 1990*).

Exchange rate volatility may affect factor mobility when relocation involves fixed costs. *Dixit (1989)* demonstrates that the volatility of the real exchange rate is positively correlated with the extent to which the exchange rate must change in order to get potential exporters to enter a new market or existing exporters to surrender their position in a market. A decrease in the mobility of capital due to an increase in exchange rate volatility, in turn, requires greater exchange rate movement to correct an initial misalignment, as shown by *Krugman (1989)*. *Bertola (1989, p. 113)* discusses how "increasing returns to stabilization policy" arise because stabilizing income, given a upper limit on exchange rate flexibility, leads to more factor mobility. These important theoretical contributions on the effects of exchange rate volatility still await empirical testing and application.

4. Conclusion

Current issues pertaining to macroeconomic coordination and economic integration in Europe come at a time when the gains of the past decade seem to be evident, while at the same time the movement towards greater linkages will be facing new sources of stress because of the inclusion of new members in the European community. We have seen that, in its early stages, macroeconomic coordination may require the suspension of certain aspects of economic liberalization, especially the free flow of financial capital. Subsequently, however, economic integration may serve as a credible commitment on the part of governments to follow stable policies. The effect of these credible commitments on agents' expectations can itself serve as a stabilizing force for members of an integrated economic community.

Even before the dramatic political events of the past year, the inclusion of new members in the European Community and the Exchange Rate Mechanism were seen as important and perhaps difficult issues facing the community. The differences in the fiscal and monetary policies of the original members of the EC from the policies of Greece, Spain and Portugal caused concerns on the viability of their membership. Corresponding concerns of the integration of Eastern European economies into the EEC, as well as the unification of Germany, run deeper since there is also the need for the establishment of well-functioning markets in these countries that can provide the necessary price signals for their economies.

The convergence in inflation rates, the dismantling of capital controls and the movement towards an integrated European market in the 1980s holds out a promise for the possible achievements of the coming decade. While the challenges facing the European community in the 1990s are manifold, recent accomplishments in European integration provide hope that these challenges can be successfully met.

Data

All data are from the International Monetary Fund's International Financial Statistics.

Real exchange rates: annual nominal exchange rates deflated by the relative consumer price indices.

Forecast errors: monthly forward exchange rates minus actual end of month nominal exchange rate.

Inflation rates: calculated from annual CPI index.

Seigniorage: annual change in reserve money (IFS line 14) divided by nominal GDP. Government revenue figures (IFS line 81) include seigniorage.

References

ARTIS,M. and TAYLOR,M. (1988). Exchange Rates, Interest Rates, Capital Controls and the European Monetary System: Assessing the Track Record, in: GIAVAZZI, F., MICOSSI, S. and MILLER, M., eds., The European Monetary System. Cambridge, England: Cambridge University Press.

BAILEY, M.J., TAVLAS, G. and ULAN, M. (1987). Exchange-Rate Volatility and Trade Performance: Evidence for the Big Seven Industrial Countries. Weltwirtschaftliches Archiv, 123, 466-477.

BAXTER, M. and STOCKMAN, A. (1989). Business Cycles and the Exchange- Rate Regime. Journal of Monetary Economics, 23, 377-400.

BERTOLA, G. (1989). Factor Mobility, Uncertainty, and Exchange Rate Regimes, in: DeCECCO, M. and GIOVANNINI, A. eds., A European Central Bank? Cambridge, England: Cambridge University Press.

CANZONERI, M; ROGERS, C.A. (1990). Is the European Community an Optimal Currency Area? Optimal Tax Smoothing versus the Cost of Multiple Currencies, American Economic Review, 80, 419-433.

CASELLA, A.; FEINSTEIN, J. (1989). Management of a Common Currency, in: DeCECCO, M. and GIOVANNINI, A., eds., A European Central Bank? Cambridge, England: Cambridge University Press.

COLLINS, S.M. (1988). Inflation and the European Monetary System, in: GIAVAZZI, F., MICOSSI, S. and MILLER, M., eds., The European Monetary System. Cambridge, England: Cambridge University Press.

CUSHMAN, D.O. (1983). The Effects of Real Exchange Rate Risk on International Trade. Journal of International Economics, 15, 45-63.

CUSHMAN, D.O. (1986). Has Exchange Risk Depressed International Trade? The Impact of Third-Country Exchange Risk. Journal of International Money and Finance, 5, 361-379.

DIXIT, A. (1989). Hysteresis, Import Penetration, and Exchange Rate Pass-Through. Quarterly Journal of Economics, 104, 205-228.

DORNBUSCH, R. (1988). The European Monetary System, the Dollar and the Yen, in: GIAVAZZI, F., MICOSSI, S., and MILLER, M., eds., The European Monetary System. Cambridge, England: Cambridge University Press.

EICHENGREEN, B. (1990). One Money for Europe? Lessons from the US Currency Union. Economic Policy, forthcoming.

FISCHER, S. (1982). Seigniorage and the Case for a National Money. Journal of Political Economy, 90, 295-313.

GIAVAZZI, F. and GIOVANNINI, A. (1989). Limiting Exchange Rate Flexibility: The European Monetary System. Cambridge, Massachusetts: The MIT Press.

GIAVAZZI, F. and PAGANO, M. (1988). The Advantage of Tying One's Hand: EMS Discipline, Central Bank Credibility. European Economic Review, 32, 1055-1075.

GIAVAZZI, F and SPAVENTA, L. (1990). The "New" EMS. CEPR discussion paper no. 369, London: Center for Economic Policy Research.

GIOVANNINI, A. (1986). Rules of the Game during the International Gold Standard: England and Germany. Journal of International Money and Finance, 5, 467-483.

GIOVANNINI, A. (1988). Exchange Rates and Traded Goods Prices. Journal of International Economics, 24, 45-68.

GRILLI, V. (1989). Seigniorage in Europe, in: DeCECCO, M., GIOVANNINI, A., eds., A European Central Bank? Cambridge, England: Cambridge University Press.

HONOHAN, P. and McNELIS,P. (1989). Is the EMS a DM Zone? - Evidence from the Realignments. The Economic and Social Review, 97 - 110.
HOOPER, P. and KOHLHAGEN, S. (1978). The Effect of Exchange Rate Uncertainty on the Prices and Volumes of International Trade. Journal of International Economics, 8, 483-511.
INTERNATIONAL MONETARY FUND (1984). Exchange Rate Volatility and World Trade, Occasional Paper No. 28. Washington D.C.
JOHNSON, H.G. (1973). The Exchange-rate Question for a United Europe, in: KRAUSE, M.B., ed., The Economics of Integration. London: George Allen & Unwin.
KLEIN, M.W. (1990). Playing With the Band: Dynamic Effects of Target Zones, in: an Open Economy. International Economic Review, 31, forthcoming.
KLEIN, M.W. (1990). Sectoral Effects of Exchange Rate Volatility on United States Exports. Journal of International Money and Finance, 9, 299-308.
KRUGMAN, P. (1989). Exchange Rate Instability. Cambridge, Massachusetts: The MIT Press.
KRUGMAN, P. Target Zones and Exchange Rate Dynamics. Quarterly Journal of Economics, 105, forthcoming.
PHELPS, E. (1973). Inflation in the Theory of Public Finance. Swedish Journal of Economics, 75, 67-82.
SVENSSON, L.E.O. (1989). Target Zones and Interest Rate Variability. Stockholm: Institute for International Economic Studies, mimeo.
THYGESEN, N. (1979). The Emerging European Monetary System: Precursors, First Steps and Policy Options, in: TRIFFIN, R., ed., EMS - The Emerging European Monetary System. Offprint from the Bulletin of the National Bank of Belgium) LIV,I, Brussels.
UNGERER, H., OWEN, E., MAYER, T., and YOUNG, P. (1986). The European Monetary System: Recent Developments. IMF Occasional Paper No. 48. Washington, D.C.: International Monetary Fund.

Vittorio Grilli

Comments on:
The European Monetary System and European Integration: An Evaluation

In this paper Dr. Klein reviews and analyzes many important issues in European monetary and exchange rate policies. Several are crucial to the understanding of the European Monetary System, both its past developments and its possible future evolution into a European Monetary Union. Dr. Klein rightly focuses on four crucial topics: (i) the disinflationary role of the EMS, (ii) the impact of exchange rate discipline on the ability of raising revenues through monetization, (iii) the presence of asymmetries in the EMS, (iv) and the success of the EMS in reducing exchange rate volatility.

As the figures presented in the paper unquestionably show, the EMS period has coincided with a substantial reduction of the average inflation rate in Europe. This has been achieved through the convergence of inflation rates within the EMS toward Germany's level. Whether the establishment of the EMS has had any special role in inducing this reduction in inflation has been debated at length. Several econometric analyses did not find any evidence that the EMS has had an independent effect in producing the disinflation. In fact, it is argued, a reduction in inflation has occurred, in this period, in most industrialized countries, whether or not members of the EMS. In my opinion, however, this type of argument underestimates the importance of the EMS since it cannot be excluded that the disinflationary policies pursued by non-EMS countries had been triggered by the establishment of the EMS. In fact, the decision of non-EMS countries to reduce inflation might have been taken, in part, in an effort not to diverge from their major trading partners, in response to the establishment of the EMS in continental Europe, and to the introduction of tight monetary policies in the United Kingdom and in the United States.

The implications of the reduction of inflation are not limited to monetary and exchange rate policies but have important effects on fiscal policies as well. As discussed by Dr. Klein, the high levels of inflation in Europe were the consequence of the widespread use of monetization to finance government deficits. The monetary discipline imposed by the EMS severely curtails the ability to resort heavily and systematically on seigniorage. As the author suggests, Greece and Portugal, which still use monetization as a main revenue source, may find full membership in the EMS very costly. It could be argued, however, that the inability to use seigniorage freely in a semi-fixed exchange rate regime, while costly in the short run, may result in a superior long run equilibrium. In general, high levels of inflation have disruptive effects on both financial and labor markets and thus are a very inefficient way of raising revenues. Nonetheless, seigniorage is widely used, as a last resort instrument, when any other alternative way of allocating of tax burden lacks the necessary social consensus. Participation in the EMS, by eliminating the tempting, but costly, option of inflation, can force social and political groups into reaching an agreement on fiscal reforms which would otherwise be postponed indefinitely.

As Dr. Klein points out, the EMS seems to suffer from some fundamental asymmetry, which tends to be associated with the hegemonic role of the Bundesbank. Dr. Klein illustrates this fact by outlining the differences in central banks' intervention policies. Other evidence of asymmetries in the system is provided by the fact that disturbances external to the EMS (such as movements of the dollar driven by U.S. monetary and fiscal policies) have led in the past to inter-EMS exchange rate tensions, usually involving the position of the Deutsche mark with respect to the other European currencies. This point of view is supported by the empirical observation that, in periods of strength (weakness) of the dollar, the Deutsche mark appears to be weak (strong) relative to the other EMS currencies.

One common interpretation of this empirical fact is that assets denominated in different currencies are imperfect substitutes in the portfolios of international investors. In particular, it is argued that the degree of asset substitutability between the dollar and the Deutsche mark is greater than the one between the dollar and other European currencies. Shocks that lead to an increase (decrease) in the demand for dollar assets will reduce (increase) the demand for the Deutsche mark more than the demand for francs, liras, or pesetas and, thus, will generate asymmetric responses in the system. If the source of this inter-EMS asymmetry is imperfect asset substitutability, then capital controls might be justified as an instrument aimed at reducing inter-EMS exchange rate tensions deriving from disturbances external to the EMS. If this view is correct, the liberalization of capital controls will exacerbate the inter-EMS tensions caused by external shocks: movements of the dollar that lead to incipient changes in the value of the Deutsche mark relative to other EMS currencies will not be dampened any more by the existing capital controls.

But there are other reasons for the existence of asymmetries in the EMS. It is a well-known fact that certain currencies (such as the U.S. dollar, the Japanese yen and the Deutsche mark) are used both as reserve assets and as vehicle currencies (i.e. currencies with which international transactions of goods and services are conducted) while other currencies (such as those of the smaller EMS countries) have a much more limited or nonexistent role as reserve assets and/or as international transaction currencies. Can inter-EMS exchange rate asymmetries be related to the fact that the Deutsche mark is such an international transaction currency while the other EMS currencies are not? In fact, it can be shown that, quite independently from the degree of substitutability of assets, demand and supply shocks external to the EMS can affect the inter-EMS exchange rates if the degree of international diversification of asset portfolios is limited and if some currencies in the EMS have a vehicle and reserve currency role that other currencies do not have *(Grilli/Roubini 1989)*.

The implications of these results are twofold. First, the liberalization of capital controls in the EMS, by allowing a greater degree of international pooling of asset, should reduce rather than increase inter-EMS tensions. From this point of view the liberalization should facilitate the objective of maintaining exchange rate stability in the EMS area. Second, while increased liberalization of capital movements might reduce inter-EMS tensions, a fundamental asymmetry in the system will persist. This asymmetry is the increasing vehicle and reserve currency role of the German mark. This is an independent and increasing source of potential inter-EMS tensions since the level of the exchange rate is affected by the relative role of different currencies in international trade transactions. In a minor measure, only the French franc has such a vehicle currency role among the EMS currencies. The particular, and so far almost unique, role of the Deutsche Mark as an international currency among the EMS is likely to remain a cause of inter-EMS tensions that have their source in disturbances external to the EMS area.

Apart from possible asymmetries in the system, the EMS played an important role in reducing exchange rate volatility in Europe. The extent of the EMS contribution to this process is particularly impressive in view of the major changes that have taken place in this period in the world financial markets. During the last decade, in fact, several countries (e.g. Japan, the U.K., Australia) deeply liberalized their capital markets. At the same time, the volume of transactions in the foreign exchange markets has risen dramatically, to an extent that cannot be explained just by the increase in the volume of trade in goods and services. In fact, most of the turnover in the foreign exchange markets is now generated by financial operations and a large part of them are of a speculative nature. This unprecedented increase in the volume of transactions has been a major shock to foreign exchange markets and could have affected the volatility of the exchange rates. From a theoretical point of view, the impact of financial liberalization on exchange rate volatility can change over time. On one side, liberalization increases both economy-wide and investor-specific uncertainty and, therefore, increases the volatility of exchange rates. On the other hand, an increase in the number of participants in the foreign exchange markets reduces volatility. In the short run, the uncertainty effect is likely to dominate, while in the medium-long run the increase in the number of traders thickens the otherwise "thin" markets and tends to reduce the volatility of exchange rates.

There is evidence that, for most non-EMS currencies, changes in exchange rate volatility have occurred, and that they have taken place close to the time in which major capital liberalization episodes have occurred *(Corsetti/Grilli/Roubini 1990)*. Changes in volatility which could be associated with worldwide capital liberalization, however, are not present for EMS currencies. These results indicate that the EMS not only has worked well in reducing the impact of intra-European shocks on exchange rate volatility, but that it has also sheltered the area from major disturbances occurring in the world financial markets as a consequence of the removal of capital controls. This evidence suggests that the broadening of membership in the EMS and its strengthening are going to be important during this period of transition toward fully integrated financial markets in Europe.

References

GRILLI, V., V. and N. ROUBINI (1989). A Model of Exchange Asymmetries in the EMS. Yale University.

CORSETTI, G., B. GRILLI and N. ROUBINI (1990). Exchange Rate Volatility in Integrating Capital Markets. Yale University.

Karl Otto Pöhl

BASIC FEATURES OF A EUROPEAN MONETARY ORDER

1. Introduction

The European Council took a decision in Strasbourg last December which will have far-reaching implications. Before the end of this year an intergovernmental conference is to be convened which is to discuss, and to decide on, the future road to European economic and monetary union and its institutional structure. It is to provide the legal basis for the necessary responsibilities which now rest with the national authorities to be transferred to Community bodies. Monetary policy will be affected most. The ruling EC treaty does not provide for any Community responsibility for monetary policy, which sufficiently explains why institutional steps towards monetary integration require an amendment to the treaty. Article 102 A, which was added to the ruling EC treaty by the Single European Act in 1986, expressly reaffirmed this requirement by stating: "In so far as further development in the field of economic and monetary policy necessitates institutional changes, the provisions of Article 236 shall be applicable." Pursuant to that article, such amendments shall be "ratified by all the member states in accordance with their respective constitutional requirements."

In most other aspects of economic policy there is no comparable requirement to establish new institutions for economic and monetary union and to transfer responsibilities to them. However, better use must be made of the existing instruments and bodies in order to achieve more convergence in economic policy and its results and to establish these permanently. The progress made so far, for example, the liberalization of the movement of goods and capital, must not be called into question again if economic and monetary union is to last. Additional binding arrangements will therefore be necessary in major sectors which make unilateral action more difficult or impossible for member states and which set a minimum standard of "good conduct" for them, particularly in fiscal policy. This will necessitate the surrender of sovereignty by the individual member states, but this need not mean corresponding gains in Community authority, that is, by the Council and the Commission, provided the subsidiarity principle is respected. As is well known, this principle provides for everything which need not be decided on at the higher levels to be decided on and implemented at the lower levels. Incidentally, the control functions of the European Parliament are to be strengthened systematically, particularly in relation to the Commission and the Council; this was a condition made by the German Federal Chancellor in Strasbourg.

2. Facing the Challenge of an EC Monetary Order

The most important issue in the menu of questions and problems which the intergovernment conference will face is no doubt the European central bank system (ECBS). Its structure must satisfy the high expectations which a future economic and monetary union arouses in the member states, namely, in the countries with stable currencies the expectation that monetary stability will not be lost in an economic and monetary union; and in countries where the value of money is being eroded to a greater or lesser degree that an end will be put to this erosion once and for all.

None other than Walter Hallstein himself, the first President of the EC Commission, saw monetary policy as the touchstone for the Community. He wrote that "monetary stability is a value of great importance, a fundamental requirement."[1] The fact is that only when those responsible in all member states are prepared to concede monetary stability this priority can the project of an economic and monetary union succeed. Only then will it be possible in the foreseeable future to fix the exchange rates between the national currencies permanently and finally to replace the national currencies by a common currency.

This ambitious goal certainly cannot be achieved in a revolutionary act, in a great leap forward, but only in an evolutionary process, which, however, should be determined by the same principles that must apply in the final stage of a European monetary order. This means that the monetary policy of the countries participating in this process must now concentrate on the task of maintaining monetary stability and of preventing inflationary pressures, a task which can be pursued with the greatest chance of success.

2.1 Lessons from the EMS

The EMS did not stabilize either until major member states accorded monetary stability the importance which was necessary for the satisfactory functioning of the system. There were no fewer than seven realignments by March 1983, which in itself is a sign of instability and divergence in terms of economic development. The decisive turnaround in the stabilization of the EMS occurred in March 1983 when the French government radically changed its economic policy objectives. It is probably not an exaggeration to say that at that time the existence of the EMS was in the balance. Since then the EMS, or at least its "hard core", has come increasingly closer to the original objective, namely to create a zone of internal and external monetary stability, which is all the more remarkable as the dollar rate was subject to extreme fluctuations in that period. The D-Mark no doubt played an important part in this. It provided the stability standard which every fixed exchange rate system needs. This is a widely held belief today. The Delors Report states, for example: "Moreover, the system has benefitted from the role played by the D-Mark as an 'anchor' for participants' monetary and intervention policies."[2]

The D-Mark has increasingly become the most important intervention and reserve currency in the EMS, not because the Bundesbank sought this role but because the D-Mark is regarded by the markets and the central banks as a stable currency which can be used internationally without restriction. Outside the EMS, too, the D- Mark is today the second most important currency after the dollar. About one-fifth of all foreign exchange reserves world-wide are held in D-Mark.

The D-Mark is becoming more important in several eastern European countries as well, and this importance is likely to increase even more, if anything. In their efforts to make their currencies convertible and to stabilize them, the central and eastern European countries will probably increasingly orientate themselves towards the D-Mark. This applies particularly to the GDR. If, after May 6, a freely elected government decides in favor of the free market economy and creates the necessary preconditions for investment capital from the Federal Republic of Germany and other countries, it could become the target of an enormous inflow of funds. This, together with an appropriate monetary and exchange rate policy, would provide the opportunity to introduce convertibility step by step. It is clear that the D-Mark must be seen as the "anchor" in such a development. In fact, the D-Mark is already a kind of parallel currency in the GDR and other central and eastern European countries.

Particularly during the seventies the Bundesbank actually resisted seeing the D-Mark forced into the function of a reserve currency as the monetary policy implications are not always very convenient. We would therefore welcome it if other currencies were to share this burden with the D-Mark as a result of the "competition of currencies" recommended by our British friends or perhaps it would be better to say: "competition of policies". The pound sterling, which has a long tradition as a reserve currency, could perhaps win back something of its old glory if the United Kingdom succeeded in solving its inflation and balance of payments problems. But particularly the French franc has in my opinion the potential of playing a far greater role in Europe and world-wide. The determined policy of the French government and the Banque de France to contain inflation could contribute to this just as much as the elimination of the last controls on capital movements and the development of Paris into one of the most important European financial centers.

On the other hand, I believe that the potential of the ECU in its present form as a basket currency is fairly limited. The private ECU has had a successful career on the financial markets, but basically it has only played a minor role in monetary integration in Europe, and as a numeraire for exchange rates its significance has at best been symbolic. During realignments it is the changes in bilateral central rates which matter, and new ECU central rates are merely derived as a second step from the changes in bilateral exchange rates. Viewed as a whole, the experience of the past ten years confirms the fact that, while an exchange rate system such as the EMS requires an agreed set of rules, its functioning depends primarily on the willingness of the partner countries to satisfy the requirements underlying stable exchange rates. These include above all the safeguarding of domestic monetary stability in all participating countries.

2.2 The Significance of Central Bank Independence

How can this basic condition of monetary union be ensured if the responsibilities for monetary policy are transferred from national institutions to a Community body? Historical experience has shown that this can best be expected of a system which is independent of political interference. This applies to the EC to an even greater extent than to national states because in a confederation such as the EC there is always a tendency to orientate oneself towards averages and compromises, but that is the worst possible compass for monetary policy. Only an independent institution is in a position to resist the ever-recurring wishes of politicians to prescribe monetary policy targets which are often inconsistent with the objective of stability, such as the stabilization of exchange rates or the promotion of growth and employment or the balancing of regional disequilibria.

If only for practical reasons a modern, efficient central bank system must be independent of the instructions and pressures of national governments and European institutions. Protracted consultation and concertation processes are not consistent with the requirements of the financial markets which need fast and flexible reactions by the central bank, as was the case, for instance, on the outbreak of the debt crisis in 1982 or after the crash in October 1987.

What is more important, however, is that only an independent central bank is in a position to pursue a monetary policy geared to longer-term requirements.[3] We know that an increase or decrease in the money stock works through to the economy only with a substantial time-lag. Interest rate measures do not affect the money stock for several months, and price movements take even longer to react to the money stock. These delays must be taken into account when monetary policy measures are being drawn up. An independent central bank is in a better position to do so than any government as it is not so much subject to the temptation to neglect the basic requirements of anti-inflationary monetary policy for the sake of short-term effects or election tactics. William McChesney Martin (Fed Chairman 1951-70) expressed this rather vividly when he said: "The Fed's job is to take away the punch-bowl just when the party gets going."

Of course, even an independent central bank cannot alone guarantee monetary stability. The financial behavior of the public authorities and the behavior of management and labor must make their contribution. But the decisions of an independent central bank about the width of the "monetary cloak" which it is prepared to provide gives an important signal for a realistic assessment of the available opportunities by all economic agents.

2.2.1 How to Achieve Independence

If it is agreed that a future European central bank system (ECBS) must be independent of governments, the Council and the Commission, the question arises of how this independence can be ensured. A corresponding legal regulation which guarantees the ECBS's independence of instructions is only one element of its independence. In addition, it requires the personal and professional independence of the members of the governing bodies of this system, that is, of both the governors of the national central banks and the members of the supreme governing body, that is to say, of the European "central bank council."

The personal independence of the members of the governing bodies can be ensured if the officials nominated by the governments (central bank governors) and the Council (members of the Board) are appointed for a sufficiently long period (14 years in the United States, eight years in the Federal Republic of Germany) and if their appointment cannot be terminated during that period. Moreover, and this goes without saying, they must have excellent expert knowledge to enable them to make independent judgments. The qualities of personal independence naturally include adequate financial arrangements during and after their term of office. This is, after all, what Professor Adolf Weber called "the continuity of responsibility and the continuity of expertise" in the discussion about the new Bundesbank Act at the beginning of the fifties.[4]

It is important that nationality takes second place to the task with which these officials are entrusted. As there can be only one self-contained monetary policy for the Community as a whole, and not a monetary policy which takes account of the special requests of individual states and regions, the central bank governors and the members of the Board must be committed to the common task and not to the interests of individual countries or regions, and this must be clear when they cast their votes.

2.2.2 Instrumental Autonomy

Above all the instrumental independence of the system must be guaranteed, i.e. its ability to fulfil its function of safeguarding monetary stability without restriction by using the necessary instruments. The instrumental independence of the ECBS must be ensured by providing it with a sufficient array of market instruments whose application is not hampered by administrative regulations and measures. These should be instruments which are linked to the markets and which use market processes to achieve their ends instead of eliminating them or falsifying them in an undesired way. It is obvious that interest rates as the price of money and credit must be of central importance. But this set of instruments should also include all the other tools of modern central bank policy, irrespective of whether they are being applied in the individual countries at present or not.

I cannot deal in greater detail with these rather technical questions in this lecture (some proposals are contained in the collection of papers submitted together with the Delors Report) but one thing should be clear: a future ECBS which is to satisfy high expectations must have the weapon which every efficient central bank must have: *the monopoly of money creation*. Monetary policy is not divisible, not even in a basically federalistic system such as the Fed or the Bundesbank. Without the monopoly of money creation, the ECBS would be a "tiger without teeth."

A system which is used only to "coordinate" monetary policy but leaves the right to decide on the price and quantity of money in circulation to the national governments and/or central banks would be "half-baked", as Alan Walters called the EMS. "Coordination" must not be orientated towards a European inflation average or any exchange rate targets, which would amount to restricting the Bundesbank's room for manoeuvre without providing a convincing alternative. Attempts of this nature have often been made in the last few years, as all those involved know. Such a system would be less efficient for achieving stability than the present regulatory framework of thc EMS. It would therefore be unacceptable to us and no doubt to other EC countries as well. This has always been the German position, and a German government which gave it up could not count on the support of the German general public which reacts very sensitively to matters of price stability. This has become very clear in the sometimes most critical reactions to the Delors Report, particularly to the proposals on "stage two" (and I quote): "At this juncture, the Committee does not consider it possible to propose a detailed blueprint for accomplishing this transition",[5] that is, for the transition from stage one to stage two in the monetary sphere. I will revert to this problem later when I describe the work programme of the Committee of EC Central Bank Governors.

With their decision to start negotiating an agreement on a European central bank system as early as the end of this year, the governments undertook to put their cards on the table and to say whether they were in fact prepared to transfer the decision on future monetary policy to an independent Community institution. In my opinion, it would have been better to gain a few years' experience with "stage one" of economic and monetary union and to implement first what has already been decided on, particularly the single market, the liberalization of capital movements, the harmonization of taxes, etc., before envisaging further-reaching institutional steps. But naturally I accept the decision of the Heads of State and Government and I understand the political motivation behind it.

2.3 Strategic Options and Organizational Aspects

If a basic consensus on the structures of a European central bank system can be achieved in the way just outlined, a number of other important questions remain to be decided on, and I would like to mention just a few of these.

First of all, what is to happen if not all governments and parliaments agree to an amendment to the treaty because of economic and monetary union as is required under EC legislation? In this case, which cannot be ruled out from the outset, there are two possibilities. One could proceed in the same way as with the EMS, which legally is an agreement between the central banks of the Community. This would give rise to a second treaty, in addition to the EC treaty. I would think this highly questionable for the cohesion of the EC and would prefer an arrangement based on the EC treaty even if it cannot be implemented by all contracting parties at the same time, as was the case with several regulations of the EC treaty some of which have still not been implemented.

Another question which is frequently raised, particularly by the French and the British, seems to me to be easier to solve: the "democratic control" of an ECBS. There is no need to wait for complete political union, a European government and a parliament with real responsibilities before an ECBS is set up even though historical experience would suggest this. Historically, central banks have always been established after the formation of states. Naturally the integration of Europe cannot be confined to monetary policy. Progress in other fields, such as the German Federal Chancellor demanded for the European Parliament, is necessary. But an independent ECBS would, in my opinion, be conceivable before the completion of political union if the governments want this and if they are prepared to surrender the corresponding sovereignty as they have done in other, albeit less important, fields. The system would have an adequately democratic legal base if it came about by an agreement between democratic governments, if the agreement were ratified by democratically elected parliaments and if the system were provided with a clearly defined mandate. In addition, the members of the Board could be appointed by the ECOFIN Council and the members of the Council by the national governments. The accounting (not the monetary policy!) could be audited by an impartial court of auditors. In my opinion it would be quite consistent with the independence of the system if the president regularly reported to the European Parliament, albeit not as frequently as is the case in the United States, and if the Chairman of the ECOFIN Council and the President of the EC Commission could attend the meetings of the European central bank council (without voting rights) just as, conversely, the chairman of the ECBS would be invited to the relevant ECOFIN meetings. In addition, the general public should be comprehensively informed, as is customary in the United States and the Federal Republic of Germany, for instance. As for the rest, the system would be measured by its success.

It is much more difficult to answer the question of which functions national central banks should retain than to answer the question of "democratic control."[6] Here, too, the subsidiarity principle should apply, that is, only those functions should be transferred to the Community body which cannot be satisfactorily fulfilled at the national level unless this affects the requirements of a consistent, self-contained monetary policy. In the first place, these are all decisions on interest rates, liquidity and the money stock, that is, monetary policy in the proper sense. This must necessarily include decisions on purchases and sales of third currencies (mainly dollars) because these have direct effects on liquidity and the money stock. It also involves the difficult problem of a transfer of foreign exchange reserves to Community institutions and the decision on who is to receive the proceeds.

In spite of these far-reaching powers, the ECBS could function with a comparatively small staff, say, a number similar to that of the Board of Governors of the Federal Reserve System, as executive functions could largely be transferred to the well-established systems of the national central banks which would then act on behalf of the Community. The settlement of payments, open market operations with the banks, business on behalf of government institutions and the like could well be taken care of by the national central banks - according to the guidelines and instructions of the ECBS. In addition, the national central banks should, in my opinion, be responsible for bank and stock exchange supervision unless this is already the case as, for example, in the Federal Republic of Germany.

This means that the national central banks would play a role similar to that of the Federal Reserve Banks in the United States or the Land Central Banks in the Federal Republic of Germany. However, they (and/or the finance ministers!) would have to give up their right to formulate independent national monetary policies. Particularly for Germany this would have far-reaching implications. The Central Bank Council, which today is the supreme decision-making body in the monetary policy field, would lose its most important function, a consequence which may not have become quite clear to every advocate of an ECBS in the Federal Republic of Germany.

Numerous other questions have to be answered, such as: how the voting rights are to be determined in a European central bank council; where the ECBS is to have its domicile; and how the profits are to be distributed, and so on. In this lecture I cannot deal with these questions in detail. There is one aspect, however, which I would briefly like to highlight.

3. The Need for Coherence of Fiscal and Monetary Policy

Even a strong and independent central bank can only fulfil its functions if its policy is not counteracted by fiscal policy. The agreement must therefore stipulate that the effective use of central bank instruments is not hindered or influenced undesirably by the nature and scale of public borrowing. Recourse to central bank credit must be ruled out from the outset or reduced to a minimum; in view of modern and free financial markets it is basically no longer up-to-date. Even if government functions are financed through the market within the appropriate limits, both the effects on the use of monetary policy instruments and the overall economic implications must be taken into account. The greater interest rate resistance of the public authorities compared with that of private borrowers must be corrected by an adequate degree of self-discipline if a crowding-out of private financing is to be avoided. And monetary policy must not be condemned to facilitate or ensure the satisfaction of the "inevitable" public borrowing needs, possibly at the expense of its proper function, the safeguarding of monetary stability.

An adequate degree of self-discipline at all government levels could reduce the necessity of binding rules for fiscal policy to a minimum or even make it superfluous. As is well known, such binding rules, with limits for the budget deficits of individual member countries, were considered necessary in the Delors Report in order to guarantee "a coherent fiscal/monetary policy mix" in the Community. There are not yet very clear ideas as to where such binding rules should come into force, how they should be determined and how they could be implemented. And, as I said before, they should not lead to all powers and control authorities being concentrated in Brussels in the future. Judging by all experience, the idea that fiscal discipline will come about quasi automatically with the aid of market mechanisms appears not to bc very realistic, however.

4. Perspectives

Experience in Germany has shown for years how important it is that the government at all levels, as well as management and labor, are willing to act responsibly under realistically assessed conditions so that the central bank can fulfil its function without undue frictional loss and safeguard the value of money, both internally and externally. As early as in the first stage of economic and monetary union it will be found out whether this willingness exists in the larger European context. It will depend on this willingness whether and when further steps are possible, including the establishment of a European central bank system. Even without amending the treaty the European Community has already an adequate institutional framework for establishing a convincing common economic and monetary policy. We have among other things the Council of European Finance Ministers and the Council of European Central Bank Governors, as well as the Monetary Committee in which our alternates work. Within this framework progress towards coordinating economic, fiscal and monetary policies is already possible and necessary today, that is, without waiting for the result of the presumably protracted intergovernment conference.

As far as monetary policy is concerned, the Committee of Central Bank Governors agreed at its January meeting on a reorganization of its work, with respect to both staffing and scope of its deliberations. Its staffing was affected in that the Chairman was elected for three years, instead of one year, thus ensuring greater continuity. Furthermore, to support the Committee, a research team consisting of competent economists will be set up; this team is to prepare problem-related studies on questions which must be answered for a common assessment of monetary trends within the Community and in relation to third countries. It will also draw up well-researched comments on relevant questions which are to be addressed to the Council or to the governments.

Regarding the content of its work, the Committee will work towards a higher degree of convergence "with a view to achieving domestic price stability, which is at the same time a necessary condition for stable exchange rates."[7] That higher degree of convergence was the aim of the amendment to the Council decision of 1964 on the cooperation between the central banks of the Community. A starting point for this is the closer coordination and convergence of the annual monetary targets of the individual national central banks. So far the most varied aggregates have been used and differing assumptions have been taken as a basis. A common monetary target for the Community will not be the result of these discussions in the foreseeable future, but it should be possible to converge the concepts and to give the Committee of Central Bank Governors the opportunity to use consistent yardsticks when consulting about the basic stance of its monetary policy. This will be of great use even if individual member countries continue to gear their monetary policy, particularly their interest rate policy, essentially to the objective of defending the exchange rate relations agreed upon within the EMS. The significance of monetary targets is thus qualified in individual cases. As a control variable the money stock nevertheless retains its significance as a money stock getting out of hand would have to be interpreted as a sign of unwelcome developments even if the exchange rate of the currency concerned remains stable.

The cooperation among the EC central banks has contributed much to the progress towards convergence in the ten years or more which have passed since the EMS was established, and it is this progress which opens up the prospect of an implementation of economic and monetary union. Compared with this, there is a considerable need to catch up in other fields, not least in fiscal policy. The Committee of Central Bank Governors will therefore not hesitate to fulfil its mandate "to express opinions to individual governments and the Council of Ministers on policies which might affect the internal and external monetary situation in the Community and, in particular, the functioning of the European Monetary System." [8]

The Committee will also comment on questions concerning the further progress towards economic and monetary union. In their capacity as members of the Delors Committee the central bank governors have created an important basis for the debate. In the meantime further considerations and ideas have come to light. The final decision naturally rests with the governments and parliaments, but it must be as well-founded as possible. The Committee of Central Bank Governors will contribute its expertise, and I am convinced that we shall thus make an important contribution to achieving European economic and monetary union. There is no way back. The task before us is to set the points correctly so that the European train reaches the destination we all want to arrive at.

Endnotes

1. *Walter Hallstein* (1973) "Die Europäische Gemeinschaft" (The European Community), Düsseldorf, Vienna, p. 133.

2. *Report on economic and monetary union in the European Community (Delors Report)*.(1989). Section 5. See also the remark made by Governor of the Bank of England Leigh-Pemberton before the Treasury and Civil Committee on June 19, 1989: "One has to acknowledge that the Bundesbank does exercise a very strong influence over the ERM at the moment. Quite honestly, we must acknowledge, too, that the successes of the ERM are due to large measure to what one might call the anchoring role of the D-Mark." Again, Italy's former Central Bank Governor and present Minister of Finance Guido Carli said: "The European Monetary System in its present form centers on the D-Mark and thus on the most stable currency; if one tried to let it break away..., one would endanger the process of achieving monetary union." (La Repubblica, July 13, 1988).

3. Alan Greenspan in a speech before the Subcommittee on Domestic Monetary Policy on October 25, 1989: "... independence enables the central bank to resist short-term inflationary biases that might be inherent in some aspects of the political process. The Federal Reserve must take actions that, while sometimes unpopular in the short run, are in the long run in the best interests of the country."

4. *Erich Achterberg, Volkmar Muthesius* (1950) "Die Bundesbank - Aufbau und Aufgaben" (The Bundesbank - structure and functions) in Schriftenreihe der Zeitschrift fuer das gesamte Kreditwesen, Frankfurt am Main, p. 14.

5. Delors Report, section 57.

6. *Milton Friedman* (1989). "The case for floating rates" in Financial Times, December 18. "A truly unified European currency would make a great deal of sense. But to achieve it requires eliminating all central banks in Europe ... except one ...".

7. See Council Decision, Doc. 10128/89, of December 4, 1989, p. 1.

8. See Council Decision, Doc. 10128/89, of December 4, 1989, p. 4.

References

ACHTERBERG, ERICH and VOLKMAR MUTHESIUS (1950). Die Bundesbank - Aufbau und Aufgaben (The Bundesbank - Structure and Functions) in Schriftenreihe der Zeitschrift für das gesamte Kreditwesen, Frankfurt am Main.

COMMISSION OF THE EUROPEAN COMMUNITIES (1989). Committee for the Study of Economic and Monetary Union. Report on Economic and Monetary Union in the European Community.(Delors Report). Luxembourg: Office for Official Publications of the European Communities.

COUNCIL DECISION (1989). Doc. 10128/89. December 4.

FRIEDMAN, MILTON (1989). The Case for Floating Rates. In: Financial Times. December 18.

HALLSTEIN, WALTER (1973). Die Europäische Gemeinschaft (The European Community) Düsseldorf, Vienna.

Daniel Gros and Niels Thygesen

TOWARDS MONETARY UNION IN THE EUROPEAN COMMUNITY: WHY AND HOW

1. Introduction

European Monetary Integration is, again, high on the political agenda. At the European Council in Dublin in April 1990, there was even an agreement that monetary union should be reached by January 1993, the date at which the internal market measures are scheduled to be completed. While it is natural for heads of government and state to push for monetary integration mainly for political reasons economists look at the economic costs and benefits. This paper therefore tries to answer the two fundamental questions an economist would like to ask about European monetary integration:

1. *Why*? That is, what are the economic reasons for advancing on the road of monetary integration?

2. *How*? That is, what "concrete steps" should be taken to take us where we want to go?

Before going into the discussion of these two fundamental questions it is necessary to sort out first one issue that in some sense determines the answer to these two questions, namely the question where the precess of monetary integration should lead.

The following section 2 therefore discusses the meaning of monetary union. It argues that "irrevocably fixed" exchange rates are not equivalent to a common currency, this implies that it is important to always clarify what one means with the term "monetary union". This section also argues that the quality of the overall monetary policy for the union is as important as fixing relativities, i.e. exchange rates. Section 3 then argues that a monetary union, with a consistent anti-inflationary overall monetary policy, should bring substantial economic benefits, even if they are difficult to measure in practice. Most of the benefits, however, would arise only through a common currency, whereas the costs arise already in an earlier stage, that is when exchange rates are fixed. Section 4 then discusses "concrete steps" towards monetary union along the lines of the Delors Report that would lead from the present EMS to a European Central Bank. Section 5 finishes with some concluding remarks.

2. Where: The Meaning of Monetary Union

It is generally agreed that the endpoint of monetary integration should be a monetary union. But the meaning of this notion is not always clear. For the Delors Report a monetary union is characterized by the combination of two elements:

i) the complete liberalization of capital transactions and full integration of banking and other financial markets; and

ii) the elimination of margins of currency fluctuation and the irrevocable locking of exchange rate parities.

The 1970 Werner plan stated explicitly that this would make national monies perfect substitutes and therefore be equivalent to the creation of a common currency. A similar view seems to underlie the Delors Report, but is not made explicit.

The purpose of this section is to argue that a system of irrevocably-fixed exchange rates would not be equivalent to a full monetary union with a common currency because as long as national currencies continue to exist there are different units of account and there are transactions costs in going from one currency to another.

These transactions costs are the most important barrier to making national currencies perfect substitutes, even with irrevocably-fixed exchange rates. For a person doing his shopping in Germany the Italian lira will not be a perfect substitute for marks if he has to exchange them for marks prior to every transaction. Exchanging currency involves a cost in the form of the bid-ask spread, which would continue to exist since financial institutions would still have to use them (or foreign exchange commissions) to cover the costs they incur by holding bank notes in different currencies and having to set up several accounting systems. This cost is not negligible; it varies with the size of the transaction. For cash it might be as high as 2-3 %.[1] This is true even for very stable exchange rates, such as the mark - guilder rate. Market size seems to be a more important determinant of the spread, since in most European countries the spread on the US dollar is lower than on other European currencies. This implies that fixing exchange rates is unlikely to reduce these costs from their present high level.

For these reasons it is unlikely that the fixing (even if it is supposed to be irrevocable) of exchange rates in Europe will make national monies perfect substitutes. Does this matter? Yes, because it has two consequences which are economically and politically important.

First, as long as national monies remain imperfect substitutes national money demands may remain stable. This implies that there is no economically compelling reason to create a common monetary institution. As long as there is agreement as to which national central bank is the leader, the system could work much like the present EMS: the leader, or anchor, national central bank would set its monetary stance (presumably geared to the objective of price stability, if it is the Bundesbank) and the other national central banks would just react. The stance of the leading national central bank would then be transmitted through the foreign exchange markets to the entire system.[2] The degree to which national currencies become substitutes has therefore important implications for the economic arguments for a European central bank.

Second, the benefits from a monetary union cannot be obtained, or at least only partially obtained in a system of irrevocably-fixed exchange rates. In contrast, the main cost associated with a monetary union, namely the loss of the exchange rate as a policy instrument, would arise even in a fixed exchange-rate system. This second point, the economic costs and benefits is discussed in more detail in the following section.

The fixing of exchange rates in a monetary union determines only relativities, i.e. the relationship between national monetary policies and price levels, per se, this has no implications for aggregate variables, i.e. the overall stance of monetary policy and the inflation rate for the entire area. There is wide agreement, however, that the European monetary union should be an area with stable prices.

Although most of the discussion of the following section is about the benefits of fixing or even eliminating the relativities (i.e. exchange rates) it is clear that these benefits could easily be swamped by the losses that arise if overall inflation is not under control. Although the costs of inflation are as difficult to measure as the benefits from monetary union it is apparent to us that even small deviations from the goal of price stability can lead to welfare losses that are of the same order of magnitude as the potential welfare gains from a common currency. We therefore take seriously the position that the goal of monetary union is worthwhile only if it leads to a zone of "monetary stability" in the sense of a stable purchasing power of money. It follows that the institutional steps discussed in section 5 below are not only designed to manage the fixing of exchange rates, but also lead to an institution that assures price stability.

3. Why: Costs and Benefits from Monetary Union

3.1 Irrevocably-fixed Exchange Rates: Costs and Benefits

Since in the present EMS, realignments of central rates are already infrequent what are the costs and benefits of formally renouncing future use of realignments between participating currencies?[3] In our view the answer comes from the general issues raised by the traditional literature of the optimum currency area and the credibility issue raised by the more recent literature on incentives for policy-makers to behave in a time-consistent manner.

Traditional macroeconomic theory suggests a general answer to the question of why realignments represent a useful policy option: governments may find realignment desirable, if the economies for which they are held to be responsible to their electorates experience differentiated shocks.[4] The shocks may be external or domestic in origin; a major energy price-hike or a domestic cost-explosion are examples that come readily to mind. Having experienced such a shock, a government would come to regret an earlier commitment to a fixed exchange rate, since accommodation of the shock through realignment may entail lower costs of adjustment than the alternative of much more gradual adjustment of relative national price-levels.

If European governments anticipated that important differentiated shocks were likely to occur in the future, *regardless of the exchange-rate regime* (and of the gradual progress of integration), they would be taking a serious risk by committing themselves to maintaining irrevocably-fixed exchange rates. The emerging acceptance of EMU as an objective is, above all, an implicit recognition by most EC governments that the likelihood of large and nationally-differentiated shocks is fading and that realignments are less useful as an adjustment instrument.

Both of these elements are important:

i) Nationally differentiated shocks constitute the only economic justification for a realignment. However, there is some recent research that indicates that for most member states of the European Community (*Stockman 1988*) the most important shocks are industry specific. Although there are large differences in the industrial structure across member states these shocks tend to cancel out in the aggregate, since most economies are based on a number of different sectors. Nationally differentiated shocks, that are not induced by (national) economic policy measures are therefore less important than is generally thought.

ii) Realignments, that is changes in the *nominal* exchange rate constitute the appropriate reaction to a shock only if there is some rigidity in nominal variables, such as prices and wages. Otherwise agents adjust prices and wages proportionally so that all relative prices and real variables are not affected by the realignment. The experience in the EMS suggests that this is indeed what happens. No country has been able to obtain a competitive advantage by relying exclusively on realignments. In the absence of accompanying measures devaluations have tended to cause mainly inflation.

Even if this recognition is widely shared, governments are correct in perceiving that their ability to conduct active stabilization policies is constrained by irrevocably fixing of exchange rates. Moreover, modern macroeconomic theory points out that since monetary expansion and devaluation are at their most effective when least expected, the short-term rewards of breaking the fixed exchange-rate commitment could well be seen as rising for a time after the declaration of an intention to keep the rate irrevocably fixed.

This suggests that governments may have incentives to opt out, if they can, in order to pursue macroeconomic objectives. For one major category of shocks to a participating economy - changes in domestic economic policy that make the fixed exchange rate unsustainable - there is clearly no independence of the exchange-rate regime. In EMU policy shocks would be limited to those that do not threaten to upset fixity. Governments that see *a priori* the remaining scope of action as too narrow will perceive a likely cost in joining EMU. Could that cost be offset by benefits?

A government which explicitly wants to retain freedom to realign its exchange rate - or a government whose commitment to fix the rate remains subject to some doubt - pays a price. Agents in the national markets for goods, labour and financial assets will assume that freedom of manoeuvre will occasionally be used. They will tend, in an economy whose currency could become subject to devaluation, to set a more rapid rate of increase of prices and costs and to add a risk premium to the required yield on assets denominated in the national currency. Higher inflationary expectations would raise actual inflation and nominal interest rates. If the exchange rate in fact remains fixed, there will be temporarily higher inflation and lower output than in the situation where the commitment to fixity had been seen as truly irrevocable. If the currency is in fact devalued, the critical perceptions of private economic agents will have been borne out and a non-inflationary reputation will be that much harder to build up in the future.

In general macroeconomic terms the basic cost-benefit assessment of irrevocably fixing exchange rates has therefore to include (1) the cost of giving up the possibility of accommodating differentiated, major and non-transitory national shocks, against (2) the benefit of more definitively strengthening confidence in the long-run predictability and stability of the price level. The verdict on how the balance between (1) and (2) comes out for any particular participant must necessarily be subjective, since its depends on the likelihood of future shocks and the degree of credibility of political agreements. All that can be said in confidence is that the balance between costs and benefits must have shifted significantly in favor of the latter as the likelihood of differentiated shocks within the EC is reduced while benefits of full convergence of interest rates and of inflationary expectations at a low level have become more clearly perceived.

Moreover, the potential costs of irrevocably locking exchange rates have already to some extent been incurred by participants in the present EMS since countries like France and the Benelux have already declared their intentions not to use realignments anymore and movements of exchange rates inside the band are too limited to have any significant real impact. The macroeconomic benefits, in the form of greater predictability and stability of the future price level and firmer protection against nationally-engineered policy shocks are still - despite the sparing use of realignments in the EMS since 1983 - some way from being realized. Nor is it obvious that they could be realized fully without the additional step of introducing a common currency to underline the definitive nature of EMU. To us the benefits of irrevocably fixing exchange rates are in themselves already sufficiently substantial to offset the costs outlined above. But the move to a common currency would in our view more decisively shift the balance of costs and benefits in favor of the latter. Hence we deal with these benefits in the following section.

Fixing exchange rates also yields the microeconomic benefit of eliminating the uncertainty introduced into international trade by exchange-rate variability. Exporters and importers can, however, hedge against this source of uncertainty at a low cost if they have access to a sophisticated financial market. With the increasing opening and sophistication of financial markets in the Community, exchange-rate variability should therefore be less of an obstacle to international trade. This is borne out in the empirical literature on the effect of exchange-rate variability on trade which has not been able to find a strong negative relationship. Moreover, the present EMS has already reduced exchange-rate variability inside the ERM to about one fourth of the level experienced in the 1970s, the elimination of this residual degree of exchange rate variability can therefore not be expected to yield substantial benefits in terms of increased intra-European trade.

3.2 Additional Benefits from a Common Currency

We see at least five sources of additional benefits from a common currency:

Elimination of transaction costs

1) The most obvious reason for expecting significant economic gains from the introduction of a common currency is that this is the only way to totally eliminate all exchange-rate-related transaction costs. The direct savings of these transaction costs arise from the bid-ask spreads and other commissions on foreign exchange-rate transactions. They are large - 2 to 5% and more for cash - but since (intra-EC) tourism does not account for a large share of the GDP of the Community their total should be small. For intra-EC trade, which accounts for about 20% of the GDP of the Community and which is handled mostly by the corporate sector the bid-ask spreads and other commissions are much smaller, depending on the currency, but generally below 0.5%.

The direct savings in transactions costs should therefore be small but not insignificant, perhaps around one-fourth to one-half of 1% of the GDP of the Community (still about 10 to 20 billion Ecu per annum in absolute terms).[5]

Elimination of information costs and of incentives for price discrimination

2) While the direct savings in transaction costs might be small, the subsistence of national currencies can still imply large indirect costs because it allows firms to engage in price discrimination between national markets. For consumers, used to evaluating prices in their own national currency, it is inconvenient and difficult to compare prices in different currencies, even if the exchange rate is fixed. The practice of retailers in border areas, using approximate "round" exchange rates several percent away from the true rates, indicates that this implicit information cost can be quite high.

An order of magnitude for the welfare gains from the suppression of exchange rates can be estimated using the range of estimates from the *Cost of Non-Europe* study which found that the suppression of all residual barriers to intra-EC trade should raise the GDP of the Community by 2.5 to 6.5 %.[6] The higher value would result from a complete elimination of price discrimination and might therefore be attainable only with a common currency. This would imply that the benefit from the introduction of a common currency could be as large as 2 % of Community GDP (about 80 bill. Ecu in absolute terms).

Dynamic efficiency gains

3) An even more speculative reason to expect large economic gains from a common currency derives from the its dynamic effects. Economists have long recognized that the most valuable benefits from integrating markets are of a dynamic nature. However, until recently these dynamic effects were difficult to measure since there did not exist an adequate theoretical framework to explain continuing growth that was not simply the result of exogenous technological progress. The models that have been developed recently to explain what factors aside from exogenous technological progress could lead to growth are still in an early stage but they can, in principle, be used to assess the dynamic impact of the introduction of a common currency.[7] While it seems very difficult to assess the exact magnitude of the increase in the growth potential of the Community through monetary union, it is clear that these dynamic effects could easily dwarf the once-and-for-all efficiency gains whose magnitude can be more easily assessed because even a small increase in the growth potential has an exponentially-increasing effect on the level of income over time.

Need for less official international reserves

4) A more macroeconomic source of benefits is the savings in terms of international reserves. As long as national currencies subsist national monetary authorities have to keep large foreign exchange reserves to be seen to be able to defend exchange rates. The direct cost of holding reserves should be small, since they can be invested in interest-bearing assets, but the cost of acquiring and maintaining confidence in the exchange-rate commitment might be large, especially for countries without a history of stable exchange rates.

Stronger European presence in the international monetary system and in global financial markets

5) Another potentially-important source of benefits from a common currency is external. A single European currency would at least partially replace the US dollar in some retail transactions around the world. The direct seigniorage gain for the European central bank that would result from this would be small, perhaps at most a once-and-for-all (as opposed to the efficiency gains which would be available year after year) gain of 30 billion Ecu (equivalent to an efficiency gain of 2.4 billion at an interest rate of 8%[8]). Much larger indirect effects could, however, result from large-scale international portfolio substitution away from the US dollar into the European currency. This might be a mixed blessing, however, since it could have an undesirable effect on the exchange rates of the European currency against the dollar, causing the latter to move temporarily below a longer-run sustainable level.

4. How: Concrete Steps

What needs to be done to achieve the goal of monetary union? In this section we discuss what concrete steps need to be taken. We start with a brief discussion of the type of measures that need to be taken in those countries that still experience large imbalances to enable them to participate in a monetary union that aims at price stability. This is followed by a discussion of the merits the institutional versus the market-led approach and finally by the steps that may be taken within the approach of the Delors plan.

4.1 Concrete Steps at the National Level: Disinflation and Convergence

A number of member countries are not even able to participate in the ERM, among those that do there are some that would have considerable difficulties in participating in a monetary union that pursues price stability. The main reason for this is inflation and inflationary expectations are still high in those countries. Both cannot be expected to be immediately brought down to zero or even close to zero since it takes some time for agents to adjust to a new environment with stable prices. Moreover, agents would be justified in adjusting their expectations and behavior slowly as long as the underlying imbalances that cause inflation have not changed. Since large public deficits and debts constitute to the main reason for governments to pursue inflationary monetary policies the disinflation effort would benefit from convergence in fiscal policy. The precise need for disinflation and convergence varies, of course, from country to country. We have therefore indicated in *Gros and Thygesen (1990)* what would need to be done in each country. We consider these measures "concrete steps" that are as important as the institutional steps along the lines of the Delors Report that are discussed below.

4.2 Institutional versus Market-led Approaches to Monetary Union

This paper has argued so far that a monetary union with a common currency would bring sizeable net economic benefits. For some observers a natural corollary has been that no further official action to create new institutions is needed because if the gains from currency unification are real they will lead markets to move spontaneously towards the adoption of a single currency. The only official action required would be to eliminate all legal restrictions that impose the use of national currency. It would not be necessary to fix exchange rates and coordinate national policies.

The economic logic behind the general idea is quite straightforward: in general competition is the best market structure; it should therefore also be applied to the choice of money. The public would then choose the best one, presumably the one that is the most convenient because it offers the most stable purchasing power. This might be called the *competing currencies approach.*

The logic of this approach is undeniable, but it implies that the monetary constitutions of almost all countries of this era are fundamentally flawed because they give the government a monopoly on the issuance of money. The proponents of this approach might argue that the reason for this discrepancy between theoretical optimum and reality is political in the sense that governments want to keep a source of potentially large seigniorage gains under their control. However, even from a purely economic point of view one could argue that there are important economies of scale in the choice of money. The benefits from a common currency discussed above are indirect expression of these economies of scale and the estimates of the order of magnitude of the potential benefits imply that they can be quite important. Free competition is in general not the optimal market structure if there are external[9] economies of scale. It is therefore possible to make a strictly economic case for a government monopoly of money and institutional steps towards monetary union.

A more popular alternative to institutional steps has focused on the private Ecu. According to this so-called *parallel currency approach* the goal of monetary union might be reached with little official action if the markets were increasingly to adopt a parallel currency, the Ecu, that gradually crowds out national currencies until it becomes *de facto* the common currency. This approach would also not rely on exchange rates being fixed. Instead, through the increasing use of the parallel currency, a common currency could be created without any need for the difficult process of convergence in national policies. The parallel currency approach was not retained in the Delors Report and we also do not believe that it represents a viable alternative, mainly because we see little prospect that markets would indeed use a parallel currency which would involve considerable transactions costs. See *Gros and Thygesen (1990)* for more details.

This market-led approach might best be thought of as substituting only for stage II of the Delors Report since if it were successful in establishing a common currency through the market there would still be a need for a common monetary institution to formulate and execute the monetary policy for this common currency.

Competing currencies

A variant of the approach to promote competition between national currencies is the essence of the UK proposal published in 1989.[10] According to this document only stage I of the Delors plan should be implemented. After stage I competition among currencies would become operational and increasingly effective because capital market liberalization and the single market for financial services would increase the available financial instruments and services.[11]

However, it is not clear from the UK document whether and how the competition between currencies or monetary policies would lead to a monetary union, in the conventional definition of a single currency. As argued in the preceding section it is unlikely that in the environment of low inflation and low exchange-rate variability which would be created by stage I, existing national currencies would be replaced either by a parallel currency or by the strongest Community currency. It is therefore highly unlikely that any further progress towards monetary union could be achieved by relying exclusively on currency competition through market forces.

Moreover, the argument that only competition between national monetary policies ensures price stability exaggerates the influence of currency competition and overlooks the difficulties in determining a stable anchor for prices and expectations that would arise in a stage I environment. Private markets do not always adopt the currency with the most stable purchasing power. The US dollar, for example, has not lost its position as the dominant international currency although it has on average over the last twenty years lost more of its purchasing power than the DM (and more recently the yen). The reason for this is again that there are economies of scale in the use of money. Stability of purchasing power is only one of the determinants of the "success" of a currency.

The most fundamental conceptual problem inherent in the UK approach is that it aims at making Community currencies increasingly substitutable. Progress towards monetary union would come through currency substitution, but widespread currency substitution would make national monetary policies less reliable and threaten the anchor role of the DM in the EMS. If there is really widespread currency substitution a common monetary institution would definitely be needed. In this sense significant progress under the market-led approaches, whether the parallel currency approach focusing on the Ecu or the UK proposal, would create a need for institutional steps.

4.3 The Institutional Approach: The Stages of the Delors Report

The Delors Committee was asked by the European Council to "Study and propose concrete stages leading towards this union" (i.e. EMU).[12] We assume the reader is familiar with the three stages of the Delors Report.

i) Stage I: tighter voluntary coordination

Stage I caused few objections when the Delors Report was on the agendas of the European Council in Madrid in June 1989. Stage I will start on July 1, 1990 - the latest date set for it in the Delors Report - while no date has yet been agreed for its completion, except that the Intergovernmental Conference to design subsequent stage(s) should permit implementation of the latter by 1993. What are the main new features of this stage and are they likely to be adequate to the tasks?

There appear to be three new features, all surrounded by some uncertainty as to the significance of their impact on policy coordination as it exists in today's EMS:

(1) New procedures for coordination in the Committee of Central Bank Governors and the ECOFIN Council;

(2) Participation of all currencies in the EMS in the course of stage I; and

(3) Experimentation with some of the procedures under negotiation for subsequent stages towards EMU.

(1) has in principle been clarified by the Decision of the ECOFIN Council to replace the 1964 Council Decision defining the mandate of the Committee of Central Bank Governors and the 1974 Council Decision on economic convergence by new Decisions guiding the form and substance of the efforts at policy coordination by central banks and in the ECOFIN Council.

The new Decisions which follow closely the proposals in the Delors Report (paras. 51-52) are difficult to evaluate, because everything depends on how the two EC bodies will make use of their mandate; those of 1964 and 1974 were never used fully. Taken literally, the Governors' Committee would develop both a more visible public profile and strengthen its analytical capacity and sub-committee structure with a view to developing an *ex ante* approach to, rather than an *ex post* analysis of monetary coordination. This would be a significant change, but it remains to be seen to what extent the Governors would actually wish to speak up in their new reports to the European Council and the European Parliament, or in collective opinions on policies in individual countries or by the EMS participants as a whole. Discussions in the Delors Committee in fact suggested that the scope for moving voluntarily, i.e. without institutional change, towards genuine *ex ante* coordination is likely to be severely circumscribed.

The Delors Committee conducted a small questionnaire study among EC central banks to clarify the scope for moving ahead without Treaty changes. Crudely summarized, the smaller participants did not see major problems in going further in the direction of submitting the policy formulations and decisions to *ex ante* coordination within the Committee of Governors; the smaller countries have few illusions of monetary autonomy left. But several of the larger countries did not see any possibility of moving significantly further without important changes in national monetary legislation and in the Treaty. The reason is either that national monetary authority is today divided between the central bank and the political authorities, with the latter unwilling to delegate to an unspecified process of central bank coordination, or that the central bank itself has an elaborate decision-making structure which makes it very difficult to conceive that it could delegate, through its President or other participants in the coordination procedures, even non-binding competence to a European body. The former of these two situations corresponds roughly to the set-up in France, and - presumably *a fortiori* - in the United Kingdom now that sterling has joined the exchange rate mechanism and the latter of that in the Federal Republic of Germany. From the perspective to either of these situations there is a need for something more well-defined than voluntary cooperation to put at the center before genuine change can be expected.

Once the Intergovernmental Conference is convened, and detailed proposals are made on further stages towards EMU, to be embodied in a revised Treaty, there may, however, be a feedback upon the first stage. Those countries least ready to envisage early Treaty revision may become the most anxious to demonstrate that voluntary coordination replicating the mandatory procedures proposed for subsequent stages can do as well as a reformed system.[13] A constructive feedback process may start which has been absent in the present EMS as long as there was no prospect (or threat) of institutional change. Such a projection into the practices of stage I of ideas for later full and mandatory coordination would obviously be unobjectionable. If successful, the process would contradict the prediction made above that the first two features of stage I - growing *de facto* symmetry and a risk of increasing instability upon enlargement - make it unlikely that the system could qualitatively improve or even retain its stability without institutional change.

Our basic assumption is therefore that preparations should be made for the eventuality that stage I might not be stable. Stage I should accordingly be as short as possible, i.e. as long as it takes to negotiate and ratify a revised Treaty. But whether there will actually be a move beyond stage I depends on the specific proposals for the next stage. Prior to moving to irrevocably-fixed rates the Delors Report proposed an intermediate stage II.

ii) Stage II: "soft" union and an emerging central bank

Why is an intermediate stage between the tighter, still voluntary, cooperation of stage I and the irrevocable locking of exchange rates, followed by the introduction of a common currency, desirable or even necessary? Would it not be possible simply to extend stage I until this final step were seen by all participants as feasible?

It seems to us unlikely that three elements necessary for the transition to irrevocably-fixed exchange rates and a collectively-managed monetary policy through a European System of Central Banks, could emerge without such an intermediate stage. They are (i) a consensus on the specific formulation of the ultimate objective(s), (ii) a common analytical framework for intermediate objectives and for the design of monetary policy; and (iii) a sufficient degree of experience with common operations. These three elements are part of a learning process in the absence of which we would doubt whether the final step could be taken. We accordingly subscribe to the view of the Delors Report that an intermediate, but not necessarily long, stage is required. In particular, experience in genuine joint decision-making is desirable, before monetary authority is fully centralized in the final stage.

It would be easier in some respects, if such an intermediate stage could be skipped, because the division of responsibility between the national central banks and an emerging ESCB is complex. A clear attribution of responsibilities assuring the cohesiveness of the system is therefore essential.

The Delors Report refrained from presenting a detailed blueprint of the intermediate stage, "as this (transition) would depend on the effectiveness of the policy coordination achieved during the first stage, on the provisions of the Treaty, and on the decisions to be taken by the new institutions." (para. 57). With preparations for the Intergovernmental Conference accelerating, there is an urgent need to examine how the intermediate stage can provide a framework for the learning process.[14]

To the extent that exchange rates become *de facto* stabilized, and recognized to be unlikely to change, national monetary policies will, de facto, become ever more severely constrained. Increasing exchange-rate stability therefore requires a framework for cooperation and coordination of national monetary policies. The more explicit the degree of exchange-rate fixity, and the higher the degree of capital mobility, the closer must be the coordination and the extent to which the overall policy stance of the participants has to be decided in common.

To implement a common policy, however, requires some consensus about the objectives - ultimate and intermediate, the design of monetary policy and the use of instruments which cannot be said to exist today, at least in any explicit form. The following pages address only the last of these three issues in a highly preliminary way, mindful that all three require very substantial efforts of macroeconomic analysis, study of empirical regularities and assessment of practical feasibility in order to be meaningfully discussed.

For the individual central bank the main operational objective in stage II would be to maintain in a credible way stable exchange rates vis-à-vis other participating currencies. *Ex ante* coordination of domestic credit expansion (DCE) objectives should make that task easier on average; in practice, the DCE objective may, in particular situations, have to be overridden to maintain shorter-term exchange-rate stability.

Collective formulation of ultimate and intermediate monetary objectives would in itself constitute a major step towards *ex ante* coordination. The participating central banks would deepen their exchange of information on their respective formulations of monetary policy by giving the reports prepared for them a more explicitly common analytical framework and by formulating joint intervention strategies and guidelines for DCE rather than simply reviewing the past record. Closer coordination could begin even while the guidelines emerging from it are not mandatory, to replicate the effects of a more advanced stage; in principle, this process begins already during stage I.

Yet it is unlikely that anything resembling closely a common monetary policy could be conducted merely through discussions, but without vesting in the ESCB genuine decision-making powers with respect to at least some significant instruments of monetary policy. But there are difficulties in determining how monetary authority might be shared between a center - the ESCB Council and Board - and the participating national central banks. The efficiency of operations requires that there should never be any doubt in the financial markets, among national policy-makers or elsewhere as to which body has the responsibility for taking particular decisions.

Three types of policy decisions could be considered as being at the core of any design of a workable pooling of instruments or responsibilities within an ESCB in stage II:

(1) adjustment of short-term interest differentials;
(2) intervention policy vis-à-vis third currencies;
(3) changes in reserve requirements.

(1) Short-term interest differentials

Adjustments of relative short-term interest rates constitute the central instrument in managing the present EMS and the main candidate for gradual pooling of authority. A high degree of coordination and occasionally *de facto* joint, or at least bilateral, decisions has already been observed.

But the gradual and partial upgrading of decision-making on relative interest-rate adjustment from the purely national level to a Community body, in the first stage the Committee of Governors, from the second stage the ESCB Council, will not in itself assure that the average level of interest rates in the participating countries is appropriate, though it should tend to make such an outcome more likely than the present system with its occasional inefficiencies of interest-rate escalations and tensions. To get a firmer grip on the average level of rates, the attribution to the ESCB of an instrument which permits a collective influence on domestic sources of money creation would be necessary. Such an instrument is described briefly below in the form of the ability for the ESCB to impose compulsory reserve requirements on domestic money creation and to develop gradually a market for a European reserve base with its own lending rate.

(2) Intervention policy vis-a-vis third currencies

A second instrument for which some degree of joint management could be envisaged is *foreign exchange interventions in third currencies*.

While in principle a common intervention policy can be achieved through joint guidelines for essentially decentralized interventions by the participating national central banks, a visible capacity to intervene jointly in third currencies, and to do so in ways that further the cohesion of the EMS, is potentially important. Without a presence in the major exchange markets the ESCB would lack the capacity to check the impact of external financial disturbances on EMS stability at source. Hence "a certain amount of reserve pooling" (Report, para. 57) as well as ample working balances in EMS-currencies would be desirable in stage II.

In a previous publication (*Gros and Thygesen 1988*) we suggested how, in the absence of an adequate operational structure, a common intervention policy could be executed through one of the component national central banks. As long as there is some exchange-rate flexibility and the ESCB does not yet have an operative arm, one national central bank could become the executing agent of the ESCB. It would not be an executing agent in the strict sense of the word, as the New York Federal Reserve Bank, but would be given some discretion in interpreting the policy guidelines formulated by the board of the ESCB. The obvious candidate to fill this position would be the Bundesbank because it already now accounts for the bulk of interventions against third currencies among the ERM countries. The Bundesbank could also be relied upon to interpret the policy of the ESCB in a way that is consistent with price stability. This alone would contribute another guarantee that the ESCB will pursue a strict anti-inflationary policy. As exchange rates get closer to becoming irrevocably fixed and the residual national competence in monetary policy disappear this freedom of manoeuvre would diminish until either the ESCB acquires its own operational arms to deal in foreign exchange markets or the relevant department of the Bundesbank is incorporated into the ESCB.

(3) Reserve requirements

A third instrument, specifically assigned to the ESCB, would be the ability to impose *variable reserve requirements* on domestic money creation.

The improved substitutability between participating currencies coming from the integration of European financial markets inexorably pushes the thinking of all monetary authorities in the direction of aggregate money creation in the area and to the formulation of intermediate objectives for domestic money creation consistent with an aggregate target and to designing procedures whereby the latter can be kept roughly on their agreed course; *Ciampi (1989)* provides an analysis of the options available.[15]

The essential feature is that the ESCB should be empowered to impose uniform or differentiated reserve requirements on either the increase in the monetary liabilities of each national central bank or on the credit extended by the member banks to their respective domestic sectors. This requirement would be met only by holding reserves with the ESCB; and the supply of reserves would be entirely controlled by the latter through allocations of a reserve asset (official ECUs) to each central bank corresponding to the demand for reserves which would arise, if agreed targets for money creation or DCE were observed. Both cost and availability considerations would provide central banks with an incentive to stay close to declared objectives. The ESCB would have to be given some discretion in extending or withdrawing reserves to provide marginal accommodation. The new system could largely replace the present method of creating official ECUs through temporary swaps of one fifth of gold and dollar reserves as well as the credits extended through the Very Short-Term Facility of the European Fund for Monetary Cooperation.

The system would create a monetary control mechanism analogous to that through which national central banks, who use reserve requirements, influence money and credit creation through their banking systems. It would introduce a certain hierarchy into the relationship between the ESCB and its constituent national central banks, while leaving some freedom for each national central bank in designing its domestic instruments.

The reserve requirements might alternatively be applied directly to DCE in the total national banking system, i.e. on the domestic sources of broad money creation. The advantage of this method would be to assign the collective monetary instrument more directly to a natural intermediate objective - DCE - underpinning fixed exchange rates, but it might introduce more slack into the control mechanism, as it would no longer apply to items that appear on the balance sheet of the central banks for which the latter could be regarded as more directly responsible.

A different approach that would allow the ESCB to have some direct impact on conditions in the financial markets could be pursued by imposing a uniform European reserve requirement on *commercial bank deposits* or on increases thereof.[16] Under this variant all community commercial banks would have to hold a certain small fraction of their deposits as compulsory reserves with the central monetary institution. The only asset that could be used to satisfy this reserve requirement would be "federal funds" which could be denominated in ECU.

The aggregate supply of these federal funds would be strictly under the control of the ESCB, since that would be the only institution that could issue them. The distribution of the total across countries and banks would be left to a federal funds market where commercial banks could trade among themselves the deposits with the central monetary institution which they need to satisfy the European reserve requirement. This scheme would therefore work like national reserve requirements, but on a European scale. The European reserve requirement could therefore be in addition to and independent of national reserve requirements.

This approach would imply that the ESCB would intervene directly in a market that reflects system-wide liquidity conditions. This might be preferable if the task of the ESCB is to be concerned with overall conditions as opposed to the specific conditions in national markets. In order to ensure a gradual transfer of authority from the national to the Community level it might be useful to impose initial limits on the total amount of open market transactions the central monetary institution would be allowed to undertake within a given period. These limits could be gradually relaxed in the course of stage II.

This approach could be implemented by giving the ESCB the power to impose a compulsory reserve requirement on all deposits of Community residents with Community commercial banks. To give banks access to deposits with the ESCB the latter could initially buy the appropriate amount of securities in the market. These securities could be denominated either in Ecu, or in national currencies, provided the proportion of the different national currencies corresponds to the Ecu weights. Once the initial amount of federal funds has been created the ESCB could regulate the total amount of federal funds in the system simply by additional open market purchases or sales.

Through its open market conditions the ESCB would be able to directly influence overall liquidity conditions in the system. If it makes an open market sale, reducing the total amount available, commercial banks everywhere in the Community would tend to restrict their deposits because the interest rate on the federal funds market would rise. By limiting the total amount of federal funds that the ESCB makes available to the system it would always be in a position to limit total liquidity creation.

This approach would be compatible with different operating procedures for the ESCB. For example, it could choose an interest rate target and restrict the supply of federal funds whenever the actual Ecu or federal funds interest rate fell below the target and vice versa if interest rates go above the target. But it could also target the quantity of federal funds by not intervening in the federal funds market and letting the interest rate adjust to bring supply and demand into equilibrium.

Different operating procedures would presumably be appropriate for stages II and III, but the mechanism in itself would not have to be modified for the passage to stage III. The subsequent evolution of the system would then be gradual and could lead to a smooth passage to the final stage without additional substantial institutional changes.

It remains to consider how the one decision in the EMS which is today subject to *de facto* joint decision-making, viz. *realignments of central rates*, could be handled in stage II. Would there be a case for vesting authority over this instrument with the ESCB as part of monetary management rather than leaving it as in the present EMS with the ECOFIN Council?

There are arguments for and against such a transfer but they suggest to us, on balance that the decisive considerations in assigning the authority to undertake realignments are how close participants have come to meeting the prerequisites for full union. It would be dangerous, if feasible, to shift the responsibility for deciding on realignments to the ESCB in stage II, if any major divergence of economic performance has persisted into that stage. But it would be desirable to shift that responsibility, if the need for realignments were generally accepted as residual only, and if adequate monetary instruments for underpinning fixed rates had been assigned to the ESCB along the lines proposed above. A tentative conclusion is that the authority to decide on realignments could become part of the mandate of the ESCB in stage II, but that this is less of a priority than the attribution of the other, day-to-day, instruments of an increasingly collective monetary policy.

iii) Stage III: "hard" union, collective authority over economic policy

The present subsection can be brief, since we have already in our evaluation of costs and benefits of EMU in Part One looked at the main features of the final stage. Relative to the intermediate stage II the main changes are the irrevocable fixing of exchange rates, in our view soon to be followed by the introduction of a common currency, full centralization of monetary authority in a European

System of Central Banks, and the transition to binding procedures in the budgetary field.

The central element of stage III is, of course, the constitution of the ESCB that has to guarantee its independence and provide incentives for its policy-making bodies to pursue the aims of price stability.

In an earlier CEPS publication we discussed how further monetary integration should be organized to guarantee a maximum of monetary stability.[17] Some of that discussion has since been superseded by the Delors Report and by much more detailed studies of how an autonomous and stability-oriented European central bank might be constituted, see notably *Louis (1989)*, there is therefore no need to elaborate further on the details of the contribution of the ESCB.

The main elements that would bring some assurance of a policy orientated towards price stability are:

1) A mandate to aim at price stability;

2) Independence of instructions from other instances and personal independence for members of the board through long terms of office;

3) No allowance to extent credit towards the public sector, whether at the European or national level.

These elements of the structure of the ESCB are by now largely uncontroversial. The only remaining task is to incorporate them in the statutes of the ESCB that will be drawn up by the forthcoming Intergovernmental Conference on EMU.

5. Summary and Conclusions

The title of this paper refers to the two fundamental questions that arise in discussions about monetary union for the European Community, namely the why and how. In this concluding section we will try to summarize briefly our discussion of both of them:

i) Why: Would the creation of a monetary union be beneficial on purely economic grounds?

Our analysis suggests that "irrevocably" fixing exchange rates involves costs as well as benefits. The main cost is the loss of the exchange rate as an adjustment instrument, the main benefit is an increase in the credibility of monetary policy and the elimination of purely financial shocks as a source of exchange rate tensions. It is difficult to establish a precise balance of costs and benefits, but it is clear that the costs should diminish and the benefits increase with the increasing integration of the economies of the Community.

The introduction of a common currency would yield substantial additional benefits, but no costs, and would therefore increase the net benefit one could expect from a monetary union.

ii) What concrete steps would be needed to establish a monetary union?

We argue that institutional steps beyond stage I would be needed to create a monetary union. Currency competition, although appealing from a theoretical point of view, is unlikely to lead to substantial progress in a stage I environment, where inflation rates can anyway be expected to converge at a lower level. There is no need to push currency competition as a mechanism for anti-inflationary discipline, as long as the proposed joint monetary policy is based on a clear mandate to aim for price stability and the institution managing the common monetary policy is politically dependent. Progress beyond stage I might also be needed because the leadership role of the Bundesbank would be weakened as other currencies become stronger because realignments are increasingly perceived as unlikely.

What institutional steps should therefore be taken beyond stage I? Following the Delors Report we recommend that the European System of Central Banks (ESCB) should be created by a revision of the Treaty. The ESCB should be an emergent European central bank. We briefly discuss the various ways in which the ESCB could use reserve requirements to mimic the structure of national central banks at a European level because this instrument might be the decisive one in allowing the ESCB to increasingly determine overall liquidity conditions in a way that allow for a smooth passage to the final stage of EMU with a common currency and a European central bank.

Endnotes

1. For inter-bank transactions the bid-ask spread is usually much lower, between most major currencies it is about 0.05 - 0.1%. For the corporate sector different national currencies (and the Ecu) might therefore more easily become very good substitutes. However, most transactions balances are held by households.

2. See *Gros (1988)* for a further elaboration of this idea.

3. *Gros and Thygesen (1990)* discusses also a number of specific issues often raised in more policy-orientated discussions in Europe.

4. See, for example, the survey by *Cohen (1989)*.

5. With intra-EC trade equal to about 20% of Community GDP, the total savings of transaction costs would be about 0.2% of EC GDP if these costs (the direct ones in the form of bid-ask rates plus the indirect, in house ones for enterprises active in intra-EC trade) were about 1%. To this one should add the savings from tourism and other retail cross-border activities.

6. See *Michael Emerson (1988)*. "The economics of 1992". European Economy 42. March.

7. See *Romer (1989)* for a summary presentation of the new theories of growth.

8. This figure is based on estimates that about 130 billion US dollar notes are used outside the US (presumably most of it in Latin America), one-third to one-fourth of which might be converted into Ecu.

9. It is crucial that the economies of scale be external. If they could be internalized by each private provider of money competition would break down, as one money would displace others and remain without competition.

10. See "An Evolutionary Approach to Economic and Monetary Union", HM Treasury, November 1989.

11. It is apparent that these elements of the UK proposal could and should be part of the internal market programme in financial services.

12. Conclusions of the Hanover European Council, 27-28 June 1988 as reprinted in Delors Report, Annex 1, p. 43.

13. Some statements by officials of the Bundesbank and the Netherlands Bank comment on the first stage in this spirit, see e.g. *Poehl (1989, pp. 146 ff)*, and *Szasz (1989)*.

14. The following draws heavily on *Thygesen (1989b)*, which is an elaboration of one of the author's contributions to the Collected Papers for the Delors Report, *Thygesen (1989a)*.

15. The following two paragraphs merely restate the main principles of the scheme, while the rest of the present subsection enlarges on it.

16. See *Gros (1989c)* for more details.

17. *Gros and Thygesen (1988)*, Part III, notably pp. 59 ff.

References

CIAMPI, CARLO A. (1989). An Operational Framework for an Integrated Monetary Policy in Europe, in: collection of papers annexed to Delors Report, 225-232.

COHEN, DANIEL (1989). The Costs and Benefits of a European Currency. Ch.7, in: DE CECCO, M. and GIOVANNINI, A. (eds.). A European Central Bank? Italian Macroeconomic Policy Group and Centre for Economic Policy Research. Cambridge: Cambridge University Press, 195-209.

GROS, DANIEL (1988). The EMS and the Determination of the European Price Level. Centre for European Policy Studies. CEPS Working Document No. 35, Brussels.

GROS, DANIEL (1990). The Ecu and Common Monetary Policy: From a Pre-monetary Union Stage to a Full Monetary Union. Centre for European Policy Studies, CEPS Working Document No. 45, Brussels, February.

GROS, DANIEL and THYGESEN, NIELS (1988). The EMS: Achievements, Current Issues and Directions for the Future. Centre for European Policy Studies, CEPS Paper No. 35, Brussels.

GROS, DANIEL and THYGESEN, NIELS (1990). Concrete Steps Towards Monetary Union. Centre for European Policy Studies. CEPS Paper No. 45, Brussels, April.

LOUIS, JEAN VICTOR ET AL. (1989). Vers un Système Européen de Banques Centrales. Collection dirigée par l'Institut d'Etudes Européennes. Editions de l'Université de Bruxelles.

POEHL, KARL OTTO (1989). The Further Development of the European Monetary System, in: collection of papers annexed to Delors Report, 131-155, September (1988).

ROMER, PAUL (1989). Increasing Returns and New Developments in the Theory of Growth. NBER Working Paper No. 3098, September.

STOCKMAN, ALAN C. (1988). Sectoral and National Aggregate Disturbances to Industrial Output in Seven European Countries. Journal of Monetary Economics 21, 387-409, North-Holland.

SZASZ, ANDRE (1989). Comment on paper: Institutional Development of the EMS. By THYGESEN, NIELS. Paper presented at the conference on The European Monetary System in the 1990s organized by the Bank of Greece and the Centre for European Policy Studies, in Athens, August 31-September 2.

THYGESEN, NIELS (1989a). A European Central Banking System - Some Analytical and Operational Considerations, in: collection of papers annexed to Delors Report, 157-176.

THYGESEN, NIELS (1989b). The Benefits and Costs of Currency Unification. Paper for 1989 Kiel Week Conference. The Completion of the Internal Market, forthcoming in volume of proceedings, Kiel Institute of World Economics.

WALTERS, ALAN (1986). Britain's Economic Renaissance. Oxford: Oxford University Press.

Alan G. Isaac

Comments on:
Towards Monetary Union in the European Community: Why and How

1. Monetary Integration: Political versus Economic Considerations

Daniel Gros and Niels Thygesen have given us a provocative and stimulating paper on the prospects of increased European monetary integration. My comments will not address their pragmatic suggestions for an EC transition to a common currency, which presuppose the desirability of further monetary integration. Nor will I focus on the relevant political considerations, which are already receiving a great deal of attention at this conference. I will focus instead on what I believe should be the core issue of concern for those considering the desirability of an EC common currency area: the economic costs and benefits of such a move.

As the authors note, European monetary integration is once again high on the political agenda. Despite the reservations expressed by Germany and by Britain, political support for the implementation of an EC common currency area continues to increase. In such circumstances, it may be useful to question whether this political agenda has convincing economic underpinnings. The authors answer in the affirmative: the costs of integration have been largely incurred and large benefits remain to be reaped.

I would like to sound a more cautious note.

2. Economic Costs

First, I would like to reconsider the costs of moving to a common currency. The authors argue that, due to the EC's increasing commitment to prevailing exchange rate parities, the potential losses associated with monetary integration have already largely been incurred. In particular, they emphasize the loss of the exchange rate as a policy instrument. Another cost, emphasized by *Canzoneri and Rogers (1990)*, *Dornbusch (1988)*, and *Fischer (1982)*, arises when irrevocable exchange rate parities constrain national seigniorage rates away from optimal tax spreading levels. Given the July 1990 implementation of the EC Directive on capital market liberalization, these costs may be summarized as the loss of the ability to conduct independent national monetary policies. If the authors wish to argue that current parity commitments already fully impose these costs of a common currency area, I will disagree only with the implicit assumption that current parity commitments are irrevocable. Unlike a common currency area, a fixed exchange rate regime allows critical leeway in the conduct of national policy.

2.1 Optimal Policy

Optimal policy will generally require exchange rate realignments in the presence of nationally differentiated shocks *(Mundell 1961; Ishiyama 1975; Grilli 1989)*. Complete monetary union, with a common EC currency, would rule out the possibility of parity shifts in response to national needs. This need not be a concern if we are confident that nationally differentiated shocks are unimportant determinants of optimal policy within the EC, but *how confident are we* that the optimum currency area is in fact the entire EC? Regional barriers in goods and factor markets, the lack of institutionalized mechanisms for income based inter-regional transfers, and the predominance of regional expenditure policies in the determination of overall EC fiscal stance--these and other fragmenting characteristics of the EC support a theoretical case against increasing monetary integration *(Leigh-Pemberton, 1990)*.

2.2 The Weight of Empirical Evidence

As for empirical evidence, the research on the national differentiation of shocks remains inadequate for an assessment of the optimal currency area. In the absence of convincing empirical evidence on this point, adoption of a common currency presents an unknown and potentially large risk. Even the optimists, who judge that the existing empirical evidence does not suggest that the EC needs to allow divergent national policies, do not have adequate assurance of the wisdom of imposing a common currency on the EC. Such evidence is inherently historical and backward looking. This century has been fraught with largely unforeseeable shocks: wars, commodity price shocks, debt crises, environmental disasters, and political upheavals. In this context, I do not believe that there is a convincing economic reason for discarding the ability to undertake decentralized monetary policy responses to unforeseen future shocks.

2.3 Flexible Exchange Rates

I would like briefly to address a side issue that arises in this context. One may wonder whether concern about nationally differentiated shocks leads logically to a position in favor of floating rates. (Such arguments can be reinforced if differing national conditions require different inflation rates to raise seigniorage revenues consistent with optimal tax spreading.) Under a floating rate regime, however, the presence of short run nominal rigidities can generate overshooting of the real exchange rate. Undesirable short run trade balance and income effects generated by overshooting can be compounded by long run hysteretical effects *(Baldwin 1988; Baldwin/Krugman 1989; Dixit 1989)*. Such considerations decrease the attractiveness of floating parities.

Of course, as the authors point out, fixed but revocable exchange rate parities also involve difficulties. In particular, such an exchange rate regime creates strategic considerations that can diminish its attractiveness. (For example, the private profitability of destabilizing speculation, the temptations of competitive devaluation, or the dynamic inconsistency in optimal public policy.) These appear to me to be the strongest of the arguments against fixed but revocable exchange rate parities, but they may speak as well of optimal crawling pegs as they do of increased monetary integration.

3. Economic Benefits

Returning to the economic costs and benefits of a common currency, I would like to address the supposed benefits. As the authors acknowledge, the empirical relationship between exchange rate variability and international trade patterns remains obscure: evidence for the widely anticipated negative correlation remains elusive. This is natural, however, given the low cost options for hedging foreign exchange risk. The authors apparently interpret the inconclusive empirical evidence as providing little evidence that EMS movement toward more rigidly fixed parities has generated large economic benefits for the EC, a point with which I concur. In contrast with the authors, however, I believe that the benefits of full monetary integration will be similarly limited. I will address the five benefits they mention in their paper.

3.1 Elimination of Currency Exchange Transactions Costs

Currency exchange transactions costs are already low, and bid/ask currency spreads give far too high an estimate of their significance. Corporate transactions are by far the most significant arena for potential gains, in terms of importance in intra-EC trade, and they involve commissions of less than one half per cent. In addition, corporations can and do maintain transactions deposits in more than one currency, thereby often avoiding commissions altogether in their multi-currency dealings. As financial integration proceeds and innovation continues, existing costs will be further diminished. The same applies to individual transactions. (As a mundane example from the tourism sector, where the relatively high bid/ask spreads for small cash transactions are often taken to be the relevant measure of transactions costs, the spread of credit card use has made much more favorable terms widely available.)

3.2 Price Transparency

The elimination of information costs and of incentives for price discrimination will generally have associated economic benefits, but it is reasonable to expect that the contribution of a common currency to such price transparency will be small. The authors appear to attribute far too large a role to increased monetary integration and far too small a role to real and financial integration, which will provide the bulk of the benefits to the EC. I am unaware of any empirical work that indicates that large economic benefits would arise directly from an elimination of information costs due to currency conversion.

3.3 Dynamic Efficiency Gains

Neither the theoretical nor the empirical literature have offered any useful guidance on the extent of possible dynamic efficiency gains obtainable from EC adoption of a common currency. While it is easy to agree with the authors that it is "difficult to assess the exact magnitude of the increase in the growth potential of the Community through monetary union," I see no reason to expect a significant contribution of monetary union per se. The real and financial integration of the Community have much more prima facie plausibility as sources of dynamic efficiency gain; how monetary integration will contribute to this remains fuzzy at best. Given the large potential economic costs of increased monetary integration, claims of significant dynamic efficiency gains from adoption of a common currency should not be allowed to motivate policy in the absence of convincing empirical support.

3.4 Reductions in Official International Reserves

Estimates of the benefits to the EC of potential reserve reductions made possible by adoption of a common currency run as high as ECU 200 billion *(Welfens 1990)*. On the face of it, this is equally an argument for a return to more flexible rates, or at least more reserve conserving forms of intervention. As the authors acknowledge, however, it is difficult to say just what are the economic costs of international reserve holding. Even if international reserves didn't pay interest, which they do, behavioral changes in this arena would largely raise intra-EC distributional considerations.

3.5 Currency Substitution into the ECU

It is possible that the ECU, as a stable alternative to the dollar with a large presence in international trade, would increasingly appear in a vehicle currency role. As the authors note elsewhere, established payments patterns are an important determinant of transactions media, and the relative confidence in the dollar cannot be overlooked as a psychological factor. Any currency substitution into the ECU should be expected to take time, but eventually might generate significant seigniorage. The extent of such effects, however, remains controversial. In addition, seigniorage is generated only by the issue of non-interest bearing high powered money, so the greater use of the ECU as the unit of account in legal international trade need not necessarily generate much seigniorage: sophisticated cash management techniques limit the extent to which use of a vehicle currency generates corresponding increases--directly or indirectly--in the demand for high powered money.

3.6 Other Benefits

In addition to the five possible benefits considered by the authors, two others have achieved some prominence in discussions of a European Monetary Union: price stability gains and increases in the overall stability of the financial system. Little work has been done on the latter, so it is difficult to anticipate the effects of movement to a single currency on stability of the financial system. My own view is that systemic changes--adequate uniformity in securities and banking laws, reporting standards, requirements of risk based insurance premia for financial intermediaries in addition to adequate risk based capital standards, and a willingness to close intermediaries when market value accounting indicates insolvency--can make a much larger contribution to financial stability than adoption of a common currency.

As for price stability, the only central bank macro-policy goal explicitly acknowledged by the authors, I would argue that it is impossible to anticipate the effects of a common currency area and a European central bank on this policy goal. Institutional design will play a critical role in determining the economic outcomes *(Welfens, 1990)*. A strong, independent European central bank committed to low inflation could indeed foster greater overall price stability in the EC. If such independence proves politically infeasible, the opposite outcome could easily ensue. A new European central bank would also lack an established reputation for commitment to price stability, and inflation expectations might therefore respond with great volatility to small changes in policy stance. In contrast, German dominance of the EMS has allowed the EC to profit from the established reputation of the Bundesbank: the well known outcome has been a convergence of EC inflation rates toward the relatively low German levels. Once again, existing monetary arrangements are associated with concrete advantages while the movement to a common currency offers only hazy promises.

4. Concluding Remarks

I have tried to argue that the economic costs of increased monetary integration for the EC are potentially large and that the potential economic benefits are small. Participants in this debate should acknowledge, however, that it is currently dominated by armchair quarterbacks. Without increases the quantity and quality of empirical work in this area, the economic desirability of a common currency area will remain moot. As noted by *Welfens (1990)*, considerations of economic desirability already seem to be displaced by political considerations in discussions of the desirability of an EC common currency area. The present commentary is an effort to dampen the political enthusiasm by focusing on the economic risks. In the absence of convincing empirical evidence of large economic gains, prudence suggests that the threat of large potential economic costs is a strong contraindication to the adoption of a common currency.

References

BALDWIN, R. (1988). Hysteresis in Import Prices: The Beachhead Effect. American Economic Review, 78, 773-785.
BALDWIN, R. and KRUGMAN, P. (1989). Persistent Trade Effects of Large Exchange Rate Shocks. Quarterly Journal of Economics, 104(4), 635-54.
CANZONERI, M. and ROGERS, C. (1990). Is the European Community an Optimal Currency Area? Optimal Taxation Versus the Cost of Multiple Currencies. American Economic Review, 80(3), 419-433.
DIXIT, A. (1989). Hysteresis, Import Penetration, and Exchange Rate Pass-Through. Quarterly Journal of Economics, 104, 205-228.
DORNBUSCH, R. (1989). The EMS, the Dollar and the Yen, in: GIAVAZZI, F., MICOSSI, S. and MILLER, M., eds., The European Monetary System. Cambridge: Cambridge University Press, 205-228.
FISCHER, S. (1982). Seigniorage and the Case for a National Money. Journal of Political Economy, 90, 295-313.
GRILLI, V. (1989). Exchange Rates and Seigniorage. European Economic Review, 33, 550-587.
ISHIYAMA, Y. (1975). The Theory of Optimum Currency Areas: A Survey. IMF Staff Papers, 22(2), 344-83.
LEIGH-PEMBERTON, R. (1990). Europe 1992: Some Monetary Policy Issues, in: Monetary Policy Issues in the 1990s. Kansas City: Federal Reserve Bank of Kansas City, 175-182.
MUNDELL, R.A. (1961). A Theory of Optimum Currency Areas. American Economic Review, 51(4), 657-65.
WELFENS, P.J.J. (1990). Creating a European Central Bank after 1992: Issues of EC Monetary Integration and Problems of Institutional Innovation, this volume.

Manfred Willms

GERMAN MONETARY UNIFICATION AND EUROPEAN MONETARY UNION: THEORETICAL ISSUES AND STRATEGIC POLICY PROBLEMS

1. Introduction

Politicians and economists in the Federal Republic of Germany are confronted with two types of monetary integration: the German Monetary Unification (GMU) and the European Monetary Union (EMU). The GMU is a new challenge resulting from the November 9, 1989 revolution in East Germany. The first ideas for monetary integration in Europe date back to the year 1970 when the former Prime Minister of Luxembourg Werner presented his plan for an EMU. In 1989 the Delors-Committee launched new efforts in this direction and outlined a plan for the realization of the EMU in three stages.

While the West German government enthusiastically pushed forward the German Monetary Unification process, the same government is much more reluctant and reserved with respect to the introduction of the EMU. At a first glance this seems to be contradictory. Is the monetary unification process with a socialist country using a non-convertible currency not much more complicated than a monetary union with a number of Western European market economies? Are the advantages of the EMU for the Federal Republic of Germany not greater than the advantages of the GMU? Another set of issues is related to the interaction between the two plans for monetary integration. Does the German Monetary Unification process delay the European Monetary Integration process? Would it not have been economically more meaningful to establish first the EMU and then extend it to East Germany?

This paper addresses these issues by a systematic comparison of the two types of monetary integration. In both cases the final goals of monetary integration are principally the same:
- The introduction of a single currency within the area.
- The conduct of monetary policy by a single central bank.
- The free movement of labor, capital, goods and services within the area.

However, as it will be demonstrated below, there exist substantial differences between the two cases in the economic and political environment which generate diverging strategic policy implications.

In this context the point of departure is the question whether the countries involved in the two monetary integration processes actually form an optimum currency area.

2. Are Germany and Europe Optimum Currency Areas?

An optimum currency area comprises regions between which a fixed exchange rate regime is more conclusive to the achievement of the ultimate goals of macroeconomic policy like full-employment, a stable price level and external equilibrium than a flexible one. Consequently, within such an area changes in the nominal exchange rate cease to be available as an instrument of economic policy. Moreover, the burden of adjustment to real and monetary shocks has to be borne by other economic variables and markets. For the determination of the size of the optimum currency area a number of criteria have been developed in the literature.

Mundell (1961) demonstrates in a model with two regions and sticky nominal wages that it is the more attractive for regions to form a currency area, the higher the degree of labor mobility among them. Under conditions of high labor mobility a shift in demand from one region to another does neither lead to unemployment, since people laid off in the depressed region can be employed in the prospering one, nor to balance-of-payments problems, since the movement of factors substitutes for the movement of goods. As a result, a high degree of labor mobility may replace the nominal exchange rate as a means to maintain internal and external balance.

Applying Mundell's criterion of factor mobility to Germany, both countries seem to form an optimum currency area, since because of the common language and cultural background the degree of labor mobility is very high. In the case of Europe, in sharp contrast, the degree of labor mobility is substantially lower and the participating countries are definitely less suited to form a monetary union.

McKinnon (1963) suggests the degree of openness measured by the importance of tradables in the individual regions as another criterion determining the optimum size of a currency area. He argues that a high degree of openness reduces the efficiency of nominal exchange rate changes as a policy instrument. In countries with a high degree of openness increases in the prices of tradables following a devaluation immediately feed through to wage increases which have a strong inflationary impact and eliminate the competitive advantage gained by a devaluation. For this reason, countries with a high degree of openness, and these are especially small countries, ought to approach a monetary union with a large country or a group of large countries.

Applying the McKinnon-criterion to the two Germanies, they do not, at the present stage, form an optimum currency area. Although East Germany is in economic terms a small country compared to West Germany (the GNP of East Germany amounts to about one-ninth of the West German GNP), its degree of openness measured by tradables as a percentage of GNP is with 25% only half as high as in the case of comparable Western European countries. As a result, under the McKinnon-criterion, the Western European countries are more suitable for a currency union than the two German countries. However, this statement neglects the fact that in East Germany trade relations have been largely determined by political forces. Under a free market system the McKinnon-criterion would be more likely to be fulfilled for Germany than for Europe.

Kenen (1969) proposes that economies with a high degree of product diversification form an optimum currency area. Countries with highly diversified production and consumption patterns experience a relatively low degree of real exchange rate variability, since many statistically independent sectorial shocks are likely to cancel out in the aggregate.

Applying the diversification criterion to the German case, a currency union between the two countries would be, at least for the moment, no optimum solution. In most sectors East Germany is far away from offering a diversified spectrum of goods and services. However, a similar situation prevails for some Western European countries which are candidates for the proposed EMU.

Vaubel (1978a, 1988) puts forward the criterion of real exchange rate variability. He argues that in a currency union with fixed exchange rates real exchange rate changes require an adjustment of national price levels. Since this is in conflict with the ultimate goal of price stability, only countries with small real exchange rate changes are appropriate candidates for a currency union. These are countries with similar preferences for price stability, similar productivity trends and highly diversified goods and financial markets. The Vaubel criterion incorporates, therefore, all the criteria mentioned before.

With respect to price stability West Germany has much more in common with East Germany than with many countries of the proposed EMU. As it will be discussed later, the rate of hidden inflation in East Germany has not exceeded the relatively moderate visible rate of inflation in West Germany over a longer period of time. In contrast, with respect to productivity growth rates an immediate currency union between the two Germanies does not seem to be appropriate. Regarding the substantial productivity gap between the two countries the difference in productivity trends are likely to be higher between East and West Germany than between West Germany and the other EMU-countries.

In summary, the theory of optimum currency areas does not deliver an unambiguous answer to the question whether the two German states or the twelve countries of the European Community are more suitable for a monetary union. In practice, almost all criteria presented here are controversial *(Ishiyama 1975, pp. 346 -359)* and to difficult to operationalize.

In this context it is meaningful to consider the distinction between the optimality of a currency union and its viability *(Vaubel 1988)*. According to economic criteria a currency union might not be optimal but viable and an optimum currency area in the economic sense might not be viable. The reason is that in addition to economic factors non-economic determinants such as the cultural background or historical experience can be important factors for the viability of a monetary union *(Cooper 1976, p. 49)*. In this respect the GMU has to be evaluated in a different manner than the EMU. In the case of the GMU a strong currency replaces a weak currency. In the case of the EMU not only weak but also strong national currencies are replaced by a synthetic, politically imposed currency, where it is not known whether this will be a strong or a weak currency.

Another important theoretical issue concerning the GMU and EMU apart from the optimality of the currency areas is the selection of the optimum currency unification process *(Vaubel 1978b, 1988)*. The benefits and costs of the two main alternative strategies for currency unification in Germany and in Western Europe, gradualism or big leap, are analyzed from a German point of view in the following sections.

3. German Monetary Unification

3.1 Economic Structure and Monetary System in East Germany

For more than 40 years East Germany has been a centrally planned socialist economy with limited access to private property. Companies were merged in large conglomerates which did not compete with each other. They were protected against foreign competition by a government agency which organized foreign trade and compensated for losses on the world market. The same government agency supervised the fulfillment of politically imposed supply obligations to the COMECON-countries.

Prices, wages and interest rates were determined politically and did not reflect the relative scarcity of goods, labor and capital. The pricing system was not targeted at the most efficient allocation of factors of production, but at distributional goals ("unity of economic and social policy"). Accordingly, prices of ordinary consumer goods were subsidized, sophisticated consumer goods were taxed. Wages and interest rates did not have much to do with productivity and factor scarcity. Consequently, prices, wages, and interest rates lost their signalling function. Furthermore, the system contained no sanction mechanism in the case of inefficient production.

The tax system focused on government-owned or quasi-government-owned companies. About 75% of total revenues were raised by duties at the company level. The official income tax contributed less than 10% to government revenues. The structure of the income tax itself was that tax-rates and tax-progressions were considerably lower for employees than for self-employed people.

The financial sector was organized in a one-stage-banking system. The existing banks functioned economically as branches of the East German central bank. Money was not primarily designed to be a means of exchange and a store of value but to be an instrument for financing and controlling the real output planned by the central bureaucracy. A market for the efficient allocation of capital did not exist. In the foreign sector, the East-Mark was a non-convertible currency. Instead of market-determined exchange rates hundreds of individual exchange rates existed.

This policy framework generated major distortions in the economy which led to labor productivity and real per capita income about 50 to 60 percent lower than in West Germany. The situation has been worsened by extremely low reinvestments such that the capital stock in infrastructure, housing and industry is largely obsolete.

After the opening of the border on November 9, 1989 a more or less communist government and the communist administration stayed in power for several months. They hindered the introduction of a free market economy wherever it was possible and prevented capital imports by a law which restricted foreign capital participation in East Germany to 49%, with some government-controlled exceptions allowed for.

Since such a policy did not set favorable prospects for the future, a daily exodus of up to 3000 people from East Germany to West Germany took place. The migration stream has caused severe shortages of skilled labor in East Germany and considerable social problems in West Germany (housing, unemployment, access to the social security system).

3.2 Necessary Reforms

There is widespread agreement that the socialist system of central planning has been inefficient. While some political groups have favored its transition to a "socialist market economy", the overwhelming majority of experts has demanded its replacement by a social market economy. As the general election of March 18, 1990 convincingly showed, also the people in East Germany want a social market economy and they want it soon.

The introduction of the social market economy requires numerous reforms. The most important are the reorientation of the pricing system and the introduction of a competitive economic order based on private property. In addition, the tax system, the social security system, the foreign trade relations as well as the money and credit system have to be drastically reorganized *(Siebert 1990c, p. 7)*. All necessary reforms are difficult to implement and will cause adjustment problems.

Free market prices are necessary in order to gain information on the relative scarcity of goods and factors of production. They are also important for the determination of the value of companies and private property. The signalling function of free market prices requires the widespread abolition or at least the significant reduction of subsidies and special taxes on long-term consumer goods.

The introduction of a competitive system requires the decomposition of the huge socialist conglomerates and "people-owned" companies. This does not constitute a severe problem in typical small business sectors where the economic units can be handed over to the present employees. It is more difficult in the industrial sector, where many companies will not be able to survive under competitive conditions. The alternatives are a closing down or a complete renewal. In both cases labor will be laid off. However, with the removal of the restrictions on capital imports and on being self-employed, unemployment should only be a short-run phenomenon. The introduction of private property and of a free enterprise system will initiate a dynamic growth process. It provides incentives for taking entrepreneurial risks, for efficient resource allocation and for additional economic activity.

The tax-system has to be shifted from taxation at the company level to the taxation of individual incomes earned under competitive conditions. The rate of progression which goes up to 90% has to be considerably reduced. In addition, it will be necessary to introduce a sales tax.

Social and economic policy have to be conceptually separated in the sense that the achievement of distributional goals has to be accomplished without direct intervention in markets. A social security system similar to West German standards has to be introduced. To this belongs the establishment of a system of unemployment insurance, previously unknown in East Germany. Moreover, the need to increase the extremely low pensions for elderly people is commonly accepted, especially, if the subsidies for housing are reduced or eliminated.

One cornerstone in the reform of the financial system concerns the establishment of a two-stage-banking system with the functions of supplying money and allocating credit separated. Another cornerstone is the introduction of the DM in East Germany. While, from the beginning, these issues were largely undisputed, the strategies towards currency unification, i.e. the question, when and under which conditions the DM should be introduced as the official currency in East Germany, has been fiercely discussed. The controversy centered around the problem whether the currency unification should be arranged by a big leap or in a gradual fashion and whether the exchange rate under gradualism should be a fixed or a flexible one. In the meantime, the decision in favor of a big leap has been taken: The DM has replaced the East-Mark on July 1, 1990.

3.3 Benefits and Costs of Gradualism

The decision in favor of the big leap strategy for the introduction of the DM in East Germany has been controversially discussed and is still in the center of political dispute. A number of economists recommended a gradual strategy for the GMU and opposed the big leap (for example *Filc 1990*; *Hoffman 1990*; and to some extent *Siebert 1990a*). These economist focus on the existing differences in labor productivity, real income and infrastructure between the two Germanies. They prefer a monetary union between countries which are economically on a similar level. Therefore, they suggested to carry out first those reforms in East Germany which lead to an increase in productivity and growth. For the reconstruction of the infrastructure a West German Marshall-Plan in the dimension of 1% of GNP or about 20 billion DM per year has been proposed *(Filc 1990, p. 135)*.

In the discussion about the preferable monetary integration strategy for Germany several types of gradualism have been proposed.

Fixed and Undervalued Exchange Rate

A first suggestion along the gradualist line has been a fixed undervalued exchange rate for East Germany. The undervaluation should encourage exports and restrict imports similar to the successful strategy of reconstruction in West Germany after the currency reform of 1948. Because of the low productivity of labor and the low quality standard of many East German products exchange rates of 5 East-Marks for 1 DM or at least 3:1 have been recommended.

Given an average wage level in East Germany of 1200 Marks such exchange rates would have implied extremely low labor costs in DM of about 400 DM per month at an exchange rate of 3:1 (2.80 DM per hour) or 240 DM at a rate of 5:1 (1.50 DM per hour). As a result, profits could have been high enough to allow for considerable growth rates of capital formation, productivity and real wages.

However, a strategy of stimulating economic growth in East Germany by suppressing wages via an undervalued currency can only work if employees have considerable exchange rate illusion or high mobility costs. Only in that case can wages be kept below labor productivity without setting an incentive to migrate. In a united labor market, as it effectively exists now in the two Germanies, neither exchange rate illusion nor considerable mobility costs seem to be a realistic assumption. Therefore, an undervaluation of the East-Mark would have only led to an increase of migration to West Germany.

Moreover, gradualism is no prerequisite for low wages in East Germany. If wages could be kept below labor productivity by an undervalued currency, the same result could also be achieved by a big leap strategy.

Quasi-fixed Exchange Rate

Instead of a fixed undervalued currency a quasi-fixed exchange rate based on a parallel central bank behavior has been proposed as another possible strategy for German Currency Unification *(Frankfurter Institute 1990, p. 19 ff.)*. In this study the adequate value of the exchange rate has been estimated between 1 and 2 East-Marks per DM. The idea was the adoption of the Austrian or the Dutch monetary policy behavior scheme: Austria and the Netherlands stabilized the exchange rate between their currencies and the DM by conducting a parallel monetary policy to the Bundesbank. Under this strategy prices, wages, pensions, interest rates and the money supply are forced to adjust to the exchange rate.

For East Germany, such a rule of monetary policy would have had the advantage of adjusting prices for traded goods immediately to world market prices and thus allowing for an optimum restructuring of the capital stock. The degree of nominal wage increases and the inflation rate would have been determined by the Bundesbank. A further advantage has been seen in the fact that foreign investors in East Germany would have had no exchange rate risk as long as the East German central bank would have followed this policy rule.

The main problem with this approach would have been that it provided no mechanism which would have guaranteed that the East German central bank would stick to such a policy. On the other hand, a formal agreement for the preliminary introduction of a fixed exchange rate system between both Germanies could not have been accepted by West Germany because the Bundesbank would have had no control over the public deficits or of the money supply in East Germany. As a result, such a system could have easily led to inflation in both countries and would have endangered the whole monetary unification process.

Floating Exchange Rate

A third suggestion along the gradualist line has been the introduction of a floating exchange rate vis-a-vis the DM. This suggestion would have had the advantage of determining the exchange rate by market forces and keeping it somehow tied to economic fundamentals. It would largely have avoided inflationary pressure on East Germany which builds up with an undervaluation and deflationary pressure resulting from an overvaluation of the East-Mark. Finally, nominal exchange rate flexibility facilitates the adjustment of real exchange rates in response to shocks. A modified floating rate system by combining flexible exchange rates between the East-Mark and the DM with a transfer of the responsibility for monetary policy in East Germany to the Bundesbank has been proposed by *Siebert (1990a, p. 20)*.

It is true that some arguments can be found in favor of gradualism for Germany. More important, however, are the general drawbacks of all gradualist strategies for the GMU. Under any of these strategies the DM would have continued to exist as a parallel currency in East Germany. This most probably would have caused instability in the money demand and problems of controlling the money supply in both countries. For the Bundesbank the large-scale use of the DM as a parallel currency in East Germany would have impeded the determination of a non-inflationary money supply target.

Another disadvantage of all gradualist strategies of currency unification in Germany would have been their relief from pressure to implement the drastic reforms necessary for a fast reconstruction of the East German economy. It is very much likely that any delay in the introduction of the DM as an official currency in East Germany would have neither relieved the economic difficulties nor would it have solved the migration problem. In reality, there has been no choice for a gradual strategy since people in East Germany simply refused to accept their domestic currency anymore.

3.4 Benefits and Costs of Big Leap

People in East Germany consider the DM as a symbol of freedom and prosperity. Due to the small degree of acceptance of the East-Mark they have not only been discriminated in Eastern European Countries but even in their own country. The fast introduction of the DM provides them overnight with one of the most reliable and stable currencies of the world. They gain the advantages and privileges of a fully convertible currency. Transformation and information costs with respect to the German-German exchange rate disappear. All prices can be compared directly. The same holds for the value of all assets and liabilities. Furthermore, the DM sets incentives for West German and international direct investments in East Germany. Because of the tremendous capital shortage large-scale direct investments from other countries are a prerequisite for a rapid recovery and an increase in the standard of living. Their positive side effect is the import of urgently needed modern technical know-how and management techniques.

However, the immediate replacement of the East-Mark will not be without costs *(Kromphardt 1990; Scharrer 1990)*. Many domestically produced goods will be substituted by imports from West Germany. The non-competitiveness of many companies will become directly visible. Due to inefficient production or to low quality standards complete production lines may have to close down. Temporary large-scale unemployment may be the case. Previously subsidized prices including rents will increase and lead to social adjustment problems, especially for pensioners. The budget cannot be financed anymore by taxes imposed at the company level. High budget deficits could be the outcome.

A key issue in the big leap strategy was the selection of an adequate exchange rate for the conversion of East-Marks into DM. The conversion rate does not only determine nominal wages and prices in the short run but also the DM value of the cash money stock, of savings and of assets and liabilities in the balance sheets of East German companies and banks. A central question with respect to the conversion rate was to what extent an excess supply of money or hidden inflation existed in East Germany.

The 1989 data (Table 1) show that the East German GNP and disposable income is between 11 and 12 per cent of the West German one. The relative cash holdings of the general public are of the same magnitude. Accordingly, the income velocity for cash money was more or less identical in both German countries.

Table 1: Income, Money and Velocity in East and West Germany - End of 1989 data -

	East Germany (Bill. Marks)	West Germany (Bill. DM)	East German as a percentage of West German data
Gross National Product (estimated)	250	2,260	11.1
Disposable Income	164	1,404	11.7
Cash Holdings of Nonbanks	17	146.9	11.6
Bank Deposits of Nonbanks	223.7	1,108.5	20.2
Money Stock M_3	240.7	1,255.4	19.2
Velocity 1 (GNP/Cash)	14.7	15.4	
Velocity 2 (Disposable Income/ Cash)	9.6	9.6	
Velocity 3 (GNP/M_3)	1.04	1.8	

Sources: Jahresbericht 1989 der Staatsbank der DDR; Statistisches Jahrbuch der DDR 1989; Monthly Report of the Deutsche Bundesbank

Contrary to this, bank deposits of the public (households, companies and government) and thus the money stock M_3 deviated substantially between the two Germanies. The ratio GNP/M_3 (Velocity 3 in Table 1) was 1.04 in East Germany and 1.8 in West Germany. Relative to West Germany the East German M_3 was almost 80 per cent higher. This could have been the indication of a hidden "cash-holding inflation" resulting from the fact that prices were politically fixed while the money stock was growing faster than the real GNP. *Cassel (1985, p. 266)* estimates the average annual rate of this type of inflation in East Germany between 1960 and 1980 of about 4.7 percent. In order to eliminate the accumulated inflation potential, with the introduction of the DM a devaluation of bank deposits in East Germany became unavoidable.

In the Treaty of a Monetary, Economic and Social Union of May 18, 1990 both German countries agreed to convert all financial assets and liabilities on July 1, 1990 at a rate of 2:1, except for 4000 Marks per capita (6000 Marks for people older than 59 and 2000 Marks for children under 15) which were to be converted at a rate of 1:1. Given the remaining population in East Germany of about 16.2 mill. people the 1:1 exchange amounted to 64.8 billion DM. Based on the financial situation on April 30, 1990 denominated in Marks the East German money stock M_3 amounted to 258.6 bill. Marks and total domestic debt to 365 bill. Marks (Table 2). According to the Treaty the money stock M_3 has been devalued to a smaller degree (1.6:1) than the domestic debt (2:1).

In relation to West Germany the favorable conversion rate of the Mark has led to an excess supply of monetary assets in East Germany of about 26 bill. DM. Instead of its share of 11.1 per cent of the West German GNP East German money holders got a share of 13.2 percent of the West German M_3 (161.5 bill. DM instead of 135.1 bill. DM). However, due to the fact that bank deposits besides a small amount of insurance savings (1989: 14.7 bill. Marks) have been the only way to hold financial assets in East Germany, it can be expected that a certain proportion of bank deposits will be transferred into more attractive forms of financial assets. M_3 may decline without a build-up of inflationary pressure.

Table 2: Money and Debt in East Germany before and after German Unification

	Marks (Bill. per April 30, 1989)	Conversion Rate	DM (Bill.)
I. Money			
1. Currency in circulation	12.6	2:1	6.3
2. Bank Deposits			
- Private	64.8	1:1	64.8
- Households	115.8	2:1	57.9
	(180.6)	1.5:1	(122.7)
- Companies	53.9	2:1	26.7
- Government	11.5	2:1	5.8
Money Stock M_3	258.6	1.6:1	161.5
II. Debt			
1. Domestic Credit			
- Private Households	2.6	2:1	1.3
- Housing	102.4	2:1	51.2
- Companies	236.4	2:1	118.2
- Government	23.6	2:1	11.8
Total Domestic Credit	365.0	2:1	182.5
2. Net Foreign Liabilities	12.6	0.6:1	19.9

Source: Deutsche Bundesbank, Statistische Uebersichten zur deutsch-deutschen Waehrungsunion, Frankfurt, July 1990

With respect to the money supply the rapid introduction of the DM in East Germany does not seem to create any problem, since the Bundesbank finally has control over its expansion process. However, a problem exists with respect to the remaining debt at the company level. Despite the fact that this debt in DM has been reduced by 50 percent many companies will have problems in serving the debt at much higher interest rates than before. Obviously, a large proportion of the debt has to be written off. This requires the introduction of equalization claims at the banking sector in addition to those which have been necessary because of the application of different conversion rates for deposits and debts. The equalization claims have to be serviced by the East German and later by the joint German government.

In summary, the big-leap introduction of the DM in East Germany is not without risks. Whereas the risk of inflation is rather small, the main challenge lies in the adjustment of the real sector. Overall, the risks seem to be limited in relation to the costs of a delay of the German Monetary Unification process.

4. European Monetary Union

4.1 Economic Structures and Monetary Systems in Europe

All member countries of the present European Monetary System (EMS) and the planned European Monetary Union (EMU) are democracies and free market economies. Prices, wages and interest rates are basically market determined. Nevertheless, the level of economic activity deviates substantially among the member countries. For example, real income differences between West Germany, some Mediterranean countries and Ireland are larger than those between the two German countries. In all countries the monetary sector is organized in a two-stage-banking system, with the central bank system providing the domestic money supply and the private banking system allocating the credit. All currencies are convertible. Capital controls still exist in some countries, but their importance is gradually declining.

The present EMS consists of 12 currencies and the basket ECU as the unit of account. Only 9 countries participate in the exchange rate mechanism, one of them, namely Spain, with special conditions. Exchange rates can deviate from the officially fixed central rate within a band +/- 2.25% and +/- 6% respectively. Central banks are obliged to intervene in the foreign exchange market in order to keep the exchange rate within the band. The intervention mechanism is supported by a system of currency swaps and official credits. Adjustments of the central rates are possible under mutual accordance.

The EMS is designed in a way that the participating countries may follow their traditional final and intermediate goals of monetary policy but cannot neglect the implications of their monetary decisions on other member countries. Since most of the member countries try to avoid the official devaluations they adjust their policy more and more to the policy of the German Bundesbank as the central bank with the most reliable anti-inflation policy. This behavior has made the Bundesbank the leading central bank within the EMS and the DM the leading currency in Europe. However, the Bundesbank has not dominated the EMS in the sense that the money supplies of the EMS countries have exclusively been affected by the German money supply. In contrast, they have also been very much influenced by the world money supply and the money supply of other EMS countries *(Fratianni/von Hagen 1990)*.

4.2 Planned Reforms

In April 1989 the Delors Committee presented a three-stage plan for the creation of an EMU. The plan is based on the idea of a step-wise expansion of the present EMS, the establishment of a European Central Bank System (ECBS) as an autonomous institution and the final introduction of a single European currency. The plan seems to be widely accepted by most European governments.

In the first stage which started on July 1, 1990 it is intended to eliminate all remaining capital controls. The three non-participating countries United Kingdom, Portugal and Greece shall join the exchange rate mechanism. In addition, the Council of the European Central Bank Presidents will be entitled to report on the monetary and exchange rate policy of the member countries and to make suggestions for money supply targets. Furthermore, three sub-committees shall be introduced for the harmonization of monetary policy, exchange rate policy and the supervision of the commercial banking system. It is also intended to grant more autonomy to those central banks of member countries which are basically dependent on the directions of their governments.

In the second stage the ECB shall be established as an own institution while the individual central banks and national currencies do still exist. The band for exchange rate changes shall be further narrowed and monetary policy is designed to be more centralized. The Delors Committee itself does neither make specific suggestions with respect to the organizational structure of the ECB nor to instruments and intermediate goals of monetary policy. It only indicates that the ECB shall be independent of instructions from national governments and Community authorities, committed to the objective of price stability, provide no credits to public-sector authorities and have a federal structure.

Detailed proposals for the conduct of monetary policy during the second stage of the EMU have been made by members of the Delors-Committee *(Thygesen 1989; Ciampi 1989)*. According to these proposals a three-stage banking system shall be introduced during stage two with compulsory reserves being the main instrument of money control. In a recent statement (April 1990) the EC bureaucracy pushed towards the introduction of stage two and the establishment of the "Eurofed" as early as January 1, 1994.

In the third stage European currencies shall be substituted as legal tender by the new European Currency Unit (ECU). The monetary system in Europe will then have to be reduced to a two-stage banking system with the present national central banks turning into subsidiaries of the ECBS and the monetary policy being determined by the European Central Bank Council.

4.3 Benefits and Costs of Gradualism

Gradualism along the route of the Delors Committee implies that 12 European currencies continue to exist as legal tender in their respective countries at least during the first two stages, while the independence of the individual central banks is reduced in a step-wise fashion. One of the main arguments in favor of a gradual strategy for the EMU is the difference in labor productivity and real income between the present EMS-member countries. A gradual strategy gives countries with lower real income a better chance to catch up with the more advanced countries by an undervalued currency and by additional infrastructure investments.

A further argument for gradualism is that those countries which tax their people by inflation like Greece, Italy, Ireland and Belgium need some time for shifting the tax system from the inflation tax to other forms of taxation. Countries with a high preference for price level stability like Germany and the Netherlands can continue their relatively restrictive monetary policy.

For Germany the attractiveness of gradualism is given by the fact that the following advantages can still exist for an undetermined period of transition *(Willms 1990)*:

- The Bundesbank will stay responsible for price level stability in Germany (and some European countries).
- The DM will continue to be the second most important reserve currency of the world.
- The real exchange rate of the DM vis-a-vis EMS-member currencies with higher rates of inflation will be undervalued so that German exporters continue to have a strong competitive position in these markets.
- The seigniorage of the Bundesbank can be used to reduce the budget deficits of the federal government and has not to be transferred to the European Community.

A disadvantage of gradualism for Germany could result from the intention to incorporate the United Kingdom into the EMS. This would reduce the German influence in shaping the future structure of the EMU in central issues like the independence of the proposed ECBS, the anchoring of the goal of price level stability and money supply control.

A further disadvantage is that the gradual approach would lead to considerable coordination problems during phase two when the ECBS has been established and the national central banks do still operate as individual decision centers. Who is then ultimately responsible for monetary policy and who guarantees that the different central banks do not act in a counterproductive way?

4.4 Benefits and Costs of Big Leap

At present, a big leap strategy with the immediate introduction of a single currency is not under discussion. It could, however, become relevant once the gradual monetary integration process does not show much progress in the near future.

A first benefit of an early big leap introduction of the ECBS is the complete elimination of transaction and information costs related to currency exchanges for intra-Community economic activities. This could encourage further trade creation and trade penetration in the member countries. A second benefit is the immediate elimination of any nominal exchange rate risk. As a result, the economic environment becomes more certain, thus encouraging further intra-Community direct investments and portfolio investments. In addition, users of financial services would gain from the rapid introduction of a single currency because the substantial differences of intermediation costs between the EC countries, which are basically the outcome of limited competition due to different currency habitats, would be considerably reduced *(Gros 1989; Thygesen 1990, p. 373)*. The third benefit is related to the avoidance of conflicts and disturbances which would accrue from the parallel existence of the ECB and the national central banks under the gradual strategy. It is probable that national central banks, despite the general agreement on the final goals of monetary policy during the period of transition, deviate considerably in the growth rates of their money supply and thus endanger the whole monetary unification process. A fourth benefit concerns the people in Community countries with traditionally high rates of inflation. They could gain from a lower inflation rate and a more predictable future price level if the ECB is credible in its policy and more committed to price level stability than their own central banks would be during the period of gradual adjustment towards the EMU.

While high inflation countries could gain, low inflation countries could lose by a soon big leap creation of a single currency if the monetary policy of the new ECBS follows a middle-of-the-road strategy with respect to inflation. Such a policy cannot be ruled out since the European Central Bank Council will consist of board members from countries with different views on the causes and costs of inflation. It is almost certain that the European Central Bank Council like the individual decision centers of the present Community central banks will soon be confronted with the traditional conflict between short-run employment effects and long-run inflation effects of monetary policy.

A general disadvantage of the big leap strategy for all member countries is that the adjustment of exchange rates cannot serve anymore as an instrument of economic policy for the correction of balance-of-payments imbalances within the Community. The burden of adjustment is then transferred to other markets like the labor, the housing and the credit market. This especially requires regionally more flexible wages and rents. Unfortunately, the European Social Charta sets signs just into the opposite direction.

Another problem is the selection of the appropriate exchange rate for the revaluation of all assets, liabilities, wages and prices. Should exchange rates be applied that exist in the EMS at the day of the big leap? These exchange rates are to a large extent determined by political decisions and not by the market. At least, they are not those exchange rates that would occur after the process of market integration has been completed. In any case, under the big leap strategy the choice of the politically fixed exchange rates shapes the future pattern of investments, production and trade and thus the growth perspectives of the Community countries *(Fuhrmann 1990, p. 100)*.

5. Big Leap for Germany and Gradualism for Europe

Viewing it superficially, both the German and the European monetary unification process would require a strategy of gradualism. It seems that in both cases the real income differentials and the differences in social and economic structures are so substantial that the instrument of nominal exchange rate changes should be kept available as a shock absorber for the period of transition. Since the Community countries are all democracies with a dominant market oriented sector whereas East Germany has been, until recently, a socialist dictatorship with a centrally planned economy, the period of gradualism should be much longer for the German monetary unification process than for the European Monetary Union.

Such a view which has a broad support also in West German academic circles neglects basic differences between the two cases. Both German countries have the same social and cultural tradition and share a common language. They had been a single currency area with identical per capita income and the same institutional setting until 1945.

The German Monetary Unification process implies in effect an extension of the DM-area to East Germany. This means that judged by international standards a successful central bank system based on the principles of independence, price stability and federalism is introduced in a country with a completely deteriorated economy where people have lost their confidence in the system and the incentive to work productively. Any delay in the introduction of the DM in East Germany means effectively for the people the continuation of a hopeless economic situation. This would either require long-lasting financial transfers from West Germany to East Germany or lead to an acceleration of migration. Without an immediate currency unification and the introduction of West German economic law in East Germany the urgently needed capital import would be very much restricted. As a consequence, productivity growth would be smaller and the severe ecological problems could not be solved within an adequate period of time. Trade creation and general economic penetration as well as the integration of East Germany into the world economy would be slowed down. On the other hand, the most important argument for a gradual strategy, namely the preservation of an undervalued currency, is not relevant between countries with almost perfectly mobility of labor. For these reasons there is no alternative to a big leap strategy for currency unification in Germany.

While for the German currency unification a big leap strategy is a rational and cost minimizing solution, for the EMU a gradual strategy is optimal. A first point is that in the German case the DM-area is extended and the Bundesbank keeps the control over the national inflation rate. In the European case the DM is finally substituted by a common currency and the responsibility for price stability is transferred to an international institution. Under these circumstances it is difficult to ensure zero or low rates of inflation without a sanction mechanism. Since Germany can easily be forced to accept a higher average rate of inflation as it existed in the past, it is better to observe the functioning of the ECBS for a while before the final stage of the EMU is installed.

A second point is that for Germany the benefits of an EMU will be relatively small anyhow. Within the European Community, most of the gains from trade creation and specialization have been obtained by the elimination of tariffs or will be obtained by the abolition of still existing non-tariff trade barriers in 1993. Some more gains from EMU will certainly result from the elimination of intra-Community exchange rate related transaction costs, information costs and risks. Consumers will benefit from more competition. But it is questionable whether these benefits justify the replacement of the DM and the closing down of the Bundesbank. In any case, these positive effects are not comparable with those productivity gains which can be expected from the extension of the DM to East Germany. Especially for this reason, people have demonstrated for the introduction of the DM in East Germany, but until now no demonstrations have occurred in favor of the introduction of the ECU in Europe.

In summary, for Germany it is rational to pursue a big leap strategy for the German Monetary Unification process and a gradual strategy for the European monetary integration process. The rapid establishment of the GMU has principally no effect on the efforts to extend the present European Monetary System to an EMU.

References

CASSEL, D. (1985). Inflation und Inflationswirkungen in sozialistischen Planwirtschaften, in: THIEME, H.J. ed., Geldtheorie: Entwicklung, Stand und systemvergleichende Anwendung, Baden-Baden, 263-294.

CIAMPI, C.A. (1989). An Operational Framework for an Integrated Monetary Policy in Europe. Delors Committee for the Study of Economic and Monetary Union. Report on Economic and Monetary Union in the European Community, Luxembourg, 225-232.

COHEN, D. (1989). The Costs and Benefits of an European Currency, in: DE CECCO, M.; GIOVANNINI, A., eds., A European Central Bank? Cambridge, New York, 195-209.

COOPER, R.N. (1976). Worldwide versus Regional Integration: Is there an Optimum Size of the Integrated Area? in: MACHLUP, F., ed., Economic Integration: Worldwide, Regional, Sectoral, London and Basingstoke, 41-53.

DELORS COMMITTEE FOR THE STUDY OF ECONOMIC AND MONETARY UNION (1989). Report on Economic and Monetary Union in the European Community, Luxembourg.

FILC, W. (1990). Devisenhilfe statt einer sofortigen Waehrungsunion. Wirtschaftsdienst, 70, 133-138.

FRANKFURTER INSTITUT (1990). Soziale Marktwirtschaft in der DDR, Bad Homburg.

FRATIANNI, M.; VON HAGEN, J. (1990). The European Monetary System Ten Years After. Carnegie-Rochester Conference Series on Public Policy, 32, 173-241.

FUHRMANN, W. (1990). Die Vision einer Europaeischen Zentralbank. Wirtschaftspolitische Blaetter, 37, 96-101.

GROS, D. (1989). Paradigms for the Monetary Union of Europe. Journal of Common Market Studies, 27, 219-230.

HOFFMAN, L. (1990). Wider die oekonomische Vernunft. Frankfurter Allgemeine Zeitung, No. 35, February 10, 1990.

ISHIYAMA, Y. (1975). The Theory of Optimum Currency Areas: A Survey. IMF Staff Papers, 22, 344-383.

KENEN, P.B. (1969). The Theory of Optimum Currency Areas: An Eclectic View, in: MUNDELL, R.A.; SWOBODA, A.K., eds., Monetary Problems of the International Economy, Chicago, 41-60.

KROMPHARDT, J. (1990). Ueber eine Waehrungsunion zur Wirtschaftsunion. Wirtschaftsdienst, 70, 128-133.

McKINNON, R.I. (1963). Optimum Currency Areas. American Economic Review, 51, 717-725.

MINFORD, P. (1990). The Path to Financial Integration in Europe, in: SIEBERT, H., ed., The Completion of the Internal Market, Tuebingen, 306-342.

MUNDELL, R.A. (1961). A Theory of Optimum Currency Areas. American Economic Review, 51, 651-667.

POEHL, K.O. (1990). Basic Features of a European Monetary Order, this volume.

SCHARRER, H.E. (1990). Schocktherapie statt Gradualismus. Wirtschaftsdienst, 70, 75-77.

SCHLESINGER, H. (1990). Die Wirtschaft der Bundesrepublik Deutschland: Vor wichtigen Weichenstellungen. Deutsche Bundesbank, ed., Auszuege aus Presseartikeln, No. 29, Frankfurt, April 6, 1990.

SCHMITZ, C. (1990). Gradualism versus Big Leap in German-German Monetary Integration. Kiel Advanced Studies Working Papers, May.
SIEBERT, H. (1990a). Die Wahlmoeglichkeiten einer deutsch-deutschen Geld- und Waehrungspolitik. Kiel Discussion Papers, No. 159.
SIEBERT, H. (1990b). Der Umstellungskurs kann nicht 1:1 sein. Handelsblatt, April 2, 1990.
SIEBERT, H. (1990c). The Economic Integration of Germany. Kiel Discussion Papers, No. 160.
THYGESEN, N. (1989). A European Central Banking System - Some Analytical and Operational Considerations. Delors Committee for the Study of Economic and Monetary Union. Report on Economic and Monetary Union in the European Community, Luxembourg. 157-175.
THYGESEN, N. (1990). The Benefits and Costs of Currency Unification, in: SIEBERT, H., ed., The Completion of the Internal Market, Tuebingen, 347-375.
VAUBEL, R. (1978a). Real Exchange Rate Changes in the European Community: A New Approach to the Determination of Optimum Currency Areas. Journal of International Economics, 8, 319-339.
VAUBEL, R. (1978b). Strategies for Currency Unification. The Economics of Currency Competition and the Case for a European Parallel Currency, Tuebingen.
VAUBEL, R. (1988). Monetary Integration Theory: A Survey and Critique, in: ZIS, G., ed., International Economics, London, 223-262.
WILLMS, M. (1990). Der Delors-Plan und die Anforderungen an eine gemeinsame Europaeische Geldpolitik. Kredit und Kapital, 23, 30-59.

John Williamson

Comments on:
German Monetary Unification and European Monetary Union: Theoretical Issues and Strategic Policy Problems

One of the many novel issues which economists have confronted during the exciting months we have recently lived through is the question of German monetary unification. When this issue first arose in February, many of us had little idea of the appropriate theory to bring to bear and almost no knowledge of the pertinent magnitudes, so that initial guesses of an appropriate conversion rate between the ostmark and the deutschemark ranged from 3:1 to 12:1. Matters have now become a good deal clearer, and the paper of Dr. Willms is very helpful in setting out current understanding of relevant factors and magnitudes.

There are basically two issues. One concerns *liquidity effects*: it seems that a conversion rate of 1:1 is likely to create some modest liquidity overhang, but that this will be manageable, especially if larger savings accounts are converted at the less generous rate of 2:1 and the new deutschemark balances are not all made available immediately. The second effect concerns factor prices, and especially the importance of ensuring that East German wages are not pitched so high as to destroy the incentive to produce and invest in East Germany. It now seems that both East German wages (measured at 1:1) and productivity are something of the order of 40 percent of the West German level, so that a 1:1 conversion rate is not unreasonable, especially in view of the fact, emphasized by Dr. Willms, that a strategy of undervaluation so as to provide an incentive for investment is unlikely to be viable given the pressures for migration that it would produce.

The other main theme taken up in the paper is the relative priority to be accorded to GMU and EMU. Dr. Willms introduces this subject by considering the battery of criteria that have emerged in the optimal currency area literature in order to pronounce on whether a particular monetary union is desirable or not. Of the four criteria that he mentions, two suggest that EMU is a better bet than GMU. I shall briefly review these four criteria.

1) *Diversification.* Willms argues that the Kenen criterion of diversification is better satisfied by the various West European economies with which the Federal Republic would be in partnership in EMU than it is by East Germany, and it would seem difficult to contest that assertion.

2) Willms declares himself unable to decide whether the Vaubel criterion of real exchange rate stability is better satisfied by EMU or GMU. To my mind the question is misguided since real exchange rate variability is largely a consequence of the exchange rate regime rather than something exogenous which can determine which regime should be adopted. (If the criterion is interpreted as referring to whether there is a greater *need* for real exchange rate variability in order to support the adjustment process, I would endorse Willms agnosticism.)

3) McKinnon's traditional criterion of openness is clearly satisfied better at the present time by the EMU countries than by Eastern Germany, although that may change in due course.

4) Willms points to Mundell's original criterion of labor mobility and argues that this points towards GMU, since labor mobility between the two Germanies is "almost perfect." I interpret labor mobility as a situation where labor flows in *both* directions, and I am unaware of any tendency for labor to flow from the West to the East. But perhaps more important is the fact that GMU was originally prompted by the hope of *stemming* the migration of East German workers to the West. It seems paradoxical in the extreme to argue that GMU is justified by the phenomenon that it is intended to prevent!

Thus the optimum currency area literature suggests rather strongly that there is a better case for EMU than for GMU. Despite that, Dr. Willms urges immediate GMU and at best a gradualist strategy for achieving EMU. This paradox is explained by the fact that he has introduced a novel criterion for an optimal currency area on page 19 of his paper. This criterion can be stated very simply as: an optimum currency area is the largest area for which the Bundesbank can act as the central bank.

This is not an unreasonable criterion. The Bundesbank has done enormously will in the forty years of its existence. It has acted as a model which other central bankers are anxious to emulate, pursuing a monetary policy firm enough to restrain inflation without being so dogmatic as to undermine other important objectives of economic policy like maintaining a healthy traded-goods sector or limiting recessions. Public opinion polls suggest that it is the most respected institution in the Federal Republic. (I am not a particular fan of German macroeconomic policy, inasmuch as Germany could have done with a tax cut for the past eight years or so, which was perpetually delayed with the promise that it would come into effect in 1990 -- just when the economy got to full employment and additional demands on it meant that a tax *increase* would have been more appropriate! But one cannot hold the Bundesbank responsible for the absurdities resulting from the German government's determination to be unKeynesian.)

It would be dangerous to take it for granted that the Bundesbank will be managed with the same competence in the future that it has enjoyed up to now. But the success of the Bundesbank depends upon more than the quality of the individuals it has been fortunate to be led by. It depends also on its constitution, and in particular on its obligation to pursue price stability and the independence it enjoys in fulfilling that duty.

One can in fact question the wisdom of central bank independence. In my ideal world both fiscal and monetary policy would be targeted *jointly* on a rate of nominal income growth calculated to strike a balance between the competing aims of reducing inflation to minimal levels (or holding it there) and permitting real growth of the economy *(Williamson and Miller 1987)*. It seems to me that there is a real danger in telling the monetary authority that it should concern itself exclusively with controlling inflation, inasmuch as this implicitly tells the fiscal authority that its responsibility is to worry about growth rather than inflation. The predictable consequence of such an assignment is precisely the combination of high real interest rates and sloppy fiscal policies that the world has experienced for the past decade.

Even though I worry about this point, I doubt very much that the best way of meeting the problem is to return central banks to being appendages of the finance ministry on the British model. Experience has shown the need for an institution with an explicit mandate to defend price stability. The challenge will be to devise institutional mechanisms which give hope of a sensible fiscal-monetary mix without endangering the objective of price stability.

So, despite the reservation, the Willms criterion for an optimum currency area seems acceptable. But does it really imply that EMU deserves to be delayed? The Bundesbank is the only conceivable model on which a Eurofed could be based at the present time, and its independence will be inevitable if it is created before a strong political executive exists. Moreover, all European central bankers are presently thirsting to be able to emulate the independence of the Bundesbank. Thus the Willms criterion seems to me to point towards early completion of EMU. Germans who are also good Europeans should not want to keep the advantages of the Bundesbank to themselves.

References

WILLIAMSON J., and MILLER, M.H. (1987). Targets and Indicators: A Blueprint for the International Coordination of Economic Policy. Washington: Institute for International Economics.

Franco Reither

LIBERALIZATION AND REGULATION IN THE PROCESS OF FINANCIAL MARKET INTEGRATION IN THE EUROPEAN COMMUNITY

1. Introduction

In 1986 the twelve member countries of the European Community (EC) signed the "Single European Act" according to which the internal market should be established by the end of 1992. The plan is to have a market without internal frontiers allowing the free movement of goods, services, labor, and capital. As an essential component, the completion of the 1992 single market program involves the realization of a genuine EC-wide common financial market. This paper is concerned with major achievements and shortcomings in the realization of the program to complete the so-called "financial dimension" of the internal market. It emphasizes the efforts towards the liberalization of capital movements and towards the creation of a new regulatory order for the community-wide supply of financial services as the two basic forces driving the process of financial market integration in the EC.

2. The Historical Record

The EEC Treaty of 1957 provides for the progressive abolishment of restrictions "on freedom to provide services within the Community" (Art. 59) and of "all restrictions on the movement of capital belonging to persons resident in member states and any discrimination based on the nationality or on the place of residence of the parties or on the place where such capital is invested" (Art. 67). It also states that "the liberalization of banking and insurance services connected with movements of capital shall be effected in step with the progressive liberalization of movement of capital".

For more than 25 years after the EEC Treaty was signed, progress in financial integration was rather modest. While, in theory, the fundamental freedoms of financial activities laid down in the EEC Treaty of Rome have been able to be invoked by individuals and corporations since the end of the transitional period (i.e. from January 1, 1970), in practice their exercise has met with considerable obstacles. In fact, financial markets have remained effectively partitioned along national lines. The establishment of branches in other member states is still subject to authorization and the general supervisory and regulatory control of the host member state. The cross border provision of services has been rendered almost impossible by the existence of exchange control restrictions and various discriminatory fiscal provisions. The prior approval of the host member state has been obligatory for such a wide range of cross border financial activities that in many cases, establishment in that other member state has effectively been required.

Circumstances started to change in 1983-84, by which time considerable progress has been made in correcting domestic and external imbalances in Community countries. Pressure for deregulation and integration was also created by financial innovation, the rapid development of international financial markets, and the decision of some Community countries to dismantle their foreign exchange controls, notably their complete elimination by the United Kingdom in 1979. It was in an effort to overcome the impasse reached, inter alia in the area of financial market liberalization, that the 1992 program was launched in 1985.

In June 1985 the Commission presented to the European Council its White Paper on "Completing the Internal Market", which sets the ambitious objective of complete integration of financial markets by 1992 and concretely identifies the steps required to achieve it. A plan for the full liberalization of capital movements was also presented to the European Council. In addition, the approval of the European Single Act introduced in the EEC-Treaty decision-making on a majority basis for a broad range of Community matters, creating the conditions for speedier approval of legislation. The formulation of a comprehensive approach to the integration of financial markets, the agreement on a final date for its realization, and the introduction of new procedures for Community decisions have created a momentum that was still unthinkable only a few years ago.

In the Commission's approach, financial market integration involves the elimination of all restrictions on capital movements and full freedom for financial intermediaries to offer their services throughout the Community. It entails the elimination of restrictions and discriminatory regulations and administrative practices concerning:

1) the right of establishment and acquisition of participations by foreign institutions in domestic financial markets;

2) permitted operation of foreign-controlled financial institutions;

3) cross-border transactions in financial services.

The first two items basically involve the freedom to supply services in EC national markets, the third, the freedom to move capital throughout the Community.

As regards the liberalization of capital movements, capital market transactions and long-term commercial credit had already been liberalized by an amendment of the 1962 Directive approved in November 1986. In October 1987 the Commission presented a draft directive providing for the liberalization of transactions in short-term securities, financial loans and credits, and of current and deposit account operations. The corresponding final Directive was passed by the Council on June 24, 1988. This Directive removing restrictions to capital movements can be said to underpin the entire financial services liberalization process. It entered into force on July 1, 1990.

Turning to the freedom to supply financial services, the new approach relies on the essential tenets of

1) minimum harmonization of prudential standards;

2) mutual recognition of national laws, and

3) home country control.

The simplicity and flexibility of this approach has permitted rapid progress in the negotiations for the Second Banking Directive which was passed by the Council December 18, 1989. It shall enter into force January 1, 1993.

3. Liberalization and Regulation in the Commission's New Approach

The Second Banking Directive deserves further consideration since it can be said to represent the prototype for future additional steps towards financial market integration in the EC. For example, the recently presented (April 25, 1990) draft Investment Services Capital Adequacy Directive is aimed to eliminate discriminatory treatments of non-bank financial traders compared with banks.

However, prior to a detailed consideration of the Second Banking Directive, certain other key legislation should be mentioned. As already pointed out, the Directive of June 24, 1988 removing restrictions to capital movements underpins the entire process of financial market integration. With certain transitional provisions being applicable to Greece, Ireland, Spain, and Portugal, this Directive entered into force on July 1, this year. It removed the remaining restrictions on transfers of capital within the Community, especially those applicable to short term capital movements.

In the securities field, the most significant proposal was the draft Investment Services Directive of December 1988 concerning the regulation of non-bank financial institutions.

In the banking sector narrowly defined, the reliance on the principle of home country control is made possible only by the simultaneous entry into force of measures ensuring a minimum degree of harmonization of prudential standards: the Own Funds Directive (passed by the Council in April 1989) and the Solvency Ratio Directive (passed December 18, 1989). Additionally, it seems likely that the Commission will seek to have its recommendations on large risk exposure and deposit guarantee schemes translated into binding texts.

These measures taken together can be considered as representing the minimum framework necessary in order for the provisions of the Second Banking Directive to be effectively implemented.

The basic idea underlying the new approach goes back to the White Paper, where a number of principles to be followed are identified. A minimal harmonization of prudential rules and standards will have to be achieved before all restrictions to the free supply of financial services can be lifted, to ensure the solvency and stability of financial institutions and equivalent standards of investor, depositor and consumer protection. Based on mutual recognition of national laws, regulations, and market practices, full freedom in the supply of services will then be allowed. Home country control will apply in that all activities of a bank or their financial intermediary are to be supervised by the authorities of the country of residence of its head office, while the authorities of the country where the service is sold will only play a complementary role.

This approach has the obvious advantage of simplifying the task for Community legislation, which is narrowed to the identification of a platform of common standards for the safeguard of the public good of financial stability. At the same time, it leaves considerable scope for accommodating different institutions, market practices, and prudential approaches. Perhaps the most important feature of this approach is that it will stimulate competition not only between private agents, but also between national institutions and regulatory frameworks. The exercise of regulatory and supervisory functions will be left with the national authorities that already perform them, and presently no attempt is made to set up supranational authorities at the Community level in this field.

The most significant feature of the Second Banking Directive is the effective institution of a single banking licence which is to be valid throughout the Community. In terms of the Directive, any bank validly established in one member state will be able to set up a branch or provide its services (without establishment) in any other member state under the proviso that it is so authorized to perform such activities in the home member state and that such activities are included in the list of qualifying activities contained in the annex of the Directive.

This list has been drawn up on a broadly defined universal banking model and includes all forms of transactions in securities. There is also provision for the amendment and updating of activities in accordance with the "comitology" procedure laid down in Article 22 of the Directive (and thus no amendment of the Directive itself is required).

As a necessary concomitant to this single licence, Article 13 of the Directive lays down expressly that the home market state is to be responsible for the prudential supervision of its duly authorized banks. Thus, endowment capital for branches will no longer be required and any EC bank opening in another member state by way of establishment or the cross border provision of services will, in general terms, have to comply only with the regulation in force in its own country.

Some home country control is without prejudice to the host state's residual powers of control over matters relating to liquidity and monetary policy. A further and extremely significant residual power of the host state concerns the mutual recognition of financial techniques.

The liberalization conceived on the basis of the aforementioned principles has only been achieved by the inclusion of express provisions in the directive for specific measures of harmonization and prudential control. These involve notably

- a minimum level for initial authorized capital;

- control over shareholdings in banks, and

- maximum levels of participations by banks in non-financial institutions.

Article 4 provides for a minimum initial capital of ECU 5 million. Member states are not precluded from insisting on a higher threshold for their own duly authorized banks, but a member state which seeks to impose a more stringent capital requirement will not be able to prevent the establishment in its territory of a branch of a foreign member state bank which applies simply the minimum ECU 5 million threshold. Consequently its banks could be placed at a competitive disadvantage in relation to such foreign member state banks operating there. This possibility of reverse discrimination is not contrary to

Community law, notwithstanding the potential distortions of competition that may be involved.

It should also be mentioned that Article 4 provides for certain derogations from the initial capital limit (understood to involve local Banque Populaires and the like), with a minimum threshold of ECU 1 million being laid down. In addition, Article 10 provides for derogations from the requirement that own funds do not fall below the said initial capital thresholds. These derogations apply to those institutions in existence at the time of implementation of the Directive with such lower levels actually in force. Detailed rules are laid down concerning any change in control or ownership of such credit institutions benefitting from this derogation. The benefit of the derogation is removed if a change of control does not involve a bank which is also beneficiary of the derogation.

Article 11 governs the acquisition and disposal of "qualifying holdings" in credit institutions (10 per cent of the capital or the voting rights). There is a general obligation of notification for such acquisitions and disposals (direct or indirect) and trigger thresholds are laid down with respect to any proposed increases or reductions in the size of the holding (total of voting rights or capital equal, exceed or fall below 20 per cent, 33 per cent or 50 per cent).

With respect to proposed acquisitions, the competent authorities (i.e., those of the home member state of the bank in question) may refuse any proposed acquisition with three months of notification of the same on the basis of a lack of suitability of the proposed shareholder, such suitability to be judged with respect to the requirements of the "sound and prudent management of the credit institution".

There is a general obligation on credit institutions to provide information with respect to any acquisitions or disposals triggering the above thresholds upon becoming aware of them. In addition, a report must be made by them at least once a year detailing all shareholders and members having qualifying holdings in the bank.

Any infringements of these provisions may involve various penalties and sanctions, including the suspension of the exercises of the voting rights attaching to the shares so held.

Article 12 governs participations held by banks in non-financial institutions with the aim of ensuring that a bank's assets are not placed in risky investments. In essence, the maximum authorized thresholds for holdings in an individual company are limited to 15 per cent, and in all non-financial companies to 60 per cent. Permissible exceptions concern temporary shareholdings in rescue, restructuring operations and other excesses in "exceptional circumstances". Additionally, there is the institution of a ten year "grace period" for those credit institutions having excess holdings at the time of implementation of the Directive. Finally, the above thresholds may be exceeded where the excess is 100 per cent covered by own funds, but such own funds may not be included in the calculation of the solvency ratio.

For the purposes of this paper it may be unnecessary to go further into the details of the Second Banking Directive (for a deeper discussion, see *Key 1989*). The elements mentioned so far can be seen as being representative for the transformation of the spirit of the new approach into concrete legislation steps. As should be noted, the driving forces towards financial integration cannot be simply characterized by "deregulation", but by a specific mixture of liberalization and the introduction of a new regulatory order. This will replace the old one which was governed by the idea of national egoism and protectionism. In contrast, the new regulatory order will seek a maximum degree of competition, not only between market participants, but also between the various institutional systems on the national level, and, at the same time, it tries to prevent excessive deregulation and to limit the risks of instability and distorted competition *(Masera 1989)*. However, the likely impact of the new approach underlying the Second Banking Directive is not free of problems, and recognition of its audacity and effectiveness should not lead to complacency about the issues that have to be tackled. In this respect, it seems appropriate to make a distinction between problems that are microeconomic in nature, and such of macroeconomic relevance. Both areas will be addressed, respectively, in the following two sections.

4. Likely Impact of the New Approach: Microeconomics

As regards the microeconomic impact of the new approach, four sets of problems seem worth emphasizing. The first one relates to existing financial market structures, especially in continental Europe, and the resulting need of change (for Italy, see, for instance, *Rondelli 1987*, for France *Melitz 1990*, for Spain, *Vives 1990*). The danger that the process of liberalization and integration will meet increasing resistance once its implications become fully apparent cannot be ruled out. Secondly, the possibility of circumventing prudential requirements by simultaneous access to a multiplicity of regulatory frameworks will be increased. This could lead to a lowering of prudential standards. Third, the remaining application of home-country control may become a vehicle for introducing impediments to the free flow of capital. Finally, specific problems may be posed by the attitude that the Commission has taken to the free supply of services on the one hand, and, on the other, to the liberalization of capital movements. As it will be shown below, the Commission's attitude will create problems of consistency. Similar difficulties will arise as a consequence of going ahead with liberalization before tax structures have been harmonized (see also *Grilli 1989*). In what follows, a closer look is taken at these issue areas.

As regards existing financial market structures in Europe, with the exception of the British system, the actual situation is still very different from the fully integrated "European Financial Area" envisaged by the internal market program. In the main, financial markets are characterized by a dominant role of banking institutions. Capital markets, instead, are rather less developed and still remain, moreover, very much confined to national operators. The operations the various agents can perform are still limited by a variety of de jure or de facto restrictions. This institutional framework, together with the low degree of cross-border competition in financial services, enters as a main determinant of the decision-making of optimizing agents at the microeconomic level. As regards the location, the degree of concentration and specialization of the financial services industry, the present state has to be seen as the outcome of these manyfold decisions on the microeconomic level. In theoretical terms, the present structure of financial markets may be characterized appropriately by the paradigm of "credit rationing", at least to some extent *(Dornbusch 1989)*. There is little doubt as to the implications of removing restrictions on capital mobility and eliminating existing barriers on the international trade in financial services. In anticipation of the coming changes in the institutional environment, some adjustments are already underway in various countries, and it can be expected that the pace of change will accelerate considerably. Since, with the sole exception of London, in the main, European financial markets have not shared in the innovation process taking place in international markets, the direction of change to be expected may be inferred by the broad tendencies already observed in this process.

Evidence of these changes is provided in the emergence of internationalization and globalization in financial markets. There has been a marked tendency towards concentration and universalization in the supply of financial services. Securitization has been an associated major trend. In many countries, structural deregulation by the authorities have accelerated these broader structural changes, intensifying competition and technology. In terms of the classification given by *Gardener (1988)*, the EC is expected to witness three types of "structural diffusion": market structural diffusion, global structural diffusion, and institutional structural diffusion. Market structural diffusion means that traditional barriers between money and capital markets are blurring in many areas of credit intermediation. Defining a neatly segmented banking or financial market will become more difficult. This process will be compounded by the emergence of the second dimension, global structural diffusion. This refers to the prospect that many important financial markets will be no longer separated by national boundaries. Finally, traditional lines of demarcation between the business conducted by different financial institutions can be expected to be eroded; institutional structural diffusion refers to the phenomenon of institutions moving into new lines of business.

As a consequence of these future developments, still existing elements of credit rationing will be eroded or de facto eliminated. This will mean that the degree of efficiency in the allocation of savings as well as in the financing of investment will be raised. Equivalently, the power of governments to crowd out business investment and consumer spending via credit rationing instruments will be weakened considerably. Up to a certain point, the efficiency gains through financial integration will be paid by governments with large deficits: the job of raising funds for the financing of the deficits will clearly become harder. But this effect also constitutes a danger for the process of liberalization and integration itself: the possibility that it will meet increasing resistance once its implications become fully apparent and make themselves felt, cannot be ruled out.

Additionally, beyond a certain point - which, unfortunately, cannot be defined exactly a priori -, a higher degree of competition and of efficiency begins to be traded for stability in financial markets *(Baltensperger and Dermine 1987)*. Therefore, the task is not to ask for maximum deregulation, but to find the optimum degree of regulation. It must be recognized that up to some extent, traditional functional barriers also had the role of reducing and separating financial risks. The system of checks and balances in different countries also provided safeguards against excessive risk taking, conflicts of interest, and market manipulation, and contributed to overall financial stability. This all may now have to undergo thorough revision. As regards prudential regulations, the attitude of continental Europe national authorities to changes has mostly been one of piecemeal, gradual adaptation of existing structures. Great weight has still been assigned to the preservation of national traditions and practices. The Commission has up to now not tried to sort out systematically this multiplicity of approaches, institutions, and national traditions. It has not taken explicit position either on the desirable direction of the developments or on the potential problems that may arise in the future. The absence of a clear concept towards optimal regulation implies that the possibility cannot be ruled out that strains will develop within national financial systems, given the specific fragility of this sector. One will not be prepared to go so far as an anonymous writer in the International Currency Review (1990) who stated: "There is now every prospect the European Commission's frantic effort to cobble together a 'unified' financial market by the end of 1992 will turn out to be a prelude to an Europe-wide financial disturbance, with global ramifications." But the need for a comprehensive approach towards an optimal trade-off of stability against efficiency cannot be denied.

A second, strongly related, but distinct area of concern is that of preserving adequate standards of investor, saver and consumer protection as the objective of the supervisory framework. In this respect, the Commission' s approach is clearly a mix of liberalization and regulation. The regulation component consists in that a minimum harmonization set of supervisory rules is imposed on all member countries. The main body of the minimum harmonization set corresponds to the framework proposed by the Basle Committee on Banking Regulation and Supervisory Practices regarding bank capital standards. The adoption of this framework implies a series of measures which in part are implemented in the Second Banking Directive, and in part are the subject of accompanying Directives, as already mentioned above.

Like quality standards in the goods market, minimum harmonization of the supervisory framework acts as a barrier to entry to the market. Given the present state of supervisory standards at the national level in Europe, for some countries the proposed minimum level may mean stronger regulation, for others it may mean less regulation, if adopted. At this point, the liberalization component of the Commission' s approach will be set in motion, as designed by the principle of home country control and mutual recognition: In the same market, institutions will supply services and compete under different conditions of supervisory rules. What will be the outcome in terms of investor, saver and consumer protection? Under such circumstances, there remains scope for competitive imbalances in favor of the institutions under less supervisory regulation. The simultaneous access to a multiplicity of supervisory frameworks will increase the possibility of circumventing prudential requirements. The opening of financial markets can lead to a dangerous lowering of prudential standards as a direct consequence of the competition between supervisory approaches, because national authorities may seek to avoid losing financial business to countries with more laxity of supervisory standards. However, there are also strong arguments against this fear. Especially, the expectation can be put forward that "the market may place value on national standards that are more stringent than those required by EC directives *(Key 1989)*.

A further problem relates to the general allowance made, in the Commission's approach, for administrative controls maintained for monetary policy and prudential objectives. This will de facto entail host-country control on a number of important aspects of intermediaries' operations. Domestic rules and administrative provisions may become a vehicle for introducing in disguise impediments for the free flow of capital *(Grilli 1989)*. Additionally, in certain areas intermediaries may be confronted with both home and host-countries regulatory requirements.

Finally, problems may be posed by the different attitude that the Commission has taken, on the one hand, to the free supply of services - where minimal harmonization is a precondition to the application of mutual recognition of national rules (starting January 1, 1993) - and, on the other, to the liberalization of capital movements to be realized - with no precondition - by July 1, 1990. In reality, we are dealing with the two sides of the same coin, the supply of, on the one hand, and the demand for financial services on the other. As a result of capital liberalization, all Community residents will gain immediate access to foreign markets on the basis of their regulatory frameworks. In a sense, the principle of mutual recognition will immediately apply to those purchasing financial services abroad. Therefore, it can be expected that the needs and concerns underlying the build-up of the minimal platform of common rules will be forestalled by immediate capital liberalization. A similar difficulty may arise in connection with the decision to go ahead with liberalization before tax structures have been harmonized. This decision is due to the difficulties encountered in making progress in this field rather than to a belief that the matter is one of minor importance. Increased tax evasion and a tendency for financial activities to move to less heavily taxed systems are likely results. Presumably, the evidence of such developments will increase pressure for the harmonization of tax structure *(Grilli 1989)*.

5. Likely Impact of the New Approach: Macroeconomics

Financial market integration will have a strong impact on the conduct of macroeconomic policies. With open frontiers for capital flows and financial services, very little room will be left for the pursuit of pure national goals by monetary or fiscal policy. Even if, in the initial stage, different currencies are maintained, financial integration will not only create the "European Financial Area", but simultaneously also a unified "European Monetary Area". In theoretical terms, this will mean that the degree of substitutability between assets dominated in different currencies will rise, and sustainable interest rate divergences will be squeezed to the amount imposed by the expectations of future exchange rate changes. Still existing impediments like transactions costs or transfer risks will be considerably lower, allowing the linking forces of arbitrage and speculation to work with very much more power and speed in eliminating profit opportunities and in equalizing interest rates and prices for tradables (including the prices for financial services and forward contracts).

As regards monetary policy, the need for abandoning the pure national orientation implies that, at the Community level, a coordination scheme has to be set up for the steering of the Europe-wide money supply. In this respect, the present functioning of the European Monetary System is a good example for such a coordination scheme. In contrast to the first years of its existence, the recent experience shows that now, even traditional weak currency countries are prepared to accept the exchange rate constraint and the leading role of the German central bank. In fact, since the last general realignment in spring 1987, there has been no adjustment of the exchange rates among EMS members who participate in the exchange rate mechanism, with the only exception given by Italy: it devaluated slightly the Lira in January 1990, simultaneously with the shift to the adoption of the narrow spread of 2.25% around the parity exchange rate (Great Britain, Portugal, and Greece still do not participate in the exchange rate mechanism). The result of this new attitude of European central banks towards the Deutsche Mark is that traditional weak currency countries defend the official exchange rate by appropriate monetary policy, i.e. high interest rates and a moderate expansion of the money supply. In so doing, the anti-inflationary stance of German monetary policy is dissipated through the whole area of the EMS. To call this situation one of "German dominance" misses the point completely. Instead, what "dominates" is price stability as the primary objective of monetary policy. In this sense, even the German monetary policy is "dominated" by this objective. Liberalization of capital movements as of July 1, this year, has already strengthened the exchange rate constraint on national monetary policy. Further progress in opening up financial markets will strengthen it additionally.

However, accepting the leading role of the German currency and fixing exchange rates is not the only thinkable coordination scheme. Admittedly, it is the most efficient and simple one if price stability is the primary objective, and if the Deutsche Bundesbank remains successful in this respect. But at the same time, it s the hardest one for other economic areas, especially for public finance. Therefore, it is not surprising that alternative approaches to monetary coordination have been developed, especially in the discussion about currency unification in Europe. The Delors Report, for example, calls for institutional coordination of national monetary policies as the main innovation of "stage two" of the three-stages approach to the creation of a European Central Bank. Institutional coordination will mean that national monetary policies will be defined on the basis of some common agreement between the member central banks. This will imply, first, that the autonomy of the Bundesbank in defending price stability will be weakened. And, secondly, the various national monetary policies will, if defined by common agreement, only by chance be consistent with market opinions at the given exchange rates. This fundamental inconsistency will necessarily destabilize the EMS.

In fact, if price stability is accepted as the primary goal of monetary policy, a system of fixed exchange rates needs one currency which bears the responsibility for this goal as the nominal anchor. Then, the job of coordinating the money supply in the other currencies will be done by the markets. There is no degree of freedom for additional criteria for monetary policies. The only alternative which will be compatible with price stability and free capital flows is that of a currency union, with one common currency replacing national monies, and establishing a European Central Bank with constitutional features like the Bundesbank, and with the legal commitment to the goal of price stability.

With fixed exchange rates, financial market integration implies serious consequences for fiscal policy. Especially, the new environment will impose strong limitations to the possibility of raising funds for the financing of large budget deficits. First, as already noted, existing schemes of credit rationing will be eroded, if not eliminated completely. Second, if monetary policy coordination is successful in realizing a low inflation level, the importance of seignorage as a source of deficit financing will vanish. Third, arbitrage in financial markets will create pressure to eliminate still existing high differences in reserve requirements for banks. Not by chance, required reserve ratios are especially high in countries with large budget deficits, and, additionally, the currencies of these countries are numbered among the weakest ones, traditionally. The worst examples for configurations of this type are given by Italy and Greece (this can best be seen by the fact that, in the process of ongoing fiscal convergence in Europe, only these two countries failed to eliminate their primary budget deficit, until now (see *Dornbusch 1989*). Elimination of the various sources of monetary financing, and the need to pay competitive market interest rates for their government debt will create serious problems for fiscal authorities in these countries. Substantial fiscal corrections will become necessary in order to reduce the deficit. But, as regards tax revenues, it seems highly questionable whether improvements can be expected, realistically (see *Giavazzi 1989*). Under these circumstances, the only way to the solution of the problem seems to consist of heavy expenditure cuts. The hypothetical alternative, the installment of a Community-wide fiscal transfer system, will presumably not be consistent with national political sovereignty (as indicated by recent experience with German unification), in the long run.

6. Conclusions

The Commission has developed an ambitious project for financial market integration in the EC. Its approach is largely based on the notion of creating dynamic disequilibria that will force action by markets and official authorities. Of course, the latter have major responsibilities to ensure that the process of integration being set in motion is governed and does not develop in a disorderly or distorted manner, both as regards the effects of increased competition on financial markets stability and the adaptation of regulatory frameworks. There is no doubt that simultaneous progress in all the areas involved - liberalization, harmonization of regulatory, prudential and tax systems - is essential for this project to succeed. At the macroeconomic level, financial market integration will bring about a higher degree of monetary interdependence. This, in turn, will call for an appropriate coordination scheme for national monetary policies, as long as a currency unification will not be realized. The scheme of hardening the EMS around the Deutsche Mark will remain a successful way to higher monetary convergence at a low inflation level. But it also requires heavy adjustments towards additional convergence in other areas, especially in fiscal policies.

References

-------------- (1990). Financial Market Instability and Crowd Behaviour. International Currency Review, 20(3), 45-54.
BALTENSPERGER, ERNST and JEAN DERMINE (1987). The Role of Public Policy in Ensuring Financial Stability, in: PORTES, RICHARD and ALEXANDER K. SWOBODA, eds., Threats to International Financial Stability. New York, 67-90.
COMMISSION (1987). Recommendation on Large Risk Exposure. (87/62/EEC) OJ L33/10, February 4.
COMMISSION (1987). Recommendation on Deposit Guarantee Schemes. (87/63/EEC) OJ L33/16, February 4.
COMMISSION (1989). Proposal for a Council Directive on Investment Services in the Securities Field. COM (88) 778-SYN 176, OJ C43/7, February 22.
COMMISSION (1990). Proposal for a Council Directive on Investment Services Capital Adequacy, April 25.
COUNCIL (1988). Directive 88/361/EEC of June 24 for the Implementation of Article 67 of the Treaty. OJ L 178/5 of July 8.
COUNCIL (1989). Directive 89/846/EEC of December 15 on the Coordination of Laws, Regulations and Administrative Provisions Relating to the Taking up and Pursuit of the Business of Credit Institutions and Amending Directive 77/780/EEC, COM (87) 715, OJ L 386/1 of December 30.
COUNCIL (1989). Directive 89/647/EEC of December 18 on a Solvency Ratio for Credit Institutions. OJ L 386/14 of December 30.
COUNCIL (1989). Directive 89/299/EEC of April 17 on the Credit Institutions Own Funds. OJ L 124/16 of May 5.
DORNBUSCH, RUDIGER (1989). Europe 1992: Macroeconomic Implications. Brookings Papers on Economic Activity 1989, 341-362.
GARDENER, E.P.M. (1988). Innovations and New Structural Frontiers in Banking, in: PHILIP ARESTIS, ed., Contemporary Issues in Money and Banking. Basingstoke, 7-29.
GIAVAZZI, FRANCESCO (1989). The European Monetary System: Lessons from Europe and Perspectives in Europe. The Economic and Social Review, 20, 73-90.
GRILLI, VITTORIO (1989). Financial Markets and 1992. Brookings Papers on Economic Activity, 301-324.
KEY, SYDNEY J. (1989). Mutual Recognition: Integration of the Financial Sector in the European Community. Federal Reserve Bulletin, 75, 591-609.
MASERA, RAINER S. (1989). Monetary and Financial Markets in Europe: Regulation and Market Forces. Review of Economic Conditions in Italy, 1, 13-42.
MELITZ, JACQUES (1990). Financial Deregulation in France. European Economic Review, 34, 394-402.
RONDELLI, LUCIO (1987). Mercato Unico Europeo: Prospettive e Problemi per le Banche e il Sistema Finanziario. Economia Internazionale, 40, 362-370.
SERVAIS, DOMINIQUE (1988). A European Financial Area. Brussels.
VIVES, XAVIER (1990). Deregulation and Competition in Spanish Banking. European Economic Review, 34, 403-411.

*Sydney J. Key**

Comments on:
Liberalization and Regulation in the Process of Financial Market Integration in the European Community

I would like to comment on one of the issues that Dr. Reither has raised about the possible impact of the EC program for financial services. Certainly, as he suggests, one could reasonably be concerned that mutual recognition and home-country control will lead to a lowering of prudential standards. But it seems to me that there are a number of reasons why this is unlikely to happen, or should it begin to happen, would be only a transitory phenomenon. To put these reasons in perspective, I would like to begin with a few remarks about the concept of mutual recognition and the way in which it is being used in the European Community.

A generally accepted principle for international trade in financial services is national treatment, which seeks to ensure equality of competitive opportunity for foreign firms entering or operating in a host country.[1] If the European Community had adopted national treatment as an approach to financial integration, the result would have been a level playing field for foreign and domestic institutions within each national market. But, even though each country's rules would have been applied on a nondiscriminatory basis, twelve separate, autonomous jurisdictions with different rules in each would have still existed. National treatment removes barriers to the provision of services that discriminate between domestic and foreign firms, but it does not address the problem of nondiscriminatory barriers. In other word, national treatment does not deal with the problem of barriers created by nondiscriminatory differences in national rules -- such as differences in permissible activities for banks or differences in the types of products that may be offered.

In creating an internal market for financial services, the European Community is trying to deal with the problem of nondiscriminatory barriers. The EC's initial approach, which was originally used with regard to products, involved complete harmonization of national rules. This was abandoned as involving too much detailed legislation at the Community level and as totally impractical to achieve within any reasonable time period.

The Community's solution was to adopt the approach of mutual recognition.[2] This approach requires each government to recognize the validity of laws, regulations, and administrative practices of other member states and precludes using differences in national rules to restrict access. Mutual recognition cannot, of course, simply be decreed among a group of countries with widely divergent legal systems, statutory provisions, and regulatory and supervisory practices. Mutual recognition of rules that differ with respect to essential characteristics would be politically unacceptable. As a result, a crucial aspect of mutual recognition is the harmonization of essential rules. In the financial sector, the process of harmonization involves identifying rules that are essential for ensuring the safety and soundness of financial institutions and the rules that are essential for the protection of depositors, other consumers of financial services, and investors. It also involves determining how detailed the harmonization of these rules must be.

The EC approach of mutual recognition could result, at least in the short run, in competitive inequalities and fragmentation of markets. However, the Community expects that over the longer run mutual recognition, in combination with market forces, will lead to a more unified regulatory structure. The process is interactive: Mutual recognition requires initial harmonization, and additional harmonization results from mutual recognition. In adopting the approach of mutual recognition in the financial area, the Community is in effect using trade in financial services to speed convergence of the regulatory policies of the member states. This is a deliberate overall strategy, which has been accepted by the national governments.

Besides leading to a regulatory convergence that would liberalize rules such as those relating to bank powers, market pressures could lead to competition in laxity among supervisory authorities, one of the concerns raised in Dr. Reither's paper. Such competition could occur either with regard to standards that have not been harmonized or that have been harmonized only in general terms or with regard to the enforcement of agreed-upon standards. Moreover, even though governments are usually permitted to impose or maintain standards stricter than the minimums set forth in EC directives, market pressures could prevent them from doing so.

One could argue that no major problems will arise with regard to competition in laxity because the scope of harmonization is sufficiently broad and because the minimum standards that the Community has adopted are sufficiently high. But even if this were not the case, I think there are additional factors that merit consideration.

1. *Political agreement on goals.* First, within the Community, there is political agreement on goals for regulatory convergence, something that is absent in discussions or negotiations in international trade in financial services beyond the Community. Such agreement involves what I believe is a crucial element: a consensus on where to draw the line between liberalization of restrictive structures, on the one hand, and laxity in regulatory and supervisory frameworks, on the other. Within the Community, there is at least theoretical agreement among the member states on the distinction between national rules that have primarily the effect of imposing barriers to trade in services and national rules that are necessary for prudential purposes or for consumer protection.

For example, a consensus exists within the Community that permitting all forms of securities activities to be conducted at a bank or its subsidiary is a positive, liberalizing measure. Banks permitted by their home country to engage in any of the activities listed in the Second Banking Directive are specifically permitted to engage in such activities anywhere in the Community through a branch or through cross-border provision of services. The Community has not required governments to give their banks the powers on the list, but it has created a situation in which regulatory convergence toward the EC list of activities as a result of market forces seems almost inevitable. Other areas, particularly if the model for convergence has not been specified in advance, could be more complicated.

2. *Coordination among national supervisors.* A second, related consideration, is the informal coordination among the supervisory authorities of the member states. Both within and beyond the European Community, the increasing internationalization of financial services and markets has necessitated and facilitated greater international cooperation and coordination with regard to supervision and regulation. The application of any principle for treatment of

foreign banking organizations operating in a host country -- whether it is national treatment or mutual recognition -- will be facilitated by the informal network of relationships among national supervisory authorities.

Under the approach of mutual recognition being used within the European Community, the role of the banking authorities is particularly important. Mutual recognition and home-country control require at a minimum that the supervisors of other member states be recognized as capable. In addition, for mutual recognition and home-country control to be acceptable in practice, there will have to be sufficient harmonization of supervisory procedures and practices beyond the general guidelines set forth for national laws or regulations in EC directives. Thus, cooperation and coordination among national authorities will be essential in defining and implementing a reasonable and generally accepted line between home- and host-country control. As part of a longstanding tradition of such contacts, EC bank supervisors meet formally in a *Groupe de Contact*. One aspect of their current work involves reaching agreement on how the provisions of EC directives regarding home- and host-country responsibilities should be implemented by national governments.

3. *Market discipline.* A third consideration involves market discipline. For example, it is possible that the market might place a value on national standards that are more stringent than those required by EC directives. In this regard, it is important to keep in mind that *governments* are the parties who are obligated to accord mutual recognition to differing national standards that have not been harmonized. *Private firms* and *individuals* are under no such obligation. Indeed, in a more competitive marketplace, firms and individuals may have even greater scope to exercise their preferences. Customers might consider a strictly regulated bank or securities firm of one member state to be preferable to institutions authorized and supervised by authorities of another member state even though the latter institutions might offer a price advantage. This assumes, of course, that firms and individuals are adequately informed about different standards of regulation and that such information is reflected in their market behavior.

4. *Ease of adjustment.* A fourth consideration involves the ease with which changes can be madc in the rules governing financial services in the European

Community. If the Community has underestimated the amount of initial harmonization that is needed, in the financial sector it is probably easier than in other sectors to make corrections. One reason, apart from the EC program, is the ongoing internationalization of financial services and markets. This has already led to cooperation among the major industrial countries with regard to bank supervision and to agreement on basic harmonization of national regulations with regard to bank capital. These accords have been negotiated under the auspices of the Committee on Banking Regulations and Supervisory Practices of the Bank for International Settlements (BIS), a committee that was established in 1974. Thus a commitment to establish and enforce adequate prudential standards exists among banking regulators both inside and outside the Community.

Another reason that ease of adjustment may be easier in the financial sector is that the rules apply primarily to the producers of financial services. By contrast, in the product sector, standards apply to the products themselves. Partly because of the intangible nature of the service being provided, the financial sector can adapt quickly to changes in the regulatory or market environment. As a result, if market forces do not produce further harmonization or if it appears that the harmonization of minimum standards is not adequate in scope or specific enough in detail, it can probably be accomplished at a later stage without major dislocations. However, because of the substantial public policy interests involving macroeconomic policy, safety and soundness, and stability of markets that are inherent in the financial sector in addition to consumer protection, a greater degree of harmonization than is necessary in the nonfinancial sector may be required to make mutual recognition and home-country control acceptable to the member states.

The element of harmonization in the EC program contrasts significantly with the work taking place on trade in financial services in the Uruguay Round negotiations within the General Agreement on Tariffs and Trade (GATT) and in the Organisation for Economic Co-operation and Development (OECD). In these fora, efforts are directed toward removing barriers to trade but without any harmonization of standards. As I have already mentioned, the harmonization that has taken place beyond the Community has been under the auspices of the BIS, where the 1988 Basle risk-based capital framework was negotiated.

5. *Possibility of a centralized supervisory function.* Fifth, at a conference devoted primarily to economic and monetary union it seems appropriate to point out the possibility of having a supervisory function in a European Central Bank. The Delors Report suggested that a European Central Bank would participate in the coordination of banking supervisory policies of the member states. Of course, if the Community were to adopt a system like that of the United States, there would be an overlay of federal and state regulators, who might not always be in agreement. For example, even *within* the United States, federal and state regulators do not always agree on permissible activities for banks.

One could imagine that the supervisory role of a European Central Bank might include matters such as licensing requirements, application of supervisory standards, issues of consolidated supervision of banks operating throughout the Community, and even deposit insurance, an area in which the EC is just beginning work on a directive incorporating the principle of home-country control. It seems likely, however, that the EC financial sector program will be in place before a central bank has been established. But, in the longer run, a supervisory role for the central bank could provide a much more formal, legalistic basis for the work now carried out in the *Groupe de Contact* and a potential forum for any additional harmonization or correction of course that might be necessary.

6. *Supranational structure of the Community.* The final point that I want to emphasize is the supranational structure of the European Community, even without a European Central Bank. The use of mutual recognition within the Community must be viewed in the context of a political movement to liberalize the economic relationships among a group of countries. The European Community is using mutual recognition in an environment of substantial coordination and common obligations established through a supranational structure to which the member states have already transferred a significant degree of sovereignty. This is a unique feature, not present in other kinds of international economic or financial agreements, and is one of the reasons that developments in the Community are so interesting.

* *Division of International Finance, Board of Governors of the Federal Reserve System, Washington, D.C. These comments reflect the views of the author and should not be interpreted as representing the view of the Board of Governors of the Federal Reserve System or anyone else on its staff.*

Endnotes

1. *Sydney J. Key (forthcoming)*. Is National Treatment Still Viable? U.S. Policy in Theory and Practice. Proceedings of a Conference on World Banking and Securities Markets after 1992. International Center for Monetary and Banking Studies, Geneva, February 15-16, 1990, currently available as International Finance Discussion Paper 385, Board of Governors of the Federal Reserve System, September 1990.

2. *Sydney J. Key (1989)*. Mutual Recognition: Integration of the Financial Sector in the European Community. Federal Reserve Bulletin, September, 75, 591-609.

Peter Bofinger

PROBLEMS OF EUROPEAN MONETARY POLICY COORDINATION IN THE TRANSITION PHASE

1. Introduction

With the Strasbourg Summit of December 8/9, 1989, the process of monetary and economic integration in Europe, which had been already quite impressive, has gained additional momentum. Before the end of 1990, the President of the European Council will convene an intergovernmental conference which will be charged with the task of preparing an amendment of the treaty with a view to the final stages of EMU.

These bold political activities which are furthered by the rapid economic and political transformation in East Europe contrast with a growing awareness that the integration process as well as the final stage of an EMU pose rather complex conceptual and procedural problems, which have not been dealt with adequately in the blueprint laid down in the Delors Committee Report. Its evident flaws prompted not a few economists to an outright refusal of the whole integration strategy *(Currie 1989, Vaubel 1989)*. This radical position prefers a competition of European currencies rather than any transfer of responsibilities on the Community level.

The following paper adopts a different procedure. It accepts the overall approach of the Delors Committee Report, especially its stepwise procedure and its final target of a federative European System of Central Banks (ESCB). It analyses the blueprint developed in the Report and related papers under the criterion of price level stability in the European currency area and the criterion of EMS stability in situations of speculative attacks. It tries to identify inconsistencies in the outline of the Report and provides some tentative solutions. As the Report has been presented and analyzed in many publications, the paper concentrates on problems of monetary coordination in the transition phase to EMU without giving a comprehensive description of its contents.

2. Open Questions in Stage One

Although stage one of the enhanced integration process is scheduled to start on July 1, 1990, it is not quite clear and until now not even a matter of intensive academic or political discussion

- whether stage one will be economically different from the Status quo characterized by the EMS and the *nominal anchor* of the Bundesbank's monetary policy *(Bofinger 1989a)*,

- how the Committee of Central Bank Governors will coordinate national monetary policies, above all which *conceptual framework* will underlie its decisions,

- how the interrelationship between the *indirect coordination* of the EMS and the *direct coordination* effected by the Committee will be structured,

- how the *stability of the EMS* can be safeguarded in situations of speculative attacks after the abolition of capital controls and with a possible membership of the Pound Sterling in the system's exchange rate mechanism (ERM), and

- if it is advisable to perpetuate the *competition of national currencies* prevailing in this stage and to renounce on stages II and III, a strategy which is suggested by the alternative proposal of the *British Treasury (1989)*.

2.1 Does Stage One Make a Difference?

Besides the liberalization of short-term capital movements in Europe, stage one will mainly result in an enhanced direct coordination of monetary policies. According to the Delors Committee Report, stage one should "gradually bring about a change from *ex post* analysis to an *ex ante* approach to monetary policy cooperation".[1] This task is complicated by the fact that a transfer of national competencies as well as institutional steps are not envisaged in this stage as this would require a ratification by national parliaments (article 102a of the EEC treaty).

The new mandate for the Committee of Governors[2], which does not fundamentally differ from the previous mandate decided upon in 1964, reflects this restriction. Nevertheless, the role of the Committee will be strengthened after July 1, 1990, not only by the establishment of a permanent research staff and three sub-committees and by a lengthening of its chairman's term from six months to three years, but above all by a specific *sanction*, which has been widely overlooked in the present debate: With stage one, the chairman of the Committee is entitled to make the outcome of its deliberations public. This gives the Committee the power to sanction individual countries by destroying their *reputation*[3] as a reliable partner in international agreements and/or as a country committed to the target of price stability. The sanction will be most efficient if it is imposed on countries following a too expansionary stance of monetary policy. The threat of a public declaration by the Committee reducing or destroying the credibility of a central bank's policy will be a very strong disincentive for national policymakers, especially as the sanction can lead to a loss of exchange reserves if market participants expect a devaluation after a negative assessment of a central bank's policy by the Committee. The Committee can also apply its sanction vis-a-vis a country pursuing a too restrictive policy stance. In this case, the negative reputational effects are not accompanied by the disciplining mechanism of the reserve constraint.

Although it is very difficult to forecast how the Committee will use this new sanction, it seems likely that its role in the process of monetary coordination will be considerably strengthened. This raises the question of the Committee's coordination concept and of the interplay between this coordination mechanism with the indirect coordination exerted by the EMS.

2.2 What Kind of Coordination?

From a theoretical standpoint, the design of a new framework for monetary policy coordination in Europe should start with the clarification of a conceptual basis determining the "*rules of the game*". After an agreement on such principles, the main task of a coordinating institution like the Committee of Governors would be to assess national policies, to identify divergences from the rules and to determine which measures are necessary to correct evident disturbances. Seen from this perspective, the Committee would act as an *arbitrator* in the field of European monetary policies.

Unfortunately, neither the Delors Committee Report nor the new mandate for the Committee give a concrete description of the conceptual framework for the coordination of national monetary policies in stages one and two. Although the Report realized the necessity to "define common surveillance indicators, propose harmonized objectives and instruments" (para. 52), it assigned this task to a monetary policy committee which is to be set up after the inception of stage one.

For the time being, the only guideline for the Committee's coordination exercise can be found in its new mandate[4], which stipulates that the governors have

> to promote the coordination of monetary policies of the member states with the aim of achieving price stability as a necessary condition for the proper functioning of the European Monetary System and the realization of its objective of monetary stability.

This important definition of the *aggregate final* target of the coordination process leaves open, however, which indicator has to be used to measure "price stability" and which *intermediate* targets have to be pursued *at the national level*. Because of

- conflicting national *sterilization policies* within the EMS,

- diverging intervention strategies of member central banks vis-a-vis *third currencies*, and

- the general problem of rather *long lags* between monetary policy actions and their impact on the price level[5],

there is no doubt that a target of domestic price stability for each country would not suffice as a guideline for the assessment of national monetary policies (see also *Gros and Thygesen 1989, p. 45*). The same applies to a proposal of *Thygesen (1989, p. 161)* who suggests the "rate of increase of some measure of *nominal income* for each participating country" as the main target of national monetary policy.[6] This indicator has the additional disadvantage that it blurs the assignment between monetary and fiscal policy and calls for a discretionary monetary policy reaction in periods of recession which might be difficult to reconcile with the target of price stability.

Thus, when the Committee will start to operate as enhanced *arbitrator* of Europe's monetary policies on July 1, 1990, it will be faced with the difficult situation that the precise "rules of the game" have not been defined in advance and are not known to the participants. This will require ad hoc decisions of the Committee's members on the general orientation of monetary policy in Europe and its implementation at the national level whenever a conflict arises. Thus, the advantages of *economies of scale* that can be realized with an international regime will not materialize in stage one. Keohane *(1984, p. 90)* puts these as follows:

> (...) establishing the rules and principles at the outset makes it unnecessary to renegotiate them each time a specific question arises. International regimes thus allow governments to take advantage of potential economies of scale. Once a regime has been established, the marginal cost of dealing with each additional issue will be lower than it would be without a regime.

The lack of a prespecified coordination concept does not only impair the internal efficiency of the Committee's actions[7], it can also reduce its *credibility* in the eyes of private market participants. As the model of *Barro and Gordon (1983)* shows, the large *discretion* that will be granted to the members of the Committee could generate higher price expectations than under the present regime. In this case, the Committee has the negative options of either validating these expectations by an inflationary monetary policy or of establishing a good reputation over time by sticking to its target of price stability thus temporarily accepting negative output effects. In the absence of any concrete rule for European monetary policy coordination, at least in the first years of stage one, the outcome of relatively high price expectations is not unlikely as almost all members of the Committee are dependent from instructions by their national governments.[8]

These theoretical findings suggest that it would be very important for the Committee to commit *itself* already from the beginning to an easily observable rule. As the experience with the Bundesbank's monetary targeting since 1975 demonstrates, such a rule must not be imposed on the central bank by law or by an external institution and must not be followed slavishly. In the context of central bank credibility, the most important element of a *self-imposed rule*[9] is the possibility to verify the central bank's decisions and the onus of proof a monetary institution is willing to bear if it considerably deviates from the targeted value.

How can such a rule be devised for European monetary policy? The most comprehensive concept for the coordination of monetary policies in a fixed rate system is *McKinnon's (1988)* proposal for a targeting of the *domestic component* (DC) of a central bank's monetary base.[10] It is equivalent with a rule which prohibits the sterilization of foreign exchange market interventions. This framework would provide a clear yardstick for the evaluation of national monetary policies. It would require the ex ante definition of non-inflationary DC target values for each central bank, which could serve as objective indicators for the surveillance of national monetary policies by the Committee of Governors. These rather simple "rules of the game" are only practical, however, if the *aggregate demand for money* in the European currency area is stable *(Spinelli 1983)*. This important issue has not yet been tested empirically.

An alternative solution for the common management of monetary policies in a fixed rate environment was developed by *Brunner (1984)*. He proposes a policy of *monetary targeting in a center country* and a strict pegging of exchange rates by the n-1 countries. In stage one, this would call for a continuation of the Bundesbank's anchor role with an enhanced monitoring of the Bundesbank's policy by the Committee of Governors. Again the "rules" could be defined rather easily: The *Bundesbank* has to target its money stock M3 in a non-inflationary way. The sanction of a public declaration by the Committee's chairman could be applied only if German M3 growth considerably exceeds or falls short of the targeted value. The *other countries* would be obliged to stabilize their respective DM-exchange rate by unlimited foreign exchange market interventions. This approach, which requires a stable money demand function in the center country[11], would be advisable if empirical tests give no evidence for a stable aggregate demand for Europe's money.

The task of defining the rules of the European monetary policy game is additionally complicated by the fact that the major players do not only follow national monetary targets but also *exchange rate targets vis-a-vis the US Dollar*. In the past, strong DM-Dollar misalignments were often paralleled by deviations from the Bundesbank's target path. Because of the deflationary or inflationary impact of real exchange rates changes, this policy was not incompatible with price stability in Germany. Therefore, an underexpansion of German M3 relative to its target value is not identical with a deflationary policy stance of the Bundesbank and would not necessarily warrant a sanction by the Committee of Governors publicly declaring the Bundesbank's policy as deflationary and detrimental to the European countries. Due to these international linkages, the rule book for European monetary coordination does not only have specify a rule for internal monetary relations but also whether the ECU-Dollar relation (McKinnon rule) or the DM-Dollar relation (Brunner rule) should be stabilized or left to the markets. This point makes it evident that the neglect of international implications, which characterizes not only the Delors Committee Report but almost all publications on European monetary integration, is a serious drawback for any surveillance of monetary policies by the Committee of Governors.

In sum, monetary coordination can neither be executed in a conceptual vacuum nor can it be left to rigid rules. What is needed evidently, is a coherent conceptual framework providing a *guideline* for the decisions of the Committee under normal circumstances. At least in the first years of stage one, which could be prone to financial shocks due to the realization of the internal market for financial services, the Committee must have the power to deviate from self-imposed rules but it must be under an obligation to justify such discretion.

2.3 How to Ensure the Stability of the EMS?

The interaction between the ERM induced monetary coordination and the coordination by the Committee is a second blind spot of the Delors Committee's blueprint for stages one and two. This has two negative implications: First, the institutional arrangements of stage one and two do not include any safeguards to ensure the stability of the EMS in an environment with liberalized financial markets and with the Pound Sterling as an additional member of the Exchange

Rate Mechanism. Second, the uncoordinated coexistence of both coordination mechanisms can erode the "real anchor" provided by the EMS and the policy of the country with the strongest currency; this aspect is discussed in section 2.4.

The growing risk of speculative attacks[12] destabilizing the EMS is widely acknowledged not only by the Delors Report (para. 12), the recent study of the *EC-Commission (1990)* but also by many academics *(Padoa-Schioppa Committee Report 1987; Portes 1989, p. 6; Gros and Thygesen 1989, p. 40)*. After the abolition of the remaining controls for short-term capital in Europe, it cannot be excluded

- that a country will be subject to large *capital outflows* although it follows a non-inflationary economic policy; due to the inherent asymmetry of the ERM, such "unwarranted speculative attacks" deplete a country of its reserves and force it to adjust its exchange rate or its monetary policy although there is no macroeconomic rationale for such steps;

- that portfolio preferences shift *in favor* of a currency although the monetary policy of the respective central bank is inflationary. This disturbance loosens the real anchor of the ERM and provides the most convincing economic rationale for an enhanced direct coordination by the Committee of Governors in stage one.

To protect countries in situations with unwarranted speculative attacks, the Delors Committee Report mentions the institutional option of a *European Reserve Fund* (ERF) which, however, was not accepted by the majority of the members. The tasks of the ERF include the "managing of the pooled reserves" and the "intervening on exchange markets as decided by the members" (para. 53). The negative assessment of this institution by the majority seems due to the fact that the proposal was not integrated within the overall coordination exercise of the Committee of Governors. The inflationary risks associated with any relaxation of the ERM's reserve constraint *(Wyplosz 1989)* can only be kept in limits if there exists a clearly defined rule book for monetary coordination.
This leads to an alternative solution where the *Committee of Governors* is empowered to relieve a country from the intervention and asset settlement obligations of the ERM. With a commonly agreed framework for monetary

policy coordination the Committee would be able to define "*unwarranted speculative attacks*": As long as a country follows the "rules of the game" according to the McKinnon blueprint, there is no need to expose it to the disincentive of a reserve loss. A speculative attack on its currency should then be handled solely by the country with the strong currency; this could be achieved by the purchase of the weak currency by the central bank with the strong currency and the (temporary) suspension of the ERM asset settlement obligations. The country with the weak currency would have no obligation to support its own currency. This approach is superior to the ERF as the amount available for interventions is quantitatively unlimited and as it is integrated in the process of monetary integration in a way which excludes the support of currencies of countries with inflationary policies. Thus, the aim of simultaneously safeguarding price level stability and the functioning of the EMS in situations with short-run portfolio shifts calls for an integrated approach which combines an enhanced coordination of macroeconomic policy coordination with the intervention and asset settlement rules of the EMS:

- As long as countries follow the "rules of the game", the stabilization of exchange rates would be achieved by a *modified* ERM. In this *symmetric* system, interventions would be executed by central banks with strong currencies only. The obligation of asset settlement would not be in force.
- For countries violating the "rules" by pursuing an inflationary policy stance, the present ERM rules (with the asymmetric reserve constraint) would apply.

It would be up to the Committee of Governors to decide whether the policy of a country is in line with the "rules of the game." Again, the Committee would have to base its decisions on a commonly agreed conceptual framework, but it should have the discretion to deviate from these rules in situations with financial shocks. If one wants to avoid that this discretion is used to undermine the ERM discipline, it would be useful that the members of the Committee are given complete political independence from the outset.

2.4 What Are the Merits of Currency Competition?

The problems associated with intra-European portfolio shifts[13] are the most compelling argument against a process of currency competition which underlies the British alternative to the Delors Committee Report.[14] In addition to their negative implications on the stability of the EMS, such speculative shocks can also distort the *market determined coordination* of monetary policies and loosen the nominal anchor of the system. These problems of any market coordination, which is based on the intervention and asset settlement rules of a fixed rate system, are completely overlooked by the British proposal.

The *anchor role* of the country with the lowest inflation rate requires a trend appreciation of its currency vis-a-vis the currencies of countries with higher inflation rates. Only then, the sanction of a reserve loss or a devaluation is exerted on high-inflation countries. The experience with internationally mobile reserve and investment currencies (Dollar, Yen, Pound Sterling, D-Mark) demonstrates that inflation differentials are a rather unreliable determinant of exchange rate paths - even in the medium and longer run. In a fixed rate system, nominal appreciations of high- inflation currencies are identical with a loosening of the nominal anchor of the system. The unlimited trust of the Treasury in foreign exchange market participants as arbitrators of European monetary policies is difficult to reconcile with the evident failure of *purchasing power parity theory* of exchange rates in the last 15 years.

A further drawback of the British case for stage one as a permanent arrangement for monetary coordination in Europe results from the unclear relationship between the *direct* coordination process, which is decided by the Committee of Governors, and the *indirect* coordination process of the ERM, which is determined by the country with the strongest currency.

Like the Delors Committee Report, the Treasury's proposal does not discuss the interplay of these two coordination mechanisms and assumes a dominance of market coordination. A priori, it cannot be excluded, however, that the market coordination of the ERM will be interfered by the *authority coordination* of the Committee of Governors. It is, therefore, an open question whether a perpetuation of stage one with a political dependent institution in the center of the coordination process is really in the interest of the British Treasury, which explicitly emphasizes the target of price stability.

3. Open Questions of Stage 2

With the establishment of the ESCB, the need for a coherent conceptual framework becomes even more urgent. Although no transfer of national competencies is scheduled in stage two, the institutional upgrading of the arbitrator will strengthen its influence on the conduct of monetary policies in Europe. As the Delors Committee Report does not call for a modification of the ERM rules in this stage, it is still necessary to safeguard the system against "unwarranted" speculative attacks. Because of the far-reaching *functional identity* of stages one and two, the main arguments of the preceding section also apply to stage two. Only in one respect, stage two is superior to stage one: the ESCB as an independent institution would be better suited for the coordination task than a Committee which consists almost completely of dependent central bank governors. However, this advantage does not necessarily call for the establishment of an ESCB. It would suffice to grant an adequate degree of autonomy to national central banks and to their governors.

The most important unresolved issue of stage two concerns the alleged need of an *intermediate institutional stage*, which would be characterized by a coexistence of a full-fledged European Central Bank System and autonomous national central banks. This raises two questions:

- Is a *training* period for the ESCB really necessary?
- Is a *sharing of responsibilities* in the field of monetary policy compatible with the autonomy of national central banks?

3.1 Is There a Need For an ESCB Without Responsibilities?

According to the Delors Committee Report, stage two will "primarily constitute a training process leading to a collective decision-making, while the ultimate responsibility for policy decisions would remain at this stage with national authorities." (para. 55). However, the Report does not explain this need for a training period. *Gros and Thygesen (1989, p. 42)*, which subscribe this position of the Delors Committee mention three arguments, which in their opinion call for a "learning process in the absence of which we doubt whether the final step could be taken":

- "a consensus on the specific formulation of the ultimate objective(s),

- a common analytical framework for intermediate objectives and for the design of monetary policy, and

- a sufficient degree of experience with common operations."[15]

The first two arguments point to the conceptual vacuum of the present plans, but these tasks have to be tackled already in stage one and they do not require the establishment of a complete European Central Bank System, especially as the Committee of Governors will be given a Monetary Policy Committee and a permanent research staff. The third argument in favor of an institutional intermediate stage seems plausible, but it depends on the projected *organizational structure* of the ESCB in stage three.

A *direct transition* from stage one to stage three could be achieved if the final ESCB would have a federative structure. The Delors Committee Report (para. 32) is evidently in favor of a decentralized system:

- "the ESCB Council would be responsible for the formulation of and decisions on the thrust of monetary policy,"

- the ESCB Board would monitor monetary developments and oversee the implementation "of the common monetary policy,"

- national central banks "would execute operations in accordance with the decisions taken by the ESCB council."

With the entry in such a final stage, the non-mandatory recommendations of the Committee of Governors (stage one) and of the ESCB Council (stage two) would be substituted by instructions of the ESCB Council,[16] which are absolutely binding for the national central banks. This transfer of responsibilities from the national to the Community level would have no direct implications for the interface between central banks and commercial banks.

Thus, the need for a training period of the ESCB is only obvious if a rather centralized system is aimed at, where specific banking functions are assigned to the central institution (ESCB Board).[17] As this structure is contrary to the outline of the Delors Committee report, its blueprint of stage two and the final stage is not consistent.

Irrespective of the organizational structure of the final stage, the advantages of a "big leap" from stage one to stage three can be also demonstrated if one analyses the present plans for the division of labour between the ESCB and the national central banks in stage two.

3.2 The ESCB as a Joint Subsidiary of National Central Banks?

Lamfalussy (1989) proposes the creation of the ESCB as a joint subsidiary of the existing national central banks.[18] In stage two, the facilities of the ESCB should be shared in performing important central bank functions ("notably the implementation of monetary policy through the domestic and foreign exchange markets"[19]). In spite of the common technical facilities, "individual member central banks would retain ultimate responsibility for the deployment of their national foreign exchange reserves, and for the supply of domestic bank reserves."[20]

As the subsidiary is given a mere *technical function*, its creation would have no direct implications on the process of monetary coordination in Europe and cannot be analyzed under these aspects.

The main advantages of this scheme would consist in the increased transparency of national central bank operations for all participating central banks, the enhanced level of trust and understanding among the staffs of member central banks, and in the political demonstration of the resolve to the goal of monetary union. The using of shared facilities could thus be regarded as a central element of the training process the Delors Committee Report asks for.

Like any implementation of an intermediate institutional stage, Lamfalussy's proposal is flawed by the fact that a joint technical facility for the execution of monetary policy in Europe is only compatible with an extremely centralized European Central Bank System, which does not correspond to the outline of the ESCB in the Delors Report.[21] Already in stage two, the centralization of central bank operations would be much more pronounced than in the German or the U.S. central bank system.[22]

Of course, the final target of an ESCB could be modified along the lines of the Lamfalussy proposal. But as long as the Delors Committee Report is regarded as the basis for further progress, the plan of a joint technical facility is leading into the wrong direction.

From a more technical perspective, the plan has the disadvantage that the common operative unit would be regionally separated from most markets where it executes its transactions. In addition, the proposal requires a politically difficult decision for a financial center hosting the ESCB's operations, which would be unnecessary under a federatively structured system. In the United States, for instance, the Board of Governors is located in Washington, DC, which is no financial center at all, and even in Italy, foreign exchange market interventions of the Banca d'Italia are executed at the Milan and Rome markets *(Bini Smaghi 1989, p. 35)*.

3.3 Can Monetary Policy Responsibilities Be Divided in Stage Two?

More ambitious approaches combine this technical arrangement with specific responsibilities of the ESCB already in stage two. Proposals for an early transfer of national responsibilities were made by the *Padoa-Schioppa Committee Report (1987)* and a recent paper of *Gros and Thygesen (1989)*. These authors suggest a limited division of monetary policy responsibilities between the ESCB and the national central banks. For stage two, they consider a possible pooling of three instruments within an ESCB:

- adjustment of short-term interest rate differentials,
- intervention policy vis-a-vis third currencies,
- the imposition of and changes in reserve requirements for national central banks or commercial banks, which should be held with the ESCB; this proposal was originally made by *Ciampi (1989)*.

In the following sections, it will be analyzed whether it is possible to define a clear assignment of responsibilities in these three areas, which is compatible with a federative structure of the ESCB in stage three and which leaves national central banks a sufficient control over their own monetary aggregates.

3.3.1 ESCB Management of Interest Rate Differentials

A precise description of the ESCB's management of short-term interest rate differentials and its interrelationship with national interest rate policies can be found neither in the Padoa-Schioppa Committee Report[23] nor in the paper of Gros and Thygesen. The latter call for a "gradual and partial upgrading of decision making on relative interest rate adjustment from the purely national level to a Community body"[24] in stage two, but emphasize at the same time that "decision-making in this sensitive area would still remain in national hands".[25]

There is no doubt that variations of money market rates constitute at present the main monetary policy instrument of all European central banks. After an assignment of responsibilities in this field to the ESCB, national authorities would have lost the ability to control the money supply process at the national level. Thus, a *pooling* of this instrument within the ESCB would be identical with a far-reaching transfer of responsibilities from national central banks to the ESCB, which the Delors Committee Report does not suggest for stage two.

It is also obvious that a *sharing* of responsibilities in this field is not possible. In the case of the Federal Republic, for instance, it will be either the Bundesbank's *Zentralbankrat* or the ESCB Council which must have the final say in the determination of the Bundesbank's lending rates.[26] This does not exclude a surveillance of the Bundesbank's policy by the ESCB and a possible sanction by a public statement of the ESCB Chairman along the lines of the general coordination process, but it is incompatible with an additional pooling of responsibilities in the field of interest policy within the ESCB.

3.3.2 Third Currency Interventions by the ESCB

Gros and Thygesen explain a genuine decision-making power of the ESCB in the area of intervention vis-a-vis third currencies with the need to avoid major misalignments and to smooth the short-term volatility of exchange rates, especially as dollar movements have a tendency to cause "unwarranted" intra ERM exchange rate movements.

A responsibility of the ESCB in this field could take two different forms:

- A certain amount of national reserves[27] could be transferred to the ESCB which it uses for interventions on its own account. In this case, national central banks would still have the right to decide on their own interventions. This arrangement would be an extension of the Lamfalussy proposal and thus be advisable only if the ESCB is to be given a centralized structure in stage three.

- The ESCB could be assigned the responsibility to determine the dollar (and other third currency) interventions of national central banks, which would be executed exclusively by these institutions. This solution could be adequate if a decentralized ESCB is aimed at in the final stage.

As the EC countries' aggregate gross foreign exchange reserves total about SDR 190 billion, a *pooling of reserves* in the order of magnitude of 10-20% would result in a portfolio of the ESCB of SDR 19-38 billion. The ESCB could use this assets, which are mainly denominated in dollar, in order to support individual EC countries, especially in periods of a strong dollar. Such interventions would substitute its dollar assets against assets denominated in individual European currencies. In order to prevent intra-ERM interventions under the disguise of third currency interventions, the ESCB should be obliged to maintain a *portfolio structure of European currencies* which is identical with the currencies' share in the ECU basket. With this important safeguard, a weakening of the ERM discipline by unilateral ESCB interventions could be avoided. At the same time, it would be ruled out that the ESCB uses its interventions in order to undermine the monetary stance of specific national central banks. Because of the large amount of available resources, the ESCB could, however, exercise an important influence on the *aggregate* thrust of European monetary policy already in stage two.

If a balanced composition of the ESCB's portfolio of European currencies were granted, a limited pooling of reserves within the ESCB and a common intervention policy of this institution would not be incompatible with the Delors Committee Report's imperative which says that "the ultimate responsibility for policy decisions would remain at this stage with national authorities."[28]

The alternative solution of a complete responsibility of the ESCB for third currency interventions, which would be formally executed by national central banks, might be adequate if an ESCB with a decentralized organizational structure is the final objective of the integration process. Under this arrangement, the lack of any quantitative limit on the ESCB's "masse de manoeuvre" would make it much more difficult for national central banks to control their money supply autonomously. It would also be impossible to protect national central banks against an unilateral ESCB interference by determining a rule prescribing a balanced composition of the ESCB's intervention activities:

Depending on the underlying portfolio shift on financial markets, it could be necessary to sell a more than proportionate amount of D-Marks in order to achieve a certain exchange rate target of the ECU vis-a-vis the dollar. As long as the ESCB's interventions only supplement the dollar interventions of national central banks ("limited pooling of reserves"), the equilibrium can be reached by larger sales of the central bank, which is mostly affected by the portfolio shift. With a sole responsibility of the ESCB for third currency interventions, an exchange rate targeting would not be compatible with a rule prescribing a rigid currency structure of its foreign exchange market sales or purchases.

In sum, any transfer of responsibilities in the field of third currency interventions requires a clear definition of the organizational structure of the final ESCB. Direct foreign exchange market interventions of the ESCB in stage two are neither necessary nor appropriate if the objective in stage three is a decentralized system where interventions are still carried out by national central banks - albeit under the aegis of the ESCB. With a complete responsibility of the ESCB for third currency interventions already in stage two, the national control over the money supply could be seriously undermined which contradicts the Delors Committee's outline of stage two.

3.3.3 Minimum Reserve Policy of the ESCB

The proposals for a minimum reserve policy of the ESCB encompass two different approaches:

- A minimum reserve requirement for European *central banks*, which would have to hold ECU reserves with the ESCB according to the domestic credit component of their monetary base or their total monetary base. This plan has been elaborated in detail by *Ciampi (1989)*.

- An EC-wide minimum reserve obligation for national *commercial banks*, which would complement national reserve systems. The reserve requirement would be imposed on the deposits of commercial banks. The banks would have to hold ESCB deposits with the ESCB.

3.3.3.1 ECU Minimum Reserve Requirements for Central Banks

Ciampi's outline of "an operational framework for an integrated monetary policy in Europe" suggests a minimum reserve system for national central banks which would be obliged to hold ECU deposits with the ESCB. Analogous to national reserve schemes, the ESCB would provide national central banks with high powered ECU assets, the supply of which is under its firm control. The ESCB Council would decide each year in advance "how much money and credit should be created overall in the Community in order to support economic activity in a non-inflationary environment. This target would then be translated into a figure for the central monetary institution's ECU supply."[29] Because of the obligation to hold reserves with the ESCB, national central banks would be tied in their policy to the overall target of the ESCB. The reserve requirements could be calculated either according to their credits to commercial banks or their total monetary base. In the first case, central banks would be free to create domestic money by foreign exchange market interventions. In the second case, they could intervene only to the extent that they sterilize the liquidity impact of the interventions by changes in the domestic credit component.

The proposal has two drawbacks. First, the analogy to the national reserve regime is flawed. Second, it does not discuss the sanctions which have to be applied if a central bank does not meet its reserve requirement.

1. It is quite obvious that the scheme leaves central banks the discretion to expand their monetary base (or the domestic credit component of the base) *less* than the target rate envisaged by the ESCB. Such a policy would result in free reserves held by the respective central bank. Whereas in the domestic banking system, a stock of non-interest bearing free reserves is an incentive for individual commercial banks to increase their lending activities, a non-profit maximizing central bank cannot be compelled by this mechanism to pursue a more expansionary monetary policy.

2. In case of an *over-expansion* of the base or the domestic component of the base, an ESCB reserve system is only superior to the general coordination procedure scheduled for stages one and two, if the infraction of the reserve requirement leads to *specific* sanctions going beyond the loss of reputation associated with a violation of the general recommendations of the Committee of Governors or the ESCB. In the domestic context, commercial banks, which do not meet their reserve requirement have to pay higher interest rates for central bank credit and may even lose their banking license. The question of adequate sanctions, which are difficult to conceive in the relationship with central banks, is neglected by Ciampi as well as by Gros and Thygesen. In contrast, Ciampi suggests a rather informal character of the new instrument, at least for stage two.[30]

On the whole, an ECU reserve system for national central banks, especially if it does not define specific sanctions, will only complicate the monetary management in Europe without enhancing the overall coordination process projected for stage two. It is also not suited to serve as a training process for the final stage: In this stage, the system would become unnecessary as the ESCB Council would have the power to instruct national central banks directly to follow certain quantitative targets.

3.3.3.2 ECU Minimum Reserve Requirements for Commercial Banks in Europe

An alternative scheme proposed by Gros and Thygesen envisages a uniform European reserve requirement on *commercial bank* deposits or on the increase thereof. European commercial banks would be obliged to hold a "small fraction" of their deposits as ECU reserves with the ESCB. In this case, the ESCB would open an EC-wide ECU refinancing facility (open market policy) for the banks. Again, the assessment of this proposal crucially depends on the *sanctions* imposed on banks which do not meet their reserve requirement. If the same severe sanctions were applied as in the domestic context, the ESCB could exert a very strong influence on the growth of monetary aggregates in EC countries (even with a low ECU reserve ratio). It could *restrain* the monetary expansion of individual countries by determining a restrictive mix of ECU base money supply and ECU reserve ratio. It would be difficult, however, to use the reserve scheme in the opposite direction as commercial banks are only constrained by their national reserve obligations.

The implementation of this variant of a European minimum reserve system would give the ESCB a very powerful tool to limit the monetary expansion in individual member countries. As the ESCB can keep its ECU supply tight, the system will work in this direction even with relatively low reserve ratios. Thus, its influence on national monetary policies does not depend on the absolute level of reserve ratios. Like a policy of determining relative interest rates, this far-reaching influence of the ESCB on monetary conditions in individual member countries is difficult to reconcile with the autonomy of national central banks envisaged in the Delors Committee Report for stage two.

3.4 An Integrated Approach

The discussion of different options for stage two shows that it is not only difficult to make a case for a training period of the ESCB, if a relatively decentralized ESCB is aimed at in stage three, but that it is also almost impossible to find an assignment of tasks between the ESCB and national central banks which leaves the ultimate responsibility for monetary policy with national authorities and which at the same time provides a sufficient training ground for the ESCB.

These considerations and the flaws of the present outline of stage one call for an *integration* of stages one and two,

- which is characterized by an autonomous status of the Committee of Governors comparable with the projected status of the ESCB,

- which includes the option of a modified EMS, which would be better protected against "unwarranted speculative attacks",

- which enlarges the responsibilities of the Committee, especially by assigning to it the power to modify the EMS rules, whenever a central bank does not comply with its recommendations (section 2.3), and

- which obliges the Committee to use its responsibilities (sanction of individual member countries by public declarations, suspension of ERM asset settlement) only after it has developed a comprehensive conceptual framework including the internal and external dimension of its coordination exercise.

From this enhanced stage one a direct transition to an ESCB with a decentralized organizational structure would be possible without a specific training period. National central banks would continue to execute all transactions with their commercial banks but they would have to follow the ESCB's decisions on interest rates, minimum reserve ratios etc.

4. Conclusions

The analysis of central elements of the Delors Committee's blueprint of monetary coordination during the process to EMU shows inconsistencies and many unresolved issues. However, the critical assessment does not call for an abandonment of the whole integration strategy or for the British alternative of a European currency competition. But it suggests that the time is not ripe for a rapid amendment of the EEC treaty determining the institutional stages two and three.

What is needed in the immediate future, is above all a comprehensive conceptual framework for an overall European monetary policy and its implementation at the national level. Only on this basis, it will be possible to define the functions of the Committee of Governors, to clarify the interplay between the EMS (indirect) coordination and the (direct) coordination effectuated by the Committee and to devise safeguards against speculative attacks on the EMS in the pre-EMU stage(s). It has been demonstrated that an (institutional) stage two is advisable only if a rather centralized ESCB is envisaged for the final stage. Although the outline of the Delors Committee Report evidently favors decentralization and the principle of "subsidiarity", its argument for an intermediate institutional stage and the various proposals for a "pooling" of responsibilities or functions put forward in related papers indicate that this issue is still unresolved. If the rule book for European monetary coordination (including adequate sanctions) has been agreed in stage one, it is difficult to see that the coordination process could be improved by introducing the minimum reserve proposal developed by Ciampi or other forms of a pooling of responsibilities in the monetary field.

Endnotes

1. Report, para. 52.

2. The final version of the new mandate determining the tasks and competencies of the Council of Governors was agreed in March 1990 by the Council of Economic and Finance Ministers.

3. The "importance of reputation as an incentive to conform to standards in world politics" is emphasized by *Keohane (1984)*. "The dilemmas of collective action are partially solved through the device of reputation. Unlike the costs of establishing bad precedents, the costs of acquiring a bad reputation as a result of rule-violations are imposed specifically on the transgressor. As long as a continuing series of issues is expected to arise in the future, and as long as actors monitor each other's behavior and discount the value of agreements on the basis of past compliance, having a good reputation is valuable even to the egoist whose role in collective action is so small that she would bear few of the costs of her own malefactions." (p. 105).

4. Council Decision amending Council Decision 64/300 EEC on cooperation between the Central Banks of the Member States of the European Community.

5. *Schlesinger and Jahnke (1987)* estimate a lag of eleven quarters for the Federal Republic.

6. See *Bradley and Jansen (1989)*.

7. See *Bini Smaghi (1989, p. 40-44)* with a survey on game theoretic and collective action literature emphasizing the disadvantages of ad-hoc coordination.

8. The German Governor, Karl Otto Poehl is the only exception.

9. The alternative is an *externally imposed rule*, for instance, a constitutional obligation to follow an n-percent rule.

10. See the detailed analysis of *Russo and Tullio (1988)* and *Thygesen (1989)*.

11. The German demand for money is rather stable (see e.g. *Smeets 1989*).

12. *Giovannini (1990)* sees additional problems because of a possible currency substitution within Europe. Experience from hyperinflations shows, however, that currencies are only substituted by currencies with lower inflation rates if national inflation rates become astronomically high.

13. See *EC-Commission (1990)*.

14. See also *Currie (1989)*.

15. *Gros and Thygesen (1989, p. 42)*.

16. The ESCB Council, which would be composed of the Governors of the central banks and the members of the ESCB Board, would be responsible for the formulation of and decisions on the thrust of monetary policy; (Report, para. 32).

17. This is the case in the German system, where the Bundesbank Act (section 7) reserves the following transactions for the Bundesbank's Directorate:
- transactions with the Federal Government and its special funds,
- transactions with banks that have central functions in the whole of the Federal territory,
- foreign exchange transactions and external transactions
- open market operations.

18. The historical antecedent of this proposal is the German postwar system from 1948-1957, where the central institution (*Bank deutscher Lander*) was a joint subsidiary of the legally independent regional units (*Landeszentralbanken*). All decisions in this monetary order were taken by a common institution (*Zentralbankrat*), which was composed of the Presidents of the Landeszentralbanken and the President and Vice-President of the Bank deutscher Lander.

19. *Lamfalussy (1989, p. 214).*

20. *Lamfalussy (1989, p. 214).*

21. Especially in the Federal Republic, a federative structure of an ESCB is regarded as an essential precondition for the transition to an EMU; see *Kloten (1988)* and *Poehl (1989, p. 137).*

22. In both systems, most domestic operations are carried out by the individual regional units.

23. This report calls for a management of national interest rates by the Committee of Governors.

24. *Gros and Thygesen (1989, p. 48).*

25. *Gros and Thygesen (1989, p. 48).*

26. A proposal of *Bini Smaghi (1989, p. 34)* suggests that "any change in national interest rates decided by a member country would be subject to the condition that partners be previously informed and an exchange of opinions take place; the announcement to market participants would be made through a joint communique, similarly to what presently occurs for exchange rate realignments within the ERM." In the German institutional setting, where the Zentralbankrat decides on interest rate changes on its biweekly meetings, this requirement would lead to an extremely long reaction lag of monetary policy.

27. *Gros and Thygesen (1989, p. 50)* suggest a percentage of 10-20%.

28. Report, para. 55.

29. *Ciampi (1989, p. 229-230).*

30. *Ciampi (1989, p. 231)*: "At an *intermediate* stage of the process, when national central banks still have primary monetary responsibility, some flexibility in the supply of official ECUs and in the way it is linked to the creation of high-powered national money would allow national member central banks to expand or contract the money supply in their countries without being rigidly tied to their ECU reserves. In these conditions, ECU operations carried out by the ESCB using the mechanism described above would serve primarily to highlight, and in part counter, divergences by individual central banks from the commonly agreed monetary and credit objectives of the Community."

References

BINI SMAGHI, LORENZO (1989). Progressing towards European Monetary Unification: Selected Issues and Proposals, unpublished paper.

BARRO, ROBERT and DAVID GORDON (1983). A Positive Theory of Monetary Policy in a Natural Rate Model. Journal of Political Economy, 91, 589-610.

BRADLEY, MICHAEL and DENNIS JANSEN (1989).. Understanding Nominal GNP Targeting. Review. Federal Reserve Bank of St. Louis, 71(6), 31-40.

BOFINGER, PETER (1989a). The EMS and Monetary Policy Coordination in Europe. SUERF Papers on Monetary Policy and Financial Systems, 7, Tilburg.

BOFINGER, PETER (1989b). European and International Monetary Cooperation: The Need for an Integrated Approach. Paper Prepared for a Conference on Reforming the International Monetary System on September 30, 1989 in Hamburg.

BRITISH TREASURY (1989). An Evolutionary Approach to EMU.

BRUNNER, KARL (1984). Monetary Policy and Monetary Order. Aussenwirtschaft, 39, 187-206.

CIAMPI, C.A. (1989). An Operational Framework for an Integrated Monetary Policy in Europe, in: Committee for the Study of Economic and Monetary Union, 225-232.

COMMITTEE FOR THE STUDY OF ECONOMIC AND MONETARY UNION (1989). Report on Economic and Monetary Union in the European Community, Luxembourg.

CURRIE, DAVID (1989). European Monetary Union or Competing Currencies: Which Way for Monetary Integration in Europe. Economic Outlook, London Business School, October 1989, 18-24.

EC - COMMISSION (1990). Report on Economic and Monetary Union.

EMMINGER, OTMAR (1986). D-Mark, Dollar, Waehrungskrisen, Stuttgart.

GIOVANNINI, ALBERTO (1990). Money Demand and Monetary Control in an Integrated European Economy, mimeo.

KEOHANE, ROBERT (1984). After Hegemony, Princeton.

KLOTEN, NORBERT (1989). The Delors Report: A Blueprint For European Integration? The World Today, 45(11), 191-194.

LAMFALUSSY, A. (1989). A Proposal for Stage Two Under Which Monetary Policy Operations Would Be Centralized In a Jointly-owned Subsidiary, in: Committee for the Study of Economic and Monetary Union, 213-219.

MCKINNON, RONALD (1988). Monetary and Exchange Rate Policies for International Financial Stability: A Proposal. Journal of Economic Perspectives, 2, 83-104.

PADOA-SCHIOPPA COMMITTEE REPORT (1987). Efficiency, Stability and Equity: A Strategy for the Evolution of the Economic System of the European Community, Oxford.

POEHL, KARL OTTO (1989). The Further Development of the European Monetary System, in: Committee for the Study of Economic and Monetary Union, 129-155.

PORTES, RICHARD (1989). Macroeconomic Policy, Coordination and the European Monetary System. CEPR Discussion Paper Series, 342.

RUSSO, MASSIMO and GUISEPPE TULLIO (1988). Monetary Cooperation Within the European Monetary System: Is There a Rule? IMF Occasional Paper, 61, 41-82.

SCHLESINGER, HELMUT and WILFRIED JAHNKE (1987). Geldmenge, Preise and Sozialprodukt. Jahrbucher fuer Nationaloekonomie and Statistik, 205, 410-426.

SPINELLI, FRANCO (1983). Currency Substitution, Flexible Exchange Rates, and the Case for International Monetary Cooperation. IMF Staff Papers, 30, 755-783.

THYGESEN, NIELS (1989). A European Central Banking System, in: Committee for the Study of Economic and Monetary Union, 157-175.

THYGESEN, NIELS and DANIEL GROS (1989). Concrete Steps Towards Monetary Union. Paper presented at CEPS Sixth Annual Conference 1989.

VAUBEL, ROLAND (1989). Ueberholte Glaubenssaetze. Wirtschaftsdienst, June 1989, 276-279.

WILLIAMSON, JOHN and MARCUS MILLER (1987). Targets and Indicators: A Blueprint for the International Coordination of Economic Policy. Policy Analyses in International Economics, 22, Washington, D.C.: Institute For International Economics.

WYPLOSZ, CHARLES (1989). Asymmetry in the EMS. European Economic Review, 33, 310-320.

*Horst Ungerer**

Comments on:
Problems of Monetary Policy Coordination in the Transition Phase

1. In his many contributions to the discussion of European monetary issues, Peter Bofinger has frequently shown a particular interest in the interrelationship between the conceptual, institutional, and procedural framework of monetary policy on the one hand and the macroeconomic aspects of monetary policy on the other hand. I agree that it is important to think about how general policy strategies and macroeconomic objectives can be translated into viable institutional structures and, eventually, into actual monetary policy decisions.

Bofinger took a close look at the Delors Report. He is pointing at certain gaps--he calls it "blind spots"--and inconsistencies which appear to exist in the Delors Report's design of a new European monetary order. He approaches the proposals of the Delors Report from the angles of the monetary policy objective of price stability and of the stability of the EMS as it is operating today. It would go beyond the scope of this contribution to discuss extensively all the points he is making. Instead I shall just make a few remarks on his paper.

2. Bofinger starts with a discussion of the institutional changes which will or have come about as a result of the decision of the European Council in Madrid in June 1989 to start the first stage of moving toward Economic and Monetary Union (EMU) on July 1 of this year.

There are people who think that the provisions for the first stage are somehow "business as usual." In contrast, Bofinger stresses in particular the possibility that the Chairman of the Committee of Central Bank Governors can sanction individual countries which stray from the path of monetary virtue by making the conclusions of the Committee public, and in this way destroy their reputation. The sanction, he says, could result in capital outflows, loss of reserves, and a possible devaluation of the currency concerned, and thus induce them to shape up.

In my view, such potential adverse developments may be exactly the reason why this sanction of public condemnation may not be used, except in very serious cases. While the Committee in its internal deliberations may heavily criticize an aberrant country and "express an opinion to it," as envisaged in the amended mandate of the Committee, the Committee may be quite reluctant to authorize its Chairman to go public, even if formally this authorization could be granted by a simple majority. Concern about the stability of the EMS, and about possible exaggerated reactions of the markets, will make the Committee very careful. In particular, it will want to avoid damaging a central bank's credibility which, after all, will be needed to successfully implement a better and more credible policy.

Having said this, I don't want to deny (and I actually hope) that the mere existence of such a sanction will be of influence and make peer pressure within the group of EC central banks more effective.

3. I come now to the subject of the "rules of the game." Bofinger deplores that this has been a "blind spot" in the Delors Report. Did he not expect too much from a committee which met only a few times over a period of six or seven months?

I found in the Delors Report some broad rules which will be important for creating EMU and will give meaning also to the transitional phase: a. The Council of the future European System of Central Banks (ESCB) "should be independent of instructions from national governments and Community authorities" (Delors Report, p. 26); and b. "The system would be committed to the objective of price stability" (p. 25).

These are two important and interrelated "Rahmenbedingungen" - framework conditions - for any monetary order, whether national or European. Many influential central bankers see it this way (*Ciampi, 1989; Duisenberg, 1989; Doyle, 1990; Poehl, 1990; de Larosière, 1990*).

In this connection, it may be of interest to take note of a recent study by *Alberto Alesina (1989)*, who explored the interconnections between politics and macroeconomics. He found a positive relationship between the degree of independence of a central bank and the inflation rate: for the period 1973-86, among 17 industrialized countries, the four most independent central banks

(Japan, the United States, and, in particular, Germany and Switzerland) have been associated with four of the five lowest inflation rates.

4. Bofinger refers, of course, to the transitional phase. But I feel, that the two "constitutional rules" will provide a good basis for the development of the "rules of the game" in a more narrow sense and are therefore also relevant for the transitional phase. This brings me to the choice of intermediate targets for monetary policy. I would like to concentrate on targets expressed in monetary terms.

I see some problems with perpetuating the present EMS practice of using the monetary target of the center country as the "anchor" to which the other countries are tied by means of asymmetrical interventions. You may recall the "asymmetry debate" among EMS countries in 1988 and 1989 which was initiated by France and Italy (*Balladur, 1988; Amato, 1988*). While an important concern was political, there were also economic arguments. There was a concern--and I think a legitimate concern--that the monetary policy which is right for one country is not necessarily equally right for countries with different economic structures and circumstances.

Whatever the merit of the debate--and there exists a whole literature--, it seems clear that an asymmetrical rule could not form a politically acceptable basis for sanctions as mentioned above or the suspension of settlement obligations as discussed later on.

With regard to common monetary targeting, that is, a strategy to stabilize aggregate monetary growth in the EC, I feel Bofinger dismisses this possibility a bit too easily. In a recent study, *Kremers and Lane (1990)* came to a different conclusion. May I quote: "The finding that . . . a well-specified ERM-wide demand for money can be identified, is striking: it suggests that monetary policy guided by money supply targets would, at least in principle, be feasible for the ERM countries collectively."

I would not want to blindly endorse the findings of Kremers and Lane. Clearly, much more work needs to be done and is actually being done. In this field lies an important task for the Committee of Governors, its Monetary Policy

Committee, and its research staff which is being assembled. Work on such problems needs to be carried on and intensified once the ESCB has been set up. This is one of the reasons--but not the only one--why the second stage of the Delors Report makes sense to me.

5. In another section, Bofinger concentrates on an important and widely discussed question: Can the EMS, as it operates now, be expected to successfully cope with possible adverse consequences of the liberalization of capital movements in the EC? He seems to join those who doubt whether EMS stability can be preserved (e.g., *Padoa-Schioppa, 1987*). He differentiates between "warranted" and "unwarranted" speculative attacks and proposes to deal with the latter by suspending settlement obligations resulting from market intervention, and in this way to avoid penalizing the well behaving country which became subject to unwarranted attacks.

I have a number of observations:

Would it be possible, even if the Committee of Governors agrees on a definition of "well behaving" and "unwarranted," to make such a differentiation at the time of a speculative attack? Monetary policy may be well intended but--in view of the inevitable time lag between taking decisions and their results--whether specific measures will bite, whether there will be overshooting or undershooting, will become apparent only much later. In the meantime, intervention will have taken place, credit facilities will have been employed, and settlement questions will arise.

Generally, my view is--and this is confirmed by the experience in the EMS in various periods of crisis: March 1983, January 1987, October 1987, August 1988--that the existing credit facilities are large and flexible enough to cope with speculative attacks. Additionally, the Basle/Nyborg agreement of September 1987 provided a framework for flexible response by means of coordinated interest rate policies and flexible use of the fluctuation margins which has been employed successfully, in particular, in October 1987. Lastly, also as regards settlement, the EMS Agreement provides flexibility which, at times in the past, has been put to good use. For these reasons, we don't need an additional rule.

With regard to the underlying issue, whether the liberalization of capital movements will destabilize the EMS, I want to mention that there are several authors who don't see a pronounced risk (*Dribill, 1988; McDonald and Zis, 1989; Joerg Mayer, 1989; Schroeder, 1989*). The basic arguments behind this view, which I tend to share, are the following:

- The achieved degree of economic convergence and credibility of central banks participating in the ERM makes speculative attacks less likely than in the past.

- The possibility of small realignments without changes in market rates (as practiced in January 1987 and January 1990) makes speculation less rewarding.

- Liberalization will exert pressure to reinforce the coordination of monetary policies, in particular interest rate policy, and will by itself enhance the credibility of central banks and the attractiveness of a currency being liberalized.

I would agree that the jury is still out, but the most recent experience with the capital liberalization in France and in Italy seems to prove that fears of destabilization might be unfounded.

In sum: I don't see great risks of speculative attacks, provided--and this is important--the efforts toward more convergence continue unabated. Should speculative attacks occur, the system is well equipped to cope with them.

6. The last question I want to comment upon is whether Stage II of the Delors Report is needed or not. There are quite a few voices who would agree with Bofinger in this respect, although for some the ulterior motives might be more of a political than economic and operational nature.

I just want to put forward the following arguments why in my own view a Stage II will be very useful if not necessary:

- The conceptual framework for a common monetary policy needs to be developed and perfected by the institution which later on will implement it. This should be done in Stage II; in this way in Stage III, the ESCB will hit the ground running.

- The ESCB needs to be built before it can operate effectively: working groups and committees; channels of information and cooperation with national central banks and so on; the creation of a staff; even the construction of a headquarters building requires time.

- An already established ESCB will make later on a common policy more credible, not less. Unless the system establishes early on a reputation as a "hard-nosed institution," the ESCB would have no business in acquiring the sweeping powers of Stage III.

- The time in Stage II will also be needed to modify the organizational structures and decision-making processes of the national central banks so as to conform with a European system. Among other things, there should be a move toward more independence of existing national central banks. How could otherwise the Council of the ESCB be truly independent of government instructions?

- Further progress needs to be made to narrow differences in the structures of national banking systems and financial markets, and in the harmonization of central bank instruments. This would alleviate the implementation of commonly decided policies on a national level.

It is my impression that it was quite deliberate that the Delors Committee left the latter question largely open. The members of the Committee probably felt that there was no point in discussing in detail monetary policy instruments and operations which later might become obsolete, in view of the rapid changes of financial markets and techniques.

Endnotes

* *The views expressed are those of the author and do not necessarily reflect those of the IMF.*

References

ALESINA, ALBERTO (1989) Politics and Business Cycles in Industrial Democracies. Economic Policy, April.

AMATO, GIULIANO.(1988) Un motore per lo Sme. Il Sole - 24 Ore, Milan, February 15.

BALLADUR, EDOUARD (1988) Mémorandum sur la construction monétaire européenne. ECU No. 3, Brussels, March.

CIAMPI, CARLO A. (1989) Lecture at the University of Macerata on November 29, 1989 in: BIS Review, December 13.

COMMISSION OF THE EUROPEAN COMMUNITIES (1989). Committee for the Study of Economic and Monetary Union. Report on Economic and Monetary Union in the European Community. Brussels.

DE LAROSIERE, JACQUES (1990). Les finalites et modalités de la creation d'un systeme européen de banques centrales. Intervention au 8e congrès du Comité des Syndicats des banques centrales européennes à Marne-la-Vallée, March 27, 1990 in: BIS Review, April 3.

DOYLE, MAURICE (1990). Economic and Monetary Union. Speech at the Association of Chartered Accountants. Cork, March 9, 1990 in: Deutsche Bundesbank Auszuege aus Presseartikeln, March 16.

DRIFILL, JOHN (1988). The Stability and Sustainability of the European Monetary System with Perfect Capital Markets, in: GIAVAZZI, ET AL (eds.), The European Monetary System, Cambridge.

DUISENBERG, W.F. (1989). Interview published in Finanz und Wirtschaft, October 11, 1989 (English translation) in: BIS Review, October 31.

KREMERS, JEROEN J.M. and LANE, TIMOTHY D. (1990). Economic and Monetary Integration and the Aggregate Demand for Money in the EMS. International Monetary Fund. Working Paper, WP/90/23, March (unpublished).

MAYER, JOERG (1989). Capital Controls in the EMS - A Survey. EPS Working Document No. 43, August.

MCDONALD, FRANK and ZIS, GEORGE (1988). The European Monetary System: Towards 1992 and Beyond. In Journal of Common Market Studies, XXVII(3), March.

PADOA-SCHIOPPA, TOMMASO (1988). The EMS: A Long-Term View, in: FRANCESCO GIAVAZZI, ET AL (eds.), The European Monetary System, Cambridge.

PÖHL, KARL OTTO (1990). Basic Features of a European Monetary Order, this volume.

Paul J.J. Welfens

CREATING A EUROPEAN CENTRAL BANK AFTER 1992: ISSUES OF EC MONETARY INTEGRATION AND PROBLEMS OF INSTITUTIONAL INNOVATION

1. Monetary and Real Integration in the EC

Founded at the end of the turbulent 1970s, the European Monetary System (EMS) goes into the 1990s with surprising (sometimes artificial) viability. Having successfully passed infancy in the 1980s the EMS now faces several challenges of adolescence, some of which are related to EC internal developments - above all "Project 1992", the elimination of capital controls and the shift to an Economic and Monetary Union (EMU) - and others which concern a rapidly changing global environment. In June 1988, the European Council entrusted the later so-called Delors Commission to prepare a report on economic and monetary union in the EC; the Delors report received support at the Madrid EC summit in June 1989 which adopted stage I of the report: the removal of capital controls and the strengthening of intra-EC policy coordination. The deliberations within the EC do not point to a basic consensus with respect to an institutional framework for an EC central bank - a dual speed monetary integration scheme in which major continental EC countries would adopt a stability-oriented common monetary policy under the leadership of the German Bundesbank (central bank) seems to be possible.

The EC Council meeting at end-March 1990 in Ashford Castle, Ireland, and the Dublin EC summit exposed the continuing rift between the stance of the hesitant British government, favoring a "hard ECU" as represented by an approach of monetary unification via the introduction of an ECU parallel currency, and the continental EC countries. The European Council agreed in Dublin to convene an intergovernmental conference in December 1990 to work out the Treaty amendments necessary for the completion of the economic and monetary union. The EC Council's decision on economic convergence of 1974 was amended in March 1990: in a first stage of greater monetary cooperation in the EC a progressive attainment of policy convergence is expected. The Council of Ministers will undertake a policy surveillance twice a year and the Committee of Central Bank Governors will assume a new role. The Committee will not only discuss principles of monetary policy but will also focus on issues that affect the stability of financial markets and the conduct of monetary policy - this implies that the Committee is to be consulted before monetary targets are set on the national level. Moreover, the Committee adopted a new set of rules of procedure - as of June 11, 1990 - where the extension of the duration of the chairmanship from one to three years and the creation of a new sub-structure were main points (sub-committees for monetary policy, for foreign exchange and for banking supervision). The EC summit of Oct. 28 in Rome proposed - against British opposition - to begin the second stage of EMU in 1994 and to issue a common ECU currency towards the end of the decade.

In contrast to many skeptical expectations the EMS has worked surprisingly well and has generated considerable momentum for further institutional change in Europe. Membership has been not only more stable than under the previous "snake regime" 1972-78 but there has been a gradual enlargement of the EMS and its integral part, the ERM (Exchange Rate Mechanism) which implies a commitment to pegging the exchange rate. The number of countries involved in the parity grid with bilateral margins of 2.25 percent - for Italy until January 8, 1990 and for Spain and the U.K. as of June 1989 and October 1990, respectively: +/- 6 percent - increased over the course of time. This occurred both by informal pegging schemes and implicit monetary cooperation as observed in Austria and Switzerland and by formal membership as in the case of the EC latecomers: Spain, Portugal and Greece; however, the latter two have yet to adhere to the ERM. In the 1980s downward inflation convergence was achieved as well as considerable exchange rate stability. Since the inception of the EMS on March 13, 1979 a total of 11 realignments have taken place, two in the years 1979, 1981 and 1982 (also in 1986) and then less frequently. More than three years of unchanged parities and increased central bank cooperation have followed the realignment of 1987.

With the Single European Act of 1985 that paved the way for the removal of all non-tariff barriers within the EC by 1992, the problem of monetary integration, already discussed in the Werner report of 1970, reemerged. A specific problem of EC integration concerns the extent to which "real integration" of goods and factor markets calls for monetary integration (and vice versa), defined on the one hand by shared institutions, rules and responsibilities in monetary policy and, on the other hand, by the removal of capital controls and more open financial market boundaries. The Delors report of 1989 emphasized parallelism between real and monetary integration, but it did not give a justification on the basis of theoretical merits nor did it focus on positive welfare effects related to static and dynamic efficiency or price stability and stable growth. With a rather optimistic perspective the Delors report develops a scenario which suggests that an EC-wide comprehensive monetary integration could be achieved in a three-stage approach of monetary cooperation and institutional integration that would ultimately lead to an EC central bank and a common currency. Thereby the policy instrument of exchange rate variations within the EC would no longer be available to achieve full employment of resources.

The topic must be raised whether expected benefits and risks of European monetary integration generate sufficient positive incentives for a sustaining monetary integration process. At the same time the ongoing real integration as represented by the convergence of national markets and a wave of intra-EC cross-border M&As that reflect the formation of "Euronationals" might support the integration of financial markets and hence influence the monetary integration process (*Welfens, 1990b*).

Proceeding towards further monetary integration in Europe makes it appropriate to take not only a look at the record of the EMS with some of its specific Germany-related problems, but also to focus on the sources of the apparent success of the EMS (section 2). One may emphasize that a successful EC monetary integration scheme could set a model for other regional monetary integration schemes.

An important topic concerns the question as to which relations exist between real and monetary integration in the EC. In this context the role of multinational corporations and foreign direct investment (FDI) will be addressed; investment flows bear significance for shaping comparative advantages and influencing trade in goods and services of which about 1/3 is intra-company trade in the world economy. From a macroeconomic point of view FDI is important for external equilibrium and spatial price competition - the latter determining the degree of price convergence across EC countries, but also the speed at which real interest rates adjust in connection with parallel inflation movements (section 3). An important point concerns the notion of the equilibrium exchange rate in the context of a worldwide allocation optimum. Since we assume that ownership specific advantages are a major explanation of FDI - together with locational advantages of host countries - a country which records FDI outflows contributes to income growth abroad and to higher wealth at home. The ensuing current account imbalance and the corresponding exchange rate do represent a disequilibrium. In a flexible exchange rate setting the capital account and the current account necessarily are in a mirror position which implies that a surplus in the former (due to net outward FDI flows) corresponds to a current account surplus - an exchange rate policy that aims to balance the currenct account by directly increasing exports and reducing imports might be inappropiate; instead the country with net FDI inflows might prefer alternative measures that lead to capital outflows in the form of portfolio investments or short-term capital exports such that the overall capital account is equilibrated (a fortiori the current account, too). As regards the stock of inward and outward FDI it is important that a network of subsidiaries abroad which partly import intermediate products from the parent company might improve the price competitiveness of subsidiaries vis-a-vis local firms, namely to the extent that in the country of the parent company the inflation rate and hence the cost push incorporated in intermediate products obtained is rather moderate.

In section 4 basic aspects of the benefits and risks of currency unification will be discussed. Among the topics are the question of EC-internal net benefits and the balance of costs and benefits for the global economy.

2. The European Monetary System in Perspective

With the first stage of closer intra-EMS policy cooperation beginning jointly with the removal of capital exchange controls in all major EC countries in mid-1990, the question arises how the switch to free capital movements in the EC - facing both increasing internal and external competition - can be reconciled with limited policy coordination to date. Moreover, the desired "hardening" of the EMS will require integrating the U.K. in the ERM and thereby raise the problem that part of the traditional shifts in global capital flows within the currency square - US dollar, yen, Deutsche mark and British sterling - would take place within a European monetary system that aims at uniform and possibly narrower spreads around parities. All this is happening in a historical phase of EC integration, namely the rapid changes of the EC industrial landscape, including a wave of cross-border mergers & acquistions in Europe, which is partly triggered by the program for a single EC market. Increasing cross-border M&A activities reflect the rising intra-EC capital mobility which in turn implies an accelerated convergence of marginal products of capital across alternative investment locations in the EC.

With serious real changes and shifts in intra-EC competitiveness ahead, the gradually acquired reluctance to adjust parities could ultimately lead to misalignment and efficiency losses in the context of an integration that aimed to improve factor allocation in Europe. Moreover, the historical setting has drastically changed since end-1989 with the fall of the Berlin wall and the German unification which will take place in the context of sweeping changes towards opening-up and marketization of East European economies and the USSR. Two basic scenarios are possible. (I) Driven by conflicts in the context of German unification new political rivalries among major EC member countries could emerge, so that consensus for further monetary integration cannot be achieved or will support only weak and unstable forms of monetary unification. (II) German currency unification can be implemented in the medium-term without a sustaining higher inflation rate in Germany, where the enlargement of the Deutsche mark area - with some positive gravity effects upon convertible Polish, Hungarian and other eastern and south-eastern European currencies - could reinforce the position of the Deutsche Bundesbank whose management of the German-German monetary merger process could be considered as an implicit test for creating greater unified currency areas in Europe. In a period of increased uncertainty in Europe, the institutional design of the Deutsche Bundesbank, with its exceptional (albeit obviously limited) independence of government's directions may be then considered a convincing model for an EC central bank; its integrative function would be a very political one because it could become an important overarching link in an EC in which political conflicts over many topics, including the German issue, might restrict sustainable cooperation schemes in other fields for many years.

However, even with agreement over the long run role of an EC central bank, the process to achieve such an institution is complicated and not least determined by expectations about benefits and risks of monetary integration. To the extent that an EC central bank's policy would be less inflationary than the average EC inflation rate in the present multi-central bank regime, a change in the long term real interest rate is to be expected in the EC. This will affect the capital flows between the EC and the rest of the world because a given world capital stock will be held by EC residents and non-EC residents in accordance with international arbitrage conditions; with a changing demand for capital in the short term in the EC and a changing supply of capital in the long term, there will be inflation-induced flow and stock effects in connection with the change of the monetary EC regime. Moreover, with the formation of an EC currency the substitutability of assets denominated in the EC currency and non-EC currencies will change which would affect the efficiency of sterilized and non-sterilized interventions in the foreign exchange markets worldwide .

2.1 The EMS Record

The EMS has experienced several surprises. The EMS in the 1980s was an asymmetric fixed exchange rate zone with West Germany playing a special, dominating role that was hardly justified by its economic size or by the role of the Deutsche mark as both a stable domestic currency and a widely used international reserve currency *(Melitz 1988)*. The Federal Republic of Germany was the center country of the continental EMS, and the Deutsche Bundesbank dominated monetary policy in the EC while being able - due to successful sterilized intervention that neutralized effects of exchange rate intervention - to pursue a domestic monetary target *(Giavazzi and Giovannini 1987)*; in turbulent periods of dollar exchange rate movements the German central bank also pursued an implicit exchange rate target vis-a-vis the dollar, where emphasis was on dampening the speed of adjustment rather than on changing the market exchange rate trend. Distinguishing short-term and long-term sterilization of the Deutsche Bundesbank, however, *Von Hagen (1989)* finds empirical evidence that the dual dollar-EMS exchange rate constraint impaired the effectiveness of monetary targeting in Germany.

The Deutsche mark was the anchor for price level stability in the whole system - a clear surprise in view of the many initial warnings of a pro-inflation bias of the EMS; low overall inflationary pressures are partly due to the fact that the burden of adjustment falls on the current account deficit countries, but this is only one element of explanation. The second surprise is the degree of internal stability achieved in terms of increased monetary cooperation and of relatively infrequent exchange rate changes in a period in which an increasing global financial interdependency along with increased capital mobility were observed. The third surprise is that there is a more parallel move of interest rates in the EMS countries *(Kath/Hennerkes 1985)* although considerable nominal and real interest rate divergences persist even with inflation rate convergence.

The EMS was founded as an attempt to create a zone of relative monetary stability in Europe, and most surveys agree that this aim has largely been achieved although a successful development cannot easily be divided between favorable external changes and intra-EC policy adjustments *(Ungerer et al. 1986; De Grauwe and Peters 1989; Wegner 1989; Claassen 1990)*. Only in the period 1979-82 did the EMS experience high exchange rate volatility which to a large extent was due to the second oil price shock and the international recession aggravated by disinflation policies in the EC. Nevertheless, compared to the "snake episode" the volatility of the external value of the Deutsche mark vis-a-vis the Belgian franc, the French franc, the Dutch guilder and the Italian lira decreased, and in the period 1983-89 it declined further (Tab. 1).

A similar development occured in non-EMS currencies that were pegged to the DM, e.g. the Austrian schilling and the Swiss franc. In marked contrast to this was the exchange rate behavior vis-a-vis the pound sterling, the dollar and the yen, where an increasing volatility both in nominal, and even more so, in real terms (except for the yen) was observed in the period 1979.II-83.I. In contrast to the yen, the real exchange rate variability increased vis-a-vis the sterling and the dollar in 1983-89. High exchange rate volatility went along with this, and it seems clear that greater interest rate shifts and hence more unstable monetary policies would have been necessary to avoid the volatility of non-EMS exchange rates.

The initially skeptical attitude of the Deutsche Bundesbank which feared a pro-inflation bias of the EMS has changed over time, although this institution has expressed reservations when it comes to initiatives for a rapid monetary integration in the EC. Moreover, the German central bank turned against soft credit arrangements in the EMS. The EMS's stability safeguards against inflationary currency market interventions were strict repayment obligations for central bank credits accorded in the context of the "very short-term financing mechanism". Compulsory interventions are financed and the balances are settled with a maximum period of 3.5 months in ECUs at the European Monetary Cooperation Fund (EMCF), where central banks make their currencies available in the required amounts. The Deutsche Bundesbank as the issuing institution of the prime creditor currency accepted the compromise of the Basel-Nyborg arrangements of 1987 which extended the very short term central bank financing mechanism (with a limit) for the so-called intramarginal interventions and called for considering exchange rate-oriented interest rate policies.

EMCF credit lines were used for intramarginal intervention only in the turbulent period of October-November 1987 when central banks worldwide created more liquidity than initially planned. Central banks' holdings of partner currencies can be increased beyond working balances only with the consent of the central bank whose currency is bought which often was the Deutsche Bundesbank. Cumulative intramarginal sales and purchases of Deutsche mark amounted to some DM 270 bill. in the period 1986-1989 *(Deutsche Bundesbank 1989)* but as central banks did not use the EMCF options and preferred investments in

Tab. 1: Exchange Rate Variability of the Deutsche Mark vis-a-vis Selected Currencies

	Belg./ Lux.fr.	French franc	Dutch guilder	Ital lira	Pound	US $	Yen	SFR
Exchange Rate Variability								
73.II-79.I								
nominal **	1.60	3.76	1.74	4.80	4.60	5.23	5.15	3.72
real ***	1.95	3.54	2.06	4.08	4.40	5.26	4.86	3.65
79.II-83.I								
nominal **	2.01	1.92	0.84	1.85	5.29	4.94	6.17	2.49
real ***	1.79	1.98	0.92	2.45	5.55	5.37	5.69	2.10
83.II-89.III								
nominal **	0.56	1.26	0.39	1.20	3.98	5.67	3.23	1.63
real **	1.03	1.04	1.10	1.24	3.85	5.47	3.08	1.60
Cumulative since start of EMS*	31.2	45.2	4.0	60*				
Change of real eff. exchange rate 1983-89 #	-12	-9	-8	8	8	-20	25	-3

* Includes the effect of the lira devaluation of January 8, 1990. Total change vis-a-vis all EMS currencies (leaving aside Spain) was +40 %.

** nominal variability is defined as standard deviations in the rate of change from the previous quarter.

*** Real variability is defined as mean deviation in the rate of change of the nominal exchange rates from the rate of change of the inflation differential (as measured by the prices of total expenditures)

Absolute change in the index (1985=100) of the IMF-defined real effective exchange rate; figures (for Germany + 3) are rounded.

Source: Deutsche Bundesbank (1989a), Monthly Report, Nov. 1989, Frankfurt/M.; IMF, International Financial Statistics, Washington, April 1990.

financial markets the liquidity policy of the Deutsche Bundesbank was not directly affected, whereas the exchange rate vis-a-vis the EMS partners and the U.S. dollar (with potential monetary policy repercussions) responded.

Due to careful institutional arrangements ("parity grid"), ideological harmonization of governments' policy goals and increased central bank coordination, a surprising inflation performance was observed. Instead of West Germany suffering from a European pro-inflation bias, it realized that the other continental EC countries enjoyed an often welcomed, DM-biased pressure towards downward inflation rate convergence; this, however, was transitorily accompanied by unemployment rate convergence at higher levels. In terms of an "international Phillips-curve" the issue arises whether a reduction of the inflation rate in Germany was imposing higher unemployment rates in the other EC countries (Tab. 2).

With parity adjustments not fully compensating for inflation differentials Germany - and other low-inflation countries - obviously enjoyed the benefit of a gradually increasing price competitiveness in the EC which contributed to higher exports and growth along with lower unemployment in Germany. Higher German growth then supported economic recovery in EC partner countries where supply-side measures as well as lower inflation rates actively favored growth. In terms of the Phillips-curve the short-run trade off became steeper in a situation in which the natural rate of unemployment gradually reduced. Due to positive structural adjustment in the OECD, the late 1980s witnessed a downward convergence of unemployment rates in the EC, without reaching, however, full-employment.

In the beginning of the 1990s there is a clear tendency in the EC that consumer price inflation is moderately increasing, where intra-EC divergences among major continental countries are not great; but the divergence between the U.K. and the other EC countries - even setting aside the methodological upward bias in U.K. figures that stems from the inclusion of mortgage rates - is considerable. As the U.K. decides to peg its exchange rate in accordance with full EMS membership, both expected inflation rates - necessarily also nominal wage rate increases - and interest rates in Great Britain are likely to come down.

With respect to public deficit-national income ratios a considerable divergence is observed among EC member countries. Italy's ratio of 10 percent is - along

Tab. 2: Convergence Indicators for ERM-Countries and the U.K.

	FRG	Belgium	Denmark	France	Ireland	Italy	Netherlands	U.K.
	Unemployment rate (in percent)							
1980	3.8	9.4	6.2	6.4	8.3	7.6	5.9	10.0
1986	9.0	16.1	8.9	10.4	18.1	11.1	10.0	11.4
1989	7.9	13.1	8.5	9.5	17.8	12.2	5.7	6.4
	Consumer prices (change from previous YEAR)							
1974-78	4.7	9.2	11.0	10.7	15.3	16.3	7.9	16.2
1979-83	4.9	7.0	10.1	11.8	15.8	17.0	5.2	11.3
1984-88	1.1	3.0	4.6	4.3	4.6	7.1	1.1	4.7
1988	1.3	1.2	4.6	2.7	2.1	5.0	0.7	4.9
1989	2.8	4.3	4.6	3.7	4.1	6.3	1.1	8.0
	Current account balance (in percent of GNP or GDP)							
1974-78	1.4	0.1	-3.3	-0.1	-5.6	-0.5	2.1	
1979-83	-0.3	-2.9	-3.6	-0.7	-11.0	-0.8	1.8	
1984-88	3.3	1.4	-3.6	-0.1	-2.0	-0.4	2.9	*-0.7
1988	4.2	1.8	-1.7	-0.4	2.4	-0.7	2.2	-3.1
1989	4.6	2.0	-1.5	-0.4	1.7	-1.4	2.3	-3.7
1990	3.3	2.3	-1.1	-0.4	1.4	-1.1	1.9	-2.8
	Financial balances of general government (% of GNP)							
1974-78	-3.0	-4.8	0.1	-1.1	-8.2	-9.6	-2.3	
1979-83	-3.0	-10.5	-5.6	-1.7	-12.4	-10.5	-5.3	
1984-88	-1.6	-8.3	-0.1	-2.3	-9.5	-11.2	-5.7	
1988	-2.0	-7.0	0.0	-1.3	-3.9	-10.9	-5.4	1.5
1989	0.2	-6.2	-0.5	-1.1	-2.9	-10.2	-4.6	0.7
1990	-2.2	-5.6	-0.4	-0.9	-1.1	- 9.8	-4.2	0.4
	Government net debt interest payment (% of expenditures)							
1981	3.2	12.4	3.0	2.5	9.0	11.9	5.9	7.5
1989	5.2	20.5	6.4	4.4	12.4	16.7	8.7	4.3
1990	5.2	20.9	6.3	4.6	13.4	16.9	8.7	4.0
	Yield difference for corporate bonds/government bonds**							
1990	0.05	0.05	-	0.98	-	-0.31	0.79	1.9
	Money stock (change from previous year; broad aggregate)							
1974-78	9.0	12.4	12.4	-	-	22.4	13.0	7.9
1979-83	6.8	7.8	11.7	11.7	15.9	18.4	6.7	21.5
1984-88	5.6	8.6	12.2	7.7	6.3	12.0	7.2	16.7

Note: Broadly defined money is M2 for Belgium, Denmark and the Netherlands, M3 for the Federal Republic of Germany, France, Ireland and Italy. U.K.: Quasi-money/line 39 IMF-IFS. As regards Belgium (Italy) the first figures refer to the period 1976-78 (1975-78).
Figures for the current account balance 1989/90 include Luxembourg for the case of Belgium. * refers to 1987; ** percentage points; figures are for beginning of April 1990.

Sources: DEUTSCHE BUNDESBANK (1989); OECD (1989), Economic Outlook, December, Paris; ECONOMIST (1990), Economic and Financial Indicators, 7-13 April, London. OECD (1990), Main Economic Indicators, Paris; IMF, International Financial Statistics, current issues. Eurostat, Luxembourg; IMF, World Economic Outlook, October 1990, own calculations.

with Greece - an extreme case, but a ratio of net debt to GNP close to unity which, roughly speaking, is also valid in the case of Ireland and Belgium implies that between 15 and 20 percent of total government expenditures are earmarked for interest payments. This is about three times as much as in other EC countries and makes the Italian government, in contrast to these, quite sensitive to interest rate changes. In Italy high inflation rates might be favored not only because of expected seigniorage gains but also because of an inflation-induced reduction of the real interest rate. However, adjustment towards lower German and French inflation rates might be necessary if the exchange rate is to be maintained within the standard narrow parity band. Shifting from a 12 percentage points band to a spread of 4.5 percent should then push down the nominal interest rate towards the lower rates of Germany and France, where governments will fear that Italy's public deficits drain their citizens' savings and push up interest rates.

Hence other EC countries are interested in Italian adjustment measures that reduce the deficit ratio. Lower public expenditures, hefty privatizations and higher excise and wage income tax rates are possible first-aid remedies for public deficit convergence in the development of EMU - measures that would have to be accompanied by some future EC monitoring principles and agreed rules on public deficits. The special problem of the public debt in Italy is obvious, given the fact that long-term government bond yield exceeded corporate bond yield in Italy. This constellation is abnormal in view of the common case that government's interest payments are usually perceived to be risk-free because government is empowered to increase effective tax rates if necessary for financing purposes. With growing opportunities for capital flight beyond the borders and an increasing share of the domestic shadow economy, the public's trust in this mechanism might indeed become so weak that government faces a risk/solvency premium in the capital market which would in itself be a strong case for immediate privatization actions in order to avoid state-owned firms facing particular disadvantages in raising capital in the market.

The contrast between high inflation countries - e.g., Italy, France (until the late '80s), Spain - and the low inflation rate members has had a long tradition in the EC. Under the implicit leadership of the Deutsche Bundesbank the continental EMS countries reached a remarkable downward convergence of their inflation rates in the early 1980s. With a technologically very competitive West German economy which recorded the relatively highest surpluses in the trade balance vis-a-vis other EC member countries, a strong pressure to reduce inflation rates was felt in other EC countries.

Low German inflation rates - ranging between 0 and 3 percent after 1983 - implied a gradually improving intra-EC price competitiveness of German firms. This happened at the expense of competitors from EC countries with a faster price increase unless a nominal devaluation of the respective currency would have fully compensated for the inflation differential; this was not typical of realignments in the EMS. However, as devaluations are conceived to be politically embarrassing and might also increase real interest rates in countries which rely on foreign borrowing (in particular Italy, France) all ERM-countries tried to avoid parity changes and instead follow the monetary stability course of the Deutsche Bundesbank.

2.2 German Dominance in the EMS?

Taking into account the convergence of inflation rates and short-term interest rates in the EMS, the degree of influence of the Deutsche Bundesbank on other central banks' policies in continental Europe can be assessed from various perspectives: (i) EMS countries - confronted with the risk of speculative attacks from the U.S., Japan and other financial centers - faced incentives to fall in line with German monetary policy and hence to reduce the exposure to external financial shocks; (ii) the short-term interest rate linkages within the EMS ran dominantly from Germany to other EC countries which reduced the effectiveness of a monetary policy, so that German monetary leadership was easier to accept; (iii) within the EC Germany's position in the fields of trade and investment was dominant and potentially reinforced by a low-inflation policy of the Deutsche Bundesbank, so that the politico-economic resistance against high inflation rates was strengthened in the EC.

All three aspects played a role in the actual developments. The Deutsche mark absorbed pressures from dollar volatility in periods of turbulence to a higher extent than other continental EC currencies *(Giavazzi and Giovannini 1986)*. Moreover, by implicit monetary cooperation in the EMS, some central banks have apparently been able to borrow reputation from the Deutsche Bundesbank and were thus able to reduce the inflation rate by more credible policies *(Giavazzi and Pagano 1988;* for a different view see *Fratianni and Von Hagen 1988)*. Changing expectation patterns in the EMS-setting as well as the policy regime adopted in the continental EC - more cooperative and with accepted German leadership after 1982 - have affected monetary policy and the inflation record in the EC *(Collins 1988)*.

As regards short-term interest linkages, empirical evidence *(Smeets 1989, 1990)* suggests that Germany indeed dominated short-term interest rates in the EC. With respect to real interest rate divergence, one may state a hypothesis: To the extent that long-term real interest rates are influenced by the marginal product of capital, the much more diverging long-term real interest rates reflect the asymmetric intra-EC distribution of technologically determined firm-specific advantages - reflected in gross foreign direct investment flows (with Germany dominating) - and hence imperfections in the trade of know-how and industrial property rights in Europe.

As a matter of fact, Germany advanced to the center country of the continental EMS which benefited as a whole from a downward inflation convergence. With the U.K. opting for flexible exchange rates, the Deutsche Bundesbank emerged as the leader in monetary policy in the continental EC which enjoyed considerable exchange rate stability in a period of high volatility of the exchange rate of the dollar, the pound sterling and the yen. The British absenteeism in the ERM was of particular importance because London's financial center role in combination with a floating sterling attracted (and perhaps generated) speculative forces of the global financial market which could otherwise have galvanized and destabilized the EMS system. The trilateral gross short-term capital flows USA-Japan-UK(or EC) are much higher than the capital flows in the continental EC, where floating exchange rates as such are likely to increase speculative flows.

The Anchor Role of the DM

With the pound sterling left outside the ERM, only the Deutsche mark remained as a major international currency in the system. With the U.K. staying outside any commitment to fixed exchange rates and central banks in France and Italy obviously being interested in borrowing credibility of monetary policy from the Deutsche Bundesbank, the large German economy strongly contributed to supplying the international public good of price stability in the EC in the 1980s.

Various factors reinforced monetary cooperation along a disinflation trajectory among the ERM countries. On the one hand, inflation prone countries faced the risk of rapidly eroding competitiveness in the case of high sustaining inflation rates; from a fiscal revenue perspective inflation-induced reductions of the real interest rates and higher "inflation-seigniorage" had to be weighed against growth-augmenting and thus revenue-increasing advantages of price stability. With low inflation rates, reduced risk for the private sector to confuse inflationary and relative price changes should encourage growth as well as a tendency to raise average maturities in capital markets so that productivity-augmenting long-term investment and innovation projects are easier to realize. Furthermore, high inflation differentials in a system with at least one stability-oriented big country would have called for periodic devaluations - that could reinforce inflationary anticipations - and also upward pressure on real interest rates (including a risk premium to reflect the uncertainty to which extent politics would allow the inflation differentials to be reflected by a corresponding adjustment of parities). The Federal Republic of Germany enjoyed the benefit of a gradual real depreciation in the EMS which reinforced the German trade balance surplus whose regional breakdown at the end of the 1980s showed the EC-11 group to amount to 3/4 while the trade volume reached only 50 %.

If an increasing current account surplus goes along with a net outflow of FDI, as in the case of Germany in the 1980s, the deficit countries do not have to increase interest rates as much to attract capital inflows as in a situation in which the current account surplus country records net inward FDI. A non-center deficit country normally has to increase the interest rate to attract capital that will finance a rising current account deficit - ultimately higher interest rates translate into reduced investment of domestic firms and lower expenditures of private households, so that with given government expenditures on goods and services a drop in absorption brings about the required correction in the trade balance. However, another approach might be taken to correct this imbalance, namely inward foreign direct investment which increases production potential and contributes to generate net exports for the host country. Big countries with a considerable demand potential (a large population with high per-capita-incomes) can thus finance high public deficits for quite some time provided the current account surplus country does not switch from an export to an import position in its foreign direct investment balance. Viewed from this unusual perspective of the German unification process which will encourage inward FDI and reduce outward FDI for quite some time, Italy as the leading public deficit country could face particular problems in the 1990s.

Political influence over monetary policy in the EC has been biased towards Germany so far. There has been German dominance in monetary policy on the European continent which has implied a loss of policy sovereignty for most other countries, while the role of the DM as a reserve currency and an important parallel currency in eastern Europe has made monetary policy control more intricate for the Deutsche Bundesbank. The French concerns of the visible loss of monetary sovereignty led in 1988 to the institutional innovation of a German-Franco Finance and Economic Council comprising the Ministers of Economics and of Finance plus the two central bank presidents; Germany's government-independent central bank accepted this institution only with reservations because its status seemed subject to erosion.

Germany's position in world industry and trade in combination with a long-standing stability-oriented monetary policy of the Deutsche Bundesbank made the Deutsche mark the anchor of the EMS. The leadership role of the Deutsche Bundesbank is surprising in view of the monetary approach to the balance of payments. It suggests that in a fixed exchange rate system high inflation rates in one big country tend to dissipate to the whole system. The direct international price mechanism pushes prices of tradables upwards - as in the case of the Bretton Woods System and inflationary U.S. policy in the 1960s - and the ensuing excess demand for money in other countries leads to capital imports or an excess supply in the tradables markets. The resulting excess supply in the currency market forces the central banks to raise the stock of money by way of intervention, where higher discount rates or other measures to sterilize the liquidity effects of intervention can help to maintain desired monetary expansion as long as domestic and foreign bonds are not perfect substitutes.

However, the EC countries are asymmetric with respect to foreign direct investment flows and the capability of its respective industry to exert price leadership in international oligopolistic markets. Germany's trade surplus vis-a-vis major EC partners reinforce its price leadership position, at least as long as increasing capacity utilization and sustaining unemployment allow further output increases under limited pressure of rising relative unit labor costs. Moreover, in a technologically leading country (Germany: 40 % of EC manufacturing output) with an elastic pool of technological opportunities that allow it to match higher interest rates with a higher marginal product of capital, the link between international financial market rates and investment is probably less weak.

In this perspective of the asymmetries of the EMS it is not so surprising that it was not the relatively inflationary policies of France and Italy which dominated the EMS but the Deutsche Bundesbank with its emphasis on price level stability. Part of the explanation for this refers to industrial economics and the role of foreign direct investment flows. A direct international price link in markets for tradable manufacturing goods can be conceived to be the result of oligopolistic price leadership exerted by that country whose industry is (more or less) dominating as evidenced by strong firm-specific advantages and high FDI. Moreover, since firm-specific advantages determine foreign direct investment, one may conclude that (big) countries with a high stock of outward FDI largely determine the development of the price level within a system of fixed exchange rates. This role was played in the Bretton Woods system by the USA.

Germany structurally benefitted from the real depreciation of the Deutsche mark, where foreign subsidiaries' higher profits, measured in domestic goods, played a particular role. Moreover, the Federal Republic enjoyed relatively strong economic growth impulses via increasing surpluses in the trade balance vis-a-vis the other EC countries - a position that might erode after German unification.

German Unification

The intra-German economic and monetary unification poses several problems for the EMS. These problems concern mainly (1) the institutional balance of power between government and the central bank in Germany, (2) the economic weight of the Deutsche mark, (3) the problems of advancing the EMS along the lines of the Delors report, (4) implications of German monetary union for further European monetary integration and (5) the history of central banking in Germany as a point of reference for the development of an EC central bank system.

German unification does not only raise questions of national internal balance of power, it also implies external political problems that are relevant for EC monetary integration. There is the risk that the German interest in supporting progress in the EC integration process will reduce as German politics shift to adopt a more national(istic) and self-centered perspective (*Welfens, 1990c*). Moreover, there is the general caveat that German unification might create political instability in Germany which would make German political leadership in monetary affairs impossible because of lack of internal consensus, and this in a period in which other EC countries become less willing to accept German dominance in any politically relevant field. Finally, the general reinforcement of national concerns over European or supranational decision-making is likely to influence the future EC central bank's institutional framework to be agreed upon in the intergovernmental conference 1990/91: Members of the central bank council might be expected to represent national interests and to take national politics into account. This would impede the functioning of an EC central bank's ability to formulate consistent monetary policies and financial regulations that focus on EC markets as a whole.

With respect to monetary integration in the EC, a rise of interest rates in connection with German unification has specific impacts: namely, that Italy, Belgium, Spain and Greece which face high public deficit/national output ratios (highest in Italy: 10 percent; in contrast to this is West Germany: 2 percent in 1990) will now find it more difficult to reconcile the liberalization of capital flows and price stability. The switch to free capital flows already implies a higher burden of interest payments for heavily indebted governments. These governments also fear the induced reduction of tax revenues that is to be expected both because of the likely downward international tax spiral and reduced investment/output growth as a consequence of higher domestic interest rates. Moreover, this increases the pressure to resort to an inflationary finance of government deficits, and this will reinforce tendencies to keep political control over central banking in the EC.

With German unification the Deutsche mark will face greater problems in its role as an anchor of stability in the EMS. Even with a prudent monetary policy of the German central bank, there is a risk that Germany - becoming more closely tied with eastern Europe - would be particularly involved in uncertainties and instabilities that surround the reform processes in Eastern Europe and the USSR. Country-specific high volatility in Germany's financial markets could mean greater volatility of interest rates and new problems for controlling monetary aggregates. Moreover, the idea of a long-run narrowing of parity spreads seems to be doubtful in a capital-control free EMS after German unification and British adherence to the ERM. For this means the double exposure to "CMEA shocks" - mostly affecting Germany and the DM - and global financial shocks that would mainly feed into London and affect via the British pound the whole EMS.

2.3 Problems of Integrating the U.K. into the EMS

Opinion polls among business leaders in the U.K. showed in the late 1980s an increasing share of proponents of full-fledged British EMS membership. Pragmatism in the field of European monetary cooperation is likely to gain ground in the U.K. in the 1990s, where an ERM membership will sharply reduce the exchange rate risk and thereby reinforce the substitutability of bonds issued in the U.K. and in the continental EC countries; thereby encouraging capital inflows, the British government might hope to reduce interest rates and spur growth. Too long, it seems, have British policies favored applying the brakes with respect to EC monetary integration so that control over the speed rather than an impact on the direction of the process was exerted.

With the U.K. fully joining the EMS institutions - with a broad exchange rate band of +/- 6 % - the system itself might, however, become much less stable than it currently is. The British position has so far emphasized three traits of the U.K.: Its status as an oil exporting country, a high stock of non-EC FDI and London's role as a global financial center *(Leigh-Pemberton 1989)*. In the perspective adopted here only the latter aspect seems to be of particular significance in the context of the EMS. British membership in the ERM would require the U.K.'s monetary policy to defend the parity of the pound sterling which is an important international vehicle currency and subject to heavy swings in global financial markets. In 1989 London as a financial center still had the highest share in the global turnover of foreign exchange: 34 percent compared to New York and Tokyo, respectively, with 24 and 21 percent; Zurich and Paris, respectively, followed with 10 and 5 percent; Brussels and Amsterdam each accounted for 3 percent *(Economist 1989)*. Moreover, foreign investors' percentage of total turnover in European stock exchanges was particularly low in Germany (9 percent), higher in Paris and Amsterdam (44 and 50 percent) and quite important in the U.K.: 21 percent at the London Stock Exchange and 48 percent at the SEAQ International in 1988.

In addition one should bear in mind that stock market capitalization as a share of national income reached 85 percent in 1988 and was thus about four times as large as in Germany and France where a restricted M&A menu has contributed to limiting the potential role of foreign influences in the stock market. Much more important than the sometimes quoted special role of the pound sterling as a currency of an oil exporting country thus seems to be London's role as a financial center. Taking due account of a traditional British lead in the insurance industry, this role might further increase as a consequence of EC 1992 and other upcoming liberalization schemes in the EC. Intra-EC competition as well as preferences on the side of external demand - mainly from professional fund managers outside the EC - could, however, lead to a single European stock market, for which the London Stock Exchange proposed to join forces with the German Federation of Stock Exchanges. The increasing demand for investment banking in connection with the formation of EC 1992 could provide momentum to build an integrated EC market system.

3. EC 1992 and Monetary Integration

The formation of a single EC market for goods and services as of end-1992 will not only affect static and dynamic efficiency as well as economic performance in the EC countries, but will also fundamentally change the structure of increasingly multinational industries with internationally diversified production facilities. Moreover, the transnationalization of industry in the sense of a more internationally diversified ownership of capital and industrial property rights plays an increasing role - leading multinationals' stocks are already quoted at major stock exchanges and could thereby reinforce international stock market linkages which became stronger in the 1980s *(Von Furstenberg/Jeon 1989)*. Vis-a-vis the U.S. major continental EC countries' "terms of capital", defined as relative international stock market prices, were more volatile in the 1980s than those of the U.K. with its combination of flexible exchange rates and more open capital markets, while the British terms of trade (for goods) were exceptionally volatile *(Welfens 1990a, p. 174)*. This could imply that capital market liberalization in combination with greater exchange rate flexibility is an impediment to greater trade in goods which suffers from exchange rate risks (empirical evidence: *De Grauwe 1987; Caballero/Corbo 1989)*. Transnationalization, multinationalization and reduced capital controls could imply greater price volatility of heavily traded blue chips, but also a greater scope of stocks traded internationally as well as a closer link between volatility of stock markets, bonds markets and foreign exchange markets.

Financial integration will induce via greater competition financial innovations, a relocation of capital and lower real interest rates. Privatization and reduction of state subsidies could stimulate at the same time innovation as well as efficiency and lead via an increase in the marginal product of capital to higher real interest rates, faster growth and increasing tax revenues - but the nations' bid for more mobile capital will reduce effective revenues from capital income. In view of the current reliance on public deficits and inflation-based seigniorage in some EC countries, economic growth is a key to creating political conditions in the EC that would allow the implementation of an EC central bank with a priority on price stability.

With greater capital mobility economic stability could be impaired by short-term flows between non-cooperative financial center regions. Due to external economies of scale or thick market externalities the challenge for London as Europe's international financial center seems to be limited *(Grilli 1989)*; however, because inter-bank deposits are much influenced by the size of the economy and, probably even more so, by the stock of FDI, German unification could intensify rivalry among financial centers but also accelerate the drive towards new joint ventures and international M&As. Stage I of the EMU in combination with the Single Market Program is likely to affect the allocation of capital-intensive resources within the EC and to change the transmission process of policy impulses. Income, employment and wealth effects might create policy problems both with respect to distributional aspects and to (regional) economic stability. The role of fiscal and monetary policy will certainly change in the context of EC 1992, where the proposals of the Delors report are so far the most discussed vision of a future EC monetary policy and a framework for fiscal policies - tax issues, however, have been neglected from the outset.

3.1 Delors Report and Resolution of the EC Parliament

The main proposals for EMS advancement were brought forward by the European Parliament and the Delors report. The political approaches of the Delors report and of the European Parliament's Resolution take the existing EC as the principle point of departure for closer policy cooperation and the formation of a currency union. There is hardly political room to achieve currency unification along the lines of an optimal currency union. Instead, one may have to ask, which institutional changes are necessary, to make such an ex ante currency union an optimal "ex post currency union".

Facing the task of developing proposals for a comprehensive monetary integration the Delors group published a study on the virtues and options of a joint economic and monetary integration process. Economic and Monetary Union was proposed as an appropriate complement to the 1992 project. There are three stages envisaged in the monetary integration process: The elimination of all capital controls in all EC countries by 1992 is foreseen as a first important step. At the same time the coordination of macroeconomic policy in the EC is to be intensified - though not meaning binding commitment -, thereby revitalizing the long-standing agreement of policy cooperation of 1974. Moreover, parity changes should be avoided by making appropriate use of other measures for external adjustment, where the Committee of Central Bank Governors - created as early as 1964 - is expected to state adequate policy proposals. National EC central banks should become more independent of domestic policy institutions. Then, in stage II, a more intensive policy coordination is to be realized, where a European System of Central Banks would coordinate monetary policy and implement narrower parity margins, while a more comprehensive EC regional and structural policy would be adopted; in the field of fiscal policies policy-monitoring on the basis of agreed medium-term policy formulations and budget deficit rules should be realized. A revision of the EC Treaty should ultimately lead to a monetary union with strictly fixed exchange rates and an institutionalized EC central banking system that implements EC monetary policy and, using the pool of national currency reserves, exchange rate interventions vis-a-vis non-EC currencies; finally a common EC currency would be introduced in stage III.

In summary, the Delors report proposes for the long run a priority of goals, a structure, organization and status of the European System of Central Banks that is akin to the Deutsche Bundesbank. The Report states that the ESCB would be based on the following principles *(Delors Report 1989, 18-20)*:

- *the system would be committed to the objective of price stability;*
- *subject to the foregoing, the System should support the general economic policy set at the Community level by the competent bodies;*
- *the System would be responsible for the formulation and implementation of monetary policy, exchange rate and reserve management, and the maintenance of a properly functioning payment system;*
- *the System would participate in the co-ordination of banking supervision policies of the supervisory authorities...*
- *a federative structure...;*
- *establishment of an ESCB Council (composed of the Governors of the central bank and the members of the Board, the latter to be appointed by the European Council), which would be responsible for the formulation of and decisions of the thrust cf monetary policy; modalities of voting procedures would have to be provided for in the Treaty;*
- *establishment of a Board (with supporting staff), which would monitor monetary developments and oversee the implementation of the common monetary policy;*
- *national central banks, which would execute operations in accordance with the decisions taken by the ESCB Council...*
- *Independence: the ESCB Council should be independent of instructions from national governments and Community authorities; to that effect the members of*

the ESCB Council, both Governors and the Board members, should have appropriate security of tenure;
- *Accountability: reporting would be in the form of submission of an annual report by the ESCB to the European Parliament and the European Council.*

The European Parliament has developed its own proposals that differ slightly from the Delors group in that currency unification is emphasized more, and, naturally, a stronger role of the EC central bank's responsibility vis-a-vis the Parliament is suggested. The European Parliament adopted on April 4, 1989 a Resolution Concerning the Development of European Currency Integration which calls for (i) the integration of all EC countries in the Exchange Rate and Intervention System of the European Currency System, (ii) an increasingly convergence-oriented intra-EC coordination of economic and social policy and a greater scope for regional policies, (iii) elimination of the parity bands of EC currencies and absolute fixity of parities provided sufficient convergence of economic policies has been reached. The resolution suggests that the Committee of Central Bank Governors should be responsible for proposing quantitative targets for monetary policy, important interest rate decisions and a common exchange rate policy vis-a-vis non-EC countries. The member countries wishing to adhere to the Exchange Rate Mechanism should institutionalize their cooperation by setting up a European Council of (Central Bank) Governors and a European Council for Fiscal and Economic Affairs which are to prepare in cooperation with the EC Commission and the European Parliament the currency union. The president of the EC Commission would participate with an advisory status in the deliberations of both Councils. By 1995 a European Central Bank should be established, where all national central banks are independent of the respective national governments. The ECU would replace all national currencies, although the existing currencies would remain valid over a transitory period until end-1997. This timing schedule proposed by the European Parliament is ambitious, but it is interesting to note that the reasoning of the EC Commission and of the European Parliament is parallel in many fields. Of the two the Delors report is certainly more influential.

Reflections on the Delors Report

The Delors report emphasizes the principles of parallelism with respect to monetary and economic (real) integration, of convergence in economic performance and policies, the principle of subsidiarity - supranational (national) policy bodies should only act in fields where national (local) policy is ineffective - and the need for cooperation. The latter concerns both a growing coordination of national fiscal policies in the ECOFIN (European Council of Economic Ministers and Finance Ministers) and closer, gradually intensifying cooperation of EC central bankers whose degree of national policy autonomy is viewed as reduced because of narrowed opportunities to conduct an independent monetary policy in an economic community with increasing capital market integration and greater capital mobility. The Delors report argues against monetary financing of public budget deficits but does not raise the question of the distribution of seigniorage.

Criticism, suggesting fields for improvements, might be voiced against various ideas and suggestions in the Delors report; in particular, it is surprising that the role of price stability as a prime goal of EC monetary policy is not more clearly evoked, although it seems clear for many theoretical reasons that the benefits of monetary integration critically depend on the ability to maintain a low inflation rate. Price stability would avoid relative price distortions that derive from the positive correlation between mean inflation rate and inflation variance. Moreover, depending on the interest rate elasticity of the money demand, a welfare-augmenting reduction (welfare-reducing increase) of the inflation rate would increase (reduce) the desired per-capita stock of money. Another critical point concerns the idea that greater convergence of economic performance through the strengthening of economic and monetary policy coordination is required *(Delors Report, p. 34)*; policy coordination in the apparent sense of policy convergence - e.g. adopting similar ranges for public deficit-GNP ratios - is one thing, convergence of economic performance another, and both are not necessarily related to each other. Project EC 1992 could indeed lead at least transitorily to a diverging economic performance of EC member countries. Convergence in economic performance might not so much be expected as a result of policy convergence across nations, but as a result of intensified market competition.

The Delors Report calls for greater political independence of national central banks as a vital ingredient for a relatively independent future EC central bank. Except for the Netherlands, Denmark and Germany, this proposal requires complicated political and constitutional shifts. Too much "consensus capital" might be used on this issue and not leave enough room for achieving consensus on a final transfer of sovereignty to the supranational EC level. Much less scarce political consensus capital would be wasted, if one had emphasized that the final stage of EMU, the creation of an EC central bank offers the unique chance to merge existing national banks under a unique superior institutional framework. Greater independence of central banks is certainly a more fundamental problem for the treasury-dominated central banks in the U.K. and France as well as for Italy, where an interministerial committee is responsible for the basic orientation of monetary and foreign exchange policy. In the Italian case the position of the central bank might be changed towards greater independence in connection with EC-1992 induced changes in the state-dominated insurance and banking industry whose status as shareholders of the Italian central bank gives them via the Consiglio Superiore the right to decide about the appointment and dismissal of the central bank management. Privatization of major state-owned insurance companies, state-owned banks (banks under public corporate law) and the Europeanization of state social insurance organizations could be a welcome point of departure in changing the status of the Italian central bank.

3.2 EMS Hardening, EC 1992 and Monetary Integration

The Italian switch - accompanied by a lira devaluation - to the standard narrow spread around parities in early 1990 as well as the removal of capital controls in all major EC countries by mid-1990 are supposed to contribute to EMS hardening. Its rules will be shared by all continental EC countries, and the EC-wide pledge to remove capital controls should then contribute to higher efficiency of capital allocation in the EC. At the same time free capital movement will put the political systems under stress because suppliers of non-tradables and owners of immobile factors located in regions that particularly attract EC capital will benefit, while other regions will suffer from downward pressure on the price of labor, goods and real assets. In this respect the Delors report suggests a center-periphery problem that might require additional EC regional funds. However, as long as exchange rates are flexible vis-a-vis the dollar and the yen, changes in the external exchange rate of "disadvantaged" countries might contribute to attracting additional inward foreign direct investment from the world's biggest FDI pools, the U.S. and Japan. The fact that the removal of EC capital controls takes place in a period of global capital liberalization - with Japan still being on the way to progressive liberalization - improves the opportunity for a successful, sustaining liberalization move in Europe. Both the negative aspect of EC 1992, namely the fear of fortress Europe, and its positive aspects, namely the creation of a bigger market with economically more prosperous private and corporate citizens will attract Japanese, but also U.S. capital inflows.

Nevertheless, EMS hardening means risks for EC governments that will face a closer interdependence of financial markets in Europe. With the narrowing of the lira spread to the standard margin of +/- 2.25 percent, the pressure for converging nominal interest rates within the EC will increase. This holds not only because profitable interest arbitrage will allow only for nominal interest rate divergences up to 4.5 percentage points, but also because a lower spread implies smaller exchange rate risks for speculative capital flows as compared to a situation of a larger spread around parity. In periods of changing exchange rate expectations speculative capital flows should therefore be expected to emerge faster and more massively than in the past. Moreover, real interest rates will converge more quickly in the EC in the future because the creation of a single EC market in combination with more mobile real capital and technology imply faster intra-EC equalization of regional marginal products of capital which should in turn be equal to risk-adjusted real bonds rates. Moreover, the increasing share of tradable goods and a growing scope of goods arbitrage should synchronize the dissipation of inflationary impulse in the EC so that in combination with deliberate monetary policy convergence real interest rates will considerably converge in the EC.

If, however, monetary (inflation) divergence would occur in an environment of increased capital mobility in the EC in the 1990s, the prospects for hardening the EMS would be bleak, and frequent adjustment of parities could be on the agenda of the EMS once again. Moreover, and this points to the importance of achieving low inflation rates in the EC, the negative link between inflation rate and average bond maturity (contract length in financial markets) means that capital mobility increases in periods of higher inflation in the sense that shorter roll-over financing periods make international reallocation of capital easier. If more frequent parity adjustments were required in the 1990s this should, however, not necessarily be taken as an indicator of a demise of the EMS. Since real developments and shifts in connection with the EC 1992 project will require parity changes anyhow, adjustments in the parity grid could do justice both to a changing intra-EC industrial landscape and to the risk of inflation-induced misalignment risks.

Various factors contribute to the risk for inflation divergence in the EC in the 1990s and inflation convergence at higher levels. Germany might adjust its objective function for monetary policy and accept higher inflation rates. Increased competition on the supply side of the loan market will create endogenous pressure to reduce reserve requirements in the countries with the highest (net) ratios, namely Italy, Spain and Portugal *(Folkerts-Landau/Mathieson 1989; Reither 1990)*. Seigniorage will consequently reduce, if higher inflation rates do not raise it again, where the non-indexation of tax schemes is an additional and probably highly relevant factor which invites inflationary policies. The ultimate test on commitment to low inflation rates in all EC countries might indeed be the willingness to adopt tax indexation schemes.

Increased competition and abolition of capital controls nevertheless do not automatically imply better prospects for efficiency and growth in the EC, but it could actually accentuate some existing distortions in the EC. The taxation of capital income still differs significantly within the EC, where one dividing-line is different tax rates for domestic and foreign residents *(Folkerts-Landau/Mathieson 1989, p. 10; Giovannini 1989)*, so that free capital flows cannot be expected to equalize gross marginal products of capital within the EC. Another impediment to this is restricted M&A menus as determined by the share of government-owned industries and banks, where privatization should increase the required and the actual return on investment. The elimination of capital controls can be expected to particularly benefit countries with no withholding tax, which means benefits for Luxembourg and Germany, where for political reasons and fear of further capital outflows the introduction of a withholding tax on bank accounts was repealed within 6 months in 1989. With increasing mobility of funds lack of intra-EC tax harmonization becomes a serious impediment for achieving optimal allocation. To the extent that different national tax schemes are reflected in the exchange rate - where, however, no unambiguous links exist - the move to a common EC currency would require as a first step the harmonization of tax codes in the EC. Moreover, for a consistent parity interlocking preceding the introduction of a common EC currency, non-distorted flows of goods and factors in the EC are a prerequisite.

3.2.1 Real Integration, Financial Markets and Monetary Integration

The early 1990s will witness more open financial and competitive markets in the EC *(Key 1989; Walter 1990)*. However, the emergence of a fully integrated EC financial market should not be expected because different currencies and multinationals headquartered in competing currency areas would still imply a certain fragmentation of capital markets. Only with currency unification and tax rate harmonization could this be expected in the EC. Impediments to European growth mentioned by *Aliber (1987, p. 389-90)* will hold for quite some time. If we add to this that segmentation discriminates smaller, often very innovative companies, that state-ownership in banking and industry still restricts the European M&A menu and that increasing intra-EC mergers increase the role of powerful multinationals whose portfolio behavior could destabilize currency markets by transactions in connection with currency substitution, the full benefit of free capital movements and a single EC market will be difficult to realize without comprehensive monetary integration.

Nevertheless, deregulation envisaged in the EC and removal of capital controls will promote the emergence of a more integrated and competitive EC financial market. The principle of home country supervision plus harmonization of basic supervision will ensure with the abolishment of capital controls that both competition in the marketplace as well as competition among regulators will be considerable. An additional factor for European interest rate convergence will indeed be intensified competition in financial markets. After 1992 increased competition in enlarged goods markets will encourage big firms as well as smaller firms to seek decidedly reduced capital costs by shifting financial funds to the cheapest source within the EC. Sharp competition among banks might induce them to take unusually high risks and realize financial innovations that could outpace the fragmented and slowly reacting supervision authorities in the EC.

Prudential supervision becomes thus quite important, and if it is true that the productivity of a country's currency is tied to the soundness of its financial system, the kind of regulatory competition observed will be important in Europe. Under the principle of a single licence for banks as well as insurance companies and the rule of home country supervision, long-term oriented conservative financial regulation schemes might be at a premium. "Regulated in Germany" (or Great Britain) could become as much an immaterial asset as the trade mark "Made in Germany". The switch to a single EC currency would, as the example of the U.S. suggests, not rule out a competitive state-based regulation of the banking and investment industry.

Financial market integration does not, however, necessarily imply that the degree of international asset substitutability within the EC will increase, although this is to be expected in the long term. As the special Italian case of government bonds paying higher interest rates than commercial ones suggests here, interest-bearing assets of different issuers cannot always be deemed to be close substitutes. Assets of various EMS countries are not necessarily better substitutes among each other than various pairings of US and EMS countries' assets. The asset market theory of exchange rate determination places, however, much emphasis on the substitutability of assets denominated in different currencies. If domestic and foreign bonds were perfect substitutes it will hold that $i = i^* + f\text{-}e/e$ (with i, i* standing for the nominal interest rate at home and abroad; f and e representing the forward and the spot exchange rate, respectively). The validity of purchasing power parity ($\pi - \pi^* = e^1\text{-}e^o/e^o$) which is doubtful in the short term implies with $i = r + \pi$ (Fisher formula) that real interest rates on bonds are equal across countries. Investment flows would adjust accordingly.

3.2.2 The Role of Foreign Direct Investment in Asset Market Equilibrium

From a theoretical point of view EC 1992 in combination with monetary integration in the sense of narrowed exchange rate margins implies that there will be a stronger convergence of nominal interest rates in the EC. Moreover, greater inflation rate convergence as a consequence of a reinforcement of the law of one price in a unifying EC market would imply a convergence of real interest rates on bonds denominated in different currencies. A convergence of real financial interest rates (r) should increase the pressure to equilibrate marginal products of capital (MPC) across EC countries, the link being profit-maximizing firms whose investment is driven by the incentive to establish r=MPC. However, the dominant impulse for financial market equilibrium could also emerge from increased real capital mobility - as represented by higher intra-EC FDI (only from a faster tendency of MPC = MPC* results then the faster equilibration of r = r* (being equal to MPC in each country)).

A specific asymmetry concerns the regional intra-EC distribution of firm-specific, mostly technologically determined advantages as well as of locational advantages that are, from a theoretical point of view, important for foreign direct investment flows. In this regard the U.K., the Netherlands (both very US-oriented) as well as Germany and France are important both as source and as host countries; the latter also include Italy and Spain. As FDI affects the marginal products of real capital in the regions/countries of the EC, the asymmetry in multinationalization is important for a "full arbitrage equilibrium" in Europe. This equilibrium means that three conditions hold simultaneously: (i) risk adjusted equality of national bond interest rates; (ii) marginal product of capital in each country equals real interest rate on bonds; (iii) and finally the marginal product of capital is equal across countries. If the real bond interest rate increases above the marginal product of capital in a major FDI source country multinational firms will shift a greater share of investment to other EC countries so that MPC abroad will decrease (with heterogeneous capital goods, FDI inflows might actually raise the host country's MPC by improving MPC in up-stream and down-stream activities).

It is interesting to put capital market liberalization and EC 1992 in the perspective of the standard asset market approach to exchange rate determination (survey: *Claassen 1980*). However, one has to go one step further and take into account the international investment dimension because a full arbitrage equilibrium can only be achieved if the marginal product of capital in all countries and hence investment is related to changes of the interest rate in bonds markets. Moreover, if the exchange rate changes, not only the relative price between tradables and non-tradables and the terms of trade change, but also the relative price and yield of assets denominated in different currencies.

An important theoretical aspect is connected with FDI and financial capital flows in a modified asset market model where a simple modification is introduced by assuming that the demand for money as well as for foreign and domestic bonds is proportional to financial wealth W and that the desired portfolio shares depend on relative returns and - entering with a positive sign in all demand equations - on real national income Y. The latter is given in the short run but can change via demand impacts in accordance with the trade balance in the medium term and in accordance with supply-side effects coupled with domestic and foreign investment in the long term (and imported input factors). In the goods market of a simple model the supply side would be determined by the capital stock K that is partly foreign-owned and labor L, while FDI flows enter on the demand side in the investment function $I(q, r, r^*)$: Both the domestic and the foreign real interest rate r and r^*, respectively, and the terms of trade $q:=eP^*/P$ which influence the real value of dividends from FDI determine the investment function here.

As a point of departure we take an expansive open market operation that shifts the money market equilibrium schedule MM and the domestic bonds market equilibrium schedule BB, respectively, to the left (Fig. 1); it is assumed that the country internationally is in a net creditor position, so that it holds a positive stock of foreign bonds F - naturally F^* is, on balance, negative in the rest of the world. Given the slope of the foreign bonds equilibrium schedule FF, the leftward shift of MM and hence the depreciation of the exchange rate e is the smaller, the greater the interest elasticity of the demand for money ; financial innovation, lower bond-money conversion costs and the growth of multinationals in the context of EC 1992 are likely to raise this elasticity. An offsetting impact, implying a steeper FF schedule, stems from a greater substitutability between domestic and foreign bonds that is to be expected in the context of capital market liberalization; a temporary reduction of the domestic interest rate induces a higher additional demand for foreign bonds than before. With respect to inflation which is disregarded in the following paragraph, we note that the intersection between the FF and the BB schedule determines the real interest rate, while the nominal interest rate i, determined by the sum of r and the inflation rate (say equivalent to BC), is relevant for the demand for money and money market equilibrium which implies that inflation lowers the real interest rate. Here, we take into account that the terms of trade $eP^*/P=q$ decrease with a switch from price stability to inflation because the reduction in desired per-capita money balances implies a once-and-for-all increase in the price level so that the trade balance deteriorates and a once-and-for-all reduction in the stock of foreign bonds occurs (upward shift of the FF schedule, passing through B).

Fig. 1: FDI and Asset Market Approach to Exchange Rate Determination

$M = m(r,r^*,B,Y)W$ (MM schedule)

$B = b(r,r^*,B,Y)W$ (BB schedule)

$eF = h(r,r^*,B,Y)W$ (FF schedule)

$W = M + B + eF$

Equilibrium condition for goods market:

$Y^S(K,L) = C(.) + I(q,r,r^*) + G + X(.) - qX^*(.)$

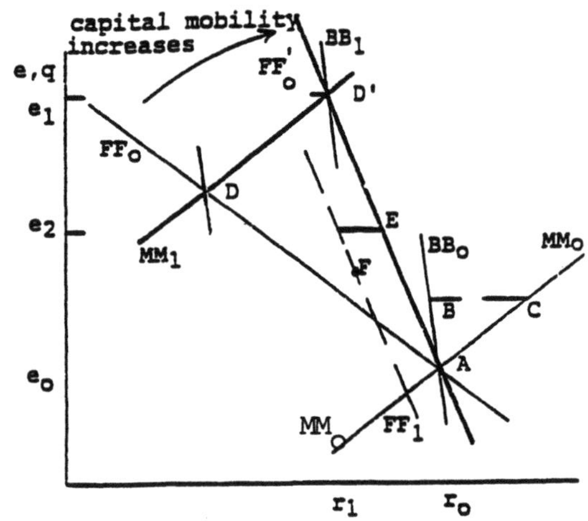

The open market operation considered here implies a new short-run equilibrium that is characterized by a higher exchange rate/terms of trade e_1 and a lower interest rate r_1. If in a fixed exchange rate regime e_1 is already above the spread margin, the excess demand for foreign bonds will partly have to be met by the central bank's selling of currency reserves/foreign bonds that offsets the initial monetary expansion. The higher the stock of inward FDI relative to the total capital stock, that is the greater the role of multinationals, and the more a correspondingly high intra-firm financial capital mobility reinforces the substitutability of domestic and foreign bonds, the steeper will be the FF curve (FF'), which in itself reinforces the need for coordinated interest rate changes. This limits the possibility of a central bank to implement an expansionary open market operation. The dominant role of German FDI in the EC supports in this view the dominance of the German central bank in monetary policy on the European continent. It is important to note: A depreciation improves the trade balance which implies increasing net capital outflows which, however, can consist of higher net FDI inflows (stimulated by changing relative profits, where q enters) combined with higher financial capital outflows which primarily react to interest rates and, not treated here, to a changing expected nominal depreciation rate of the currency. Situations in which MPC > (<) MPC* can be combined with r falling short or exceeding r*. Both a trade surplus and net FDI outflows can reflect an improved competitiveness which makes an FDI-adjusted basic balance concept meaningful.

If the trade balance was in equilibrium initially, the depreciation in connection with the J-curve effect means a short-term deterioration of the trade balance, but a long-term improvement. In the case of flexible exchange rates or within the margins of the parity spread a corresponding capital export in the long run is required. The immediate impact of the expansive open market operation is a lower interest rate and an excess demand in the money market that falls on foreign bonds and is fully absorbed by a corresponding depreciation - in the case of low capacity utilization that allows higher exports partly by a depreciation, partly by an increase of the stock of foreign bonds F and a corresponding appreciation (e_2). In terms of foreign goods the real depreciation (e_0 is here the point of reference) makes the acquisition of companies cheaper for foreigners (also because of the drop of r). It will be restored by higher net capital inflows which means that F reduces and the depreciation increases furthermore in the medium term; or, to put it in the explicit perspective of the stock market: foreigners will swap a given amount of foreign stocks for a greater share of K which might be dubbed an improvement of the foreign countries' "terms of capital". Net FDI inflows amount together with higher domestic investment, both stimulated by a lower interest rate, to a positive supply-side effect. The supply-side effects tend to support the terms-of-trade induced improvement of the trade balance so that F will increase in the long-term (downward shift of the FF schedule), and higher output and national income will shift the MM-curve and the BB-curve to the right (point F). With a *Metzler*-type savings behavior that implies savings as a function of the divergence between target wealth and actual wealth, a medium-term increase in the price level and hence a reduction of M/P would stimulate savings and lead via a reduced absorption to a transitory reinforcement of the trade balance improvement.

For a given exchange rate depreciation observed in the asset market it holds: The higher the international FDI elasticity - and here capital import controls, state-ownership and location quality divergences enter the problem -, the greater the increase in the production potential and the higher the actual and anticipated long-term trade surplus. Taking into account the impact of 1992, the conclusion to be drawn is that short-term exchange rate volatility as measured by the first-round impact of monetary policy is likely to increase, but that more elastic foreign direct investment is likely to support self-corrective and largely anticipated exchange rate adjustments. Due to the "FDI-supply side effect", greater short-term exchange rate volatility will then imply only transitory problems for central banks' commitment to defend parity. In this sense a high degree of investment mobility supports the case for fixed exchange rates and ultimately for currency unification.

3.2.3 Market Integration and Intra-EC Price Adjustment

The EC 1992 project will create a single EC market without significant barriers to trade, and this facilitates regional price arbitrage. This development should reinforce the law of one price for tradable goods, and by reinforcing parallel price movements across EC countries the intra-EC process of adjustments in the real interest rates will be affected. From the theoretical perspective of the monetary approach to the balance of payments, the speed with which national price increases for tradables translate via increasing "world market prices" into an excess demand for money in other countries pertaining to a fixed exchange rate system is particularly important.

With respect to monetary policy the greater scope for the purchasing power parity implies that a given monetary impulse in some EC country will translate more rapidly into price increases in the whole EC. Especially if the share of tradable goods is rising, national central banks might turn to non-cooperative policies that pay less attention to price stability than so far - an argument in

Tab. 3: Regional Price Divergences in the U.S, the EC and West Germany

1988# P		1988 y*	1988 P		1987 P	1978 P
USA	EC countries			cities/towns in Germany		
	DK	144.9	121.5	Hamburg	n.a.	101.7
	FRG (Bonn)	135.1	(100)	Bonn	100	100
	F	116.0	93.0	Karlsruhe	101.5	98.9
					94.1**	
	B	103.2	88.7	Frankfurt	n.a.	101.6
	NL	104.5	87.2	Duisburg	n.a.	n.a.
	IRL	61.1	85.2			
	I	98.0	80.7	München	103.0	100.7
					110.3**	
	LUX	122.2	79.9	Pirmasens	n.a.	98.2
	UK	96.0	79.9			
	SP	59.5	65.3			
	GR	36.3	62.1			
	P	28.9	48.5			
				Weiden		96.0
				Berlin	102.2	100.9
	------------				117.3**	
	AUT		100.8	München	103.0	100.7
263	CDN		76.9			
urban	USA	137.4	74.0			
areas	J	160.0	116.9			
0.093	coefficient of variation	0.391 (EC)	0.218 (EC)			0.018 ***0.02-0.09

* EC average = 100.
** Index which includes housing (weight: 1/3).
*** Coefficient of variation for regional price index samples as calculated by the Statistisches Bundesamt for various consumption goods (specific brands) in unpublished samples.
Sources: Figures for the USA in 1988.III are based on ACCRA (1988), Cost of Living Index, 21, No. 3, 1988. Index for real GDP per capita according to EC Commission; national figures for purchasing power parities (June 1988) are from Eurostat, Economy and Finance, Series B, Consumer price index, supplement 2, 1988, 5; Figures for the Federal Republic of Germany are based on: ROSTIS, W. (1979), Zwischenörtlicher Vergleich des Verbraucherpreisniveaus in 31 Städten, Wirtschaft und Statistik, 1979/6, 403-410. ANGERMANN, O. (1989), Vergleich der Verbraucherpreisniveaus in Bonn, Karlsruhe, München und Berlin (West), Wirtschaft und Statistik, 1989/4, 258-261. Own calculations.

favor of tighter institutionalized policy cooperation in the EC. Figures for absolute regional price comparisons are difficult to obtain in the EC and methodological differences among countries complicate an analysis focussing on the strictness of the law of one price. Tab. 3 shows the standard deviation for regional price index values in Germany, the U.S. and the EC. As might be expected - setting aside methodological caveats - the standard deviation of composite price indices within Germany and in the U.S. is much smaller than among EC countries. Obviously migration and mobility on both the demand and the supply side would have to rise considerably in a post-1992 EC to reduce the present EC price variation. However, there is no doubt that the law of one price will be reinforced in the future. This might also imply a steeper (international) Phillips-curve in the future as inflationary impulses in a more open economy tend to quickly reduce the respective country's price competitiveness.

It will certainly take time until EC markets for goods and factors have become more integrated. One cannot exclude that EC firms that face reduced opportunity for price discrimination within the EC will try to enforce price discrimination schemes in other regions of the world economy.

A survey by *Runzheimer Mitchell Europe (Financial Times 1990, p. 4)* showed for the case of individual products large intra-EC price differences. The ratio of the highest to the lowest pre-tax price in the EC varied between 1.36 and 2.37; the price - without taxes - of the Financial Times itself ranged from only ECU .67 in London to ECU 1.54 in Denmark. Price differentiation of multinational corporations plays a significant role in reality, but companies are likely to try to segment European markets along income and quality profiles rather than along the vanishing national borders and currency areas.

3.3 EC-External Aspects of European Monetary Integration

If EC firms - favoring in the 1990s cross-border EC M&As as domestic concentration opportunities have been rapidly exhausted between 1986 and 1990 - were to adopt a similar price discrimination strategy as Japanese multinationals which adjust in periods of global demand changes mainly export prices while leaving higher domestic prices relatively unchanged, the effectiveness of stabilization policy could increase in the EC. This holds namely because expansive monetary policies can more easily be combined with expansive fiscal policies, where extra public demand would then imply limited upward pressure on prices in the EC and a marked increase of EC export prices - hence a real appreciation which stimulates output growth via cheaper imported input factors. Moreover, upward pressure on interest rates might also be limited. With the EC being in a net creditor position vis-a-vis the rest of the world, net wealth in terms of domestic goods would reduce which in turn could stimulate EC savings in the context of a METZLER-type household with a given wealth target.

The EC's aim to adopt narrower spreads around central rates while maintaining nominal exchange rate stability faces not only EC-internal difficulties, but also problems that stem from the relations with the U.S., Japan and other countries. There is above all the question whether EC monetary integration will not periodically lead to greater volatility of the dollar exchange rate which in turn could have destabilizing effects upon the EMS currencies' exchange rates *(Giavazzi and Giovannini 1986)*.

This argument might support the idea of a common EC currency which will be perceived by financial market participants as distinct from a system of national EC currencies connected with adjustable, although fixed exchange rates. Moreover, an interesting question is, whether proposals *(Williamson and Miller 1987)* for an indicator-guided exchange rate policy could not gain more global support with fewer but greater currency areas in the world economy.

As regards the international distribution of the burden of adjustment in the real and the monetary sphere, capital market integration as well as EC currency unification implies a greater future need for changes in the U.S. The old interest rate parity in its long run version becomes doubtful, namely that in the EC the nominal interest rate plus the rate of exchange rate appreciation is equal to the marginal product of capital in the U.S. plus the expected U.S. inflation rate = long term U.S. interest rate (MPC in Europe would then adjust to the difference of EC nominal interest rates minus expected inflation). In the future EC interest movements will affect U.S. interest rates and investment decisions. From a theoretical point of view the locking of exchange rates should take place only after complete removal of internal barriers to trade in goods and assets in the EC.

4. Creating an EC Central Bank

It is obvious that EC financial market integration in connection with project EC 1992 poses serious problems for progress in the EMS along the lines of the Delors report. If the transition phase to a common central bank with a common EC currency is long and burdened with recurrent strains, a European System of Central Banks might never become reality at all. An attractive vision of an EC central bank and a common currency would be important to generate the necessary politico-economic momentum for the formation of an EC central bank.

4.1 Benefits and Risks from Currency Unification and EC Central Banking

With respect to currency unification a traditional approach in economics is connected with the literature on the optimum currency area, where "currency area" means either a monetary union with strictly fixed exchange rates among currencies or the adoption of a single currency.

Focussing on the problem that a currency area renounces the policy instrument of exchange rate changes within the area and thus foregoes the benefits of using exchange rate changes as an instrument to achieve or restore full-employment, the classic approach of *Mundell (1961)* emphasizes that those regions/nations should not renounce the option of changing exchange rates to restore competitiveness that are characterized by low factor mobility. Taking into account changes of residence by the respective domestic citizens plus the immigration rate, labor mobility in Germany, France and the UK was found to be lower in 1980 than in the US or Japan *(OECD 1987, p. 136)*. Intra-EC mobility across national borders is certainly even lower than within the countries themselves. Project 1992 as well as the greater role of multinational EC companies are likely to somewhat increase labor mobility, and further legal and illegal immigration from North-Africa and Eastern Europe might indeed raise factor mobility even more. An open question is whether a relatively low degree of labor mobility cannot be compensated by considerable price differences of non-tradable services and real estate as well as a high mobility of complementary factors, in particular real capital and technology. Indeed, due to the closing human capital gap within the EC as a result of a generally increased capital mobility (high-tech is not tied to natural resource sites as it was typically for heavy industries) and as a consequence of EC 1992 the complementary factors are more mobile in the EC than before. Moreover, one may argue that a currency unification implies a decisive shift towards a less fragmented capital market and hence increased pressure in the European capital markets which should further raise the mobility of real capital.

It is doubtful that the EC is an optimum currency area *(Thygesen 1987, 1990)*. But if one presumes that for political reasons the 12-country EC is the relevant region to be conceived as a common currency area, one may restate the optimum currency area approach by supposing the area as pre-defined and then asking for the necessary institutional reforms in the respective countries that would ex post make the EC an optimum currency area. Following this line of reasoning, the mobility of production factors in the EC should be systematically encouraged by an adequately tailored political framework and systematic incentives for avoiding unemployment risks. Stronger incentives to reduce unemployment risks can be provided by encouraging greater real wage diversity, higher regional and greater upward "skill-mobility". More important than exchange rate flexibility would be new unemployment insurance schemes along true insurance principles, namely partial refunds of contributions for full-employment regions and regional contribution rates that depend on past and present unemployment records. Currency unification does not necessarily imply higher unemployment if monetary unification is connected with superior insurance schemes and if one adds to this a greater EC regional policy fund - being also useful to sanction non-compliance with agreed upper limits on national deficit-spending - that allocates public investment and seed-financing to regions in which high sunk costs of investment in physical and human capital imply considerable negative welfare effects of idle production factors.

Another criterion for an optimum currency area is related to the degree of openness of the economy as measured by the share of tradables: *McKinnon (1963)* argued that a small open economy that faces given terms of trade will record only a higher price level as a consequence of a devaluation - a risk that rises with the share of tradables in overall output. However, as exchange rates are largely determined by capital flows, the tradability of real and financial assets could be considered to be an important additional criterium. Exchange rate changes become a less powerful instrument of economic policy if no capital controls exist - and hence, capital market liberalization supports the case of currency unification. This holds because exchange rate shifts imply then not only changes of the terms of trade but of international relative asset prices (the terms of capital) as well; the asset market effects can run counter to the goods market effects, where overshooting or undershooting effects related to the contrast of high adjustment speeds in financial markets and low adjustment speeds in the real sphere imply a danger of misallocation and protectionism in countries with sharp appreciations.

Kenen (1969) proposed the product diversity criterion for constituting a currency union. If there is low product diversity in a country's output, international relative price shifts and hence exchange rate changes will be important to compensate internal or external price shifts that impair the profitability of specialized firms and production locations. Hence, countries with high and increasing product diversity in output are candidates for joining in a currency area; EC 1992 indeed is likely to reinforce intra-industry trade and product diversity in the EC, so that this aspect supports the currency unification goal.

Another argument in favor of establishing a common EC currency is related to currency substitution (CS) whose impact on exchange rates are as yet ambiguous *(Miles 1978; Isaac 1989)*. With increasing currency substitution there is a risk of higher induced exchange rate volatility that might translate in an EC with increasing emphasis on nominal exchange stability into severe misalignment. While the currency substitution problem is not directly important for money demand shifts within the EC, indirect currency substitution will concern major EC currencies. Moreover, establishing a common currency in connection with the establishment of an EC central bank would avoid the risk of non-cooperative central bank behavior in Western Europe *(Cohen 1989)*.

The benefits of a project 1992 might not fully be realized if exchange rate volatility prevents the full exploitation of opportunities for a greater intra-EC division of labor and the use of scale economies. The counter-argument is that financial market integration and innovation offer market-based options to cope with exchange rate risk; however, restriction in these markets and problems of overshooting cannot be overlooked. Moreover, if a single EC currency would reduce exchange rate volatility vis-a-vis the dollar and the yen, the risk of periodical exchange rate overshooting and induced (irreversible) protectionism in countries with a real appreciation could be reduced. Positive external effects, i.e. growing world trade, could support EC currency unification.

The visible positive external effects of German monetary union show in principle the significance of a convertible and stable currency: With the adoption of the West German currency East Germany (then the GDR) achieved immediate access to all goods of the world market, but, of course, at the same time its industry became subject to world market competition which implies adjustment pressure; the shift to world market prices amounts to a relative price shock and translates via induced obsolescence of part of the capital stock into negative wealth effects. However, facing a much bigger variety of goods and assets that could be bought with the DM, savings incentives increased, work incentives improved and better investment opportunities attracted both internal and external capital.

In principle it is conceivable that - after the creation of a convertible stable EC currency - the German-German currency unification could have a European analogy. Introducing a convertible ECU in Poland, Hungary and other East European countries could be a decisive step to integrate these countries (after supply-side adjustments) into the EMS as market-based economic systems. This could happen within a treaty among European central banks or by joining the EC. Such an East-West currency unification could yield considerable benefits provided it contributes to price stability and growth in the whole of Europe. This idea, however, is a proposal for the long term only.

A prudent monetary integration scheme in the EC that would lead to a sustaining containment of the EC-wide inflation rate could have economic benefits which are not just tied to economizing on transaction costs but also to reducing the risk of inflation in the EC as well as to increasing the global currency competition between the dollar, the yen and the ECU (and in some distant future: an internationally accepted currency of the NICs). While higher unemployment risk due to wage inflexibility could become a more serious problem after currency unification, it seems to be clear that providing a price stability assuring EC currency as a competitor vis-a-vis the dollar and the yen will be beneficial for several reasons (see exhibit 1).

(I) A low inflation rate means a smaller relative price variance and hence a reduced risk of misallocation, compared to a situation with high inflation rates; this is an argument in favor of currency unification provided that only an EC central bank could realize price stability to a greater degree than the current EMS regime.

Exhibit 1: Benefits of Currency Unification and EC Central Banking in Connection with 1992 Program

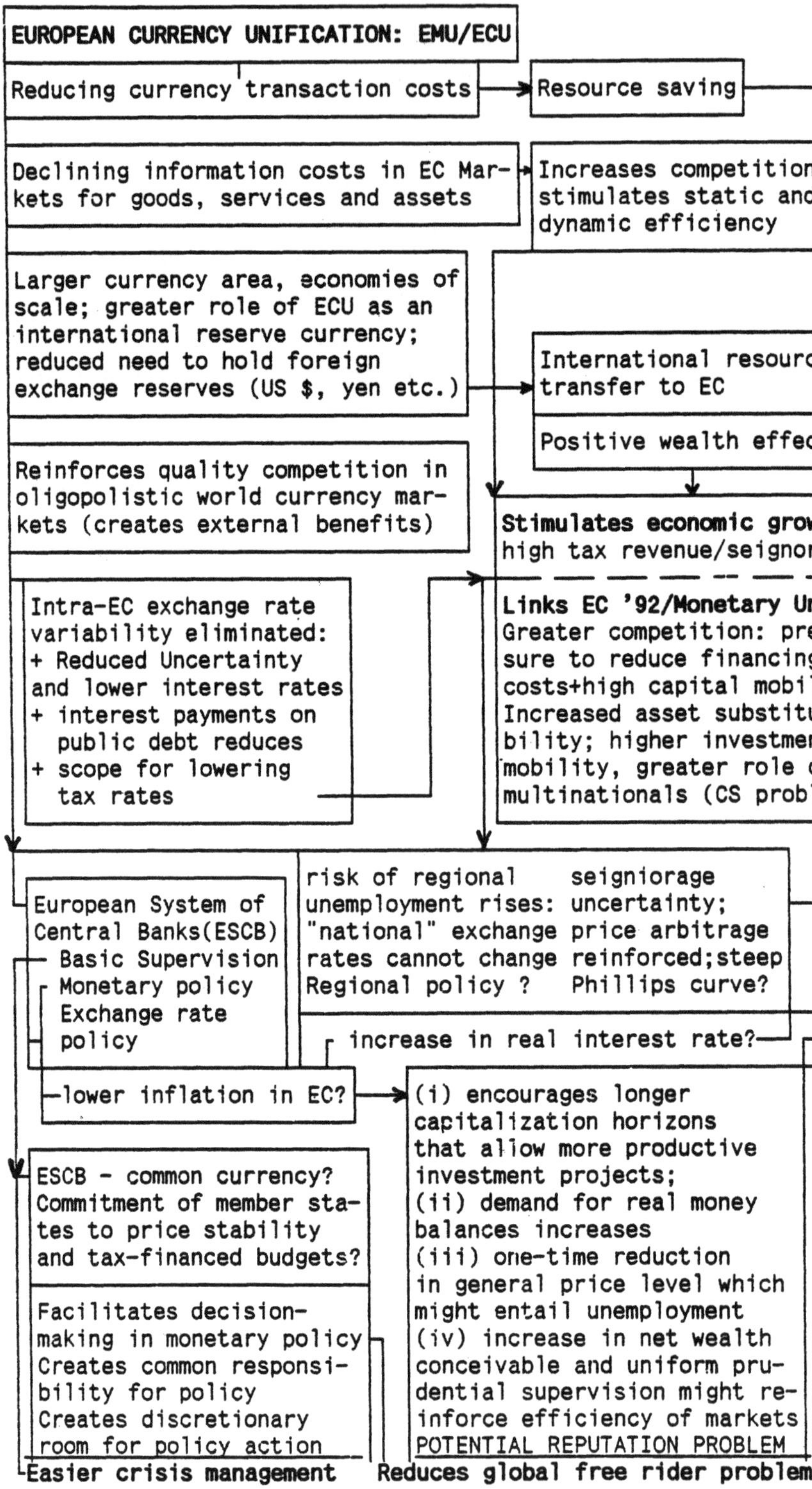

(II) Currency unification as well as narrowing the margins around parities should promote trade, efficiency and growth by eliminating exchange rate risks.

(III) In a unified currency area a stable foreseeable monetary policy can be more easily implemented than in a potentially non-cooperative EMS regime with many currencies; reduced uncertainty should reduce real interest rates as suggested by *Mascaro and Meltzer (1983)*.

(IV) The lower the inflation rate and the nominal interest rate, respectively, the higher the desired per-capita amount of money which offers prospects of a positive wealth effect; since capital market integration implies a higher interest elasticity of the demand for money, a reduction of the current EC inflation rate will bring considerable positive welfare effects.

(V) The ECU could achieve an increasing role as an international reserve asset, while EC member countries could drastically reduce their official foreign reserve holdings. With an outstanding amount of global official reserves of $ 600 billion, a share of the ECU of 1/3 and a reduction of EC reserve holdings to the US-level of end-1989 ($ 48 bill.) would amount to considerable benefits.

(VI) Greater price transparency in the markets for goods, factors and assets as well as the increasing scope of markets themselves offer benefits; risks emerge from a narrowing of competition among monetary regimes in the EC, but also as a consequence of potential reputation problems for both an ECU currency and an EC central bank.

(VII) An oligopolistic rivalry between the ECU, the dollar and the yen creates a globally welcome competitive pressure for the provision of stable currencies. With reduced inflation risks in the EC, North-America and Japan, the advantages of flexible nominal exchange rates in the triangle US-Europe-Japan can be fully exploited - monetary cooperation in crisis periods within that triangle is facilitated by the visible interdependence among the small (and reduced) number of central banks.

4.2 Problems of Institutional Innovation: Policy Failure and Market Failure

The formation of an EC central bank will be a unique and historical exercise in institutional innovation. Problems of an EC central bank and a common monetary policy have been discussed in the literature only recently *(e.g. De Cecco and Giovannini 1989; Hasse and Schaefer 1990)*. It is obvious that such a new institution poses risks and offers benefits, where the balance is much determined by the institutional design adopted.

A major driving force behind the move towards an EC central bank is certainly the desire of major EC countries to realize greater influence in monetary policy and to be less dominated by German policies and politics. The creation of a common EC currency poses some technical as well as some psychological problems (where national pride of the traditional domestic currency can be taken into account with an ECU layout on the face side and the respective national symbol on the back).

A common EC central bank that would replace the current overlordship of the Deutsche Bundesbank in the continental EC countries is desired, but it is difficult to set up a new institution with equal reputation, especially if one takes into account the task of supplying a high-quality ECU. If the Bundesbank's reputation capital could be somehow transferred to the new institution, all EC economies would benefit from high credibility of monetary policy in Western Europe that would otherwise have to be accumulated over many years; less uncertainty over monetary policy strategies will then pay off in the form of less uncertainty in financial markets, and this should reduce real interest rates - welcome not least by governments with a high debt burden. Reputation and credibility are also important assets for interventions in the foreign exchange markets. Credibility in turn can be based both upon certain rules and the incentives faced by "monetary management".

An EC central bank will most likely grow out of a system of closer monetary cooperation in a transition phase. The governors of the present EC central banks will cooperate systematically and develop a very specialized organizational human capital which implies high personal "career sunk costs" that would add to the stability of cooperation schemes developed. Specialized human (political) capital in an organization where conflicts in decision-making would reduce the viability and status of the EC central bank implies low incentives for opportunistic behavior of the leading persons in such a new central bank unless they would face control by a national policy body. The more likely version, however, is that the supranational EC parliament will gain more responsibility. Moreover, the complex field of monetary policy could bring for EC monetary policy more room for discretionary policies, especially because in the field of the much politicized nationally-rooted fiscal policies problems of cooperation and harmonization are very high. Latent conflicts within the ECOFIN could indeed increase the degree of freedom for an EC monetary policy.

A key issue of a transition to EC central banking is in most countries the apparent loss of policy autonomy. But in most cases this issue is a rather subjective and fictitious one because financial market forces today are so strong and international monetary policy interdependence so visible that the transfer of formal national rights to the supranational EC level would mean only at first sight a substantive loss of policy autonomy; on the contrary, transferring formal national decision rights to the supranational EC level could mean for some EC countries greater policy control. With multinational and transnational industries and banking, the supranationalization of policy might indeed become a strategy of policy-makers to regain some policy autonomy and effectiveness.

The institutional setting for the envisaged EC central bank would be decisive for the success or failure of the supranational system. If the new institution would represent less policy failure (and, as regards prudential supervision, less financial market failure) than the sum of current national policy failures, the supranational monetary regime could be deemed a success.

The theoretical discussion about the complex aspects of institutional innovation in the EC has only begun. The politico-economic situation in the EC in the 1990s seems to lead to a European System of Central Banks in the long run - possibly in the form of an integrated EC central bank or a system of national central banks acting within the overarching framework of common goals, principles and instruments. An integrated EC central bank with a sub-structure of dependent national central banks which assume more or less technical functions seems desirable to the extent that coordination of monetary policy within a more loose institutional framework faces systematic instability or rising consensus costs. With now 12 EC member countries and probably more to join in the distant future, an ever-present varying EC election calendar implies the problem that nationally responsible central banks would burden consensual decision-making with factors derived from short-term political pressure. This aspect is particularly true with respect to government-dependent central banks, where even the German central bank with its particular status testified in the context of German currency unification that election calendars have an impact on central banking. Furthermore, with an ever faster and sometimes unstable global financial market system one could argue that delayed stabilizing intervention in a period of potential financial market crisis would bring high opportunity costs that could be avoided only in an ECBS with options for a rapid decision-making process.

Reduced competition among European currencies in the EC as a consequence of currency unification could imply that Western Europe will face on average a "quality of money risk", especially higher inflation rates, in the future. However, intensified competition in a more levelled global currency market could counter-balance this effect. Also, rules and incentives might be stated in a way so as to ensure priority to the goal of price stability, although not all EC member countries attach as high a priority to it as does the German central bank.

If we take into account the rivalries among major EC countries and their respective "strong traditions", an EC central bank could have the following traits: a chairman of a board responsible for monetary policy from one of the smaller countries; a British chairman for prudential supervision; and Frankfurt or Paris as the seat of the EC central bank - the selection of Frankfurt could be intended to achieve a transfer of stability reputation to the new EC central bank. If Italy was to receive a special once-and-for-all transfer of EC regional funds, the question might arise what Spain as a new important player in the EC could expect: Fortunately, the new EC treaty will have to be signed in a major capital.

References

ALIBER, R.Z. (1987). Financial Markets and the Growth of Europe, in: LAWRENCE, R.Z.; SCHULTZE, C.L., eds., Barriers to European Growth. Washington: Brookings.

CABALLERO, R.J. and CORBO, V. (1989). The Effect of Real Exchange Rate Uncertainty on Exports: Empirical Evidence. World Bank Economic Review, 3, 263-278.

CECCO, M.; GIOVANNINI, A., eds. (1989). A European Central Bank? Cambridge: Cambridge University Press.

CLAASSEN, E.M. (1980). Grundprobleme der Geldtheorie. 2nd ed., Heidelberg: Springer.

CLAASSEN, E.M., ed. (1990). International and European Monetary Systems. New York: Praeger.

COHEN, D. (1989). The Costs and Benefits of a European Currency, in: CECCO, M.; GIOVANNINI, A., eds. (1989). A European Central Bank? Cambridge: Cambridge University Press, 195-209.

COLLINS, S. M. (1988). Inflation and the European Monetary System, in: GIVAZZI, F.; MICOSSI, S.; MILLER, M., eds., The European Monetary System. Cambridge: Cambridge University Press, 112-136.

COMMISSION OF THE EC (1990). XXXIIIrd General Report on the Activities of the European Communities 1989. Luxembourg 1990.

DE GRAUWE, P. (1989). International Trade and Economic Growth in the European Monetary System. European Economic Review, 31, 389-398.

DE GRAUWE, P. and PEETERS, T., eds. (1989). The ECU and European Monetary Integration. London: Macmillan.

DELORS REPORT (Committee for the Study of Economic and Monetary Union, 1989). Report on Economic and Monetary Union in the European Community, Brussels.

DEUTSCHE BUNDESBANK (1989). Exchange Rate Movements within the European Monetary System. Monthly Report of the Deutsche Bundesbank, 41, November, 28-36.

ECONOMIST (1989). A Survey of Europe's Capital Markets, December 16, London.

FINANCIAL TIMES (1990). Counting Costs of Dual Pricing in the Run-up to 1992, July 9, 4.

FOLKERTS-LANDAU, D. and MATHIESON, D.J. (1989). The European Monetary System in the Context of the Integration of European Financial Markets. Washington: IMF.

FRATIANNI, M. and VON HAGEN, J. (1988). German Dominance in the EMS - The Empirical Evidence. Indiana University.

GIAVAZZI, F. and GIOVANNINI, A. (1986). The EMS and the Dollar. Economic Policy, 2, 455-473.

GIAVAZZI, F. and GIOVANNINI, A. (1987). Models of the EMS: Is Europe a Greater Deutschmark Area? in: BRYANT, R.; ET AL., eds., Global Macroeconomics. London: Macmillan, 237-270.

GIAVAZZI, F. and PAGANO, M. (1988). The Advantage of Tying One's Hand: EMS Discipline and Central Bank Credibility. European Economic Review, 32, 1055-1075.

GIOVANNINI, A. (1989). National Tax Systems versus the European Capital Market. Economic Policy, 9, 345-386.

GRILLI, V. (1989). Europe 1992: Issues and Prospect for the Financial Markets. Economic Policy, 9, 387-422.

ISAAC, A.G. (1989). Exchange Rate Volatility and Currency Substitution. Journal of International Money and Finance, 8, 277-284.

KATH, D. and HENNERKES, W. (1985). Internationale Zinsübertragung bei flexiblen Wechselkursen, in: FILC, W.; KÖHLER, C., eds., Stabilisierung des Währungssystems. Berlin: Duncker & Humblot, 161-176.

KEY, S.J. (1989). Financial Integration in the European Community. Board of Governors of the Federal Reserve System International Finance Discussion Papers No. 349, Washington.

KENEN, P.B. (1969). The Theory of Optimum Currency Areas: An Eclectic View, in: MUNDELL, R.A.; SWOBODA, A.K., Monetary Problems of the International Economy. Chicago: University of Chicago Press, 41-60.

LEIGH-PEMBERTON, R. (1989). The Future of Monetary Arrangements in Europe. IEA Occasional Paper, 82, London.

MASCARO, A. and MELTZER, A.H. (1983). Long- and Short-term Interest Rates in a Risky World. Journal of Monetary Economics, 12, 485-518.

McKINNON, R. (1963). Optimum Currency Areas. American Economic Review, 53, 717-725.

MELITZ, J. (1988). Monetary Discipline, Germany and the European Monetary System. Kredit und Kapital, 31, 481-512.

MILES, M.A. (1978). Currency Substitution, Flexible Exchange Rates and Monetary Interdependence. American Economic Review, 68, 428-436.

MUNDELL, R.A. (1961). A Theory of Optimum Currency Areas. American Economic Review, 51, 657-665.

OECD (1987). Structural Adjustment and Economic Performance, Paris.

REITHER, F. (1989). Fiskalische Restriktionen für die Europäische Währungsintegration, in: SCHÄFER, W.; HASSE, R., eds., forthcoming.

SCHÄFER, W. and HASSE, R., eds. (1990). Europäische Währungspolitik im Wandel, forthcoming.

SMEETS, H.-D. (1989). Does Germany Dominate the EMS? University of Bayreuth, mimeo.

THYGESEN, N. (1987). Is the European Economic Community an Optimal Currency Area? in: LEVICH, R.M.; SOMMARIVA, A., eds., The ECU Market. Lexington: Lexington, 163-185.

THYGESEN, N. (1990). The Benefits and Costs of Currency Unification, in: SIEBERT, H., ed., The Completion of the Internal Market. Tübingen: Mohr, 347-375.

UNGERER, H. et al. (1986). The European Monetary System: Recent Developments. Washington: IMF.

VON FURSTENBERG, G. M. and JEON, B.N. (1989). International Stock Price Movements: Links and Messages. Brookings Papers on Economic Activity, 125-167.

VON HAGEN, J. (1989). Monetary Targeting with Exchange Rate Constraints: The Bundesbank in the 1980s. Federal Reserve Bank of St. Louis Economic Report, September, 53-69.

WALTER, I. (1990). European Financial Integration and its Implications for the United States. Paper prepared for AEI conference The United States and Europe in the 1990s, Washington, D.C., March 5-8.

WEGNER, M. (1989). The European Monetary System: A Regional Bretton Woods or an Institutional Innovation? in: VOSGERAU, H.-J., ed., New Institutional Arrangements for the World Economy. Heidelberg: Springer, 89-111.

WELFENS, P.J.J. (1990a). Internationalisierung von Wirtschaft und Wirtschaftspolitik/ Internationalization of the Economy and of Economic Policies. Heidelberg: Springer.

- (1990b), Privatization, M&As, and Inter-Firm Cooperation in the EC: Improved Prospects for Innovation?, paper presented at the Schumpeter Society Meeting, Airlie House, Virginia, June 3-5, 1990.

- (1990c), EC Integration and Economic Reforms in CMEA Countries: Germany as a Bridge Between East and West?, paper presented at the conference Economic Aspects of German Unification, AICGS/The Johns Hopkins University, Washington D.C., Nov. 13/14.

WILLIAMSON, J. and MILLER, M.H. (1987). Targets and Indicators: A Blueprint for the International Coordination of Economic Policy. Washington: Institute for International Economics.

WILLMS, M. (1990). Der Delors-Plan und die Anforderungen an eine gemeinsame europäische Geldpolitik. Kredit und Kapital, forthcoming.

George M. von Furstenberg

Comments on:
Creating a European Central Bank after 1992: Issues of EC Monetary Integration and Problems of Institutional Innovation

The paper probes many issues surrounding the establishment of European monetary union in a manner that is imaginative and suggestive of further thought. I would like to expand on just three of the points that I regard as particularly important.

1. The first worrisome issue is: "How Would Fiscal Policies Be Disciplined in the Final Stages of European Economic and Monetary Union?"

The working document of the EC Finance Ministers assembled at Ashford Castle at the end of March 1990 waffles eloquently on this point. It claims that "it is vital that Member States retain the capacity to use their budgets to respond to diverse economic problems." Among these problems, one may presume, is the political inability to cut government expenditures, including subsidies to industry and agriculture, and/or to raise taxes. What these corrective actions would be supposed to have accomplished during prosperous periods is to reduce the rate of growth of government debt to well below that of GNP. Few of the European or North American countries are likely to achieve any such outcome under current circumstances. The last thing we need, therefore, is further to facilitate government deficits.

Under these circumstances it appears necessary to ask what the integration of financial markets and home-country issuance of community-wide passports to financial institutions may mean for fiscal discipline in the EC. Most likely discipline will decline unless bank regulators are empowered to downgrade central government debt and focus keenly on country tax-risk. The Second Banking Directive leaves much prudential regulation to national authorities. The common solvency-ratio and capital-adequacy standards envisaged under it do not discriminate the quality of different central governments' debts. Competition between national regulators, mentioned by Welfens, will not help make such distinctions.

Concretely, for countries such as Italy one may therefore wonder whether its banks will ever be able to balk at Italian government debt the way New York City banks balked at New York City debt about 15 years ago. And if not, will their local-deposit taking foreign branches--among others--not, in fact, provide for direct foreign financing of Italian government debt in the future, with only minimum scrutiny and public risk awareness? Contrary to what Welfens tried to deduce from the volatile, and sometimes inverted interest-rate spread between corporate and government bonds, capital-market discipline certainly has not yet arrived in Italy. For sovereign debts I doubt it ever will arrive in time within any country as long as the home-country principle of prudential regulation remains paramount.

To conclude this point, it is not the capital markets first and foremost, but the politics and economics of taxes and tax competition that may ultimately set an effective limit on how much debt a government can afford to owe. For governments must tax more the higher their debt if they are to meet their debt-service obligations under conditions where real interest rates exceed the average growth rate of their economies. Capital markets can help in a timely way to hold public-debt exposure to below the danger point only if rating services are free and their verdict is respected by changing the terms and allocation of credit. This, however, rating services and prudential guidelines on banking-grade investments are not likely to accomplish with regard to central government debt under current circumstances.

2. The second question I would like to raise is: "Should One Hurry European Monetary Union in a Period of Increased Uncertainty Brought on by Supply (Factor-Endowment) and Demand Shocks in Eastern Europe, Particularly Those Attending the Unification of Germany?"

Welfens recognizes that uncertainty has been increased by recent developments. He also raises the question of whether EC monetary integration will, by itself, lead to greater or lesser volatility of the dollar exchange rate without committing to a particular point of view. The Ashford Castle document mentions currency substitution of ECUs against dollars and points to reduced demand for international reserves, particularly dollar-denominated reserves, in Europe. This would lead one to expect a decline in exchange-rate stability with the dollar during the period of international portfolio adjustment. What I would like to focus on in the second point, however, is whether this is a good time to move toward greater exchange-rate fixity between the currencies of the exchange-rate mechanism in Europe.

There is now much uncertainty about where the real exchange rate between the DM and other major currencies should be in the coming months and years. If the higher real interest rates that may now have to prevail in Germany for some time are not to be shared, almost equally, with other European countries, a real appreciation of the DM would be required to maintain portfolio balance. This, at least, is the prediction which all model simulations have produced whose specifications are based on the normal Dornbusch-type intertemporal mechanism with its tie back to PPP. On the other hand, if uncertainty has risen about almost every economic and some political aspects of the outlook for Germany, there might be a higher risk premium on the DM. Such a risk premium could prevent real appreciation of the DM in spite of a rising differential of Germany's real interest rates over those in other EC countries.

Perceptions of uncertainty, and how they are being resolved, are themselves volatile and subject to frequent modification from the intense flow of news surrounding Germany at this time. Under these circumstances, the appropriate real exchange rate for Germany may prove especially hard to pin down. In particular, to assume that this rate is the same as it has been, say with the French Franc, for the last 4 years would be an act of pure, and quite possibly tragically mistaken (in view of Germany's rigid and union-dominated "insider" labor markets) faith. Hence, for the good of both Germany and its neighbors, this is not a safe time for eliminating the option of realignments, or for moving to yet greater exchange-rate fixity within Europe.

The Franco-German competition about "who has the hardest currency of them all" is admirable in broadening the continental coalition against inflation that has long included several smaller countries besides Germany. However, exchange-rate fixity should not become a fetish when major changes in real exchange rates may be called for. Such changes can and should not be produced through anything other than nominal exchange rate changes since inflation rates should stay at similar low levels in Germany and France.

3. The third and last question I would like to address relates to the roles of pound sterling and Swiss franc in Europe: "Can the Pound and the Swiss Franc Remain Competitive if it Appears that an ECU Zone Could Be Formed Without Either?"

Welfens notes that the pound/DM rate has been about as variable as the yen/DM rate since the transition to generalized floating among the major currencies in 1973. He infers from this that bringing the pound into the EMS and subsequently into the DM zone could be destabilizing. In fact, it would more likely be stabilizing to the extent the ECU financial asset mix would come much closer to equality with the world portfolio if is included a major (for some more years, at least) oil exporter. Adding such a country's assets would diversify holdings within the ECU zone. In the past, having a common currency with continental Europe would have protected the U.K. against "Dutch disease," so that it would have been beneficial for the U.K. as well. Britain is needed for greater balance also in another way. A Great Britain that adheres to deregulation and the competitive-market paradigm is an indispensable complement to the Western European continent and its ever-present anti-market reflexes.

Perhaps the British themselves have no choice about joining the final stage of EMU. As long as they continue to use price stability like the Romans used the feather -- to throw up a little bit of disinflation just so they can sit back and reflate -- the pound, on its own, will be an uninteresting currency compared with the future ECU. At the same time, the abolition of capital controls in the EC would make London less needed as a xenocurrency center, dealing in ECUs. Realistically, therefore, the pound will have to follow absorption into the ECU if the ECU would otherwise become the common currency of continental Europe without it. I do not believe that London will be able to safeguard its preeminence as Europe's financial center in any other way.

A currency that has much better prospects for survival and should be kept around to provide competition to the future ECU is the Swiss franc. Together with the yen, the Swiss franc may well be the champion of price stability in the future, setting the standard of aspiration for the ECU from outside that the

Bundesbank, hitherto, had set to some degree from within. Hence while the British are right to want currency competition in Europe, they do not have the currency values to provide it. The Swiss do.

Jürgen von Hagen and Michele Fratianni

MONETARY AND FISCAL POLICY IN A EUROPEAN MONETARY UNION: SOME PUBLIC CHOICE CONSIDERATIONS

1. Introduction

European Monetary Union (EMU) has long been considered an important part of the European integration process, albeit a highly ambitious one. Provisions for the coordination of monetary policies in the European Community (EC) were already included in the Common Market Treaty of 1958, which obliged all member states to regard their exchange rate policies as a matter of common concern (Art. 107) and created an advisory currency commission (Art. 105). But it was not before the Bretton Woods System ceased to furnish monetary and exchange rate stability externally to the EC in the late 1960s, that the process towards EMU gained strength. EMU was first adopted as an official goal by the EC at its Hague Summit in 1969, which lead to a number of significant steps. The *Werner Report (1970)* presented a first proposal of how to achieve EMU. It lead to the unsuccessful Snake arrangement of 1972, the European Monetary Cooperation Fund of 1973 and a number of directives to institutionalize monetary policy coordination in the EC *(Christie and Fratianni 1978)*. The *Marjolin Report (1975)* discussed the relationship between trade and goods markets integration and monetary integration in the EC. It argued that monetary union should be postponed until the achievement of a high degree of economic integration in the Community. Reducing barriers to trade and factor mobility would create a unified internal market which would be a sound basis for subsequent monetary unification. The *MacDougall Report (1977)* discussed the possibility of monetary integration from the perspective of fiscal federalism. The Report stressed the role of a unified fiscal system in a monetary union and concluded that a EMU would not be viable without a sufficiently large Community budget available for fiscal stabilization policies.

The concept of building a EMU gradually and on the basis of economic union was criticized by the Commission's President Roy Jenkins in his Florence speech of 1977 (*Jenkins 1978*). He advocated a big leap forward to EMU instead of a laborious "politique des petits pats". Monetary union would become the driving political force to reach economic integration.

The Community took its next important step towards EMU in 1978 with the creation of the European Monetary System (EMS). Like the Snake, the EMS focuses on exchange rate policies to achieve policy coordination. The main purpose of the EMS was to promote monetary stability in the region, in the form of both exchange rate and price stability. Its creators regarded the EMS as a new kind of exchange rate system, one that was *flexible* enough to support inflation differentials among the members, and *symmetric* in the sense that no single country would be forced to adjust its monetary policy unduly to the policies of other members (e.g. *van Ypersele 1979*).

In view of the large inflation differentials prevailing among the member countries at the time, the creation of the EMS met general skepticism (see *Fratianni and von Hagen 1990a*). In 1978, for example, EMS inflation rates measured in terms of consumer price indices varied between 2.7 percent in Germany and 12.1 percent in Italy. In this regard, the EMS has surprised many by the sheer fact of its survival over the past decade. Inflation rates have gradually declined in the member countries and converged at a low level of two to five percent in the late 1980s. But a similar decline and convergence of inflation rates can also be observed outside the EMS, so that the European disinflation cannot be easily attributed to the EMS. On the other hand, the EMS has resulted in a significant reduction of real and nominal exchange rate uncertainty among the member currencies. However, this reduction has been achieved at the cost of greater exchange rate uncertainty in relation to non-member currencies. The welfare implications of the EMS are therefore ambiguous (see *Fratianni and von Hagen 1990a*).

Following a period of stagnation in the early 1980s, the process of EMU has regained momentum in the course of the Community's current efforts to complete its internal market, the "Europe 1992" program. In its latest step, the Council adopted the *Delors Report (1989)* as the official blueprint for monetary unification (see *Fratianni and von Hagen 1990c* for a detailed review). This report discusses the relationship between economic and monetary integration again at length. In what appears to be a compromise between the positions of the Marjolin and MacDougall Reports and the political position of *Jenkins (1978)*, the Delors Report develops the concept of parallelism: Monetary and economic integration are two aspects of the same process and have to be pursued simultaneously. The Delors Report also deals extensively with the role of fiscal policy in a monetary union, calling repeatedly for fiscal policy coordination and the imposition of binding restraints on members' budgetary policies. Like the Werner Report, the Delors Report proposes to build monetary union in three stages and outlines institutional arrangements for each step. The Report advocates an enlarged EMS as the foundation of a future EMU. With all its emphasis on EMU and the implied fiscal arrangements, however, the Report is conspicuously silent on what will determine the inflation trend of the monetary union.

In this contribution, we review and discuss some of the main policy issues facing a future EMU. We do not dwell on the process of achieving EMU, but take it as the starting point: The Community has adopted a common currency or irrevocably fixed exchange rates. In Section 2, we discuss the determinants of EMU inflation. Building on a public choice approach, we interpret monetary union as a form of collusion among national central banks. In contrast to the standard economic argument about collusion, however, we argue that such collusion can improve or diminish the quality of monetary policy, depending on the institutional design of a EMU. We discuss some important conditions for achieving price stability in the monetary union. In Section 3, we address the role of fiscal policy in a monetary union. We discuss, and reject, the Delors Committee's recommendations for greater coordination of fiscal policies in a EMU. The final section summarizes the main conclusions.

2. Determinants of Inflation in a Monetary Union

2.1 Monetary Union and Central Bank Collusion

Public choice literature regards monetary union as a form of collusion among central banks (e.g. *Vaubel 1980, 1989*). This view contrasts the monetary union with the alternative of a "competitive scenario" of policymaking. In a world of free currency convertibility, unrestricted capital mobility, and flexible exchange rates, central banks are subject to the pressures of competition among independent national monetary policies. A high-inflation central bank promotes the erosion of the use of its money, as the private sector would prefer to hold assets denominated in more stable currencies. With fewer people holding its money, the central bank's benefits from inflation--revenue from seigniorage and the ability to conduct stabilization policies--disappear. In contrast, a low-inflation central bank is rewarded by an increasing use of its currency. Competition of monetary policies therefore exerts an important disciplinary force on central bankers and prevents them from inflating too much.

According to this view, the creation of a monetary union reduces the degree of policy competition. By fixing the relative prices of their currencies and, possibly, issuing a common currency, central bankers eliminate differences in "product quality" and adopt a common monetary policy instead. As a result, the threats and rewards from competition disappear. Monetary union destroys the disciplinary power of policy competition and thereby worsens the quality of the product, that is, it results in higher average inflation.

This negative assessment of monetary union based on the competitive scenario rests on three assumptions. First, each central bank can pursue a credible low-inflation policy under competitive circumstances. Second, collusion among the members of the monetary union reduces the degree of effective competition in the international arena. Third, the individual incentives to inflate are the same for each central bank in the monetary union; collusion only reduces the cost of high inflation and the reward for low inflation. To assess the consequences of a EMU, the important question is, how valid these assumptions are.

2.2 Central Bank Credibility: EMU as a Commitment Mechanism

Governments generally cannot enter credible precommitments to ex-ante optimal, low-inflation policy rules, because, in practice, they face no formal punishment for deviating from prior announcements. *Barro and Gordon (1983)* have shown that, if nominal wages are rigid and markets understand policymakers' incentives, the non-enforceability of policy announcements biases monetary policy outcomes towards positive inflation. Equilibrium inflation is positive although it generates no output or employment gains, because a zero- or low-inflation policy rule is not time-consistent and its announcement therefore is not credible.

The source of the inflation bias and the lack of credibility is a deficiency in the political institutions, namely the lack of an effective commitment mechanism.

Thompson (1981) and *Rogoff (1985)* propose to cope with this deficiency by delegating monetary policy to an agent whose preferences with regard to inflation, output and employment differ significantly from the politicians' preferences. They argue that the appointment of a "conservative" central banker, who puts the most emphasis on fighting inflation will lead the public to reduce inflation expectations and thereby lower the equilibrium inflation rate. Implicitly, they assume that, once appointed, the central banker can conduct monetary policy independently from the politician and cannot easily be removed from office (*Lohmann 1989*; *von Hagen 1990b*). If this is true, his appointment allows the politicians to precommit indirectly to a low-inflation policy.

More generally, the credibility argument emphasizes that monetary policy should be viewed as the result of a struggle between the conflicting interests of elected government politicians, who are mostly concerned with using monetary policy to ensure levels of output and employment favorable for re-election, and central bank officials who are more concerned with price stability. The more the central bank has to give in to political pressure, the less credible is the commitment to price stability and the higher is the inflation rate. Thus, the quality of domestic monetary policy is endangered by the lack of a commitment mechanism and the influence of domestic politicians on the central bank, a point neglected by the competitive framework above.

The delegation of monetary policy need not be limited to a domestic central banker. Alternatively, a central bank may decide to fix the exchange rate between its currency and the currency of a country whose central bank is well known for its strong commitment to price stability. This is the basis of a recent interpretation of the EMS, which holds that traditional high-inflation countries, like France and Italy, have used the EMS to submit their policies to the authority of the Bundesbank. By fixing their exchange rates with the DM, these countries have adopted the Bundesbank's low- inflation policy and gained additional credibility of their own, new commitment to price stability (*Giavazzi and Giovannini 1989*; *Giavazzi and Pagano 1988*). The fixed exchange rate relieves these central banks from some of their domestic political pressures and thus improves their inflation bias.

The interesting point of this interpretation of the EMS is that international collusion can provide countries with a commitment mechanism not available domestically. The credibility argument implies that monetary union serves to improve the average quality of monetary policy if it facilitates precommitment to a low-inflation policy. Neglecting this possibility, the competitive scenario implicitly assumes that all central banks enjoy a large degree of independence from domestic political pressures to begin with, an assumption that seems unrealistic in the European case.

It is worth noting that a monetary union is likely to be a more efficient device of policy delegation than an exchange rate system with a dominant low-inflation country. The functioning of the exchange rate system is complicated by a conflict of interest between the high-inflation countries and the low-inflation country, which results from the fact that the fixed exchange rate alters the inflation incentives for the low-inflation central bank (*Fratianni and von Hagen 1990a, b*). Being the "leader" of the system, the low-inflation central bank can partly export the inflation consequences of a monetary surprise in its own economy to other members. With fixed exchange rates, this central bank therefore faces a larger unemployment-inflation trade off, so that the incentive to generate surprise inflation rises. As the private sector understands this change, inflation expectations increase, and so does the inflation rate. The low-inflation country therefore ends up with a higher inflation rate under fixed exchange rates than with independent monetary policies. But this higher inflation rate results from the assumption that national monetary authorities pay no attention to the inflation cost of domestic monetary expansions in other countries. In a monetary union, this externality would not occur, if monetary policy is conducted by a common authority concerned with price stability in all member countries. Provided that the monetary authority of the union is as committed to price stability as the central bank in the low-inflation country, the EMU would result in less inflation than the EMS.

Compared to an independent, national policy environment, a monetary union produces an important change in the number of players involved in the monetary policy game. In the national environment, each central bank has its own government as the opponent. In contrast, the monetary authority in a monetary union faces Community officials and all national governments together as opponents. As long as elections are not synchronized and there are national idiosyncrasies in the timing of business cycles, the political interests of the individual governments are likely to be different and the resulting political pressures are likely to neutralize each other to some extent. This would leave the EMU monetary authority with more freedom to follow its own preferred policy than national monetary authorities currently enjoy. Provided that central bank officials in a EMU share similar preferences for low inflation, this improved strategic position raises the attractiveness of the monetary union. As a corollary, monetary union appears again to be a more attractive delegation device than an exchange rate arrangement.

However, monetary union can only improve the average quality of monetary policy, if its institutional design facilitates credible precommitment to low-inflation policies. Two important requirements must be fulfilled. On the one hand, the EMU monetary authority must be fully independent from political pressure. On the other hand, the credibility of the EMU itself must be assured.

There are three main conditions for central bank independence (*Neumann 1990*). First, national and Community politicians must have no jurisdiction in interfering with the conduct of monetary policy. In particular, the monetary authority must have full control over the assets and liabilities of its balance sheet. This excludes compulsory lending to public-sector authorities and the monetization of public debt, which undermine the credibility of the central bank's commitment to price stability and are likely to increase inflation in the long run (*Barro 1983*). The example of the Bundesbank demonstrates that efficient monetary control is possible even without open market operations of significant size, as the central bank can control the monetary base by lending to the banking sector. Balance-sheet autonomy also excludes that a government or the Community can impose exchange rate policies of the EMU with non-member countries on the monetary authority, whose autonomy would be weakened. Recent experience with international policy coordination has shown that governments all too willingly engage in efforts to manipulate exchange rates without regard to the future inflation consequences (*Funabashi 1988; von Hagen 1989*). The second condition is that the monetary authority must not be obliged to follow instructions by governments or Community authorities. This includes general clauses, such as a prescription to support the Community's economic policies, which create opportunities for government officials to exert pressure on the monetary authority.

The third condition is that central bank officials in the union must have personal independence. This entails that their appointment be sufficiently long-term to be removed from the short-run orientation of electoral interests. On the other hand, there should be no re-appointments, otherwise central bankers would be inclined to serve political interests to assure a second term. As a practical solution, *Neumann (1990)* proposes to set a minimum age for appointment to the central bank board and terms which are long enough for the appointee to reach normal retirement age. Furthermore, central bank officials should be paid salaries which are commensurable with top management positions in the private sector. Otherwise, there is a danger that central bank positions will be primarily regarded as stepping stones to more lucrative private sector jobs, in which case central bankers would be eager to seek good contacts and understanding with private interest groups. Personal independence also conflicts with accountability to national governments or the European Parliament. As demonstrated by the US example, the need to report to political authorities on a regular basis creates incentives for central bank officials to bow to political pressures. This does not exclude, of course, that the monetary authority be audited and supervised to assure that its policies are conducted on sound banking and accounting principles.

Even if these conditions are fulfilled, the monetary union does not provide an effective solution to the precommitment problem, if politicians can regain control over monetary policy relatively easily and at their discretion. Under such circumstances, the private sector would rationally foresee that politicians revert to discretionary monetary policies under politically opportune conditions, and the EMU commitment to price stability would not be credible. Indeed, the failure to identify plausible and significant sources of the cost of reneging on the pre-announced, low-inflation exchange rate target is one of the main reasons why most credibility interpretations of the EMS in the literature remain unconvincing (*von Hagen and Fratianni 1989, von Hagen 1990b*). EMU as a commitment mechanism requires that the political or economic cost of regime reversals be large enough to outweigh their potential short-run gains. This brings in two further requirements. First, politicians must find it very hard and costly to change the status of the monetary authority, so that its independence is not subject to the discretion of the political sector. This could be achieved by elevating the monetary statute of the EC to the rank of constitutional law. Second, since the individual member states retain their formal sovereignty to withdraw from the union, their commitment to membership must be rendered credible by making withdrawal sufficiently costly to outweigh the potential short-run gains from leaving the union and returning (temporarily) to an independent and more inflationary monetary policy. To raise the cost of withdrawal, EMU membership should therefore have constitutional status in all member countries. Furthermore, the monetary union should have very visible institutions such as a common central bank, so that voters would regard membership withdrawal as a loss of reputation of their country. Finally, the adoption of a common currency would enhance the credibility of the EMU commitment by raising the cost of reverting to an independent monetary regime.

In light of these requirements, the Delors Report did not propose an adequate institutional framework for a EMU. In para. 32, the EMU monetary authority is required to support the general economic policies of the EC, a provision which is mediated somewhat by the monetary authority's commitment to price stability. The same para. 32 foresees that the chairman of the monetary authority shall report to the European Parliament and the European Council. Finally, instead of advocating a single currency, the Report speaks of "irrevocably fixed exchange rates" in the final stage of monetary unification. The authors of the Report obviously failed to recognize that to have "irrevocably fixed exchange rates" among national currencies seems a contradiction in itself, and hence lacks credibility.

2.3 EMU and the Degree of Effective Policy Competition

The competitive hypothesis objects to monetary unification because it restricts competition among monetary policymakers. *Vaubel (1989)* elaborates on this point referring to Hirshman's principles of "exit" and "voice" *(Hirshman 1970)*. "Exit" is the ability to invest in assets denominated in different currencies. EMU reduces the opportunities for "exit" by replacing a variety of national monies with a common one, or by introducing fixed exchange rates. "Voice" refers to the voter's ability to disapprove of erroneous monetary policies through the ballot box. EMU dilutes "voice" because collusion among policymakers makes political responsibilities more diffuse and eliminates the demonstration effect that a successful monetary policy in one country has on other countries. Vaubel argues that, in the context of monetary union, "exit" is a more powerful principle than "voice", because elections are decided over a variety of issues.

Even in the competitive scenario, "exit" is limited by the fact that citizens of one country are forced to use their home currency for transactions such as tax payments or are required to accept their home currency in payments, i.e., national monies are legal tender. But to what extent would EMU limit the power of the "exit" principle even further? The important issue is how large the EMU is relative to the remaining non-member economies. Central bank collusion in a EMU clearly restricts some competition of monetary policy, but it does not create an international monopoly. "Exit" opportunities will remain through the availability of non-EC currencies such as the US dollar, the Swiss franc, and the Japanese yen, to name a few. Monetary policies in non-EC countries can still impart "good lessons". The effectiveness of "exit" does not require the largest possible number of individual policies, just as competition in goods markets can prevail even if the number of firms is not very large.

On the other hand, EMU promotes the elimination of barriers to competition by favoring the dismantling of exchange and capital controls vis-a-vis non-members. The Community has proposed and begun the dissolution of such controls *erga omnes* (that is, with respect to all countries) as part of the process of financial integration. By opening individual financial markets to more outside competition, EMU thus actually strengthens the force of and opportunities for "exit" in some member countries. Capital and exchange controls may be reintroduced in the future only if governments perceive that short-run capital movements cause significant strain in foreign exchange markets and disturb the conduct of monetary policy in a member country (*Bofinger 1989, p. 433; Key 1989, p. 596*). Although, with provisions like this, the return to restrictions remains an explicit possibility, their reimposition would likely be subject to the consent of all members, and therefore be removed at least partly from the discretion of national politicians.

2.4 Seigniorage and the Incentive to Inflate in a EMU

Recent literature on optimal taxation views inflation as part of a nation's tax system. Contrary to the conventional view of inflation as an inefficient source of government revenue, this literature argues that, in a world with transaction and distortionary costs in collecting taxes, inflation becomes part of a second best tax structure (*Klein 1978, p. 81*). Its optimal rate is obtained at the point where the marginal social costs of raising revenues through inflation and through other distortionary taxes are equal to each other (*Mankiw 1987; Gros 1990*). To illustrate, let t_y be the distortionary tax rate on income, m_y the ratio of base money to income, b_y the ratio of debt to income, g the ratio of government expenditure to income, π the inflation rate, and r the real interest rate. Let the social cost of collecting revenues from income taxes and inflation be quadratic in the tax rate and the inflation rate, and assume that the authorities have the following preference function: $L = \int (zt_{ys}^2 + v\pi_s^2)\exp(-rs)ds$, where v and z are fixed weights. The optimal inflation tax rate is found by minimizing L subject to the steady state government budget constraint $g + rb_y = t_y + m_y$ (*Gros 1990*). This yields:

$$(1) \qquad zt_y(m_y + b_y) = v\pi .$$

Taking g as given for the financing decision, the optimal steady-state inflation rate is

$$(2) \qquad \pi = (g + rb_y)\left(m_y + \frac{v}{z(m_y + b_y)}\right)^{-1}.$$

The larger the collection cost ratio z/v, the lower the money base velocity and the higher the debt ratio, the larger is a country's optimal inflation tax.

It is plausible to assume that, in a EMU, delegates of each country represent their different national interests and tax systems, or that the common authority maximizes the sum of the individual preference functions. This implies that the monetary authority will have to find a compromise between different target inflation rates for its members. Table 1 shows the 1988 values of t_y, m_y and b_y

for most of the EC countries. If, for the sake of simplicity, the values of z/v are assumed equal for all members, we can infer from the computed value of $t_y(m_y + b_y)$ that representatives of Belgium, Greece and Italy would have higher target rates than those of France, Germany and the United Kingdom. In essence, the less fiscally strong a EMU member and the more highly indebted its government, the higher the target inflation rate it would prefer for the monetary union (see e.g. *Tanzi and Ter-Minassian 1987; Council of Economic Advisors to the German Ministry of Economics 1989; Giavazzi 1989*). The table indicates that all countries would prefer inflation rates larger than the preferred German rate. Unless the Bundesbank were to set the EMU inflation rate unilaterally, which is politically improbable, the monetary authority is bound to target a higher rate than the lowest one currently achieved.

But there is no reason to believe that the EMU members would want the same target inflation rate for the union as they would for themselves when they conduct independent monetary policies. The reason for this is a familiar free riding problem. In a monetary union, seigniorage accrues to the common monetary authority, and all countries would share its revenues. This implies that any single country can effectively tax citizens of other countries through a higher union inflation rate. The preferred union inflation rate for each country becomes

$$(3) \qquad \pi_E = (g + rb_y)(\theta mE + \frac{v}{z(\theta m_E + b_y)})^{-1}.$$

where E is the base money to income ratio for the entire union and θ is the ratio of a country's share of EMU seigniorage to the country's share of EMU income. A country's preferred union inflation rate is higher than the country's preferred steady-state inflation rate with independent policies if

$$(4) \qquad H = (m_y - \theta m_E)(v/z - (m_y + b_y)(\theta m_E + b_y)) \qquad < 0.$$

The term $(m_y - \theta m_E)$ represents the change in the country's tax base for the inflation tax from joining the union. It is negative when the country obtains more seigniorage for a given inflation rate inside the union than it would domestically, that is when free riding occurs.

Given the data in Table 1, the term $v/z - (m_y + b_y)(\theta m_E + b_y)$ is likely to be positive. Consequently, a country prefers a higher union inflation than its own, independent one, if it can increase its inflation tax base in the union. The only distribution scheme assuring that the inflation incentives be the same with and without EMU is with $\theta = m_y/m_E$, which implies that seigniorage is distributed among the union members according to their shares in the monetary base of the EMU.

Table 1 displays values of H under two alternative distribution schemes for union seigniorage. H_E distributes seigniorage according to countries' weights in the ECU based on January 1987 par values. Given the 1988 tax and inflation rates, condition (4) is satisfied for almost all countries. Only Italy and Greece, the two relatively high-inflation countries would desire a lower union inflation rate than their preferred independent rate.

More significantly, the lowest-inflation countries--Germany, Belgium, and the Netherlands--would have the strongest preference to raise the union inflation rate above their own. With such a distribution scheme, EMU would most likely raise average inflation compared to independent policies. In comparison, H_Y assumes that seigniorage is distributed according to each country's share in regional real income.

Table 1: TAXES, MONETARY BASE, DEBT AND INFLATION RATES

Country	Tax rate (t_y)	Monetary base (m_y)	Net debt (b_y)	$t_y(m_y + b_y)$
		(as a proportion of GDP)		
		1988 values		
Belgium	0.460	0.077	1.233	0.603
Denmark	0.605	0.041	0.246	0.174
France	0.489	0.066	0.243	0.151
Germany	0.443	0.100	0.235	0.148
Greece	0.362	0.200*	0.644	0.305
Italy	0.401	0.150*	0.879	0.413
Netherlands	0.543	0.087	0.554	0.348
Spain	0.381	0.220	0.299	0.197
U.K.	0.391	0.033	0.387	0.164
	Relative inflation target**	H_E	H_Y	
Belgium	4.07	-6.70	-0.24	
Denmark	1.18	-0.20	-0.15	
France	1.02	-0.04	-0.09	
Germany	1.00	-0.12	0.22	
Greece	2.06	0.23	0.19	
Italy	2.79	0.77	0.48	
Netherlands	2.35	-4.33	0.35	
Spain	1.33	--	0.54	
U.K.	1.11	-0.04	-0.15	

* indicates 1987 values
** compared to the German rate

Source: OECD, *Economic Outlook* N. 45 data diskettes for net debt; IMF, *International Financial Statistics* for the monetary base; and European Commission, *European Economy*, Supplement A, N. 2, July 1989 for average tax rates.

Here the outcome is more favorable to a lower union inflation; in particular, the low-inflation Germany and Netherlands as well as Italy and Greece would prefer lower union inflation. The important conclusion from this exercise is that the long-run inflation rate in a EMU depends critically on the way seigniorage is distributed among the members. This is independent of the institutional arrangement by which seigniorage is actually collected and distributed. In practice, redistribution can take indirect forms such as additional programs for regional policies or structural policies--as proposed in the Delors Report (para. 32) as part of a EMU--financed with seigniorage revenues, which allow for revenue transfers among the EMU members. An "inadequate" distribution scheme would provide incentives for an inflation-biased union. The normative implication is that, in developing the institutions of the EMU, the seigniorage distribution scheme should be engineered in such a way to bias the outcome towards low union inflation.

To settle on a particular target inflation rate, the rules of the EMU must specify a voting mechanism allocating voting power to each member. The results of this section indicate that the optimal design of the voting mechanism should be considered together with the design of a seigniorage distribution scheme. For example, with $\theta = m_y/m_E$, a simple majority *cum* one-state-one-vote rule among the countries of Table 1 would result in an EMU inflation of at least one third above Germany's preferred inflation rate. With Spain as the pivotal voter, the same voting rule would result in a lower inflation rate if combined with the distribution scheme of H_Y.

Furthermore, the results suggest that a low EMU inflation rate can be achieved by allocating the majority of the votes to the fiscally strong countries, while compensating the fiscally weak countries with the largest shares in seigniorage revenue. In this way, seigniorage considerations would not be permitted to distort the fiscally strong countries' incentives towards more inflation, while the fiscally weak countries' interest in higher inflation would not carry enough weight in the common decision-making process to raise the union's inflation rate.

3. The Role of Fiscal Policy in a Monetary Union

The Delors Committee spent much time and effort to discuss the fiscal arrangements it deemed necessary for a EMU. The two most controversial elements of its proposal are the provision for close coordination of national fiscal policies and the advocation of binding rules limiting the size of national government budget deficits. In this section, we discuss the need for fiscal coordination, first, and then turn to the role of fiscal restraints.

3.1 Harmonization, International Transfers, and Fiscal Policy Coordination

Recent literature has pointed to the potential damages international inconsistencies of tax systems can cause of an economic union (e.g. *Isard 1988; Tanzi and Ter-Minassian 1987; Vegh and Guidotti 1989*). Taxes on goods, services and factors of production distort relative prices which trigger inefficient flows of goods, services, capital and labor and produce regional trade imbalances. The harmonization of national tax laws is a critical element in bringing about the EC's internal market. Monetary integration reinforces the importance of this element in that exchange rate changes can no longer be used to rectify regional imbalances. One can go further by saying that the harmonization of tax systems is itself a precondition of monetary unification as long as the union retains individual national currencies tied together by fixed exchange rates which have to be maintained by foreign exchange market intervention. Persistent trade imbalances due to inconsistent tax laws would undermine the sustainability of the union. A basic degree of harmonization is therefore indispensable in a EMU.

The traditional literature on optimal currency areas stresses the role of fiscal policy in a monetary union as the primary instrument for absorbing regional economic shocks (e.g. *Kenen 1969*). This was also the position of the MacDougall Report. Since monetary policy can no longer be used autonomously in the various parts of the union, and exchange rates no longer adjust, fiscal policy has to play the role of equilibrating regional differences in the fluctuations of output and employment. Say an adverse supply shock hits Belgium without affecting other European countries. With flexible exchange rates, the Belgian franc would depreciate, allowing for a real depreciation of the currency. The resulting increase in export demand would help Belgium to recover from the shock. In a monetary union and with sluggish prices, adjustment can occur through a lower tax burden or the migration of labor to more prosperous regions. Since, in the presence of mobility cost, migration is an inefficient response to transitory shocks, the fiscal system has to serve as the principal shock absorber. It must facilitate income redistribution within the union in response to regional shocks. The lack of such a system would cause strain to develop in the union along with dissatisfaction with the fixity of exchange rates.

Such a system can be implemented in a EMU in two alternative ways. The first one operates via government spending and has been advocated by the MacDougall Report. The EC would allocate a sufficiently large fiscal budget in Brussels, which would allow its central administration to direct funds to areas of relatively weak economic performance. Since the budget would be funded by all members, the necessary degree of income redistribution would be achieved by an appropriate regional distribution of EC spending. The MacDougall Report concluded that, in view of the size of regional shocks and the central government budgets commonly available for such purposes, EMU remained infeasible without a Community Budget of at least five to seven percent of Community GNP. The Delors Report, and *Lamfalussy (1989)* in one of the contributions to it, follow the same approach, but argue that the EC is not politically ready to accept such a large Community budget. Instead, close coordination of national spending policies is required to serve the same purpose.

It is important to understand, however, that a fiscal redistribution system can work alternatively on the government revenue side and without any need for centralized government spending. Income redistribution to equilibrate regional shocks can be achieved through a Community-wide income tax and transfer system. The system would have to be designed such that relatively depressed regions are taxed less heavily than relatively booming regions, e.g. by progressive income taxation, and would have to facilitate the transfer of tax revenues from the latter to the former. Like in other federal systems, e.g. West Germany, regional income redistribution can be achieved with rules of sharing tax revenues among the individual member states. In combination with national institutions such as unemployment compensation, the tax system would execute automatic transfers among regions, without requiring any appropriations and spending authority at the Community level nor coordination of national spending policies.

From a political economy point of view, however, the two alternatives are not equally desirable. Increasing the Community budget means to increase the power of the central administration both in comparison to the national governments and to the EMU monetary authority. It raises the pay-off for and encourages lobbying at the central administration and creates new opportunities for log-rolling and influence-peddling. Based on the experience with government spending programs at the national level, the efficiency of centralized or coordinated spending to buffer transitory regional shocks is highly questionable, given the sluggishness of the political process and the well-known difficulty to phase-out regional subsidies. A redistributive tax system, in contrast, would not make the actual transfers subject to political discretion. In addition, it would leave the spending power with the national administrations. The theory of fiscal federalism suggests that national administrations would recognize better the priorities and needs of the individual member countries. Finally, a tax-based redistribution with decentralized spending would favor competition among fiscal authorities and help preserve the independence of the common monetary authority.

The drive towards building a significant central budget or, as a politically more promising substitute, towards the coordination of national fiscal policies in a monetary union arises from very different grounds. Assuming that the "Europe 1992" program is successful in promoting goods markets and financial markets integration, this will increase intra-EC trade and raise the share of exports and imports in each country's GNP. Financial markets integration will tend to increase the international substitutability of financial assets within the region, particularly at the shorter end of the market. Thus, each economy becomes more "open" and more closely integrated in the regional capital markets.

The important implication of these trends is that national fiscal policies are likely to lose much of their power to control national output and employment, even in the short run. Greater openness implies greater spill-overs of aggregate demand between the economies and, hence, reduces government spending multipliers. National fiscal policymakers will therefore see their power and influence diminish as economic integration proceeds in Europe. Public choice theory suggests that these policymakers will seek ways to regain their leverage and restore the effectiveness of their policy instruments. Coordination of national policies and centralization of fiscal policy at the Community level are both promising strategies to achieve that goal. Both are in essence forms of collusion among fiscal policymakers and both serve to increase the clout of fiscal policy relative to monetary policy in a monetary union. Both raise the probability of fiscal dominance of the monetary union which in turn tends to endanger its usefulness as a commitment mechanism for price stability. For this reason, greater fiscal coordination is not only unwarranted, but counterproductive for the performance of a EMU.

The Delors Committee may have feared that uncoordinated fiscal policies in a monetary union would yield inconsistent fiscal activism at the national level, and put a strain on the monetary system. The Committee's recommendation of coordination *cum* binding constraints on fiscal policies may be interpreted as an attempt to prevent such inconsistencies while limiting the clout of fiscal policy by imposing constraints. But there is little reason to follow this approach. The reduced effectiveness of fiscal policy due to integration and the greater competition national governments will face in the capital markets reduce the benefits and raise the economic cost of national fiscal activism. Greater economic integration and competition among national fiscal policies therefore tend to induce governments to adopt more stable fiscal policies compatible with stable monetary policy in the union. In contrast, the Committee's regulatory approach most likely invites fiscal policymakers to find ways around the constraints and use coordination as a way to maximize their own influence over the EMU's monetary and economic policies.

A rather different impetus for greater fiscal centralization or coordination in a EMU arises, if EMU is understood to lead inevitably to the political unification of the Community. With political unification, the Community would have to provide basic public goods such as a common defense, police and justice systems, that require a sufficient Community budget. But, apart from such political considerations, EMU does not require centralization nor coordination of government spending.

3.2 The Role of Fiscal Restraints in a Monetary Union

The Delors Report calls repeatedly for "effective upper limits on budget deficits of individual member countries" and "the definition of the overall stance of fiscal policy over the medium term including the size and the financing of the aggregate budgetary balance" (para. 33). Fiscal restraints are regarded as one of the "basic elements" of an "economic union in conjunction with a monetary union" (para. 25). This reasoning focuses on a moral hazard problem in a monetary union which reduces the fiscal discipline of its members. Individual members may be tempted to raise public debt beyond levels considered sustainable outside the union because they can expect the common monetary authority to come to their rescue should a debt crisis emerge. Such rescue operations would tax citizens of other member countries either explicitly or through a higher inflation rate in the monetary union (*Lamfalussy 1989*), and make the EMU unacceptable for the fiscally disciplined governments. Fiscal restraints, such as balanced budget provisions or ceilings on deficits, are required to guarantee the soundness of fiscal policies in the union.

The basic flaw in this argument is that the moral hazard problem is a consequence not of the exchange-rate regime but of closer international coordination and integration. Recent experience with the debt of the LDCs and Eastern European countries is clear evidence of this point. Industrial countries have agreed to reschedule and forgive debt, irrespective of the exchange rate arrangement linking debtor and creditor nations. Solidarity, not monetary union, is the source of bail-outs. Certainly, monetary union will raise the degree of solidarity among the members. But it is misleading to attribute the moral hazard problem to the monetary union itself.

On the other hand, there are forces at work in a monetary union which enhance fiscal discipline and work against the negative incentive effect. Reputational considerations suggest that excessive debt is incurred by governments that have direct access to the printing press. As argued above, joining a monetary union with an independent monetary authority eliminates such access and reduces deficits and debt (*Goodhart 1989*). The assured independence of the common monetary authority can indeed be regarded as an institutional substitute for fiscal restraints. EMU has no need for fiscal restraints, if monetizing public debt by the common central bank is credibly excluded.

Even if one assumes that solidarity and reputational effects together work towards raising public deficits and debt, binding rules can only be justified if capital markets in the Community do not price individual country risk differentials adequately to offset the incentive for higher deficits by larger risk premia. The Delors Report in fact takes this position:

> To some extent market forces can exert a disciplinary influence...[but] market perceptions do not necessarily provide strong and compelling signals and that access to a large capital market may for some time even facilitate the financing of economic imbalances...The constraints imposed by market forces might either be too slow and weak or too sudden and disruptive. (Para. 30).

Therefore, governments must rectify a market failure with an administrative rule. Again, we note that the market failure argument does not pertain to monetary integration; it arises with independent monetary policies as well. A monetary union--in which international interest rate differentials are not clouded by exchange rate expectations--would raise the visibility of risk premia imbedded in interest rate differentials and, thus, would enhance the efficiency of market forces (*The Council of Economic Advisors to the German Ministry of Economics 1989*).

On the other hand, there is no reason to assume a priori that fiscal restraints imposed by the Community would be more effective than market forces. Public choice theory suggests that national policymakers would seek and find ways to circumvent such rules, if doing so serves their own political interest. At the same time, the rules and the enforcement mechanisms designed by the Community would emerge from a political process at the Community level that would not necessarily reflect the best economic rationale. Historically, the performance of the Community in enforcing common rules has been rather poor (*Mortensen 1989, p. 69*). To shed some empirical light on the effectiveness of formal fiscal restraints in a monetary union, we present some evidence from the United States.

3.3 The Effectiveness of Fiscal Restraints: Evidence from the US

Formal fiscal restraints exist in the US in the form of statutory or constitutional balanced budget requirements and limitations to state debt. 49 states have some form of balanced budget requirements (BBRs), ranging from the simple provision that the Governor has to submit a balanced budget (12 states), to the explicit ban on carrying over a deficit into the next fiscal year (29 states). 32 states have state debt limits in the form of nominal limits, percentage limits relating to state funds, tax revenues, taxable or state property, or total appropriations; 38 states have debt limits of this kind and/or special legislative restrictions such as a referendum requirement to create debt.

A recent study by *ACIR (1987b)* provides an index of the stringency of the legal constraints implied by the BBRs. The index ranges from zero (no requirement) to 10, with a distribution that is heavily skewed towards the higher values: 36 of the 50 states have a ranking of nine and ten. To assess the effectiveness of these restraints, we divide the states into groups with and without debt limits, and groups of low (index value zero to four), medium (five to eight) and high (nine and ten) degree of fiscal stringency. Table 2 shows the averages of four indicators of fiscal performance for these groups, state debt per capita, state debt-to-income ratios, state debt growth and the mix of guaranteed and non-guaranteed state debt. The latter indicator is important because fiscal restraints only limit the size of fully guaranteed debt and do not apply to off-budget activities. States with high stringency have a significantly lower average state debt per capita than states with low stringency, but there is no significant difference between states with medium and high (or low) stringency. The only other significant difference is in the allocation of debt between fully guaranteed and nonguaranteed debt. Here the evidence is clear: Fiscal restraints induce state governments to change their debt mix towards more nonguaranteed (unrestricted) debt.

The risk of a central bank bailing out an insolvent Treasury depends even more on the probability of particularly deviant fiscal behavior than on average fiscal performance. To see how fiscal restraints change this probability, we have isolated the three largest observations for each of the four indicators.

The three states with the fastest debt growth and the largest ratios of nonguaranteed to guaranteed debt fall into the group with the highest stringency index and with formal debt limits. Two of the three states with the largest per capita debt and debt income ratios, respectively, also belong to the group with the highest fiscal stringency and formal debt limits (for more details see *von Hagen 1990a*). Fiscal restraints obviously do not preclude extreme fiscal performance.

The lesson we draw from this simple empirical exercise is that fiscal restraints do little to change average fiscal performance and do not significantly lower the probability of extreme outcomes. This broad conclusion is in line with the more detailed evidence provided in other studies (*ACIR 1987b; von Hagen 1990a; Heins 1963; Abrams and Dougan 1986*).

Despite the obvious fact that the US differs structurally and institutionally from the EC, this evidence casts doubt on the promise that formal fiscal restraints can enhance fiscal discipline in a EMU and reduce the monetary authority's risk of being called upon to bail out an insolvent member government. In conclusion, there are neither theoretical nor practical reasons to believe that binding rules can rectify alleged market failures in restraining the growth of government debt.

Table 2: FISCAL RESTRAINTS AND FISCAL PERFORMANCE IN THE US (1985)

		Debt Limits I		Debt Limits II		BBR Stringency Index		
		Yes	No	Yes	No	Low	Medium	High
Debt per capita ($)	Mean	1203.5	1290.1	910.7	2267.7	1576.6**	1723.5	919.2
	StD	1904.0	775.0	654.8	2813.3	406.7	2714.8	752.8
Debt/ income ratio (per cent)	Mean	9.4	9.3	7.5	15.1	11.1	11.9	7.7
	StD	11.5	5.8	5.2	16.6	4.4	16.0	5.7
Debt growth (per cent)	Mean	4.5	2.9	4.2	2.9	4.1	2.7	4.5
	StD	4.2	3.0	4.2	2.1	4.1	2.1	4.4
Debt mix (per cent)	Mean	3.5*	2.4	3.5**	2.5	1.9**	2.0**	4.0
	StD	2.6	1.5	2.5	0.8	0.2	1.2	2.6

Note: Debt Limits I are nominal debt limits and percentage limits relating to state funds, taxable property, tax revenues, or total appropriations. Debt Limits II add to Debt Limits I special legislative requirements. Mean and StD denote group averages and standard deviations; * and ** denote statistical significance of a t-test for equal means at the five and one percent levels, respectively. Debt growth denotes the 1975-1985 growth factor of total nominal state debt. Debt mix denotes the ratio of non-guaranteed state and local debt to fully debt.

Source: *von Hagen (1990a)*

4. Conclusions

Monetary union is a form of collusion among central bankers. While collusion is unambiguously bad if compared to an ideal competitive scenario with independent central banks, we have argued in this paper that there are reasons why EMU could contribute to improving the quality of monetary policy in Europe. EMU would not create a monopolistic scenario, as there will remain strong competitive forces in the international monetary policy arena. The positive impact of EMU stems from its potential as a commitment mechanism to price stability which many countries may not have available domestically. The important task therefore is to design the institutional arrangements of EMU such that it becomes an efficient commitment mechanism. The most important requirement is to guarantee the independence of the monetary authority in a EMU. Voting rules and rules for distributing seigniorage revenue have to be designed in a way to set the correct incentives for low-inflation policies.

The proper functioning of a monetary union requires the harmonization of tax laws to avoid incongruent distortions of relative prices and provisions facilitating income redistribution among the members to buffer regionally diverse economic shocks. Both features can be achieved by an appropriate design of the tax system. Unless EMU is interpreted as a first step towards political union in Europe, there is no need for any greater coordination or centralization of government spending in the monetary union. In contrast, such tendencies arise from the relative loss of power national fiscal policymakers face as a consequence of greater economic and financial integration in Europe. But fiscal coordination and centralization would be invariably counterproductive for the monetary union, as they weaken the relative strength and independence of the monetary authority.

Finally, we reject the call for fiscal restraints in a EMU. Imposing formal constraints on budget policies does not seem to be a more promising way to prevent unreasonable budget deficits than market forces. However, fiscal restraints invite politicians to seek ways to circumvent the budgetary rules and ultimately make the public control of government more difficult.

References

ABRAMS, B. A. and W. R. DOUGAN (1986). The Effects of Constitutional Restraints on Governmental Spending. Public Choice, 49, 101-116.

ACIR (Advisory Commission on Intergovernmental Relations) (1976, 1987a). Significant Features of Fiscal Federalism. Washington, D.C.: U.S. Government Printing Office.

ACIR (1987b). Fiscal Discipline in the Federal System: National Reform and the Experience of the States. Washington, D.C.: U.S. Government Printing Office.

BARRO, R. J. (1983). Inflationary Finance under Discretion and Rules. Canadian Journal of Economics, 16, 1-16.

BARRO, R. J. and D. B. GORDON (1983). A Positive Theory of Monetary Policy in a Natural Rate Model. Journal of Political Economy, 91, 589 - 610.

BOFINGER, P. (1989). Zum Bericht zur Wirtschafts- und Währungsunion in der Europäischen Gemeinschaft des Ausschusses zur Prüfung der Wirtschafts- und Währungsunion - Delors Bericht. Kredit und Kapital, 22, 429 - 47.

CHRISTIE, H. and M. FRATIANNI (1978). EMU: Rehabilitation of a Case and Some Thoughts for Strategy, in: M. FRATIANNI and T. PEETERS (eds.), One Money for Europe. London: MacMillan.

COMMISSION OF THE EUROPEAN COMMUNITIES (1975). Report of the Study Group "Economic and Monetary Union 1980". [Marjolin Report]. Brussels, March.

COMMISSION OF THE EUROPEAN COMMUNITIES (1977). Report of the Study Group on the Role of Public Finance in European Integration. [MacDougall Report] Volumes 1 & 2, Brussels.

COMMISSION OF THE EUROPEAN COMMUNITIES (1989). Committee for the Study of Economic and Monetary Union, 1. Report on Economic and Monetary Union in the European Community. 2. Collection of Papers Submitted to the Committee for the Study of Economic and Monetary Union. [Delors Report] Luxembourg: Office for Official Publications of the European Communities.

COUNCIL OF THE EUROPEAN COMMUNITIES (1970). Interim Report on the Establishing by Stages of Economic and Monetary Union. Supplement to Bulletin 11-1970 of the European Communities, the Werner Group, under the chairmanship of Pierre Werner. Luxembourg: Office for Official Publications of the European Communities.

COUNCIL OF ECONOMIC ADVISORS TO THE GERMAN MINISTER OF ECONOMICS (1989). Europäische Währungsordnung, Bonn.

FRATIANNI, M. and J. VON HAGEN (1990a). The European Monetary System Ten Years After, in: A. H. MELTZER and C. PLOSSER (eds.) Carnegie-Rochester Conference Series on Public Policy, 32, Amsterdam: North-Holland.

FRATIANNI, M. and J. VON HAGEN (1990b). Asymmetries and Realignments in the EMS, in: P. DE GRAUWE and L. PAPADEMOS (eds.), The European Monetary System in the 1990s, forthcoming.

FRATIANNI, M. and J. VON HAGEN (1990c). Public Choice Aspects of European Monetary Unification. forthcoming: CATO JOURNAL.

FUNABASHI, Y. (1988). Managing the Dollar: From the Plaza to the Louvre. Washington, D.C.: Institute for International Economics.

GIAVAZZI, F. (1989). The Exchange Rate Question in Europe, in: R. C. BRIANT, D. A. CURRIE, J. A. FRENKEL, P. R. MASSON and R.

PORTES (eds.), Macroeconomic Policies in an Interdependent World. Washington, D.C.: Brookings Institution, CEPR and IMF, 283-304.

GIAVAZZI, F. and A. GIOVANNINI (1989). Limiting Exchange Rate Variability: The European Monetary System. Cambridge: Cambridge University Press.

GIAVAZZI, F. and M. PAGANO (1988). The Advantage of Tying One's Hands. European Economic Review, 32, 1055-82.

GOODHART, C. (1989). The Delors Report: Was Lawson's Reaction Justifiable? London School of Economics, Typescript.

GROS, D. (1989). Seigniorage and EMS Discipline, in: P. DE GRAUWE and L. PAPADEMOS (eds.) The European Monetary System in the 1990s, forthcoming.

HEINS, J. A. (1963). Constitutional Restrictions Against State Debt. Madison: University of Wisconsin Press.

HIRSHMAN, A. O. (1970). Exit, Voice, and Loyalty. Cambridge, Massachusetts.

ISARD, P. (1988). The Implications of Fiscal Conditions and Growing Internationalization for Monetary Policies and Financial Market Conditions. IMF Working Paper 88/52, Washington, D.C.

JENKINS, R. (1978). European Monetary Union. Lloyds Bank Review, January.

KENEN, P. B. (1969). The Theory of Optimal Currency Areas: an Eclectic View, in: R. A. MUNDELL and A.K. SWOBODA (eds.), Monetary Problems of the International Economy. Chicago: University of Chicago Press.

KLEIN, B. (1978). Competing Monies, European Monetary Union and the Dollar, in: M. FRATIANNI and T. PEETERS (eds.), One Money for Europe. London: MacMillan.

LAMFALUSSY, A. (1989). Macro-coordination of Fiscal Policies in an Economic and Monetary Union in Europe, in: COMMISSION FOR THE STUDY OF ECONOMIC AND MONETARY UNION (ed.), Report on Economic and Monetary Union in Europe, Luxembourg: European Commission.

LOHMANN, S. J. (1989). Optimal Commitment in Monetary Policy: Credibility Versus Flexibility. Working paper 88-89-88, Graduate School of Industrial Administration, Carnegie Mellon University.

MANKIW, G. N. (1987). The Optimal Collection of Seigniorage: Theory and Evidence. Journal of Monetary Economics, 20 September, 327-341.

MORTENSEN, J. (1989). Macroeconomic Policy in the Community: Federalism vs. Co-ordination; Where do we stand? Typescript.

NEUMANN, M. J. M. (1990). Precommitment to Stability by Central Bank Independence. Working Paper. Institut für Internationale Wirtschaftspolitik, University of Bonn.

ROUBINI, N. and J. SACHS (1989). Government Spending Deficits in the Industrial Countries. NBER Working Paper No. 2919, April.

TANZI, V. and T. TER-MINASSIAN (1987). The European Monetary System and Fiscal Policies, in: S. CNOSSEN (ed.), Tax Coordination in the EC. Deventer: Kluwer.

VAN YPERSELE, J. (1979). Operating Principles and Procedures of the EMS. in: P. H. TREZISE (ed.), The EMS: Its Promise and Prospects. Washington, D.C.: Brookings Institution.

VAUBEL, R. (1980). The Return to the New EMS, in: K. BRUNNER and A. H. MELTZER (eds.), Monetary Institutions and the Policy Process.

Carnegie-Rochester Conference on Public Policy, 13, Amsterdam: North Holland, 173-221.
VAUBEL, R. (1989). Currency Unification, Currency Competition, and the Private ECU: Second Thoughts. Working Paper, University of Mannheim.
VEGH, C. A. and P. E. GUIDOTTI (1989). Optimal Taxation Policies in the EMS: A Two-Country Model of Public Finance. IMF Working Paper WP/89/40.
VON HAGEN, J. (1989). Monetary Targeting With Exchange Rate Constraints - The Bundesbank in the 1980s. Federal Reserve Bank of St. Louis Review, 71(5), 53-69.
VON HAGEN, J. (1990a). A Note on the Empirical Effectiveness of Formal Fiscal Restraints, forthcoming: Journal of Public Economics.
VON HAGEN, J. (1990b). Policy Delegation and Fixed Exchange Rates. Working Paper. Indiana University School of Business, January.
VON HAGEN, J. and M. FRATIANNI (1990). Credibility and Asymmetries in the EMS, in: P. DE GRAUWE and V. ARGY (eds.), Choosing an Exchange Rate Regime: The Challenge for Smaller Industrial Countries. Washington, D.C.: International Monetary Fund.

Robert Solomon

Comments on:
Monetary and Fiscal Policy in a European Monetary Union: Some Public Choice Considerations

I am not in sympathy with the public choice approach to economic analysis and policy. In fact, as I read the present paper with its obvious distrust of the political process, I could not help wondering whether the authors would agree with Churchill's well known quip that "democracy is the worst form of Government except all those other forms that have been tried from time to time." But, oddly enough, despite my philosophical differences with von Hagen and Fratiani, I am in agreement with many of the conclusions they reach regarding European Monetary Union (EMU).

I do, however, want to quarrel with their starting point to monetary union; namely their interpretation of the inflation bias in modern central banking. They state that "the credibility argument emphasizes that monetary policy should be viewed as a result of a struggle between the conflicting interests of elected government politicians, who are mostly concerned with using monetary policy to ensure levels of output and employment favorable for re-election, and central bank officials who are more concerned with price stability. The more the central bank has to give in to political pressure, the less credible is the commitment to price stability and the higher is the inflation rate."

What bothers me about this approach is that it regards the objectives of high output and employment as somehow of secondary importance. Politicians have to care about these objectives because they want to be re-elected. The implicit assumption is that the output objective is of no importance to central banks, which would, if not influenced by politicians, pursue price stability regardless of the costs in terms of lower output and employment. That is not, in my view, the world we are living in.

In any event, according to von Hagen and Fratiani, a central bank can achieve credibility by tying its currency to that of a central bank that does have credibility, as in the D-mark dominated EMS.

According to the authors, a monetary union could be even less inflationary than the EMS, provided that "the institutional design facilitates credible precommitment" of the union's monetary authority to low inflation policies and therefore independence from political pressures. This requires, among other conditions, that the officials of the union's central bank be well paid and elderly; well paid so that they do not regard their central-bank posts as stepping stones to more lucrative jobs in the private sector and elderly so that the end of their terms coincide with retirement age. With all respect, I find these conditions to be ludicrous. Having spent a good portion of my life at the Federal Reserve Board, I am undoubtedly viewed by public choice theorists as incapable of being objective. But, my close association with top policymakers in the Federal Reserve System over a good many years turned up very little evidence to support these views. Nor do I agree that the requirement for the Federal Reserve to report to political authorities--that is, the Congress--creates incentives to bow to political pressures.

But these are minor matters. I have no disagreement with the authors' belief that the central bank of a monetary union should be independent. As noted earlier, in my view an independent central bank has in its objective function not only price stability but also output and employment.

With respect to fiscal policy in an economic and monetary union, the authors consider how regional economic shocks would be alleviated. They compare handling such problems via government spending and via taxes and transfers. Possibly for different reasons from those that motivate von Hagen and Fratiani, I agree that the latter method is preferable.

They also note that closer economic and financial integration among the nations of the European Community will increase the international spillover effects of fiscal policy and reduce its domestic impact. Public choice theory suggests to the authors that the fiscal policymakers will wish to regain their lost power and will therefore opt for coordination of national fiscal policies and centralization of fiscal policy at the Community level. These forms of "collusion" are rejected by the authors on the grounds that "fiscal dominance" would endanger the commitment to price stability.

Von Hagen and Fratiani see no need for a fiscal policy in a united Europe. This is related to their single-minded focus on monetary and price stability noted earlier. What they do not consider is the international relationship of the EMU to other parts of the world, especially North America and Japan. While exchange rates within Europe will be fixed, Europe's exchange rate with the North American dollars and the Japanese yen may require some management. That, in turn, would engage the European central bank, possibly influencing its monetary policy. Many of us believe that target zones should not be considered until and unless there is an active fiscal policy to assure that domestic objectives are met when monetary policy is aimed at stabilizing exchange rates. For the same reason, the EMU may need a fiscal policy.

The authors also reject the Delors Report's recommendation of limits on the fiscal deficits of member countries of the EMU. Once again I agree with them but for reasons that differ from their reasons. They argue that such rules are unenforceable, and buttress their case with an analysis of the experience of individual American states with such limits. Their analysis is not easy to follow and therefore to appraise. What is clear is that the authors would prefer to rely on the capital market to discipline the individual members nations of the EMU in their fiscal behavior.

Once again they do not recognize that the EMU may need a fiscal policy if it has an exchange-rate objective vis-a-vis the rest of the world.

Tamim Bayoumi and Paul R. Masson

WHAT CAN THE FISCAL SYSTEMS IN THE UNITED STATES AND CANADA TELL US ABOUT EMU?[1]

1. Introduction

The Maastricht Treaty on the move towards Economic and Monetary Union (EMU) raises the prospect of the establishment of a common currency area among EC countries without there being a common fiscal policy. Some have argued (notably, *Sala-i-Martin and Sachs, 1992*) that a community-wide tax and transfer system would be desirable in order to cushion regional shocks, since member countries in a monetary union are not be able to use the exchange rate instrument for that purpose. Indeed, according to those authors, such a federal system may be essential for the survival of EMU. In contrast, the EC currently has no fiscal mechanisms at the Community level for offsetting short-run, or cyclical, fluctuations--such as unemployment insurance or an EC-wide income tax.

Another aspect of fiscal policy in a federal system is the capacity to make continuing income transfers from richer to poorer countries or regions. Such transfers could, in principle, finance investment needed to promote the development of poorer parts of the monetary union. The EC has recognized the problem of long-term regional income differentials, and has fashioned several programs aimed at reducing them. In particular, in 1988 the EC decided to double the transfers from "structural funds" by 1992.[2]

The experience of existing currency areas seems likely to be of some relevance for EMU; in particular, fiscal federations like the United States and Canada, since they are composed of regional governments with some of the characteristics of EC countries, may be of interest. The two countries, though both federations, have quite different divisions of powers between federal and sub-national governments.[3] A looser federation, with fewer provinces than states, gives the Canadian provinces more discretionary fiscal powers than their U.S. counterparts. On the other hand, the Canadian constitution, unlike that for the United States, explicitly grants to the federal government a responsibility for "equalization"--transfers from rich to poor provinces in order to enable them to provide similar government services at similar tax rates.

In what follows, the fiscal systems in the United States and Canada are analyzed in some detail. The next section considers the structure of the fiscal systems in the United States and Canada, focusing on the different functions of the federal and lower levels of government in the two countries. Section 3 looks at the nature of the disturbances to personal income experienced by regions in the two countries, measuring the degree to which variations in regional real personal income are due to asymmetric shocks, which affect regions differently, as opposed to common shocks across the entire country. Section 4 then summarizes some results on the importance of federal fiscal flows aimed at redistribution and at stabilization in the United States and Canada, while Section 5 does the same for the EC. The last section contains conclusions and implications.

2. The Fiscal Systems in United States and Canada

Table 1 shows the structure of the tax and transfer system in the U.S. and Canada. It reports payments of taxes and levels of spending on transfers as a percentage of GDP for 5 year intervals starting in 1965, differentiating between federal fiscal flows and those flows to and from other levels of government.[4] We focus on spending on transfers rather than overall government spending for several reasons. Transfer payments represent spending that is often explicitly directed at reducing income inequalities of one type or another; it is also easier to identify on a regional basis than other types of federal spending, such as those for national defense; finally, preliminary work using state by state data on federal procurement and wages and salaries in the United States since 1981 indicates that nontransfer spending has no significant correlation with relative per capita income levels.

There are certain important differences between the situation in the United States and in Canada, which might cause the federal tax system to operate in different ways. Canada has a considerably looser federation than the United States, and its federal taxes make up only about half the percentage of income that they do in the United States.[5] In addition, while almost all U.S. states are constrained by balanced budget provisions,[6] Canadian provinces have considerable fiscal freedom, which they can, and do, use to operate their own counter-cyclical policies. On the other hand, the Canadian welfare system is more highly developed, and the Canadian constitution gives the federal government a responsibility for "equalization" transfers to poorer provinces in order to enable them to provide similar levels of government services at similar tax rates. Hence, while the stabilization role of the federal government in the economy may be smaller, it may have a more important role in the redistribution of regional incomes.

In the United States in 1990, federal income taxes on persons were the most important source of government revenue, followed by another national tax on labor income, namely social insurance payments.[7] These two sources accounted for over half of total tax revenues for all levels of government; by contrast, federal taxes on income from business and indirect taxes were relatively unimportant revenue sources. Total nonfederal tax receipts were significantly less important than those from federal taxes (including social insurance payments), raising only half as much money. They were dominated by indirect tax revenues, which made up over two-thirds of all nonfederal tax revenues, followed by direct taxes on persons and direct taxes on businesses. Overall, tax revenues made up about 30 percent of GDP.

The Canadian tax structure in 1990 showed both similarities with, and differences from, that in the United States. As in the United States, federal income taxes on persons were the largest source of revenue. However, indirect taxes were the next most important federal revenue, while social insurance payments, which were so important in the United States, were a relatively unimportant source of revenue. Another major contrast between the two systems is the importance of nonfederal taxes. In Canada, nonfederal governments collect almost as much money as the federal government, compared to half as much in the United States. As a result, taxes make up a significantly larger proportion of GDP in Canada than in the United States (36 percent as opposed to 30 percent). Finally, the structure of nonfederal revenues is also different. While indirect taxes are the most important source of non-federal tax revenues in both Canada and the United States, income taxes on persons and businesses raise almost as much money as indirect taxes for lower levels of government in Canada, while in the United States they are much less important.

The two tax systems show similar trends over time. Measured as a ratio to output, personal income taxes and social insurance payments have risen in both Canada and the United States, income tax revenues from business and federal indirect tax revenues have fallen, while revenues from non-federal indirect taxes show no trend. Overall, then, the picture is of a Canadian tax system which is significantly more decentralized (in the sense of channeling more flows through lower levels of government) than that in the United States, which relies more heavily on indirect tax revenues, and which raises more overall revenue. All of these differences are likely to be even more pronounced for any European fiscal system under Economic and Monetary Union (EMU) in Europe.

Table 1 also shows data on the structure of transfer payments in the two fiscal systems. Three types of recipients for federal transfers are identified: persons, businesses, and other levels of government. The two countries have a similar overall level of transfers; however, the distribution among the recipients is somewhat different. In the United States federal transfers to individuals in 1990 represented the vast majority of all transfers, around three-quarters of the total. Lower levels of government were the other main recipients, with around one fifth of the total, while transfers to businesses were relatively important.

The Canadian system shows the same overall ranking between the recipients; however, transfers to other levels of government and to businesses were significantly more important, and transfers to individuals less important, than in the United States. This may well reflect structural differences between the economies. The constitutional provision for "equalization" of government services and the government-run health care system may tend to boost intra-governmental transfers, while a policy approach which puts more weight on a mixed economy may result in higher levels of transfers to business. Again, all of these differences are likely to be even more important in Europe. Finally, transfers from lower levels of government to both individuals and businesses are larger in the Canadian fiscal system, presumably reflecting a looser federation than in the United States.

Both systems show significant upward trends over time in transfers to individuals from all levels of government, presumably reflecting the expansion of the welfare state over the period. In the United States, after rising significantly in the 1970s, transfers to non-federal levels of government fell during the 1980s. The Canadian data show a similar rise over the 1970s; however, a retrenchment in the 1980s is less clear-cut. Transfers to business in the United States show no trend over time, while in Canada there is a marked upward trend over most of the period which appears to have been reversed in the 1990 data. As with the data on taxes, the differences between the Canadian fiscal system and that in the Unites States are likely to be much smaller than differences of either country relative to a European fiscal system under EMU.

The overall impression from a study of the two tax and transfer systems is of two systems with relatively different structures, corresponding to the different economic and political objectives they are designed to serve. It appears likely that the structure of a European fiscal system under EMU would differ even more significantly from those of these two other federations, and in particular from the relatively centralized system in place in the Unites States.

3. The Relative Importance of Asymmetric Shocks

We now consider the issue of the size and distribution of inter-regional shocks. If shocks hit regions symmetrically, then relative price changes are not likely to be needed in adjusting to those shocks. Therefore the loss of the exchange rate instrument is unlikely to add to adjustment problems. In contrast, the existence of large regionally-differentiated shocks will put strains on a monetary union; in the absence of wage/price flexibility or labor mobility, high unemployment in adversely-affected regions is likely to result (*Kenen, 1969; Cohen and Wyplosz, 1989; Masson and Taylor, 1992*). In order to assess the nature of shocks, we first examine the extent that variation in real, per capita personal income (from which federal transfer payments have been excluded) occurs across regions and over time. Because of the unavailability of separate price deflators for all of the U.S. regions, U.S. variables are deflated by the national consumer price index. For Canada, provincial CPI series are available from 1979 on; they are spliced to the Canadian CPI before 1979.

For convenience and in order to create units that are more similar in size to EC countries, the U.S. states are grouped into eight regions, using the groupings of the U.S. Bureau of Economic Analysis. For Canada, data for the 10 provinces were collected. In this way, we have a sample of sub-national governments for each of the two countries that is close in number to the 12 member countries of the EC, although in terms of population the Canadian provinces are only the size of the smaller EC countries.

The data in Table 2 suggest that persistent regional differences are much more important than asymmetric shocks to regional income. When the standard deviations of detrended levels are compared for the United States, the cross section variation exceeds the variation over time (for the average region) by a factor greater than two. Data for the first differences of the logs of the series (i.e., for growth rates) give quite a different picture. The cross-sectional variation is very small, suggesting that income differences across the U.S. regions are very persistent, and vary little over time. When growth rates are compared, variation over time exceeds that across regions by a factor of eight. So the time series variation in a region's income is highly correlated with movements of personal income for the Unites States as a whole, and not specific to that region.

The data in Table 2 give a similar picture for Canada. Again, the time series variation in detrended levels is lower than the variation across provinces, and the ranking is reversed when first differences are compared. Most of the time series variation in a province's per capita income is correlated with movements in Canada's per capita income, producing similar standard deviations for all provinces. The one outlier is Saskatchewan, which is heavily dependent on agricultural and resource revenues (wheat, oil, and potash) and whose standard deviation is roughly twice that of Canada in levels and more than three times in first differences. Fig.1, which shows personal income relative to the national average for the 8 regions of the United States used in the analysis and for 10 Canadian provinces, illustrates some of these features.

A conclusion that emerges is that these two federations do not face large short-run, region-specific shocks for which nominal exchange rate changes would be useful. Instead, they face problems of regional development related to long-run factors--resource endowments, geography, climate, and infrastructure--which exchange rate flexibility is unlikely to ameliorate. In principle, such differences in per capita income could be compensated, at least in part, by fiscal flows. However, their persistence implies that fiscal flows would have to be consistently in a single direction for each region, and permanent subsidies from richer to poorer regions require a high degree of solidarity among residents.

It is difficult to compare the results in Table 2 with similar data for the EC countries. However, *Bayoumi and Eichengreen (1993)* analyze the importance of asymmetric shocks across U.S. regions and across the EC countries using slightly different techniques. They conclude that the EC has a core set of countries, made up of Germany, France, the Netherlands, Belgium and Denmark, which have a similar level of symmetry in their shocks to those of the United States. The first principal component explains 74 percent of the variance in the growth of output across 8 U.S. regions and 73 percent of the variance in growth across these 6 "core" E.C. countries.

The other EC countries, however, face significantly larger idiosyncratic shocks, with the first principal component explaining only 49 percent of the variance in growth. Measures such as OECD estimates of per capita GDP across the EC also appear to indicate that, measured at purchasing parity exchange rates, income differentials between EC countries have been large and extremely persistent over time, as in the United States and Canada. However, such a conclusion is less clear-cut when market exchange rate values are used.

4. The Impact of Federal Taxes and Transfers in the United States and Canada

Regional Data on Taxes and Transfers

For the United States, detailed data on personal incomes by state are available on an annual basis from the Commerce Department. In addition to pre-tax personal incomes, it is also possible to get data on payments of direct federal taxes and social insurance payments. These make up the vast majority of federal tax revenues. The two important sources which are missing are corporate tax payments and indirect taxes and excise duties, which, as can be seen from Table 1, make up some 20 percent of federal revenues. In addition, the personal income tables provide data on personal transfer payments. Unfortunately, these flows are reported in terms of function rather than source, hence the level of federal transfers has to be constructed by making assumptions as to the source of the payments. Data on federal grants to state and local government were also collected. Clearly, not all government grants are directed at the personal sector, and hence the inclusion of all grants may imply some overestimation of the objectives of the federal government in redistributing personal income.[8] The data on personal taxes, social insurance and transfers are available from 1963, those on government grants from 1969.

Transfers and grants together make up some 65 percent of U.S. government expenditure, with the balance going to wages and salaries and government procurement. Data on federal wages and salaries and procurement by state were collected from 1981 onwards. Regressions using this expanded definition of government expenditure gave similar results to those using only transfers and are not reported.

Canadian data on personal incomes,[9] federal personal direct taxes, federal transfers to persons, and federal government grants to provincial and local governments were collected for each of the 10 Canadian provinces; Alberta, British Columbia, Manitoba, New Brunswick, Newfoundland, Nova Scotia, Ontario, Prince Edward Island, Québec, and Saskatchewan. The data correspond to those collected for the U.S. states, except that social insurance payments are not reported separately. Employer and employee contributions to public service pensions plans and to unemployment insurance are included with direct taxes, while federal transfers to persons include unemployment insurance benefits, public service pensions, old age security, and miscellaneous other transfers. However, Canada and Québec pension plan (CPP/QPP) contributions and benefits are excluded from our data.

The data are illustrated in Fig. 1, which shows per capita personal income, personal income adjusted by federal taxes, and personal income adjusted by taxes, transfers and grants, all measured relative to the national average. The data are shown for the 8 regions of the United States and the 10 Canadian provinces used in the analysis, and illustrate the role of taxes and transfers in reducing income differentials both across regions and over the cycle within a region.

Estimates of the Size of Redistributive Flows

There are many reasons why a federal fiscal system may tend to support the relative income of poor regions and reduce that of rich regions. For example, to the extent that taxes are higher in regions with higher incomes, they will tend to equalize after-tax incomes across regions. Businesses also pay taxes which are likely to be related to income. Similarly, to the extent that poor regions are in more social need, their residents are more likely to receive personal transfer payments associated with the alleviation of poverty (such as social security payments). Finally the government may deliberately redistribute income for political reasons, such as social cohesion.

The importance of the redistributive flows can be measured using cross-sectional regressions which estimate the relationship between personal income net of federal taxes and transfers and pretax personal income. The regression coefficients obtained give a direct measure of the degree to which the federal tax system reduces inequalities in incomes. In addition, by running intermediate regressions it is possible to estimate the contribution of different elements in the fiscal system (such as the federal tax system, personal transfers, etc.) to the overall total.

Bayoumi and Masson (1993) report results from the following specification:

$$(Y\text{-}TAX+TRAN)_i/(Y\text{-}TAX+TRAN)_{US} = \alpha + \beta\, Y_i/Y_{US} + \epsilon_i \qquad (1)$$

where Y is per capita personal income (less all transfers from the federal government), TAX and TRAN are per capita federal taxes and transfers, respectively, subscript i refers to the individual states and "US" indicates the aggregate U.S. value. The equation measures the relationship between personal income before and after the influence of federal fiscal flows. The difference between the coefficient ß and unity represents the size of the offset to personal income caused by these flows. Hence, for example, a coefficient of 0.80 would indicate that 80 percent of the initial differences in relative incomes remained after federal fiscal payments had been taken into account, indicating that the federal government redistributes 20 cents of any dollar difference between richer and poorer states within the United States.

The results from this estimation are shown in Table 3, measured as the degree of redistribution in cents per dollar. Hence, for the United States the coefficient ß when all offsets were included was estimated at 0.781 (with a standard error of 0.028). Hence U.S. total federal fiscal flows reduce long-term income inequalities by some 22 cents in the dollar. Fig.2, panel A, shows a scatter plot of the raw data, with pre-tax relative personal income on the vertical axis and personal income adjusted for all federal flows on the horizontal axis. It is clear from the chart that there is an extremely close connection between the two series, which is essentially linear.

The relative importance of the individual elements in the overall redistributive process is also shown.[10] The results indicate that all parts of the U.S. federal fiscal system have a role in redistributing income. The largest roles in this redistribution are due to federal taxes and transfers (which reduce inequalities by some 7 1/2 cents and 10 cents in the dollar, respectively), with the contribution from federal grants being 4 cents.[11] Given the relatively small role played by federal grants in the redistributive process, the issue of whether they should be interpreted as giving support for personal income or not does not have a large effect on the results. Even if all grants were excluded from the analysis, the redistributive effect would still be 18 cents in the dollar.

As in the United States, the results for Canada indicate that all of the elements of the fiscal system produce significant redistribution. Direct taxes provide an estimated 2 cents in the dollar of redistribution, somewhat smaller than in the

United States. Transfers provide around 15 cents in the dollar of redistribution, and grants 22 cents, much larger than in the United States, presumably reflecting the more highly developed social services and the effect of the equalization grants. At 39 cents in the dollar, the total effect in Canada is almost double that in the United States. The basic data are given in Fig.2 panel B, which shows a scatter plot of relative personal incomes before and after personal taxes, transfers, and grants. Panel B indicates that, as is the case for the U.S. data in panel A, there is a close (essentially linear) relationship between the variables, while the flatter slope of the line illustrates the larger role of redistributive flows in the Canadian data.

Estimates of the Size of Stabilization Flows

The level of stabilization across regions in the United States and Canada can also be measured using a time series version of equation 1. The results, also summarized in Table 3, indicate that in the United States taxes stabilize incomes by around 9 cents in the dollar, almost identical to the estimate of the redistributive effect from the cross-sectional regression. When the dependent variable is adjusted for taxes, personal transfers, and grants, this estimate rises to 30 cents in the dollar, larger than the 22 cent estimate of the redistributive effects provided by the cross-sectional regressions, reflecting the fact that personal transfers and grants vary more in response to short-term fluctuations than to long-term income differentials. More detailed results indicate that this difference is largely due to personal transfers, which play a significantly larger role in stabilization of short-term economic fluctuations than they do in reducing long-term income differentials, while the role of U.S. federal taxes, social insurance payments, and grants appears similar across the two sets of regressions.

These results from *Bayoumi and Masson (1993)* can be compared with those from earlier studies using U.S. regional data by *Sala-i-Martin and Sachs* (SS) and *von Hagen* (vH). Two features stand out. In terms of the size of the stabilization effects, our estimate of 30 cents in the dollar is within the range suggested by SS, who estimated a value of 30-35 cents, but very different from the estimate of under 10 cents in the dollar produced by vH. In terms of the composition of the stabilization effects, the results in this paper are radically different from both of the earlier studies, which concluded that almost all of the stabilization comes from the tax system and very little from transfers. As discussed in more detail in our earlier paper, we believe that the estimation procedure used by both SS and vH may have tended to overstate the role of tax payments and understate that of transfer payments.

The stabilization regressions for Canada indicate that when taxes, transfers, and grants are all included the overall stabilization effect is 17 cents in the dollar, with transfers accounting for some 11 cents of that, and taxes and grants 3 cents each. The total effect is much smaller than the 39 cents in the dollar estimated for the redistributive flows, largely due to the much smaller role of federal grants in the stabilization regressions. As a result, while the Canadian data show a higher level of federal redistribution across regions, the overall stabilization role is considerably smaller than in the United States.

5. Redistribution and Stabilization in the EC

It is useful to compare the results for the United States and Canada with redistribution and stabilization across EC states. Redistribution across EC states is primarily carried out through the EC budget.[12] The small size of this budget (EC budgetary receipts were 1.1 percent of EC GDP in 1992), and the wide differences in income levels across EC countries, means that the potential for redistribution across EC states is small. *Gordon (1991)* estimates that redistribution of the order of 1 percent occurred in the EC in the late 1980s. Taking into account the doubling of the size of the Structural Funds by 1992, and allowing for the establishment of the Cohesion Fund created in the context of the Maastricht Treaty on EMU, one comes up with a figure of at most 4 percent of the variations in income. This is the estimate given in Table 3 for the EC.

Unlike redistribution, which requires cooperation across countries, stabilization of cyclical movements in income across EC states can be carried out at the national level. Notwithstanding the EC growth initiative announced at the December 1992 Edinburgh summit (EIB loans for infrastructure investment, and increased national spending, totaling ECU 35 billion), the EC has virtually no stabilization role.

In order to measure the level of national stabilization, annual data were collected on personal income, taxes, transfers and population for Germany, France, the United Kingdom, the Netherlands and Belgium from the OECD National Accounts for the period 1970-89. It is important to note a difference between the data for EC countries and the data for U.S. and Canadian regions. Changes in federal fiscal policies have a limited impact on data for the U.S. and Canadian regions, measured relative to the national aggregate, since all of the regions in each country face the same policy change. This is not true for the EC data since each country operates an independent fiscal policy, and hence changes in the fiscal system in one country do not reflect a common EC policy change.

Estimates of stabilization across five EC states, reported in *Bayoumi and Masson (1993)* imply that, on average, taxes and transfers reduce fluctuations by 31 cents in the dollar in these countries. This is very similar to the estimate obtained for the United States, and higher than that found for Canada. Disaggregated results indicate that 10 cents of the stabilization comes from the direct tax system, with the other 20 cents coming from transfers. This ratio of two-to-one in the relative impact of taxes and transfers is very similar to the results found for the United States and Canada.

The issue arises as to whether the EC would continue to be able to perform the same degree of stabilization as in the past. There are two considerations that are most relevant here. One is tax harmonization and greater integration, which together may restrict the scope for fiscal deficits. The other is the Maastricht fiscal criteria, which set reference values for government deficits and debt to prevent them from exceeding 3 percent and 60 percent of GDP, respectively. Depending on how strictly they are applied, these criteria may prevent stabilization in response to new adverse shocks.

On the first point, it seems likely that enhanced mobility of tax bases will make it more difficult to maintain widely divergent tax rates--at least for taxes which are not linked to benefits.[13] However, this would have implications mainly for discretionary spending increases, which would require permanently higher taxes. Stabilization policy, however, should balance out over the cycle, and should mainly involve the operation of such automatic stabilizers as unemployment insurance payments. If correctly designed and transparent in their operation, deficits resulting from the operation of automatic stabilizers should not be a problem to finance; they would not call into question the sustainability of the government's fiscal policy. Of course, there may be uncertainty about the extent to which deficits are structural versus cyclical, but unless the level of government debt is very large the government should have an adequate margin to operate its stabilization policy.

On the second point, the Maastricht criteria may be constraining for countries which are in a situation of large deficits and debt--unfortunately the case currently for a number EC members. The Treaty does provide for discretion in the application of the criteria, but it is unclear at the moment how this will operate. However, if the criteria are to be strictly applied under monetary union, it will be important for countries to aim for a deficit target that is considerably below 3 percent when averaged over the cycle, in order to allow for an adequate stabilization role.

6. Conclusions

This paper has investigated the fiscal systems in the United States and Canada with the aim of seeing what they can tell us about EMU. A comparison of the relative roles of the federal government and lower levels of government indicates that, while similar in some respects, the two tax and transfer systems have relatively different structures, corresponding to the different economic and political objectives they are designed to serve. Canada has a more decentralized system, with non-federal levels of government raising more taxes, using more diversified sources for these revenues, and providing more transfers. In addition, federal transfers to other levels of government are also significantly larger in Canada than in the United States, presumably reflecting the requirement for equal provision of government services across provinces.

These differences in fiscal structure do not appear to reflect differences in the nature of the disturbances hitting the two economies. Both economies appear to be primarily affected by common disturbances which affect all regions at the same time, rather than by region-specific shocks. Parts of the EC, on the other hand, may well be faced with significantly larger idiosyncratic disturbances.

Next, evidence on the role of the federal government in both long-term redistribution of income across regions and in short-term stabilization of regional income was discussed. As might be expected given the differences in the fiscal systems, the results indicate that the size of federal fiscal transfers varies with the type of function (stabilization or redistribution) and across countries. In the United States, where there is no federal mandate to equalize per capita incomes, redistributive flows from all federal sources [14] amount to around 22 cents in the dollar, while stabilization flows are somewhat larger at around 30 cents in the dollar. In Canada, where the federal government is a smaller factor in the economy but has certain responsibilities to "equalize" the levels of government services provided across regions, the redistribution flows are around double those in the United States (39 cents in the dollar) but the stabilization flows are smaller (17 cents in the dollar). Taxes and transfers both play important roles in these flows.

Finally, the situation on the EC with respect to redistribution and stabilization was discussed. In the EC, there is very little "fiscal federalism"; the EC budget is small and redistribution is limited. However, national governments carry out stabilization of personal income using domestic fiscal instruments to an extent comparable to that in the United States and Canada.

These results suggest three considerations that may be relevant in the context of EMU. First, the size of the federal flows varies significantly depending on the institutional structure of the country concerned, so that neither the United States nor Canada provides a "blueprint" for the EC. In Canada, where the individual provinces have more fiscal independence than U.S. states, the flows related to federal stabilization are smaller. Similarly, the relative size of redistributive flows appears to reflect the differing roles of the two federal governments; the Canadian federal government does considerably more to equalize long-term income differentials than the U.S. Government.

Second, the stabilization performed by national governments in the EC is comparable to that which occurs in the U.S. or Canadian federal fiscal systems. Therefore, there does not seem to be a case for a federal system among EC countries on stabilization grounds, unless increasing integration limits their ability to carry out stabilization policies (for instance, because of increasing tax harmonization and factor mobility), an issue which is beyond the scope of the paper.

Third, both federations however have significant redistributive functions. Even in the case of the United States, where there is no specific requirement for the federal government to equalize incomes, the federal fiscal system reduces long-term income differentials by 22 cents out of every dollar, which is considerably larger than the amounts involved in the EC Structural and Cohesion Funds. Clearly it is a political choice as to how much redistribution should occur across countries, rather than an economic necessity related to monetary union. However, political pressures for such redistribution may grow in the EC in response other forces leading to increased integration, in particular the Single Market and EMU itself.

1 The views expressed here are personal to the authors and do not represent those of the International Monetary Fund.
2 See *Gordon (1991)* for a detailed description of the operation of these structural funds.
3 There is a large literature on fiscal federalism. See, for example, *Krasnik (1986)*
4 The data come from national accounts sources.
5 However, in Canada provincial income taxes are integrated into the federal system and are collected by the federal government for all provinces except Québec. Hence federal tax changes induce automatic changes in provincial government revenues, unless offset by deliberate changes in tax rates or tax credits.
6 State-by-state details of these provisions can be found in "Significant Features of Fiscal Federalism," an annual publication of the Advisory Council on Intergovernment Relations (ACIR).
7 Strictly speaking, social insurance revenues are not defined as taxes. However, the balance on the social insurance fund is included in the federal budget, hence, to all intents and purposes, it can be regarded as a federal tax.
8 Though such grants may not be targeted at redistribution, they have that effect in practice.
9 Adjusted to exclude federal transfers, as in the case of the U.S. data.
10 They were calculated using intermediate regressions in which pre-tax income was adjusted by different elements in the fiscal system in turn (federal taxes, social insurance payments, personal transfers, and grants to state and local government). The difference between the successive coefficient estimates indicates the effect of including that fiscal flow in the regression.
11 The *EC Commission (1977, Vol. 2, p. 130)* estimates the level of redistribution in the United States to be slightly higher than our estimates (23-28 cents in the dollar); the main difference appears to be the larger estimated role for personal transfers, which they estimate to contribute 12-14 cents in the dollar, as opposed to 10 cents in our analysis. The significant role played by transfers and grants in the equation is noteworthy, since other empirical results *(Sala-i-Martin and Sachs, 1992; and von Hagen, 1992)* did not find a significant role for these elements.
12 In theory, redistribution could occur through direct revenue sharing agreements across member states, of the type that operate between German Länder, but there are no proposals for such a system in the EC.
13 See *Bovenberg, Kremers, and Masson (1991)*. If levies are linked to services, e.g. to future pensions or to municipal infrastructure, then arbitrage need not operate to equate tax rates.
14 Taxes, transfers and grants to state and local governments

References

BARRO, R. and SALA-I-MARTIN, X. (1992), Journal of Political Economy, Vol. 100, 223-251.

BAYOUMI, T. and EICHENGREEN, B. (1993), Shocking News about European Monetary Union, in: Giovaninni, F. and Torres, F., eds., The Transition to Economic and Monetary Union in Europe, Cambridge University Press.

BAYOUMI, T. and MASSON, P.R. (1993), Fiscal Flows in the United States and Canada: Lessons for Monetary Union in Europe, mimeo, International Monetary Fund, April 1993.

BOVENBERG, A. L., KREMERS, J.J.M. and MASSON, P.R. (1991), Economic and Monetary Union in Europe and Constraints on National Budgetary Policies, International Monetary Fund Staff Papers, Vol. 38, 374-398.

COHEN, D. and WYPLOSZ, C. (1989), The European Monetary Union: An Agnostic Evaluation, in: Bryant, R., Currie, D., Frenkel, Masson, P, and Portes, R., eds., Macroeconomic Policies in an Interdependent World, Washington DC: International Monetary Fund.

EC COMMISSION (1977), Report of the Study Group on the Role of Public Finance in European Integration, collection of studies, Economic and Financial Series Nos. A12/B13, Brussels.

EC COMMISSION (1990), One Market, One Money, European Economy, No. 44, Brussels.

GORDON, J. (1991), Structural Funds and the 1992 Program in the European Community, IMF Working Paper, WP 91/65, June 1991.

KENEN, P.B. (1969), The Theory of Optimal Currency Areas: An Eclectic View, in: Mundell. R.A. and Swoboda, A., eds., Monetary Problems of the International Economy, Chicago: University of Chicago Press.

KRASNICK, M. (1986), Fiscal Federalism, Toronto: University of Toronto Press.

MASSON, P.R. and TAYLOR, M.P. (1992), Common Currency Areas and Currency Unions: An Analysis of the Issues, Parts I and II, Journal of International and Comparative Economics, Vol. 2: 3 and 4, 1992.

SALA-I-MARTIN, X. and SACHS, J. (1992), Fiscal Federalism and Optimum Currency Areas: Evidence for Europe from the United States, in: Canzoneri, M., Grilli, V. and Masson, P.R., eds., Establishing a Central Bank: Issues in Europe and Lessons from the U.S., Cambridge: Cambridge University Press, 150-219.

US DEPARTMENT OF COMMERCE (1984), State Personal Inocme: Estimates for 1929-1982, February 1984.

VON HAGEN, J. (1992), Fiscal Arrangements in a Monetary Union: Evidence from the US, in: Fair, D. and de Boissieux, C., eds., Fiscal Policy, Taxes and the Financial System in an Increasingly Integrated Europe, Deventer: Kluwer.

Table 1. U.S. and Canada: Taxes and Transfers

(As a percentage of GDP)

	Direct Taxes					Indirect Taxes		Net transfers (excluding Interest Payments)				
	Paid by Persons		Paid by Business		Social Insurance	Federal	Other	Federal to Persons	Federal to Business	Other to Persons	Other to Business	Federal to Other
	Federal	Other	Federal	Other								
United States of America												
1965	7.6	1.2	4.1	0.3	3.8	2.4	6.6	4.3	0.5	1.3	-0.4	1.6
1970	9.1	1.7	3.0	0.4	5.2	1.9	7.4	6.1	0.6	2.0	-0.4	2.4
1975	7.9	2.0	2.7	0.5	6.4	1.5	7.3	9.3	0.4	2.5	-0.3	3.4
1980	9.5	2.1	2.6	0.5	6.9	1.5	6.4	9.1	0.4	2.4	-0.2	3.3
1985	8.5	2.3	1.9	0.5	7.7	1.5	6.7	9.1	0.5	2.5	-0.3	2.5
1990	8.7	2.5	2.0	0.4	8.1	1.2	6.8	9.0	0.4	3.0	-0.4	2.4
Canada												
1965	5.8	1.9	3.8	0.9	--	5.6	7.7	4.0	0.8	1.9	0.2	2.5
1970	8.3	3.4	3.4	0.9	1.5	4.5	8.9	4.6	0.8	3.2	0.3	3.8
1975	8.9	4.1	4.4	1.2	1.6	4.6	7.8	6.2	2.1	3.3	0.7	4.5
1980	7.6	5.1	3.9	1.2	1.8	4.0	7.5	5.3	2.1	3.7	0.9	4.1
1985	8.9	5.6	3.3	0.8	2.1	4.0	8.3	6.6	2.0	4.1	1.3	4.5
1990	10.9	7.2	1.6	0.8	2.3	3.9	9.0	6.3	0.9	4.2	1.1	4.0

Source: U.S. and Canadian National Accounts

Notes. For Canada, social insurance payments are defined as the sum of payments to the federal and Quebec pension funds. For the U.S., the data come from the national accounts, which differ slightly in terms of definition and coverage from the regional data used in the estimation.

Tab. 2: United States and Canada: Standard Deviation of Logarithm of Real Per Capita Personal Income*

	Over Time		*Across Regions*	
	Detrended Levels	First Differences	*Levels*	*First Differences*
USA (1965-86)				
North East	0.041	0.027		
Middle East	0.036	0.023		
Great Lakes	0.050	0.036		
Plains	0.053	0.040		
South East	0.049	0.030		
South West	0.042	0.025		
Rocky Mountains	0.048	0.025		
Far West	0.031	0.026		
Total	0.038	0.027	0.104	0.0033
Canada (1966-88)				
Newfoundland	0.072	0.032		
Prince Edward Island	0.071	0.053		
Nova Scotia	0.051	0.023		
New Brunswick	0.056	0.024		
Quebec	0.067	0.027		
Ontario	0.045	0.021		
Manitoba	0.053	0.033		
Saskatchewan	0.123	0.083		
Alberta	0.076	0.038		
British Columbia	0.080	0.031		
Yukon/Northwest Territories	0.046	0.042		
Total	0.058	0.023	0.209	0.0056

* *(Transfers from the Federal Government to persons have been netted out of personal income)*

Tab. 3: Estimates of the Impact of the Federal Fiscal System
(Cents per Dollar)

	Redistribution			Stabilization		
	USA	Canada	EC	USA	Canada	EC
Taxes*	7.7	2.4	na	8.6	3.4	10.4
Transfers	9.9	15.2	na	14.4	10.9	20.4
Grants	4.3	21.6	na	7.2	3.1	na
Total	21.9	39.2	4	30.2	17.4	30.8

* *Including social insurance payments*

Fig. 1: (a) United States: Personal Income per Capita Relative to U.S. Average

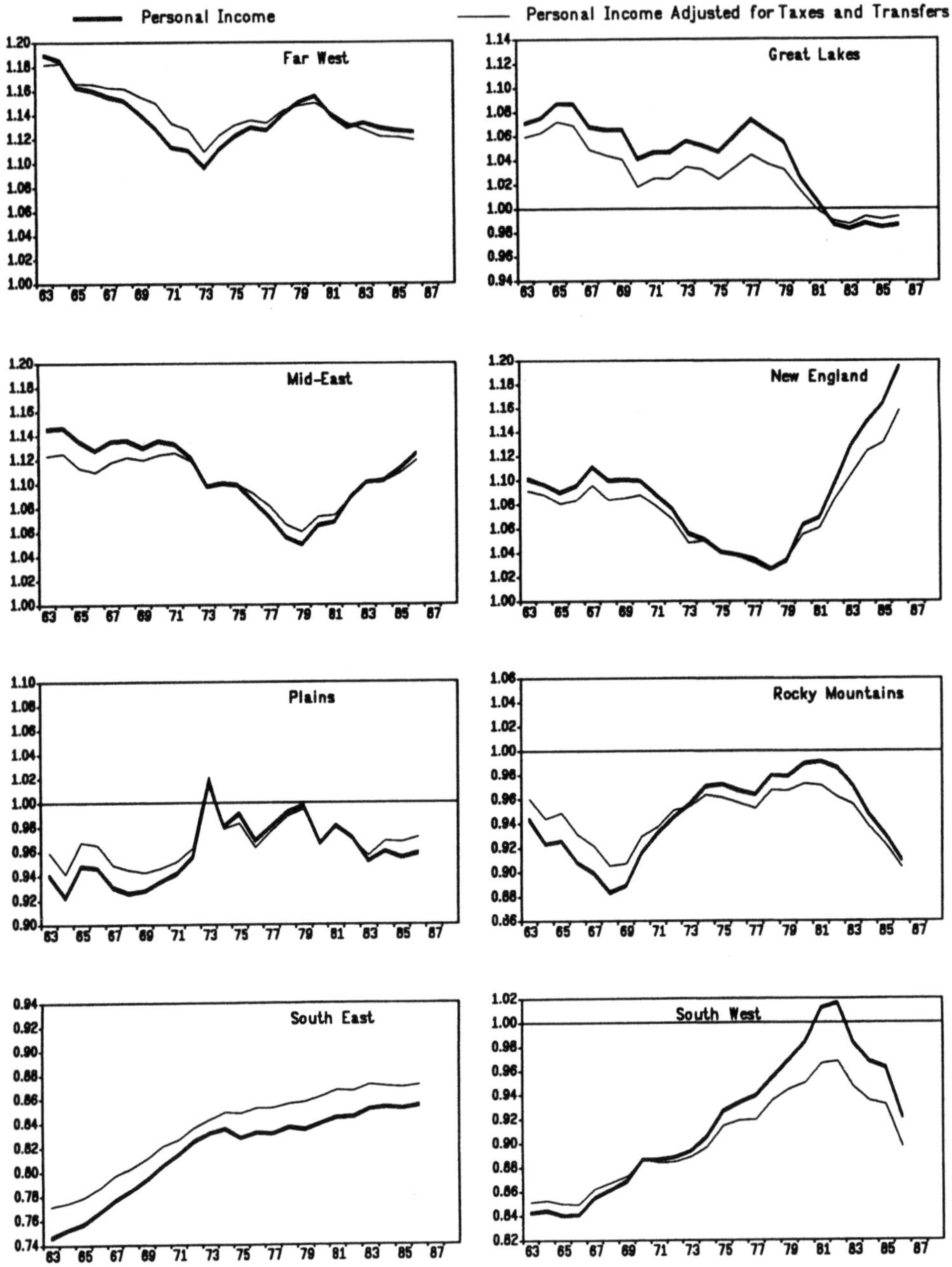

Fig. 1: (b) Canada: Personal Income per Capita Relative to Canadian Average

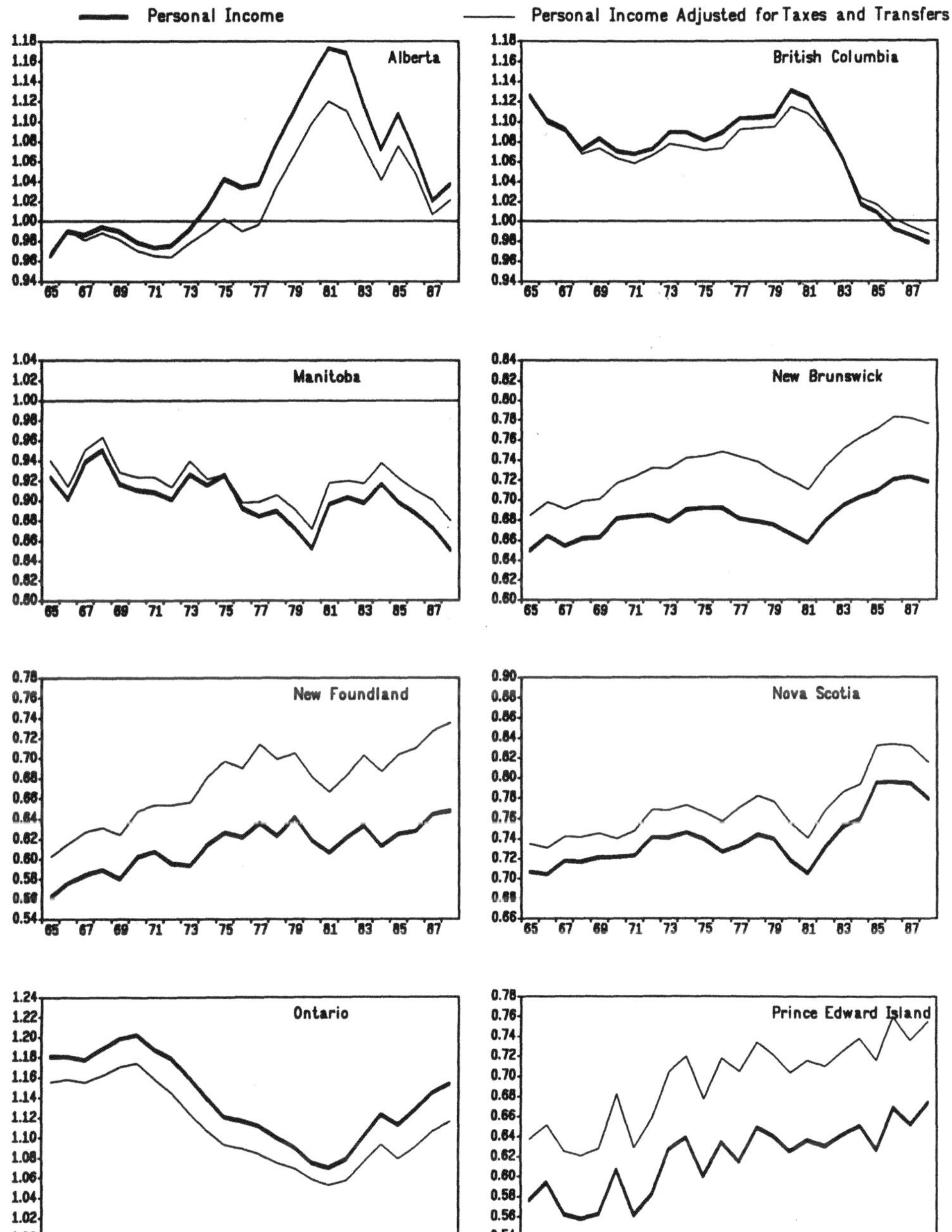

Fig. 1: (b; continued) Canada: Personal Income per Capita Relative to Canadian Average

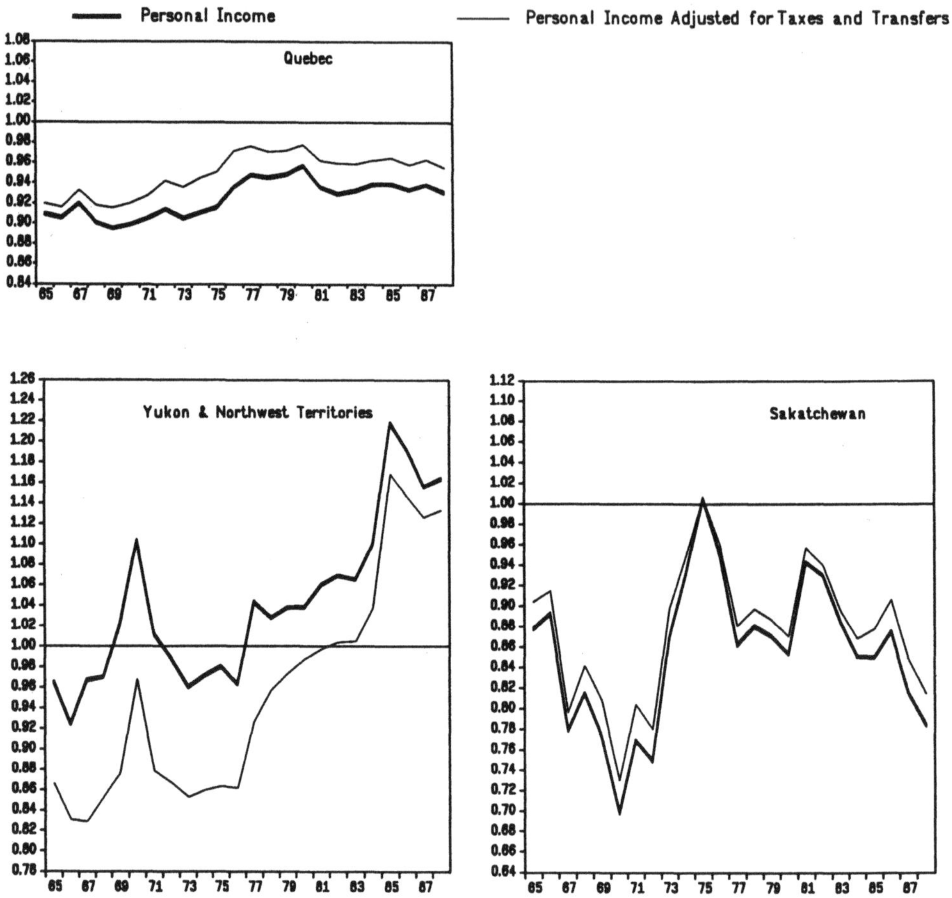

Fig. 2: Federal Fiscal Flows and Personal Income

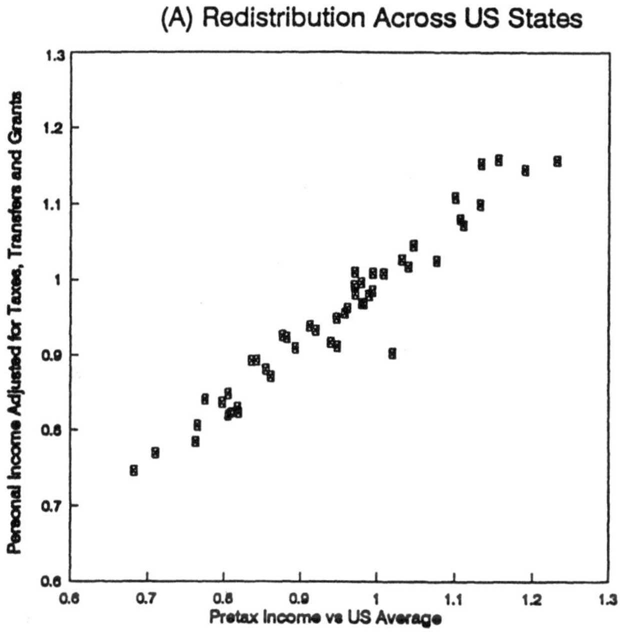

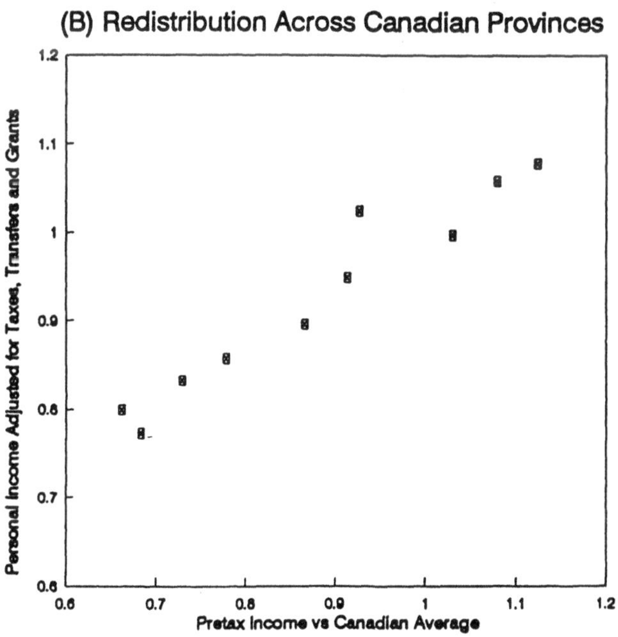

Susan M. Collins

Comments on:
What Can the Fiscal System in the United States and Canada Tell Us About EMU?"

This is an interesting and informative paper and I enjoyed reading it. The work is motivated by the often heard claim that lack of a common fiscal policy among European countries will compromise their ability to establish a common currency area. In my view, the issue at hand is somewhat more general than that. Not only is it relevant for a monetary union, it is relevant in a milder form for the sustainability of a multilateral fixed exchange rate system which is difficult to realign, such as the EMS post 1987. Perhaps additional scope for fiscal transfers would have enabled EMS members to weather the asymmetric shock of German unification without a need to "unswaddle" bilateral exchange rates. Thus, I believe that the issues discussed here remain of considerable importance for understanding the likely constraints to further monetary integration -- even though establishing a common currency in Europe is unlikely to happen over the next few years.

I initially commented on a related paper by the same authors.[1] Although, the discussion here has been modified in a way that reflects two of my main concerns about the other paper, my guess is that my overall view about the importance of fiscal transfers remains somewhat different from theirs. Since there is now some discussion of this issues in this version, let me simply mention both briefly. First, I believe than an extension of the role for cross-country fiscal transfers would be critical for the sustainability of further monetary integration among EMS members. However, the central concerns that I raised in my initial comments about the politics of maintaining an integrated monetary system among democratic nations are acknowledged more fully here. Second, I have been (and am!) skeptical that the nations could continue to follow the same types of discretionary fiscal policy in response to cyclical developments in national economic performance that they have conducted to date. (As discussed below, this assumption was one of the factors underlying the authors' conclusion that additional fiscal transfers among countries would not be necessary.) The paper now mentions that "the Maastricht criteria may be

1 The paper extends the discussion in T. BAYOUMI and P. MASSON, "Fiscal Flows in the United States and Canada: Lessons for Monetary Union in Europe," mimeo, International Monetary Fund, April 1993.

constraining for countries which are in a situation of large deficits and debts". In my view, the point should have been taken further. Some type of federal mechanism may well be necessary so as to compensate national constituencies for the loss of national policy makers to conduct stabilization policies.

The paper makes four main points. I will discuss each point in the order it was presented. First, the paper argues that a comparison of fiscal transfers within the U.S. and Canada provide interesting lessons for the potential role of redistribution within EC states. I agree wholeheartedly, and found the information presented in this part of the paper both useful and interesting. In particular, the paper shows that redistribution plays a very different role in the two federal systems, so that there is no particular reason to assume that one model (e.g. that of the U.S.) is the appropriate "blueprint" for a more integrated EC. However, it also notes that even with the doubling of the structural funds, the EC provides for considerably less potential redistribution than is the norm in either the U.S. or Canada.

I would have carried this discussion further, to explore whether conditions in Europe appear to be inconsistent with significantly less redistribution than we observe in other fiscal systems. On the one hand, voters may tolerate less redistribution across countries than within countries, especially over long time horizons. On the other hand, getting back to the "sustainability" issue, voters may be less likely to continue to support membership in an integrated EC without more redistribution to offset regional differences. Putting these two together, my guess is that European voters in prosperous regions will not tolerate large, persistent transfers to less prosperous regions in other countries. However, without such transfers, voters in less prosperous regions may vote to pull out of a fixed exchange rate system, so as to spur national growth through devaluation. I view the limited scope for fiscal transfers in the EC as a major constraint on further monetary integration. The Bayoumi and Masson discussion has not convinced me otherwise.

Second, the paper argues that it is important to distinguish between redistribution (long-term) and stabilization (short-term) when examining fiscal transfers. Although this is not a new point, it is clearly made, and the authors' use of both cross section and time series data to distinguish between the two is nicely done.

Third, the results reported in the paper are based on a different means for decomposing the redistributive effects of taxes versus transfers than the approach followed by other authors in the literature. Unlike those previous studies, Bayoumi and Masson find that transfers are relatively more important than taxes as a means of redistribution. But is this the "correct" decomposition as they claim? In my view, this depends on whether one believes that individuals care about stabilizing their income relative to the average national income, or about stabilizing the absolute level of income.

The point that can be made clearly if we think of taxes as being proportional to income while transfers are fixed amounts (as the authors do in their example). Transfers will be relatively more effective in stabilizing relative incomes than in stabilizing the difference between a state's income and the national average -- for which the equal transfer payments will simply cancel out. However, taxes, which are automatic stabilizers, will be relatively more effective in offsetting shocks that cause a state's income to deviate in absolute value from the national average than in stabilizing the ratio of a state's income to the national average. Bayoumi and Masson focus on relative income, and thus assert that their decomposition that emphasizes the role of transfers is "correct". As should be clear from the above discussion, this is not at all clear to me. I would have liked to see some discussion of what governments do -- and should - try to stabilize as background to an evaluation of the alternative decompositions.

Finally, the paper argues that stabilization policies need not be conducted at the supranational level of the EC. In fact, countries in Europe currently undertake quite a bit of stabilization -- comparable to that undertaken in the U.S. and Canada. Again, I agree this an important point, and these authors have made it clearly and convincingly. However, as discussed above, they do not carry the discussion as far as I would have liked in terms of whether these countries would be able to continue undertaking as extensive counter-cyclical policies under the Maastricht formulation of macroeconomic integration.

In sum, this paper spells out some key lessons from U.S. and Canadian experience for the role of fiscal transfers in a more integrated Europe. Although there are some places where I would have pushed the arguments in a somewhat different direction, I found the paper to be extremely useful and interesting overall.

Stephen Overturf

THE EUROPEAN COMMUNITY AS AN OPTIMUM CURRENCY AREA

1. Introduction

The intensity of debate associated with economic and monetary union (EMU) in the European Community (EC) highlights the core question of how valuable irrevocably fixed exchange rates, or a common currency, would be for its members. This is at heart an economic concern, one to which political objectives and motivations must be compared.[1]

In late 1992 the European Monetary System (EMS), before this time viewed as quite stable, became splintered by a series of forced devaluations and withdrawals from the system. Prior to this, and certainly still to a large extent, it was generally agreed that the EMS had worked well to its purpose of establishing a zone of monetary stability in Europe.[2] It is important to emphasize that the exchange rate mechanism (ERM) of the EMS is not one of fixed rates (*Wihlborg and Willett 1990*). Instead, what is generally considered to be the institutional base for movement on to EMU was in its earlier years characterized by frequent realignments of exchange rates, while even without realignments the ERM allows for larger (6 percent) or smaller (2.25 percent) margins within which rates may fluctuate, depending upon prior designation for each member country. It is, naturally, arguable that continuation of the flexibility inherent in the EMS[3] would serve its members better than would EMU and a common currency.

When movement toward a common currency in Europe is addressed, guidance is often sought from what is termed optimum currency area theory.[4] As noted by *Tower and Willett (1976)*, however, it is probably inappropriate to refer to a single theory of optimum currency areas given the multitude of criteria that have been advanced in the large literature on the subject, and perhaps better to consider an optimum currency area approach to the question of a common currency. Moreover, the discipline has diverted from the original consideration of characteristics that would apply to countries that would make them better or worse candidates for currency union to the nature and source of disturbances that might impact a particular country, or group of countries, and the insulation properties of fixed versus flexible exchange rates *(Edison and Melvin 1990)*.

Optimum currency area theory, in other words, seem to have lost some of the appealing simplicity which made it attractive as a model, a model that promised direct application to policy.

In addition, although initial empirical verification of the approach was encouraging, this body of research was not conclusive, nor was it ever fully developed.[5] *Edison and Melvin (1990, p.8)* feel that the underdevelopment is "...owing in part to the difficulty of developing empirically testable hypotheses."

This paper seeks to reexamine one of the seminal papers in this area, both with an eye to extending its vision and encouraging its application to the present concern over whether the individual member states of the EC might benefit economically from a common currency. This revisit, as it were, of an early paper by McKinnon (1963) is seen as anything but exhaustive regarding optimal currency areas; rather, it is an attempt to focus on and examine empirically what might be one perceived benefit to arise from EMU for individual countries within the EC. In this way, a more precise definition of one particular benefit may, in a much broader calculus, be weighed along with other economic as well as political costs and benefits of the sacrifice of sovereignty involved in accepting a common monetary policy and currency.

2. Model in a McKinnon Setting

Briefly, McKinnon's thesis is that the degree of openness, as measured by the ratio of an economy's tradeables to nontradeables, is important in the choice of the proper policy mix needed to reconcile external and internal balance. His particular contribution is to consider explicitly the increasing impact that exchange rate changes may have on price level instability, this in addition to any ineffectiveness such a policy may have on external balance arising from a high level of openness of the economy. Because of the potential impact on the overall price level, in other words, it would be advisable for more open economies to peg their exchange rates to those of their trading partners, and leave it to monetary and fiscal policies to directly deal with external balance through absorption control.[6]

This approach thus provides an explicit and measurable characteristic of countries to aid in their decision to fix or not, or at least to allow for less than full flexibility to their exchange rates. Its use avoids some of the difficulty associated with the application of another notion, factor mobility, that is also associated with the optimum currency area approach, as originally developed in the major contribution of Mundell (1961).[7] The two, that is openness and factor mobility, are not mutually exclusive, of course, with at least one connection being that capital mobility itself can be expected to be influenced by the degree of exchange rate flexibility. Similarly, diversification, also not unrelated to openness, is not explicitly considered by McKinnon,[8] nor are public finance issues (*see, for example, Canzoneri and Rogers 1990*). Following the notion of focusing the discussion on openness as related to price stability, this paper will also not comment on the rich literature developed around discipline, and credibility concerns, nor will it deal with political economy arguments *(Burdekin et al. 1991)*.

Establish a loss function (L) for an economy, with a Lagrange multiplier, defined in terms of the relation between inflation (p), entered here quadratically, and real income growth (y) which falls below the rate of natural real income growth (y_n), weighted by the importance of the tradeoff (d):

$$(1) \qquad L = 1/2\, p^2 + d(y_n - y) - T(t + e_1 p_t - e_2 y)$$

The change in the trade balance (t) in equation (1) is effected by a change in the price of tradeables (p_t) and/or income (y). The price elasticity of the trade balance (excess demand for tradeables) is e_1, while the income elasticity of the demand for tradeables is e_2. The price change includes implicitly some absorption change (unless there is an entirely dominant supply response to the tradeable price change), which may be supplemented by the impact of monetary-fiscal policy on absorption through a direct reduction in income. The decision thus involves the proper mix of policies (exchange rate and monetary-fiscal) that can minimize the loss function, which explicitly involves the attitude of the economy to any short and medium term tradeoff between inflation and real income growth, as constrained by the reaction of the trade balance to the two policy options.[9]

If b designates the (presumably absorption) weight of the impact of tradeable price changes (again, p_t) on overall price level changes (p), then:

$$(2) \qquad p = bp_t$$

In equation (2) the term b serves as a measure of the level of openness of the economy, as it reflects the proportion of total absorption composed of tradeables. The more open the economy the closer b approximates the value of one, and the more completely the overall price level is influenced by tradeable prices.

Next, in order to demonstrate the impact that exchange rate devaluation (k) has on prices, let:

$$(3) \qquad p_t = k$$

The law of one price is, of course, represented in equation (3), as tradeable prices adjust fully to any change in the nominal exchange rate. Also, note that there is nothing in the equation that constrains the system under which the exchange rate is to move. The exchange rate may change either by fiat in the alteration of a fixed rate, or by intervention or market pressure in a system either with established margins, or without them.

Inserting equation (2) into (1), and equation (3) into (1); solving for the impact of exchange rate change and income change on the loss function; and, finally, rearranging terms, yields:

$$(4) \qquad k = e_1 d / e_2 b^2$$

This parsimonious model (for which both the first and the second order conditions for a minimum are satisfied) can be seen to demonstrate the essential nature of the McKinnon framework for determining the degree of appropriate exchange rate response as part of the adjustment mechanism to external imbalance, with direct inclusion of the impact exchange rate changes on price instability. Equation (4) indicates that the appropriate rate of exchange rate change depends negatively on the square of the degree of openness. The term b is especially pertinent in that it represents not only the proportion of tradeables in an economy, but in the model it directly measures the impact of exchange rate changes can have on the price level through the change in tradeable goods prices. Therefore, openness affects a country's attraction to limiting exchange rate changes because of their potential impact on prices.

Also note that the price elasticity of tradeables enters positively, while the income elasticity enters negatively. The greater the price elasticity of the excess demand for tradeables the more attractive exchange rate changes become, as they have a greater impact on the trade balance, and can imply both a reduction in the size of any necessary realignments as well as a reduced need to curtail absorption directly through countercyclical policies. The greater the income elasticity of tradeable demand, on the other hand, the less the necessary impact on income of any monetary of fiscal policy action, and, therefore, a reduced need to use the exchange rate instrument, with its implications for price level stability.

Finally, from equation (4) it may be determined through the term d that the more critical is the value of maintaining real income in the face of increased inflation, the more the economy will willingly resort to exchange rate changes. This term may be seen to be important given the possibility of quite different acceptance levels of inflation, a point especially applicable to the European experience.

2.1 Model Extension

The model represented here, therefore, seems to capture well the nature of the openness criterion as an approach to determining the optimal level of exchange rate flexibility for a country. It shares with much of the literature, however, an inherent problem in application of the criterion. Specifically, it helps to direct a country as to how much exchange rates should be relied upon (again, within the price stability-adjustment context), but it does not give guidance regarding other states with which it should join for an optimal currency area. In other words, the model is implicitly a two-country model.

It is possible to extend the notion of openness, however, to that of open commerce with a country's several trading partners. In this way, it should be possible to delineate which of those partners might make better potential members of a currency union.

Define the loss function as before, but substitute for the price of tradeables a weighted sum of the change in price of tradeables for various countries' goods:

$$(5) \qquad p_t = \sum_c w_c \, p_{tc}$$

The way equation (5) is intended to be read is that overall tradeable goods prices are impacted severally by the price changes of goods traded with other countries (p_{tc}). The weight for each country (w_c) thus represents not only the proportion of influence on total tradeable goods prices, but also the level of trade with that country.[10] The greater the level of trade with another country, in other words, the more influence that country has on the internal price level of the original country through its impact on the price of tradeables.

Next, define the price of tradeables with other countries to be directly influenced by the *individual* exchange rates with those countries:

$$(6) \qquad p_{tc} = k_c$$

Again inserting equation (2) in the original model into equation (1), and then substituting equation (6) into equation (5), and equation (5) into equation (1) yields:

$$(7) \quad L=1/2b^2 \sum_c (w_c^2 \, k_c^2) + d(y_n-y) - T(t+e_1 \sum_c (w_c \, k_c) - e_2 y)$$

Taking the first differential of equation (7) with regard to the exchange rate with any one particular country (c) as well as with the level of income changes, setting the results equal to zero and solving for k_c yields:

$$(8) \qquad k_c = e_1 d / e_2 b^2 w_c$$

Equation (8) denotes that the appropriate exchange rate change of a country with one of its trading partners is related to the same variables as before, including the negative relation to the overall level of openness. In addition, however, there is a term (w_c) that indicates a negative relation with the weight of the other country's trade with the original country. Besides openness, and the elasticity and attitude toward inflation considerations examined above, a country will be less inclined to use exchange rate changes with its larger trading partners. Again, this makes sense, as these countries will have the greater impact on prices of any exchange rate realignment. Here, however, it adds a criterion to the more standard one which might help direct a country in how to manage its adjustment policies versus individual nations.

Such a standard allows a measure of how to treat some versus others in regard to establishing a potential optimum currency area. Moreover, it may help to explain why some countries in Europe might be more or less anxious to move onto EMU with the entire spectrum of EC countries (including potential new entrants), or might be more satisfied with a currency union composed of a smaller group of countries. Memories of the snake arrangement of the 1970s, which at the end of its existence included a grouping of smaller countries, not all of whom were EC members, around the DM seem pertinent to this notion. Finally, such a concept might shed some light on the political-economic cost-benefit analysis associated with moving towards EMU.

2.2 Empirical Results

The earlier empirical work in this area tended to include a wide variety of variables, developed in the optimum currency area approach, as explanatory in the choice of exchange regime.[11] While certainly useful, it may be that such an approach contributed to the lack of focus noted above. There is also the question of how applicable exchange regime results are to the decision of establishing a currency union with a set of particular countries.

The empirical section of this paper, therefore, will concentrate on openness as a criterion for allowable exchange rate flexibility, and, in addition, will extend the concept to openness, or trade, with individual countries in order to determine their attractiveness as currency partners.

As the interest of this study is Europe, and on the EC as an optimum currency area, the data set will be limited to these 12 European countries (with Belgium and Luxembourg already constituting currency union), plus the US and Japan representing external industrialized countries. In addition, the dependent variable will throughout be the coefficient of variation of the pertinent exchange rate over a period of five years, using yearly averages as observations in the coefficient determination. The driving force behind this choice of variable was twofold. First, it was presumed that over the longer run countries choose the level of exchange rate flexibility that they find acceptable. Shorter term measures of exchange rate variability may, of course, diverge from what is considered acceptable, but the sense of the measure is that over the longer term countries are able not only to choose but to control the level of flexibility with which they feel comfortable. Second, such a measure avoids some of the ad hoc nature of attempting to define type of regime into which countries fall as a dependent variable. In the case of the EMS, for example, it is especially critical not to lump all of the members together, for there is a great deal of variability not only within the bands, but also in the size of the bands themselves. Actual exchange rate variability over a longer period directly reflects, then, the revealed preference of these countries for exchange rate flexibility.

The period under consideration covers the five years from 1986 to 1990, so as to be able to comment upon the current preferences of a group of countries that moved, especially since the French policy decisions of 1983, to a level of commitment to very moderate levels of exchange movement between the members of the EMS. This allows for some beginning analysis on the willingness of these countries to move beyond EMS towards EMU; an analysis that could not so well be based on earlier data from a period of significant and frequent realignments in the system (especially between 1979 and 1985).

The first estimation is one concerning equation (4), which poses a simple negative connection between openness and the degree of exchange rate change. Using the 12 EC member states, Japan and the US, and employing double log OLS for the 1986-1990 period, the coefficient of variation of the exchange rate[12] is regressed on the percentage of imports plus exports of goods and services to 1988 GDP,[13] giving the a_2 coefficients in the following (with t statistics in parentheses):

a1	a2	F	R^2
-3.686	-.614	5.15	.301
(16.891)	(2.272)		

In support of earlier empirical studies on optimum currency areas using a broader spectrum of countries and a greater selection of variables, openness enters here as a statistically significant variable, at the five percent level.[14]

Next, it is possible to extend the model, as in equation (8), to individual EC countries and the degree to which their exchange rate variability with each of their EC trading partners over the period is influenced by the level of trade with those same partners. This is done by regressing for each country the log of the coefficient of variation of the exchange rate with each of its trading partners[15] on the log of the proportion of total 1988 import trade with those partners.[16] (Each country's global level of openness, as well as its attitude toward inflation, of course, remains invariant across its trading partners.) The results are presented in Table 1, and they are instructive.

In the table the proportion of trade variable is significant and of the expected sign for six of the 11 countries: Belgium/Luxembourg, Denmark, Germany, the Netherlands and Spain. Italy is very close to significant at the five percent level, with a coefficient itself well within the range of the others; while Greece carries a significant but positive coefficient. There is some evidence here, therefore, in support of the proposition that not only is openness a criterion that influences the way in which EC countries choose to manage their exchange rates, but also that the proportion of trade with individual countries is important to how exchange rates are managed country by country. This lends, then, empirical support not only to the simple theoretical characterization of the McKinnon criterion, but also to the extension of the criterion to intraregime rate setting. EC economies, in other words, not only appear to prefer less exchange rate variability as their level of openness increases, but also seem to prefer greater fixity with their larger trading partners.

Tab. 1: EC Exchange Rate Variation on Trade Proportions by Country
(Period 1986-1990)

COUNTRY	a_1	a_2	F	R^2
Belg./Lux.	-4.845 (6.591)**	-0.423 (2.235)*	4.99	0.333
Denmark	-5.128 (7.114)**	-0.513 (2.716)**	7.38	0.425
France	-4.432 (6.158)**	-0.364 (1.793)	3.22	0.243
Germany	-6.047 (5.066)**	-0.780 (2.296)*	5.27	0.345
Greece	-1.676 (7.769)**	0.140 (2.345)*	5.50	0.355
Ireland	-1.776 (8.274)**	0.061 (1.158)	1.34	0.118
Italy	-4.373 (7.147)**	-0.348 (2.148)	4.61	0.316
Netherl.	-5.886 (6.333)**	-0.694 (2.837)**	8.04	0.446
Portugal	-2.557 (11.185)**	0.008 (0.140)	0.02	0.002
Spain	-3.799 (8.411)**	-0.280 (2.273)*	5.17	0.341
UK	-3.369 (6.246)**	-0.218 (1.410)	2.00	0.166

a_1 = constant; a_2 = proportion of imports with trading partner
t statistics for coefficients in parentheses (95 percent significance; ** 99 percent)*

Another interesting result emerges from closer examination of Table 1. The trade coefficient (for those with significant coefficients plus Italy) ranges from a low of -.280 for Spain to a high of -.780 for Germany. In fact, the progression is: Spain (-.280), Italy (-.348), Belgium and Luxembourg (-.423), Denmark (-.513), the Netherlands (-.694), and Germany (-.780). France at -.364, would fall here between Italy and Belgium/Luxembourg. This relation is suggestive that not only do the coefficients represent the expected negative correlation, but they also reflect the attitudes of the states toward inflation. It will be remembered that the model includes a term for the attitude of a country to inflation, and the willingness to accept a greater degree of income constraint in the adjustment process to external disequilibrium. This seems to be represented in the coefficient of trade (and to some extent the constants as well). Spain, here, again according to these results, is ready to accept a greater degree of exchange rate change than is Germany, presumably due to somewhat less of a concern over the price destabilizing impact of such exchange rate changes.

With an acceptance of this reading of the results, one may then proceed to use the regression equations to determine, from their revealed preferences coupled with the actual proportions of trade for each country, which other EC countries each nation would consider an appropriate candidate for currency union. Using Germany's equation in Table 1, for example, it is possible to enter Germany's actual proportion of trade with the Netherlands in order to decide an acceptable level of longer term exchange rate fluctuation with that country. If this level of fluctuation falls within a suitable narrow range, say, 2.25 percent (borrowed from the smaller band of the ERM), it would seem to constitute at least a country with which one would be tempted to establish pegged rates with a very narrow margin, and perhaps even union.

Table 2 represents the results of this experiment. It shows for each country that carries a significant coefficient (of the correct sign), and Italy (with a t-statistic only .031 off significance at the five percent level), the countries that satisfy the 2.25 percent criterion for exchange rate variation.

Tab. 2: EC Currency Groupings

COUNTRY	ASSOCIATIONS
Belgium/Lux	France; Germany; Netherlands
Denmark	Germany; Netherlands
France	(Germany)
Germany	Belgium; France, Italy, Netherlands, UK
Greece	(no guideline)
Ireland	(no guideline)
Italy	Germany
Netherlands	Belgium; France, Germany; UK
Portugal	(no guideline)
Spain	none
UK	(no guideline)

Table based on size of trading partner entered in country equations from Table 1 (see text for explanation). No guideline for a country follows from lack of a significant relationship.

The table seems to fit generally some heuristic sense of the partner countries within the EC for optimum currency sharing. It is not surprising, for example to find some of the smaller northern European countries associated with neighbors which are large trading partners. Belgium/Luxembourg, therefore is linked here with France, Germany and the Netherlands, while Denmark is associated with Germany and the Netherlands. The Netherlands, again evidencing no little aversion to inflation, and hence by these criteria opening it to more rather than fewer countries for exchange rate linkage, is related in Europe to Belgium/Luxembourg, France, Germany, and the UK.

An important question in the development of the EMS, as well as EMU, is the attraction of some of the larger states to currency union, or at least a peg with fixed and narrow margins.[17] In this sample Spain, in fact, has no countries with which it would find it good to associate, probably reflecting a more benign attitude toward inflation, and less to income losses, than the more northern states. Italy is in a similar position, although the level of its trade with Germany evidently outweighs a greater insouciance toward exchange fixing. Incidentally, although France does not posses a significant coefficient, when the standard is applied to France it indicates Germany as a good partner.

Perhaps the most interesting result is that of Germany itself. Given the low tolerance for inflation (as represented by the regression coefficients), within Europe Germany would be open to an area of very reduced exchange rate variation with no fewer than six countries, including Belgium/Luxembourg, France, Italy, the Netherlands, and the UK. Given the self-imposed constraints on both the theoretical and empirical model in this paper, it is nonetheless significant that such a rationale may be employed to help explain the consistent participation of Germany in the snake arrangement during the 1970s, the fact that Germany was instrumental in establishing and maintaining the EMS even during turbulent years, and, more recently, the willingness of the country actively to consider movement toward EMU, even at the risk of losing sovereignty over the creation of its own currency. Indeed, it is noteworthy that it is here exactly the well-known German concern, over imported inflation, that would actually drive Germany toward EMU, and have it consider establishing a currency union with at least many of its EC trading partners. Another possible interpretation, of course, is that it might be most satisfied with an arrangement where it establishes relatively fixed rates through a disciplined EMS with low margins, and yet still retains its monetary sovereignty.

Finally, two points regarding this approach to the question are worth making. First, it follows from the model in this paper that as intra-EC trade grows (say, following upon the implementation of a successfully expanded single market), a common currency becomes more attractive. Second, the fact that many of the groups reported in Table 2 seem to involve more northern EC states may speak to an inherent willingness within the Community to establish a two-tier currency structure within Europe.

3. Conclusion

In conclusion, this paper has revisited one specific criterion for the establishment of an optimum currency area, openness, and assessed its value in addressing the future of EMU among the EC states. Using a simple theoretical construct involving adjustment in general, and the cost of price instability in particular, it is possible to demonstrate not only that openness is a useful guide, but also, through an extension of the model, that the proportion of trade with partner states is an effective criterion for deciding on greater exchange rate fixity with particular nations. A sample empirical analysis applied to recent EC experience reinforces the openness standard, and also demonstrates how small and large (especially northern) EC countries might be expected to benefit from narrowly fixed exchange rates, or perhaps even monetary union. Whether or not this economic benefits coupled with other economic and political benefits, are viewed as adequate to outweigh other economic and political costs, is, of course, the key question in a much broader analysis of whether or not there might eventually be a single currency for much of Europe.

References

BURDEKIN, R.C.K., WESTBROOK, J. and WILLETT, T. (1992), The Political Economy of Discretionary Monetary Policy: A Public Choice Analysis of Proposals for Reform, Presented at the Western Economic Association Conference in San Francisco, 1992.

CANZONERI, M.B. and ROGERS, C.A. (1990), Is the European Community an Optimal Currency Area? Optimal Taxation Versus the Cost of Multiple Currencies, American Economic Review, Vol. 80, 419-433.

COMMISSION OF THE EUROPEAN COMMUNITIES (1990), One Market, One Money, European Economy, 44, Brussels: DG for Econ. and Fin. Affairs.

CORDEN, W.M., Monetary Integration, Essays in International Finance, No. 93, Princeton, NJ: Princeton University, 1972.

EDISON, H.J. and MELVIN, M. (1990), The Determinants and Implications of the Choice of an Exchange Rate System, in: HARAF, W.S. and WILLETT, T.D., eds., Monetary Policy for a Volatile Global Economy, Washington: AEI Press.

EICHENGREEN, B. (1989), Is Europe an Optimum Currency Area?, Presented at the Conference on European Economic Integration and External Relations, Basle, August 1989.

EUROPEAN COMMUNITIES (1990), Basic Statistics of the Community, Luxembourg: Office of Publications of the EC.

FELDSTEIN, M. (1992), Europe's Monetary Union: The Case Against EMU, The Economist, June 13, 1992, 19-22.

FRATIANNI, M. and VON HAGEN, J. (1990), The European Monetary System Ten Years After, in: MELTZER, A.H., ed., Unit Roots, Investment Measures and Other Essays, Amsterdam: North-Holland.

FROOT, K.A. and ROGOFF, K. (1991), The EMS, the EMU, and the Transition to a Common Currency, NBER Working Paper No. 3684, Cambridge, MA: NBER, April 1991.

HELLER, H.R. (1978), Determinants of Exchange Rate Practices, Journal of Money, Credit, and Banking, Vol. 10, 308-321.

HOLDEN, P., HOLDEN, M. and SUSS, E.C. (1979), The Determinants of Exchange Rate Flexibility: An Empirical Investigation, The Review of Economics and Statistics, Vol. 61, 327-333.

INTERNATIONAL MONETARY FUND (1991), International Financial Statistics Yearbook, Washington DC: IMF.

KAUFMANN, H. (1989), Toward a European Central Bank, Business Forum, 14(4), Fall 1989, 49-53.

KAUFMANN, H. and OVERTURF, S. (1991), Progress Within the European Monetary System, in: HURWITZ, L. and LEQUESNE, C., eds., The State of the European Community, Boulder, CO.: Lynne Rienner.

McKINNON, R.I. (1963), Optimum Currency Areas, American Economic Review, Vol. 53, 717-725.

MUNDELL, R.A. (1961), A Theory of Optimum Currency Areas, American Economic Review, Vol. 51, 657-665.

THYGESEN, N. (1987), Is the European Community an Optimal Currency Area?, in: LEVICH, R.M. and SOMMARIVA, A., eds., The ECU Market, Lexington, MA: Heath, 163-185.

TOWER, E. and WILLETT, T.D. (1976), The Theory of Optimum Currency Areas and Exchange Rate Flexibility, Special Papers in International Economics, No. 11, Princeton, NJ: Princeton University.

WHILBORG, C. and WILLETT, T. (1990), Optimum Currency Areas Revisited, Presented at the Gothenburg Conference on Financial Regulation and Monetary Arrangements after 1992, May 1990.

1 *Feldstein (1992)*, for example maintains that the question should be reversed from whether the political costs of EMU outweigh the economic gains to whether the political gains outweigh the economic costs. For the official view see *Commission of the European Communities (1990)*.
2 It is a heavily debated point in the literature on the nature and reason for this perception of success, with a good deal of the debate centering more on the reduction and convergence in inflation rates than on the reduction of exchange rate variability. See, for a summary, *Kaufmann and Overturf (1991)*, and, for some recent contributions to the debate, *Fratianni and von Hagen (1990)* and *Froot and Rogoff (1991)*.
3 Or expandable, considering a proposal to widen the bands, thus making permanent the "temporary" actions in response to the August 1993 ERM crisis.
4 See *Tower and Willett (1976)* and *Wihlborg and Willett (1990)*, and the sources referred to in those works, for surveys. For more recent applications of the approach to Europe see *Thygesen (1987), Kaufmann (1989) and Eichengreen (1989)*.
5 The *Commission of European Communities (1990, p.46)* finds that "Empirical applications of this [optimum currency area] approach are scarce and hardly conclusive."
6 *Corden (1972)*, similarly, treats currency union through consideration of the increased price stability offered by fixed exchange rates, and the impact on trade as well as protection for those countries averse to inflation, whereas McKinnon is concerned more with the usefulness, or liquidity value, of money. Corden's discussion of the possibility of insulation of an economy to the instability of foreign prices (through flexible rates) is especially interesting.
7 See *Commission of the European Communities (1990, p.46)* for some of the problems in application of the mobility criterion, especially to the case of the EC.
8 Although interindustry trade mobility, as well as more general factor mobility, is.
9 An implicit assumption here is some degree of short and medium term wage and price inflexibility, or else there would be little need for the discretionary macroeconomic policy response. On this point see *Burdekin, et al. (1992)*. Also, even though it is perhaps easiest to imagine the response called for in the policy decision to be in reaction to an external real shock affecting the trade balance, there is no reason policymakers would not be faced with similar dilemma in reaction to an internal policy shock created by the authorities themselves. Thus, a Barro-Gordon style engineered surprise inflation would then require a policy response to deal with the trade implications of the prior policy decision.
10 There is introduced in this construct a level of independence of the markets for goods from specific countries.
11 See specifically the papers by *Heller (1978)* and *Holden, Holden and Suss (1979)*. *Edison and Melvin (1990)* note the empirical tension between testing for source of disturbance versus overt country characteristics.
12 The nominal effective exchange rate over the five years, from *IMS (1991)*.
13 From the national accounts in the *IMS (1991)*.
14 Again, see *Edison and Melvin (1990)* for reference to source of disturbance empirically dominating openness and other optimum currency area approach characteristics. Also, a run of the same equation here, but using a broader grouping of OECD countries increased the t-statistic for openness to 2.900. With attention to missing variables the equation was also run including a proxy for the "d" term in equation (4), as the difference in the inflation rate of each country from the average inflation rate for the population. Neither did the coefficients change in value or in significance, nor was the new term significant. Also, the influence of price and income elasticities, again represented in equation (4), is expected to be captured in the openness variable. The expectation is, reinforcing the way in which they enter in the equation, that price elasticities increase with openness. See *Tower and Willett (1976)*.
15 Period averages of market rates run through the US dollar over the 5 years, from *IMS(1991)*.
16 Data from intra-Community trade and total import tables as contained in *European Communities (1990)*. Export data are not included by country in this source.
17 In a a somewhat similar vein *Thygesen (1987, pp. 167-8)* finds it easy to explain why the smaller European states have chosen to manage their exchange rates, as they "...are all very open by the McKinnon criterion," and yet finds that it does not explain why some of the "...larger European countries have chosen to set up the EMS in preference to less complex methods."

Karen H. Johnson

Comments on:
The European Community as an Optimum Currency Area"[1]

Stephen Overturf's paper is an interesting additional contribution to the literature on the proposed European Monetary Union (EMU) and on the question of whether the EC member countries constitute an optimum currency area. Given the enthusiasm with which this topic has been addressed in the literature, it is no easy task to find something new to say about is: but Overturf does so.

The paper addresses only one dimension of this question and is very explicit about limiting the discussion to this one dimension: the author acknowledges that as a consequence his treatment does not provide a complete answer to the question whether the EC is or is not an optimum currency area.

The dimension that the paper pursues, that of the degree of openness as a criterion for the members of an optimum currency area, dates back to *McKinnon's (1963)* contribution to the optimum currency literature. McKinnon's proposition was that the degree of openness of a given economy, which is itself a well-defined currency area, should matter in its choice of whether to have a flexible exchange rate or a fixed exchange rate with respect to the currency of its trading partner. In the event that a fixed exchange rate regime is chosen, the two have in effect become a single currency area. The underlying objective is to stabilize the domestic price level in the given country. If the economy is sufficiently open, the prices of tradeable goods have a dominant effect on the domestic price level. In that case, a fixed exchange rate stabilizes tradeable goods prices, and so the price level, provided that the trading partner's prices for tradeables are themselves stable.

One of the strengths of Overturf's approach to this question is that it allows him to distinguish among the EC countries. From his perspective, the question is not whether the EC taken together is an optimum currency area, but rather for which EC countries does this criterion imply that a fixed rate with certain other EC countries is advisable. Such an approach helps the reader to recognize that among the EC countries, some may choose to join the EMU for one reason, while others mays reject that reason, but choose to join for another. These differences among the EC countries are often overlooked in the literature on EMU; for example the gains to Germany, in contrast to all other EC countries, of participating in an EMU or in the existing ERM are often questioned in the literature, but the question of how the benefits to France from participating in an EMU compare with those of Belgium or Luxembourg is seldom addressed.

The particular model that Overturf uses to motivate his empirical work is very simple and so has some drawbacks. For example, the price and income variables are all in rate of change terms. As a result, his loss function compares the rate of growth of actual income to that of "natural" real income, i.e., potential. The size of the gap between the levels of potential and actual output does not enter. Growing at potential contributes the same to the loss function (zero) whether that gap in terms of levels is large, small, or zero. When the model is extended to allow for several trading partners, the simplifications made imply an assumption that each tradeable good can be identified with one trading partner and its exchange rate, or something equivalent. The model is used only to motivate the intuitive conclusion that the appropriate degree of exchange rate responsiveness depends inversely on the degree of openness.

In the empirical test of the model, Overturf again makes some simplifications. In the theoretical derivation, the measure of openness is the elasticity of the domestic price level with respect to the price of tradeables. In the regression analysis, he uses instead the ratio of exports plus imports to GDP in 1988 for the joint cross-country estimate, and for the individual bilateral equations he uses total 1988 imports of the given country from the partner country. As the regressions are essentially cross-section in nature and each EC country has only 10 possible EC trading partners (Belgium and Luxembourg are combined), the estimates seem to suffer from lack of degrees of freedom.

Overturf finds some interesting results that basically support McKinnon's original hypothesis but also distinguish among the EC members. For about half of the EC countries, he finds a statistically significant coefficient of the expected sign on the openness measure; the results for Denmark and the Netherlands are strongest. When he uses his estimated results to conclude which countries are candidates for monetary union with each of the EC countries, he obtains no suitable countries[2] for Greece, Ireland, Portugal, Spain and the United Kingdom. Other than Ireland, none of these countries were in the ERM for a significant portion of the 1986-1990 period from which he drew his data. (The peseta joined in mid-1989, and sterling, in late 1990.)

With the recent widening of the margins for exchange rate fluctuations within the ERM and earlier withdrawal of the lira and the pound from the system, it would seem that a review of the reasons for and benefits from exchange rate stability among the currencies of the member countries would be useful. If EMU is to be implemented, it may well be done in a two-tier manner; a review of which countries are best suited to be partners in a monetary union with which others would again be useful in formulating such an approach to EMU.

Overturf's paper is a contribution to this process. It revives the earlier McKinnon idea and establishes that the degree of openness of an economy is one of the criteria that should be considered in making decisions about the exchange rate regime. With a very simplified regression used to capture the influence of openness and with significant results for about half of the countries, however, the paper is only an initial step in addressing these issues. The regressions as presented confound the effects of openness per se and officials' preferences with respect to inflation versus growth. An attempt to estimate separately the effects of these two variables would be worthwhile. In addition, it would be informative to learn how the coefficients Overturf has estimated have evolved over time; a panel data approach might shed light on this question.

On balance, the paper is a stimulating, but perhaps simplified, attempt to insert an old idea into a very timely debate.

References

McKINNON, R.I. (1963), Optimum Currency Areas, American Economic Review, Vol. 53, 717-725.

Endnotes

1 The author is an Assistant Director of the Division of International Finance, Board of Governors of the Federal Reserve System. The opinions expressed above are those of the author only and do not necessarily represent the views of the Board or any members of its staff.

2 The finding of no suitable countries resulted either from a lack of statistical significance in the given country's equation or from the data for the given country's trade with the other EC members not implying exchange rate variability of less than 2.25 percent.

INDEX

EUROPEAN MONETARY INTEGRATION

List of Contributors/Conference Participants and Panel Participants*

**** indicates participants at panel B6: European Communities Studies Association's international conference "European Integration after 1992 and Maastricht"***

*Dr. Tamim Bayoumi**
Economist, International Monetary Fund

Dr. Peter Bofinger
Professor of Economics, Universität Würzburg

Dr. Matthew Canzoneri
(session chairman) Professor of Economics, Georgetown University

*Dr. Susan Collins**
Senior Fellow, Economic Studies, The Brookings Institution and Associate Professor of Economics, Georgetown University

Dr. Michele Fratianni
Professor of Business Economics and Public Policy
Graduate School of Business, Indiana University

Dr. Klaus Friedrich
(session chairman)
Institute of International Finance

Dr. George M. von Furstenberg
Rudy Professor of Economics, Indiana University,
and Visiting Senior Economist, U.S. Department of State

Dr. Vittorio Grilli
Professor of Economics,
Birbeck College, University of London

Dr. Daniel Gros
Senior Research Fellow at CEPS, Brussels;
and Economic Advisor DG II
(EC Directorate General for Economic and Financial Affairs)

Dr. Jürgen von Hagen
Professor of Economics, Universität Mannheim

*C. Randall Henning**
Senior Research Fellow, Institute for International Economics, Washington DC

Dr. Dale Henderson
(session chairman) Senior Research Fellow, Board of Governors of the
Federal Reserve System

Dr. Alan G. Isaac
Assistant Professor of Economics, The American University

*Dr. Keren Johnson **
(session chairwoman) Assistant Director, Board of Governors of the
Federal Reserve System

Dr. Sydney Key
Senior Fellow, Board of Governors of the Federal Reserve System

Dr. Michael W. Klein
Assistant Professor of International Economics,
The Fletcher School of Law and Diplomacy, Tufts University

Dr. Robert Gerald Livingston
Director,
American Institute for Contemporary German
Studies at the Johns Hopkins University

*Dr. Paul Masson**
Assistant Director, European I Department, International Monetary Fund

Dr. Nadine Mendelek
(Paris) Princeton University

*Dr. Stephen Overturf**
Ferguson Professor of International Economics, Whittier College

Dr. Eckard Pieske
German Ministry of Finance, Bonn

Karl Otto Pöhl,
former President, Deutsche Bundesbank
Guest of honor at the AICGS, 1990

Dr. Franco Reither
Professor of Economics, HWWA Institute for Economic Research, Hamburg

Dr. Robert Solomon
Senior Fellow, The Brookings Institution, Washington DC

Dr. Niels Thygesen
Senior Research Fellow at CEPS
and Professor of Economics,
University of Copenhagen

Dr. Horst Ungerer
Advisor, European Department, International Monetary Fund

Dr. Paul J.J. Welfens(*)
Professor of Economic Policy/International Economic Relations, University of Potsdam
(1990/91: McCloy Distinguished Research Fellow, American Institute
for Contemporary German Studies/The Johns Hopkins University, Washington DC)

Dr. John Williamson
Senior Research Fellow, Institute for International Economics, Washington DC

Dr. Manfred Willms
Professor of Economics and Director, Institute for Economic Policy
Chistian-Albrechts-Universität Kiel

Appendix: Demand for Money and Currency Substitution in Europe

Deutsche Bundesbank (reprinted with permission from Monthly Report 1995/1)

In the past, the international interdependence of the financial markets has become progressively closer. World-wide, investors have increasingly diversified their portfolios. Against this background, it might seem reasonable to assume that progress has likewise been made in the internationalisation of holding liquid funds. This might be expected to be particularly true of Europe, where the goods and financial markets have largely coalesced to form a single market. If different currencies become more readily interchangeable, the question arises as to whether monetary growth can be assessed solely on the basis of domestic developments or, alternatively, whether the domestic money stock can still be regarded as a suitable yardstick for the operation of monetary policy. The point has in fact already been made that German monetary policy at the present time should orient itself less towards a domestic money stock and, instead, rather more towards a pan-European monetary aggregate. The present study constitutes an attempt to establish whether and, if so, to what extent factors due to currency substitution in Europe have affected German demand for money. The findings suggest that currency substitution effects have hitherto generally played only a minor role in Germany, so that it is appropriate for the Bundesbank to continue to gear its policy stance to the movements of the German money stock.

Currency substitution and the demand for money: some theoretical considerations

Currency substitution is defined as a situation in which foreign money acts as a partial or full substitute for holding liquidity in national currency. Regarding the role of money as a means of payment, it is to be presumed that the interchangeability of currencies in the demand for money is being enhanced by the internationalisation of merchandise trade. Growing foreign trade turnover, mounting foreign travel and increasing cross-border investment income payments are likely to result in a greater diversification of money-holding at home and abroad. This applies in particular measure within Europe, as the bulk of the EU countries' foreign trade is intra-EU trade, and market interdependence is accelerating. As is evident from the adjacent table, however, the need for transaction-induced liquidity-holding in foreign currency would appear to be less pressing for German enterprises than for undertakings in many other European countries. In line with the currency pattern of German foreign trade, the greater part of German exports and imports is invoiced in Deutsche Mark, followed by the US dollar. In the aggregate, only 12 % and 10 %, respectively, of German exports and imports are invoiced in other EU currencies. Incidentally, these proportions have changed but little over time. No major repercussions on the trend of domestic monetary growth are to be expected from this angle, not even in the medium run. Altogether, this type of currency substitution is therefore likely to be of minor relevance for the description of German demand for money.

Tab. 1: The currency structure of German foreign trade in 1992

Percentage share

Currency	Exports	Imports
Deutsche Mark	77.0	55.9
US dollar	7.3	18.4
French franc	3.4	3.1
Pound sterling	3.2	2.2
Italian lira	2.2	1.7
Japanese yen	0.6	1.7
Other	6.3	17.0
All currencies	100.0	100.0
of which EMS currencies[1]	89.1	65.8

1 Including Italian lira and pound sterling, excluding Austrian Schilling.
Deutsche Bundesbank

In capital transactions, in contrast to merchandise trade and services transactions, currency substitution is of major significance.[1] Money is used here not only as a transaction vehicle, but above all as a store of value and a medium for speculation. In this function, one currency is substituted for another whenever the cost of and the return on money-holding shift in its favour.

Broadly speaking, the „cost“ of money-holding means the opportunity cost of alternative types of investment. The closer substitutes these „competing products“ are for the monetary aggregate in question, the more sharply the demand for money will respond to changes in that cost. In studies of the demand for money, it is customary to consider domestic alternative investments. For theoretical reasons, a wide range of „opportunity costs“ ought to be taken into account here. However, the usual statistical estimation methods are soon stretched to their limits at this point. In general, studies of the demand for money therefore confine themselves to considering only one or two variables for measuring the opportunity cost - say, a short-term interest rate in the case of narrowly defined monetary aggregates such as the money stock M1, or a long-term interest rate, possibly adjusted for the interest on the interest-bearing components, in the case of broadly defined monetary aggregates such as the money stock M3. These traditional arguments of a money demand function have to be supplemented if the role of currency substitution is to be examined. After all, in addition to potential domestic alternatives, foreign investments then have to be taken into account as well. Accordingly, the range has to be extended to include both (expected) exchange rate changes - the alternative investment is a non-interest-bearing bank deposit or cash held in the form of foreign currency - and foreign currency interest (adjusted for expected exchange rate changes) - the alternative investment is an interest-bearing bank deposit in foreign currency. If currency substitution is a major phenomenon, even relatively small changes in these variables will have an appreciable impact on domestic demand for money. In these circumstances it would be doubtful, for example, whether the achievement of a monetary target derived entirely from domestic variables could be viewed as an indication of an appropriate monetary policy. An internationally aggregated money stock might then be a more informative indicator of the stance of monetary policy. These considerations have been set forth in the form of a simple portfolio model in the box on page 368.

Practical problems posed by an empirical review of currency substitution

Any attempt empirically to review the above-described theoretical relationships between currency substitution and money demand comes up against a number of serious problems. As will be shown below, these are attributable, firstly, to the fact that, while there may be a close substitutional link with investments of funds in various currencies, these do not affect the statistical growth of the

Figure 1: A simple portfolio model

The phenomenon of currency substitution, as described in the article, can be formalised in a simple portfolio model containing interest-bearing and non-interest-bearing monetary components for two countries that can be aggregated to yield national money stocks. The model is thus oriented towards the money stock M3, which comprises (non-interest-bearing) currency and sight deposits plus (interest-bearing) time deposits and savings deposits. Both money stock components may be held by residents and non-residents alike. In addition, there is the option of investing funds in long-term debt securities.

The overall assets M and M^* held by residents and non-residents consist of domestic and foreign interest-bearing (T and T_a respectively) and non-interest-bearing (M1 and $M1_a$ respectively) components, all of which are considered to be interchangeable. The foreign holdings are translated into domestic units using the exchange rate e.

$$(1) \quad M = M1 + T + e(M1_a + T_a)$$

$$(2) \quad M^* = M1^* + T^* + e(M1_a^* + T_a^*)$$

The total amount of domestic assets is marked by a "tilde" and is generated as follows: 1

$$(3) \quad \tilde{M}1 = M1 + M1^*$$

$$(4) \quad \tilde{T} = T + T^*.$$

Equation 4 means that domestic time deposits ($\tilde{T}$) are held by residents (T) and non-residents (T^*). The return on the foreign non-interest-bearing component equals the expected rate of appreciation of that currency E(e), whereas the nominal return on the domestic non-interest-bearing money stock component is zero. For the domestic interest-bearing money stock component, the interest rate is i. The corresponding foreign investment yields the foreign interest rate i_a plus the expected appreciation E(e).

The demand relationships can be derived from profit maximisation. For market equilibrium conditions (with small letters for the demand functions) in nominal units, the following equations are then obtained for the domestic money stock components (the "+" and "-" signs above the arguments indicate the signs of the partial derivatives):

$$(5) \quad m1\,[\overset{-}{E(e)}, \overset{-}{i}, \overset{-}{i_a + E(e)}, \overset{-}{r}, \overset{+}{Y^n}] + m1^*\,[\overset{-}{E(e)}, \overset{-}{i - E(e)}, \overset{-}{i_a}, \overset{-}{r}, \overset{+}{eY_a^n}] - \tilde{M}1 = 0$$

$$(6) \quad t\,[\overset{-}{E(e)}, \overset{+}{i}, \overset{-}{i_a + E(e)}, \overset{-}{r}, \overset{+}{Y^n}] + t^*\,[\overset{-}{E(e)}, \overset{+}{i - E(e)}, \overset{-}{i_a}, \overset{-}{r}, \overset{+}{eY_a^n}] - \tilde{T} = 0.$$

The first four arguments in the demand functions are the nominal returns on the respective alternative investments (in each case, in absolute form): E(e) is the alternative return on the foreign non-interest-bearing investment; i, i_a+E(e) and i-E(e), respectively, are the expected nominal returns on the domestic and foreign interest-bearing money stock component for residents and non-residents. For the sake of simplicity, only a single rate of return r of a non-money investment in the capital market is analysed. This assumption can be explained by the close interdependence of international capital markets or the domestic interest rate dominance in the capital market. In line with the usual portfolio behaviour, the demand for a component rises if the return on it increases or if the return on the alternative investment declines. In addition, all demand functions are positively affected by the nominal income Y^n or Y_a^n. 2

Currency substitution is summarised in arguments E(e), i_a+E(e) and i-E(e), respectively. If an appreciation of the foreign currency is expected, the demand for the two domestic money stock components falls, other things being equal – specifically, both via the direct effect of E(e) and via the indirect effect through the exchange-rate-adjusted interest rates i–E(e) and i_a+E(e), respectively.

1 For the sake of simplicity and because of the limits to the empirical part, the foreign components of the overall portfolio are disregarded. — 2 As only a segment of the overall portfolio decision is being analysed, the assumption of a positive income dependence of the demand functions poses no problems.

domestic money stock. Secondly, it is not impossible that phenomena which are at least closcly associated with currency substitution influence domestic monetary growth without this being identifiable by the methods of analysis used here.

In Germany the definition of the monetary aggregates is based on their being held by residents. On the other hand, a differentiation by currency is not made. Consequently, it is irrelevant for monetary growth measured in this way if, for example, a domestic enterprise holds its sight deposits at a German bank in French currency rather than in Deutsche Mark. Similarly, the German money stock is not affected - at least directly - if a non-resident opens a Deutsche Mark account with a German bank. To the extent that currency substitution has these results, it thus fails to affect statistical monetary growth. Accordingly, in these cases it cannot be said that the indicator function of the monetary aggregates is being impaired, either. An exception in this respect is the demand for cash. In the past few years there have indeed been recurring indications that the movement of currency in circulation has been distorted by cash-holding abroad. The demand for Deutsche Mark notes abroad is determined not only by the high inflation rates in many countries but often also by special circumstances, such as political uncertainty or changes in tax legislation. A crucial factor here is, of course, that (unlike bank deposits, which are included in the money stock) currency in circulation comprises, if only for statistical reasons, all notes and coins denominated in Deutsche Mark, irrespective of whether they are held by domestic non-banks or by non-residents.

In the past, the switching of money holdings to the Euro-markets has occasionally been linked to currency substitution. This is correct to a limited extent only. German non-banks' deposits abroad are mostly denominated in Deutsche Mark. The table on page 370 shows German non-banks' foreign currency deposits at home and abroad. The very modest size of these bank deposits, relative to the money stock M3 (which size, moreover, does not fluctuate very sharply) does not suggest that the currency substitution is highly significant. This applies in particular to the links with the European currencies, as the foreign currency assets are denominated primarily in US dollars.

Tab. 2: Domestic non-banks' foreign currency deposits

DM billion; annual averages

Year	at domestic credit institutions 1	in the Euro-market 2		Compare	
		Total	US dollar share 3	Euro-deposits, total	Money stock M3 4
1988	1.2	9.0	5.2	63.2	1,122.8
1989	1.5	16.3	5.8	94.6	1,185.6
1990	1.7	17.8	6.2	123.6	1,240.8
1991	1.7	16.0	5.8	152.8	1,489.4
1992	1.7	14.4	9.1	174.6	1,616.1
1993	1.8	15.4	9.7	228.4	1,748.4

1 Foreign currency deposits in EC currencies. — 2 Foreign currency deposits at domestic credit institutions' foreign branches and subsidiaries. — 3 End-of-year levels. — 4 Calculated from end-of-month levels; until 1990 western Germany.

Deutsche Bundesbank

Conversely, it is also true that phenomena which at least in a broad sense constitute currency substitution may have an impact on monetary developments in Germany even though no evidence of this can be adduced by the traditional means of tracing currency substitution. This is true in particular of the effects of substitution between Deutsche Mark securities and securities denominated in foreign currency; this process is as a rule discussed under the heading of portfolio substitution or international capital mobility. If, for example, non-residents' demand for Deutsche Mark securities increases at times when the Deutsche Mark is expected to appreciate, and if this causes the capital market rate to decline and consequently prompts residents to prefer holding liquid funds to investing resources in the securities markets, the resultant faster monetary growth actually owes something to external influences. However, in this case the tests usually performed with the aid of money demand functions will provide no evidence of substitution effects as the impact is exerted via the domestic capital market rate. The customary partial analysis fails to capture such causalities. Hence the studies presented here cannot be regarded as being fully representative of all external influences on domestic monetary developments, especially not in periods of speculation.

Another problem in reviewing currency substitution is posed by the quantification of expected exchange rate changes, which are of crucial importance in this context as an argument in the money demand function. Measuring expectations of (changes in) exchange rates is indeed difficult, and empirical studies are invariably subject to the condition that the assumptions made in respect of the expectations of exchange rate changes are fairly plausible. In the empirical studies described below, an attempt has been made to allow for this problem by taking due account of several common hypotheses about the formation of exchange rate expectations.

Earlier empirical studies

In recent years quite a number of studies of the implications of currency substitution for the demand for money in individual countries have been carried out. In line with the considerations outlined above, these studies have analysed, firstly, the implications of foreign interest rates and of expectations of exchange rate changes for the respective national demand for money. Secondly, tests have been made to establish whether there is a link between the money demand functions for different countries from which currency substitution may be inferred. In this connection, the authors have tried to find out, in particular, whether trends in the monetary expansion of a given country which cannot be explained by traditionally formulated money demand functions are accompanied by mirror-image „errors“ in the monetary growth of a partner country.

In earlier studies of the impact of currency substitution on German demand for money, the focus was on the role of the Deutsche Mark/US dollar exchange rate or of the US dollar interest rate. While the findings do not point unambiguously in a single direction, these studies provide some evidence of the existence of currency substitution effects. More recently, attention has been focused more strongly on relations with European partner countries. This owes something to the perception that currencies will probably become more interchangeable in the course of the European unification process, and that monetary aggregates based on Europe-wide definitions are likely to play a major role in monetary policy in any future monetary union. However, only in isolated cases do the findings of these studies endorse the thesis that currency substitution has exercised an impact on national money-holding (see the table on page 372).

Tab. 3: Impact of currency substitution in the EC on German demand for money

Author	Estimation period	Estimation method	Monetary aggregate	Currency substitution variables	Currency substitution effects identified
Brillembourg, Schadler [1]	1973–1978	Full Information Maximum Likelihood	M2	Foreign interest rates, exchange rates (French franc, Italian lira, pound sterling, Swiss franc)	For Swiss franc only
Melvin [2]	1973–1980	OLS, sensitivity analyses	M1, currency	Foreign inflation rate (pound sterling, Italian lira, French franc), foreign interest rate	For Italian lira only
Batten, Hafer [3]	1972–1983	Output equation with OLS	M1	Effective exchange rate	None
von Hagen, Neumann [4]	1973–1987	Error correction equation	M1	Dollar interest rate, dollar exchange rate	Currency substitution for interest-bearing dollar component only
Artis et al. [5]	1979–1990	OLS with Goldfeld lag	M1	Swap rate (US dollar, French franc, Italian lira, ECU)	For Italian lira only
Lane, Poloz [6]	1972–1990	(1) Error correction models (2) SUR estimation (3) Correlation of residuals of national money demand functions	M1	Exchange rates (French franc, Italian lira, pound sterling), foreign GNP (France, United Kingdom, Italy)	(1) Long-run: ambiguous (depending on specification) Short-run: French franc, pound sterling (2) For French franc only (3) French franc, pound sterling
Angeloni et al. [7]	1982–1990	GLS estimation	M1, M3	ECU exchange rate	None
Monticelli [8]	1979–1992	Error correction models, Granger causalities	Europe-wide money stock aggregates including/excluding cross-border deposits	EU countries excluding Luxemburg, Portugal, Greece	Minor impact of currency substitution as European aggregate excluding cross-border deposits best
Mizen, Pentecost [9]	1976–1990	OLS	Pound sterling held in European countries	Foreign interest rates (Germany, France, Belgium, Netherlands, Italy, Denmark, Ireland)	None

1 A. Brillembourg, S. M. Schadler, A Model of Currency Substitution in Exchange Rate Determination, 1973–78, IMF Staff Papers, 1979, Vol. 26, page 513 ff. — 2 M. Melvin, Currency Substitution and Western European Monetary Unification, Economica, 1985, Vol. 52, page 79 ff. — 3 D. D. Batten, R. W. Hafer, Money, Income and Currency Substitution: Evidence from Three Countries, Federal Reserve Bank of St. Louis Review, 1985, Vol. 67/5, page 27 ff. — 4 J. von Hagen, M. J. M. Neumann, Currency Substitution and the Demand for Money: Further International Evidence, 1990, mimeo. — 5 M. J. Artis, R. C. Bladen-Hovell, W. Zhang, A European Money Demand Function, in: P. R. Masson, M. P. Taylor (eds.), Policy Issues in the Operation of Currency Unions, Cambridge, 1993, page 240 ff. — 6 T. D. Lane, S. S. Poloz, Currency Substitution and Cross-Border Aggregation, IMF Working Paper 92/71, Washington. — 7 I. Angeloni, C. Cottarelli, A. Levy, Cross-Border Deposits and Monetary Aggregates in the Transition to EMU, IMF Working Paper 91/114, Washington. — 8 C. Monticelli, All the Money in Europe? An Investigation of the Economic Properties of EC-Wide Extended Monetary Aggregates, BIS Working Paper No. 19, Basle, 1993. — 9 P. Mizen, E. J. Pentecost, Evaluating the Empirical Evidence for Currency Substitution: A Case Study of Demand for Sterling in Europe, The Economic Journal, 1994, page 1057 ff.

Deutsche Bundesbank

These studies, which cover the period from the early seventies to the mid-eighties, provide little evidence of currency substitution within the EC. Effects of this kind were identified, if at all, only vis-à-vis the Italian lira. In these analyses, money demand equations were specified with a partial adjustment process as a matter of principle. A more recent study, which covers the period up to the end of 1987, and which explicitly tries to sift out the impact of the setting-up of the EMS on the Deutsche Mark/US dollar relationship, is based on the assumption of a broader dynamic structure. But this approach, too, failed to identify short or long-run currency substitution in the stricter sense, i.e. in terms of M1. On the other hand, such effects were clearly discernible among the interest-bearing components - on a growing scale, indeed, from the beginning of the eighties. The impact on the money stock in Germany, however, was but small.

Those studies which cover trends extending into the nineties are more likely to yield findings in some areas which imply currency substitution in Europe. Currency substitution effects were identified here for the demand for M1 with respect to French franc, the pound sterling and, with reservations, the Italian lira. As far as the money stock M3 is concerned, by contrast, only very minor „external influences" of this kind were identified. Altogether, it is therefore often claimed that currency substitution has hitherto had little impact on the demand for money in Germany. This does not rule out the possibility of such effects increasing in importance in future.

Empirical evidence gathered by the Bundesbank

The Bundesbank studies presented bellow analyse the extent to which the demand for the money stock M3 in Germany may have owed something to factors which might indicate currency substitution within Europe. Firstly, it is assumed that a long-run relationship exists between the domestic money stock and the usual domestic variables to be taken into account here, such as GNP and Deutsche Mark interest rates. This approach is justified insofar as there is reasonable evidence of such a long-run relationship. Secondly, it is assumed that this long-run relationship is obscured by short-run relationships between monetary growth and its determinants. It is examined whether these determinants also include variables which might be interpreted as indicating currency substitution. Accordingly, the traditional specification of money demand equation with a domestic opportunity cost and transactions variable is supplemented by two arguments which are simultaneously added to the estimation equations (for a more detailed description, see the annex):

- the expected appreciation or depreciation of the foreign currency, to capture currency substitution in the narrower sense (reference point: non-interest-bearing money stock components)
- the exchange-rate-adjusted (expected) return on a foreign interest-bearing (short-term) financial investment, to capture currency substitution in the broader sense (reference point: interest-bearing money stock components).

In line with the theoretical considerations, the impact of these variables on M3 should be significantly negative, i.e. an expected Deutsche Mark appreciation should increase demand for M3. Conversely, higher foreign interest rates should curb domestic monetary growth because an investment in Deutsche Mark appears to be less attractive.

The study thus analyses the bilateral relationship with the French franc, the Dutch guilder, the pound sterling, the Italian lira, the Danish krona, the Belgian franc and the ECU (representing the EMS as a whole) from the early seventies to 1994. Admittedly, such a separate study, broken down by individual currencies, has the disadvantage that the currency substitution variables of the countries not included exert no impact in the equations. On the other hand, if all variables were incorporated in a single estimation equation, the total number of variables to be taken into account would increase to such an extent that the findings would be unlikely to be informative.

As the exchange rate expectations actually prevailing in the market are unknown, empirical studies are forced to rely on plausible assumptions. Thus, in many studies the swap rate or the gap between domestic and foreign interest rates is used as a measure of expected exchange rate changes, or perfect foresight is assumed. The former poses problems because of „covered interest parity“. This method implies that, in the final analysis, the foreign arguments virtually coincide with the domestic interest rate arguments, and hence that an empirical study along the lines described here is impossible. If, on the other hand, actual exchange rate trends are used, obvious errors of measurement will give rise to distortions. Even so, perfect foresight was included in the empirical studies as a possible hypothesis and, accordingly, the exchange rate changes occurring in the following period were used as the (expected) rate of return for the non-interest-bearing component and, in conjunction with a foreign interest rate, for the interest-bearing component. Alternatively, the assumption that the future exchange rate can best be predicted on the basis of the exchange rate last observed is regarded as an exchange rate hypothesis.

When comparing forecasts, this random-walk hypothesis of exchange rate movements has proved to be superior to alternative attempts at explanation in a large number of econometric studies. This means that exchange rate changes follow a random path. Under this hypothesis, only the foreign interest rate remains as the currency substitution variable. Finally, as a third variant, an assumption of the expectations entertained of exchange rate changes is used which implies that the expected future changes in the spot rate are identical to its past trend (adaptive expectation formation). For the sake of econometric operationalisation, exchange rate expectations are depicted in terms of the current appreciation or depreciation of the domestic currency in relation to the previous quarter.

The second constituent of the currency substitution argument (foreign interest rates) is captured by the three-month Euro-market rate, which is intended to provide a proxy for the return on the foreign currency. Short-term interest rates are likely to depict the relevant return on foreign financial investments. The use of Euro-market rates circumvents the problems posed by differing national interest rates and capital controls, which used to be of significance in the past.

In the relationships with the French franc, the pound sterling, the Dutch guilder, the Belgian franc or the Danish krona, neither the non-interest-bearing nor the interest-bearing components of M3 provided any evidence of external influences that could be associated with currency substitution, under any of the three expectation hypotheses. In some cases, the coefficients of the (adjusted) foreign interest rates and of the expectations of exchange rate changes did not differ significantly from zero in the statistics. Some of them even had „wrong", i.e. positive, signs. In other words, no evidence of currency substitution effects was found among the countries in question. The findings are no different if the observation period for the hypothesis with adaptive expectations of exchange rate changes does not start until 1985. Only in relation to the Dutch guilder does the net interest variable with a negative sign become significant. This might be due to the close interest and exchange rate linkage between the Netherlands and

Germany. Broadly speaking, however, the thesis that currency substitution has been posing increasing difficulties over time for German monetary policy makers is not tenable.

The relationship with the Italian lira apparently constitutes a special case. Evidence of currency substitution can be found for all three hypotheses of exchange rate movements. If the Italian currency is expected to appreciate and/or if Italian „net interest income“ increases, demand for M3 declines. There is thus a temporary shift out of the official German monetary aggregate. Both the interest-bearing and non-interest-bearing components of M3 are affected.

These findings are consistent with the fact that, almost throughout the period covered by the study, inflation rates and nominal interest rates in Italy were higher than in Germany. As expectations of stable parities within the EMS have prevailed in the market since the realignment in 1987, and until 1992, Italian assets yielded ex ante and ex post correspondingly higher returns. Thus the lira appreciated against the Deutsche Mark in real terms between 1988 and 1991 because of inflation-induced high nominal interest rates. In addition to this speculative motive, intensive German-Italian travel is likely to have contributed to the interdependencies described.

There is also evidence of small-scale currency substitution effects in Germany's relations with the EU countries as a whole (which were depicted by including the Deutsche Mark/ECU exchange rate and ECU interest rates in the German demand for money). On the one hand, this is rather surprising, as such effects tended not to be confirmed for the individual currencies, viewed in isolation. On the other hand, one explanation could be that, in the ECU orientation, not only Italy but also the other higher-inflation countries Spain, Portugal and Greece were included with some weight.

As mentioned above, it cannot be taken for granted that the demand for the money stock M3 is affected by currency substitution phenomena, if only because this monetary aggregate does not distinguish between currencies. Basically it would therefore seem to be more promising to attempt to trace such influence in the case of the demand for cash. German currency in circulation encompasses all Deutsche Mark notes and coins outside the German banking system, irrespective of whether these funds are held in Germany or abroad.

Switching out of foreign currencies into Deutsche Mark or vice versa is therefore fully reflected in currency in circulation as shown in the statistics. In point of fact, even less evidence of any impact on the demand for currency which could be associated with currency substitution can be identified than in the case of the overall trend of M3. Only in relation to the Italian lira and only for the abbreviated period from 1985 can significant and, in terms of their order of magnitude, major influences be detected. It should be noted, however, that the estimations of the demand for currency have generally yielded less satisfactory results, so that these conclusions are necessarily subject to major reservations. Moreover, these studies do not take due account of conditions in eastern and south-eastern Europe, i.e. those countries in which presumably a large part of the Deutsche Mark cash balances lodged abroad is held.

The generally small empirical evidence of currency substitution in the EU may owe something to the fact that quarterly data have been used as part of a money demand estimation. Currency substitution processes may play an appreciable role in strictly limited periods only, such as in a situation of strong expectations of exchange rate changes, which, moreover, are not captured properly by our models of the formation of expectations. This is why what are known as „impulse dummies“ have been defined for individual countries for the exchange rate realignments of 1987 and 1992. They, however, likewise failed to provide any significant explanation. Hence it is not impossible that the use of monthly or even weekly data might have provided stronger evidence of such effects. On the other hand, one factor arguing against the use of monthly data is that no suitable monthly variables for recording transaction volumes exist. Anyway, even monthly data might well prove to be too long-term.

Summary and conclusion

The findings of the present study suggest that, basically, the significance of the phenomenon of currency substitution in Germany can be assumed to be low. In most cases, no such effects could be identified, regardless of the expectat formation process assumed for exchange rate movements in demand estimations for the money stock M3. Changes in interest or exchange rate conditions in other European countries apparently fail to induce German non-banks to engage in large-scale switching of their currency holdings.

On the other hand, the studies presented here do not rule out the possibility of such influences playing a major part over very short periods of time. Moreover, it is not unreasonable to presume that external influences have not been of major relevance only because German monetary policy has been able to operate in Europe within a framework of mostly fixed but still adjustable exchange rates. After all, the approaches outlined here provide no indication of whether domestic monetary growth was influenced indirectly by external factors, such as the repercussions of foreign interest rate movements on domestic interest rates.

Annex: Empirical test of currency substitution

Econometric methodology

The currency substitution hypothesis is verified for Germany with the aid of a money demand function which is supplemented by currency substitution effects. For this purpose, money demand functions are formulated within the framework of general dynamic structures as what are known as error correction equations. In this way, long-run equilibrium relationships are combined with a high degree of dynamism. The concrete model framework is provided by the two-tier procedure developed by Robert Engle and Clive Granger.[2] There,currency substitution variables are included in the short-run dynamics which are superimposed upon the long-run (cointegration) relationships.

The data

In the study, unadjusted data based on quarterly observations are used. The estimation period covers the years from the early seventies (for further details, see the estimations) to the first quarter of 1994. From the third quarter of 1990, all-German data are used. The logarithm of real demand for money (mr) is estimated, with the GNP deflator (p) being used for deflating. The domestic variables used comprise a scale variable, the logarithm of real GNP (yr) and an opportunity cost coefficient, viz. the yield on domestic bearer debt securities outstanding (r) or, for the interest-bearing money stock components represented by the time deposit rate for deposits of between DM 100,000 and DM 1 million (it), an interest rate differential (zd=r-it). The changes (Δ) are the changes from the corresponding period of the previous year, i.e. they are fourth differences (year-on-year growth rates).

M3 has been adjusted for statistical breaks. By eliminating statistical breaks, illusory correlations are avoided, as is the risk of deriving economic effects (such as structural breaks) from changed statistical definitions. In addition, foreign currency deposits included in M3 have been adjusted for changes in value caused by exchange rate changes. Currency substitution effects are therefore not mistakenly attributed to differing valuation effects. The hypothesis of currency substitution is verified by reference to interest and exchange rate influences. The currencies studied are the French franc (F), the Italian lira (I), the pound sterling (GB), the Dutch guilder (NL), the Danish krona (DK), the Belgian franc (BE) and the ECU (EC). The foreign interest rate variables are denoted by ix, the exchange-rate-adjustment returns by nfx in the case of perfect foresight and by nzx in the case of adaptive expectations of exchange rate changes (with x ≡ F, I, GB, NL, DK, BE, EC). The focus of the presentation of the empirical findings is on the estimations with adaptive expectations of exchange rate changes. Moreover, the results derived from the alternative exchange rate hypotheses, which are more frequently used in the literature, are given for Italy and for the EC.

Tab. 4: Stationarity tests

Variable	Test specification	t-value (absolute)
m3r	C, T	1.82
Δm3r	C, T	4.99 ***
y	C	0.49
Δy	C	3.40 **
r	C	2.00
Δr	C	3.69 ***
zd	C	2.72 *
Δzd	C	5.13 ***
iDK [1]	C	1.54
ΔiDK	C	4.35 ***
iF	C	2.09
ΔiF	C	4.77 ***
iI	C	2.67 *
ΔiI	C	5.48 ***
iGB	C	3.31 **
ΔiGB	C	5.65 ***
iNL	C	3.14 **
ΔiNL	C	5.44 ***
iBE [1]	C	1.90
ΔiBE	C	3.56 **
iEC [2]	C	1.38
ΔiEC	C	2.51 **
eDK	C	1.85
ΔeDK	C	4.82 ***
eF	C	1.59
ΔeF	C	4.46 ***
eI	C	1.82
ΔeI	C	4.19 ***
eGB	C	2.48
ΔeGB	C	5.58 ***
eNL	C	2.80 *
ΔeNL	C	6.22 ***
eBE [4]	C	2.12
ΔeBE	C	4.32 ***
eEC [3]	C	1.71
ΔeEC	C	3.23 **

Estimation period 1970/1 to 1994/1 unless indicated separately. — Comparison of t-values with the critical values of J. G. MacKinnon, Critical Values for Cointegration Tests, in: R.F. Engle and C.W.J. Granger (eds.), Long-Run Economic Relationships, Oxford 1991; test with 2 lags. — ***/**/* significant at the 1 %/5 %/10 % level. — C = constant, T = deterministic trend. — 1 1978/3 to 1994/1. — 2 1980/1 to 1994/1. — 3 1973/1 to 1994/1. — 4 1979/3 to 1994/1.

Deutsche Bundesbank

Long-run relationship for German demand for money

First, the degree of integration of the time series used, as required as part of a cointegration analysis, is investigated. As is evident from the adjacent table, all variables are integrated from degree 1 (I(1)), so that the stationarity of the variables is ensured by simple differentiation. The basic precondition for the application of the methods used here is thus satisfied.

After the preliminary statistical work, the long-run equation covering the period from the first quarter of 1970 to the first quarter of 1994 is estimated first. Besides GNP and the capital market rate, three seasonal dummies (seas1, seas2, seas3) are included to capture seasonal effects, each of which has the value one in the first, second or third quarter and otherwise is zero. In line with the procedure used for many studies, real equilibrium equation is estimated. A price homogeneity of the demand for money of degree one is thus assumed, ensuring freedom from money illusion. The basic structure of the results equation corresponds to that obtained in other studies. It reads as follows:

$$m3r = -6.40 + 1.40\,yr - 1.22\,r + 0.12\,seas1 + 0.07\,seas2 + 0.05\,seas3 + \varepsilon$$

$R^2 = 0.98$ (adjusted determination coefficient)

DW = 0.48 (Durbin-Watson statistic)

ADF = 2.50 (Augmented Dickey-Fuller test with four lags)

ADF (4) = 3.78** (ADF test only with fourth lag)

[The critical value of the ADF test at a significance level of 10 % (5%) is 3.52 (3.84).]

Income elasticity is above one, reflecting the falling trend of the velocity of circulation of money. The negative (semi-)interest elasticity of - 1.22 is likewise statistically verified. The findings of augmented Dickey-Fuller tests in respect of the cointegration of the variables are admittedly not unequivocal, but it has been shown that such tests are of a relatively poor quality, and that it is better to use the t-value of the error correction term as a cointegration test in the dynamic equation.[3] As described below, the findings of such a test argue in favour of the existence of a cointegration relationship.

Estimation of the dynamic models

The residual of the long-run regression are used as equilibrium errors in the error correction models. For stability reasons, the sign of this error correction term (ECT) should be negative, so that existing disequilibria are reduced over time. Owing to the seasonal pattern of the money stock and the income variable, these error correction terms are modelled not as a simple lag but as averages of the four previous quarters.[4] The other variables are included in the estimation in the form of annual growth rates.

In all estimations, the simultaneous values and up to four lags of the endogenous and exogenous variables are initially taken into account. In the subsequent selection process the coefficients which are not significant are successively set at zero. Of the currency substitution variables, however, one variable is retained in the equations, even if it is not significant, in order to provide an idea of the order of magnitude of these influences. Depending on the availability of data, the estimation period ranges from the first quarter of 1973 (as a maximum) to the first quarter of 1994. In some cases it has been adjusted forward (for further details, see the explanatory notes to the table on page 382).

In the columns of the table the t-values come after the estimated coefficients. The test statistics' properties are satisfactory. All equations are free from first-order auto-correlation (Durbin-Watson statistic). The explanatory value of the equations specified is high (adjusted determination coefficient). In all estimations, the standard error of the regression is between 1.4 % and 1.6 %. In the test statistics for autoregressive heteroscedasticity (ARCH effects), the White test points to the existence of corresponding effects for the Netherlands and the United Kingdom. According to the Jarque-Bera test for normal distribution, the equation residuals found are consistent with the normal distribution hypothesis.

A feature common to all estimations is that the coefficients of the domestic variables have the theoretically expected signs and differ significantly from zero. For instance, the coefficient of the simultaneous income variable is positive and relatively high, at about 0.80.[5] In the aggregate, correction with lagged values yields a value of about 0.40. The coefficients of the domestic capital market rate are negative. For the short run, semi-interest elasticities of an order of magnitude ranging between - 0.30 and - 0.50 are observed. The coefficient of the error correction variable is negative and mostly significant at the 5 % level, so that in the long run the coefficients of the cointegration relationship are operative.

These test and estimation results substantially remain valid if the other two hypotheses about exchange rate expectations in Germany demand for money are analysed.[6] The test statistics do not change markedly. The standard error of the regression is about 1.5 % in each case. The determination coefficient is 0.80. No significant currency substitution influences were found for the currencies of France, Belgium, the Netherlands, Denmark and the United Kingdom.

Tab. 5: Estimation results of error correction models for M3*

Variable [1]	Italy	France	Netherlands	United Kingdom	Denmark	Belgium	EC
C	0.02 (5.30)	0.02 (5.15)	0.02 (4.93)	0.02 (5.76)	0.02 (4.88)	0.02 (4.27)	0.02 (5.37)
Δm3r (−1)	0.49 (6.17)	0.49 (5.94)	0.55 (6.73)	0.48 (6.12)	0.44 (4.86)	0.52 (4.81)	0.39 (5.54)
Δm3r (−4)	−0.24 (4.29)	−0.25 (4.59)	−0.24 (4.29)	−0.25 (4.70)	−0.24 (3.92)	−0.25 (3.58)	
ECT	−0.24 (3.32)	−0.26 (3.88)	−0.26 (3.77)	−0.28 (4.28)	−0.22 (2.76)	−0.29 (3.46)	−0.30 (3.70)
Δy	0.75 (9.51)	0.80 (10.08)	0.82 (10.01)	0.78 (9.96)	0.84 (9.69)	0.87 (8.66)	0.77 (8.90)
Δy (−1)	−0.35 (3.26)	−0.34 (3.08)	−0.44 (4.08)	−0.36 (3.45)	−0.36 (2.99)	−0.48 (3.42)	
Δy (−2)							
Δy (−3)							−0.45 (6.09)
Δy (−4)							
Δr			−0.37 (2.44)	−0.39 (2.71)	−0.46 (2.56)	−0.39 (1.84)	
Δr (−1)		−0.36 (2.41)					−0.46 (2.12)
Δr (−2)							
Δr (−3)							
Δr (−4)	−0.27 (1.99) [2]						
Δnzx [3]			0.05 (1.10)	0.04 (1.69)			
Δnzx (−1)	−0.09 (2.62)						
Δnzx (−2)						0.04 (0.30)	
Δnzx (−3)		0.09 (2.38)			0.20 (2.72)		0.35 (2.94)
Δnzx (−4)							
Δex [3]						−0.28 (2.18)	
Δex (−1)				0.05 (1.89)			
Δex (−2)		0.12 (1.09)					
Δex (−3)	−0.13 (3.14)						
Δex (−4)							

Test statistics [4]

	Italy	France	Netherlands	United Kingdom	Denmark	Belgium	EC
R^2	0.82	0.82	0.83	0.84	0.84	0.84	0.84
DW	1.61	1.64	1.72	1.72	1.68	1.74	1.94
Std	0.014	0.014	0.015	0.014	0.015	0.016	0.015
ARCH(4)	0.97	1.92	1.50	0.55	0.76	1.00	4.69
White	0.85	1.68	1.94	1.78	0.57	0.86	1.89
JB	0.82	0.09	0.34	0.36	1.19	1.90	1.52

* Estimation periods: I: 1975/2 to 1994/1; F, NL, GB: 1973/ 1 to 1994/1; DK: 1979/3 to 1994/1; BE: 1980/1 to 1994/1; EC: 1981/1 to 1994/1. — 1 Absolute t-values in parentheses after coefficients. — 2 For Italy, the interest rate differential zd = r-it was used instead of r. — 3 x ≡ I, F, NL, GB, DK, BE, EC. — 4 R^2: adjusted coefficient of determination; DW: Durbin-Watson test statistic; Std: standard error of regression; ARCH (4): autoregressive conditional heteroscedasticity with 4 lags; White: White test for heteroscedasticity; JB: Jarque-Bera test for normal distribution of residuals.

Deutsche Bundesbank

Tab. 6: Estimation results of error correction models for M3 (Italy and EC)*

	Country					
	Italy			EC		
	Hypothesis					
Variable 1	Random walk	Perfect foresight	Adaptive expectation	Random walk	Perfect foresight	Adaptive expectation
C	0.02 (5.10)	0.02 (5.57)	0.02 (5.30)	0.02 (5.25)	0.03 (7.30)	0.02 (5.37)
Δm3r (−1)	0.52 (6.10)	0.47 (5.57)	0.49 (6.17)	0.35 (4.57)	0.30 (4.61)	0.39 (5.54)
Δm3r (−4)	−0.25 (4.19)	−0.25 (4.46)	−0.24 (4.29)			
ECT	−0.26 (3.38)	−0.25 (3.34)	−0.24 (3.32)	−0.37 (4.49)	−0.43 (5.14)	−0.30 (3.70)
Δy	0.75 (9.16)	0.75 (9.28)	0.75 (9.51)	0.85 (9.74)	0.65 (8.68)	0.77 (8.90)
Δy (−1)	−0.37 (3.37)	−0.32 (2.77)	−0.35 (3.26)			
Δy (−2)						
Δy (−3)				−0.49 (6.18)		−0.45 (6.09)
Δy (−4)					−0.47 (6.86)	
Δr				−0.42 (1.81)	−0.30 (1.67)	
Δr (−1)						−0.46 (2.12)
Δr (−2)						
Δr (−3)						
Δr (−4)	−0.22 (1.52) 2	−0.20 (1.79) 2	−0.27 (1.99) 2			
Δix 3	−0.06 (1.66)			−0.18 (1.33)		
Δix (−1)						
Δix (−2)						
Δix (−3)						
Δix (−4)						
Δnfx 3		−0.07 (2.06)				
Δnfx (−1)						
Δnfx (−2)						
Δnfx (−3)					0.40 (3.22)	
Δnfx (−4)						
Δnzx 3						
Δnzx (−1)			−0.09 (2.62)			
Δnzx (−2)						
Δnzx (−3)						0.35 (2.94)
Δnzx (−4)						
Δex 3					−0.46 (4.02)	
Δex (−1)						
Δex (−2)						
Δex (−3)		−0.10 (2.41)	−0.13 (3.14)			
Δex (−4)						
Test statistics 4						
R^2	0.80	0.81	0.82	0.82	0.86	0.84
DW	1.63	1.69	1.61	1.66	1.72	1.94
Std	0.015	0.014	0.014	0.016	0.014	0.015
ARCH(4)	0.98	0.83	0.97	1.25	1.74	4.69
White	1.19	0.83	0.85	1.51	1.58	1.89
JB	0.73	0.63	0.82	0.62	0.19	1.52

* Estimation periods: I: 1975/2 to 1994/1; EC: 1981/1 to 1994/1. — 1 Absolute t-values in parentheses after coefficients. — 2 For Italy the interest rate differential zd = r-it was used instead of r. — 3 x ≡ I, EC. — 4 See footnote 4 to the table on page 47.

Deutsche Bundesbank

Endnotes

1 Deutsche Bundesbank, Germany's securities transactions with non-residents in the second half of the eighties, Monthly Report, April 1991, page 14ff.
2 R.F. Engle, C.W.J. Granger, Cointegration and Error Correction: Representation, Estimation, and Testing, Econometrica, 1987, Vol. 55, page 251ff.
3 See J.J.M. Kremers, N.R.Ericsson, J.J. Dolado, The Power of Cointegration Tests, Oxford Bulletin of Economics and Statistics, 1992, Vol. 54, page 325ff.
4 Consequently: $ECT = 0.25 \sum \varepsilon_{-i}$ für $i = 1,...,4$.
5 If a dummy variable which has the value one in the third quarter of 1990 and the value minus one in the third quarter of 1991 is included in the equations, the coefficients of the income variables decrease. The coefficient of their lag will even become insignificant in some cases. In addition, the coefficient of the error correction term falls at the same time. However, this change in specification does not result in the coefficients of the foreign variables becoming significant. To this extent, the empirical evidence of currency substitution remains low.
6 See the table on page 383 for the relationships with the Italian lira and the ECU.

International Economics

R. Tilly, University of Münster, Germany
P. J. J. Welfens, University of Potsdam, Germany (Eds.)

European Economic Integration as a Challenge to Industry and Government

Contemporary and Historical Perspectives on International Economic Dynamics

1995. X, 558 pp. 43 figs., 68 tabs. Hardcover **DM 198,-**
ISBN-13:978-3-642-79971-6

The EU single market and the opening up of eastern Europe offer new opportunities for creating a truly pan European market economy. What lessons can be drawn for this opportunity from early 20th-century developments in Europe? With this question in mind, the fragility of international trade, financial investment and foreign investment relations in and across Europe are analyzed here from both a contemporary and historical perspective.

P. J. J. Welfens, University of Potsdam, Germany (Ed.)

Economic Aspects of German Unification

Expectations, Transition Dynamics and International Perspectives

2nd rev. and enlarged ed. 1995. XVI, 527 pp. 34 figs., 110 tabs.
Hardcover **DM 198,-** ISBN-13:978-3-642-79971-6

This book analyzes the German unification after five years with respect to expectations, international impact and internal adjustments – including dramatic structural shifts. German unification is changing central Europe, the EU and international economic and political relations generally.
It raises many new questions for Germany itself, Europe, and the whole international community.

Springer

Prices are subject to change. IN EU countries the local VAT is effective.

Springer-Verlag, P.O. Box 31 13 40, D-10643 Berlin, Fax 0 30 / 82 07 - 3 01 / 4 48 e-mail: orders@springer.de tm.BA95.09.06

European and Transatlantic Studies

B. Eichengreen, University of California, Berkely, CA, USA
J. Frieden, University of California, Los Angeles, CA, USA
J. v. Hagen, University of Mannheim, Germany (Eds.)

Politics and Institutions in an Integrated Europe

1995. VII, 228 pp. 15 figs., 13 tabs. Hardcover **DM 120,-**
ISBN-13:978-3-642-79971-6

B. Eichengreen, University of California, Berkely, CA, USA
J. Frieden, University of California, Los Angeles, CA, USA
J. v. Hagen, University of Mannheim, Germany (Eds.)

Monetary and Fiscal Policy in an Integrated Europe

1995. VII, 242 pp. 26 figs., 28 tabs. Hardcover **DM 120,-**
ISBN-13:978-3-642-79971-6

In these volumes, a group of distinguished economists and political scientists analyzes the political economy of European integration. The authors evaluate recent developments of the European Monetary and Fiscal Policy. They consider the current situation, and assess prospects for the future of an Integrated Europe. These books will be of great interest to observers, scholars, and students of European economic and political affairs, macroeconomic policy, institutional analysis, and comparative and international political economy. The books are unique in combining perspectives from economics and political science and provide an in-depth analysis of the new European institutions.

Springer

Prices are subject to change. IN EU countries the local VAT is effective.

Springer-Verlag, P.O. Box 31 13 40, D-10643 Berlin, Fax 0 30 / 82 07 - 3 01 / 4 48 e-mail: orders@springer.de tm.BA95.09.06

MIX
Papier aus verantwortungsvollen Quellen
Paper from responsible sources
FSC® C105338

If you have any concerns about our products,
you can contact us on
ProductSafety@springernature.com

In case Publisher is established outside the EU,
the EU authorized representative is:
Springer Nature Customer Service Center GmbH
Europaplatz 3, 69115 Heidelberg, Germany

Printed by Libri Plureos GmbH
in Hamburg, Germany